JOHN CLARE

JOHN CLARE IN 1820

From the portrait by William Hilton, R.A., in the National Portrait Gallery

JOHN CLARE
A LIFE

J. W. AND ANNE TIBBLE

*"Biography alone has no convention
save the sober one of truth."*
A. J. A. SYMONS

LONDON
COBDEN-SANDERSON
1 MONTAGUE STREET

PRINTED IN GREAT BRITAIN FOR
R.   COBDEN-SANDERSON   LTD   AT
THE CAMELOT PRESS, SOUTHAMPTON
MCMXXXII

CONTENTS

Spring

Summer

Autumn

Winter

ILLUSTRATIONS

ACKNOWLEDGMENTS

WE are deeply in debt to Mr. Edmund Blunden. The importance of his public contributions to Clare's fame is realised by all who are interested in the poet. His private enthusiasm, his zeal in collecting and his generosity in giving away information, his patient devotion of valuable time to answering our many requests and to reading and re-reading the manuscript of this Life, we record here with a sense of lasting obligation. Without Mr. Blunden the work could not have been begun, much less brought to a conclusion.

We are indebted to Professor Lascelles Abercrombie for his interest in this book, and for his reading of it in manuscript.

We are very grateful to Mr. J. W. Bodger, the untiring secretary of the Peterborough Archæological Society and keeper of the Peterborough collection of Clare manuscripts. For some years we have had access to these, and have been allowed opportunity to transcribe at leisure. Mr. R. Brown, the chief of the Northampton Public Library, and his assistants, have given us kindly and unfailing help in our work among the Northampton documents. We thank, too, Mr. J. S. Billingham, who, out of his inspiring collection of Clariana, has provided us with details of knowledge that we might otherwise have missed; and Mr. T. R. Hughes, who has read the proofs and supplied items of information from his work on the *London Magazine*.

Finally, we owe thanks to the following, who have answered queries, given us the benefit of their knowledge, or supplied us with Clare documents or transcripts: Mr. R. J. Goodfellow of Helpston, Clare's grandson and his family of Northborough, Miss K. A. Cary, Mr. R. W. King, Professor Ernest Weekley, Mr. Alan Porter, Mr. E. Leslie

Griggs, Mr. E. V. Lucas, Mr. G. H. Drury, Mr. R. N. Green-Armytage, Mr. J. C. Thornton, Mr. W. Beattie of the Department of Printed Books at the National Library of Scotland, Messrs. Birrell & Garnett, Messrs. Elkin Matthews, the editor of the *London Mercury*, the editors and staff of the *Bedford Times and Independent*, the director of the Municipal Libraries of Bath, Mr. W. D. Saunders of the *Peterborough Citizen*, the librarians of the Central Library of Hull, Mr. H. T. Kirby for the photograph of the Grimshawe portrait and Mr. R. S. Parr for the photograph of Swordy Well.

FOREWORD

IN 1820 John Clare took the literary world by storm as
the peasant-poet of Northamptonshire. He had then
lived for twenty-seven years in the poverty and obscurity
which were the natural lot of one born into the lowest
stratum of society. In the following pages may be read the
story of those years of obscurity, of the swift turn of Fortune's
wheel which carried Clare to the dizzy heights of success and
fame, of the slow descent on the other side until, after seventeen years, the wheel came full circle and condemned Clare
once more to twenty-seven years of obscurity, the grimmer
obscurity of an asylum for the insane.

The story of Clare's after-fame is almost as strange as that
of his life. His death in 1864 revived memories of the peasant-
poet of 1820. In 1865, thirty years after the appearance of the
last of his five volumes of poems, was published a Life by
Frederick Martin. In 1873 came another Life by J. L.
Cherry, with a selection from the asylum poems. In 1893 a
Centenary Exhibition of manuscripts was held at Peterborough ; some ninety of these manuscripts of all kinds and
sizes, from rough drafts scribbled on the backs of letters and
bills to neatly written, finely bound manuscript-books, found
a permanent home in the Peterborough Museum. A smaller
collection was acquired by the Northampton Public Library.
Six large volumes of letters written to Clare had been bought
by the British Museum in 1873. In 1901 a selection from the
published poems was prepared by Mr. Norman Gale, and in
1908 Mr. Arthur Symons edited another selection, which
included sixteen previously unpublished poems. During
these years, anthologists had not neglected Clare, and the
story of his life had been many times briefly told in introduc-
tions to the selections, in encyclopædias, and in newspaper
articles.

Yet, despite this collection of the manuscripts in accessible places and these activities of his admirers, it was a new Clare that the enthusiasm and research of Mr. Edmund Blunden and Mr. Alan Porter revealed to the literary world of 1920, one hundred years after his first rise to fame. For not only were they able to include in their selection a large number of poems previously unpublished, many of them among Clare's best work, but in his Introduction Mr. Blunden revealed the inadequacy of all previous accounts of the poet's life. This inadequacy was due to the fact that writers about Clare accepted Martin's Life as the authentic biography, and based their accounts on his.

Frederick Martin yielded to none in his enthusiastic appreciation of Clare ; but a biography founded on enthusiasm alone is a house built on the sands. Martin had access to all the manuscripts and letters mentioned above, but he used them as a novelist rather than as a biographer. There is scarcely a page without its errors and mis-statements, and he invented freely—thoughts, emotions, scenes, conversations, incidents, and copious tears. His biography is therefore valueless as an authority, though for sixty years its romancings were generally accepted as facts. The few who mistrusted the biographer and disliked his "bastard-Carlylese" were sometimes led to belittle Clare as well; among them was Charles Dickens, who wrote indignantly of "such preposterous exaggeration of small claims."

J. L. Cherry's brief account of Clare in his *Life and Remains* is more trustworthy, though his editing of texts was careless. He gave some quotations from the Journal and letters and expressed his doubts of Martin's accuracy. But, unfortunately, he was unable to consult many of the manuscripts, and had to rely on Martin for much of his information.

Thus it was left for Mr. Blunden to point the way to the first authentic biography of Clare by revealing the rich stores of autobiographical material hidden away in the manuscripts at Peterborough and Northampton. Some passages—notably Clare's vivid pen-pictures of the authors he met in London—

have been printed since 1920 in periodicals, and again in *Sketches in the Life of John Clare*, where they accompanied an account of his early life written by Clare for his publishers in 1820. The sketches of the *Londoners* are reprinted again in this book; apart from brief extracts, the other autobiographical passages are now printed for the first time, among them the full story of his early life and his rise to fame, his Journal for 1824–5, his observations as a field naturalist, his opinions of men and books, of religion and politics, his pictures of village life and society, extracts from his asylum notebooks, and many quotations from unpublished poems. The letters in the British Museum have enabled us to corroborate Clare's story at many points and to fill in the gaps in his narrative ; we have also quoted from references to Clare by his friends and acquaintances.

We have been glad to allow Clare to tell his own story wherever possible. The qualities which made him a poet and naturalist did not desert him in his prose sketchings of men and events. He is always a faithful chronicler ; although he had no pretensions as a writer of prose, and often felt that Priscian's art was black magic, his native idioms and quaint turns of phrase give a freshness and individuality to his prose ; and there are some passages of a strange and moving beauty, where the poet in him guided his pen. Following Clare's instructions to his editors, we have supplied punctuation and regularized spelling; otherwise the text is as it stands in the rough and fragmentary jottings of the manuscripts.

The many articles and reviews since 1920 testify to the interest which Clare has aroused in this generation; yet the contradictions and divergencies found in what Mr. Blunden calls this "puzzling profusion of good and bad critiques" are astonishing; the traditional view of Clare dies hard. One writer thinks he is too well read in the poets of the eighteenth century, and imitates them continually; another notes the immense gulf which divides him from those same poets. To one his poetry is "mere picturesque description"; another sees in him always "a poet of the spirit." One finds no "principle of inner growth" in his work; another comments on the "continuous growth of the poet's mind, strangely crowned in the Asylum period." Here we read of the "pure imagination of a hundred enchanting phrases," there that there is "not one startling felicity, one concentrated ray in the whole body of his work." And in his life some see a miserable record of failure due to weakness of character, lack of business acumen, and dissipation, while others see a gallant struggle against great odds and a life rich in achievement, despite apparent failure.

With these problems in mind, we have endeavoured to give in this book a complete and faithful record of Clare's life, and the reader may, if he wishes, disregard our occasional interpretations and judgments, and base his own conclusions upon first-hand evidence. We are confident that the new light thrown upon Clare's mind and character and achievements will reveal the crudities and falsities of the century-old traditional picture of him; and we believe that the following pages give light and shade and colour to that simple self-portrait which he sketched in the lines:

> *A silent man in life's affairs,*
> *A thinker from a boy,*
> *A peasant in his daily cares,*
> *A poet in his joy.*

There, in essence, is the real John Clare, as he himself wished to be remembered; and for the rest we may set down here a remark which he made in a letter to a friend: "If life had a second edition, how I would correct the proofs!"

SPRING

I

JUMPING TIME AWAY
1793–1805

Poet of Nature, thou hast wept to know
That things depart which never may return:
Childhood and youth, friendship, and love's first glow,
Have fled like sweet dreams, leaving thee to mourn.

. . . .

In honoured poverty thy voice did weave
Songs consecrate to truth and liberty.
Deserting these, thou leavest me to grieve,
Thus, having been, that thou shouldst cease to be.

SHELLEY : "To Wordsworth."

WHAT may be called the "John Clare country" is that
north-east corner of Northamptonshire which lies
between the valleys of the River Welland on the north and
of the River Nen on the south. Here, as in Tennyson's
Lincolnshire, are two distinct types of country. There is the
dyke-sown, treeless fen, and the wooded midland, with its
sunny, eventful field-corners.

A glance at the modern Ordnance map will show that
the dividing-line between the two types of country is sharp
and clear. The main road from Peterborough to Lincoln
seems to make the boundary between fen and midland.
Once, the boundary may have been the Roman road of
King Street. On the east, in years past, sea marshes may have
crept up as far as this; for the land still retains some likeness
to the sea itself. As late as 1810 the Peterborough Great Fen
lay between Peterborough and Crowland Abbey. A tract
of level land of six or seven thousand acres, and capable of
the highest output of crops, it was, up to then, undivided
and uncultivated. Writing after the drainage, Charles
Kingsley lingered in fancy

BJ

" over the shining meres, the golden reed-beds, the countless waterfowl, the strange and gaudy insects, the wild nature . . . where the coot clanked, and the bittern boomed, and the sedge-bird, not content with its own sweet song, mocked the notes of all the birds around."

Round the small town of Market Deeping, which is eight miles north of Peterborough, the fenland penetrates westward to the main line of the London and North-Eastern Railway. On the south-west side of the railroad, only fifty feet above sea-level and just outside the bounds of the fen, is the small village of Helpston. Here, on the 13th of July, in 1793, John Clare was born. To the west and south of the village lies the district that Clare was later so untiringly to wander in, with its woods and heathy common-land. To the east and north the fen "spread its faint shadow of immensity." Clare wrote of both these kinds of country; he described again and again "the flaggy forest and the flood" ; but that which he loved and clung to, as Michel loved and clung to the plain of Montmartre, was the wooded, softly swelling midland, with its many grey spires, to the south and west of his home.

Helpston[1] has perhaps not altered greatly in the last hundred years. It is a long, straggling village, seven miles from Peterborough, and picturesque because of the excellent grey stonework of most of its houses. The parish adjoins that of Barnack, for some years Charles Kingsley's home, and birthplace, in 1830, of his brother Henry. In 1793 Helpston had accommodation for sixty families. On the right-hand side of the village street running south the cottage where Clare was born stands, made of grey stone and thatched like the rest of the older dwellings. To-day it is one of a row of three. Originally there were only two, both of which belonged to an old retired farmer named Gee. He lived in one and the Clare family in the other, they having the whole of the garden at the back. There were elm-trees in the hedgerow, one so huge that it "turned a whole day's rain,"

Where ring-doves from their nest would call,
And the vein-leaved ivy grew.

Each of the original cottages probably had four rooms, two up and two down. The ladder which led to the rooms above is still used instead of a staircase. Yet the cottage, Clare records in his autobiographical fragments,

"was as roomy and comfortable as any of our neighbours', and we had it for forty shillings, while an old apple-tree in the garden generally made the rent. The garden was large for a poor man, and my father managed to dig it night and morning before the hours of labour, and lost no time. He then did well; but the young farmer that succeeded our old landlord raised the rent, and the next year made four tenements of the house, leaving us a corner of one room on a floor for three guineas a year, and a little slip of the garden which was divided into four parts; but as my father had been an old tenant, he gave him the choice of his share and he retained our old apple-tree. Though the ground was good for nothing, yet the tree still befriended us and made shift to make up the greater part of our rent."

Clare's father was Parker Clare. The family of Clare was a large one, the name being common in the district and throughout the county. Perhaps residence in or near the small town of Clare, in Suffolk, originated the surname, though its corruption from "Clayer," meaning "clay-worker," sounds more feasible. Clare himself knew and cared little about it :

" I cannot trace my name to any remote period ; a century and a half is the utmost, and I have found no great ancestors to boast in the breed. All I can make out is that they were gardeners, parish clerks, and fiddlers, and from these has sprung a large family of the name, still increasing, where kindred has forgotten its claims."

Parker Clare was born on the 14th of January, 1765, "one of fate's chancelings, who drop into the world without the honour of matrimony."

His surname was that of his mother, doubtless the daughter of that "John Clare, Clark," whose flowing signature in the Helpston parish registers is now all the trace that can be found of him. Parker was the name of the child's unworthy father, John Donald Parker, a Scotsman who stayed for a while at Helpston as schoolmaster. He disappeared at the inconvenient birth of his son.

Notwithstanding the circumstances of Parker Clare's birth, he was in his youth a man of great strength, whose usual means of a livelihood was day-labouring among the farmers round about. He was noted at the village feasts and among his acquaintances as a wrestler, and he loved in later years to show his scars.[1] His conversation, like that of most men who work close to the soil, was full of pith, virility, and aptly coloured phrases. His memory was stored with old ballads and songs, and his boast was that he could sing or recite over a hundred. So he was in social demand because of this, too. For his strength he was chosen as a thresher, and threshing with a flail became his chief labour. While he was hale and strong, his living, if meagre, was at least regular and assured.

He married Ann, the daughter of John and Elizabeth Stimson, of the neighbouring village of Castor. She was eight years older than her husband, having been born on the 14th of April, 1757.[2] Unlike Parker, who could read a little in the Bible, Ann did not even know her letters. A prudent woman and an indulgent mother, she showed great courage and endurance under the dropsy with which she became afflicted some few years after John's birth. The bond of understanding between her and her only son was strong and lasting.

Clare was the elder of twins. The other child was a "bouncing girl, while John might have gone into a pint pot ";[4] but the younger, more promising child died soon after birth, as we know from a sonnet of Clare's published in the London Magazine for August, 1821, "To a Twin Sister who Died in Infancy." Though Clare apostrophised her as "Bessey," there is record in the registers of neither her baptism nor her death, so it is probable that she was given the

unceremonious burial by night accorded to unbaptized
babies. Another child, Elizabeth, was christened on the
7th of July, 1796, but she did not live to grow up. A third
daughter, born on the 1st of April, 1798, and ten days later
christened Sophy, lived with her father and mother in the
cottage at Helpston until at least 1824. She afterwards
married an innkeeper named Kettle, of Newborough, a fen
village about five miles away. Sophy worshipped her brother,
and many times saved him from trouble because she knew
where to find him at bedtime. Later she saved from
destruction poems which he used to hide in the wall of the
cottage beside the fireplace.

Before the most dire poverty overtook the family at Helpston and Parker Clare was unable to work through rheumatism, they struggled along happily enough. The children,
through the mother's industry, were decently, if meanly,
clad. "And housewife's care in many a patch was seen";
often, perhaps, ends met so hardly that the parents gave
their last mouthful so that the children might not go short.
Frequently, "that sad fiend" necessity was at their backs
to oppress them, while the farmer, like Stephen Duck's
employer, was no friend, but an enemy, to the hireling
thresher. Yet, in spite of all this, John's childhood, and
especially his early childhood, was gloriously happy. Times
without number after he grew up he recalled its joys:

> *O, I could tell for aye and never tire*
> *The simple trifles infancy supplies;*
> *O, I could view for ever and admire*
> *The gilded prospects of its painted skies.*

When he was a very small boy, the line where those
painted skies met the earth so stirred his fancy that he set
out to find the horizon:

> *To the world's end I thought I'd go,*
> *And o'er the brink just peep adown*
> *To see the mighty depths below.*

He records this attempt to outwit distance:

"It cost my parents some anxiety. It was summer. I started off in the morning to get rotten sticks, and I had a feeling to wander about the fields, and I indulged it. I had often seen the large heath called Emmonsales stretching its yellow furze from my eye into unknown solitudes where I went with the mere-openers, and my curiosity urged me to steal an opportunity to explore it that morning. I had imagined that the wood's end was at the horizon and that a day's journey was able to find it; so I went on with my heart full of hopes of pleasant discoveries, expecting when I got to the brink of the world I could look down like looking into a large pit and see into its secret the same as I believed I could see heaven by looking into the water. So I eagerly wandered on and rambled along the furze the whole day till I got out of my knowledge and the very wild flowers seemed to forget me. I imagined they were the inhabitants of new countries. The very sun seemed to be a new one and shone in a different grandeur in the sky. Still I felt no fear; my wonder-seeking happiness had no room for that. I was finding new wonders every minute and was walking in a new world and expecting the world's end; but it never came. ... The sky still touched the ground in the distance, and my childish wisdom was puzzled. Night came on before I had time to fancy the morning was by, which made me hasten to reach home. I knew not which way to turn, but chance put me in the right track, and when I got back into my own fields I did not know them, everything looked so different. The church peeping over the woods could hardly reconcile me. When I got home I found my parents in the greatest distress and half the village about hunting me. One of the woodmen in the woods had been killed by the fall of a tree, and it seemed to strengthen their terrors that some accident had befallen myself."

Although Clare might, writing later, in certain moods remember himself as a lonely boy with little relish for the games and fun and rivalry of companions, it seems clear that this love of solitude did not distinguish him till after the first boisterous discovery of the countryside as a playground. No small child with an imagination like Clare's, turned loose

in all seasons among lanes and meadows, could keep all the
exciting adventures and inventions to himself. Later on, but
still in boyhood, when his feeling for the country deepened,
he wanted the earth for his own thoughts only. But meanwhile he and his nameless companions played all the games
that happy, unconfined country children have played always.
In summer they cut the stalks from mushrooms and floated
them for mimic boats down the streams ; or, in days when
rumours of war reached their heedless ears, they waded slyly
through the farmer's wheat to get the corn-cockle for a
" wild cockade," tore through the woods to pull kecks for
bugles, and, when they were hungry, stole peas from the fields,
and ate crab-apples and hazel-nuts, " shells, pith and all."
Sometimes their imaginations supplied the feasts ; they made
houses of clay and sticks and stones, hoarded bits of broken
pot for pottery, spread on a " table-stone " their burdock-
leaf of a table-cloth, had mallow-seeds for cheeses and the
seedbox of the sinister henbane for loaves of bread ; flowers
of the greater bindweed made enviable drinking-horns.
 Their games and pastimes were endless :

> *We shot our arrows from our bows,*
>   *Like any archer proud,*
> *And thought when lost they went so high*
>   *To lodge upon a cloud;*

>   .   .   .   .

> *We often tried to force the snail*
>   *To leave his harvest horn*
> *By singing that the beggarman*
>   *Was coming for his corn.*
> *We thought we forced the lady-cow*
>   *To tell the time of day,*
> *'Twas one o'clock and two o'clock,*
>   *And then she flew away.*

> *We bawled to beetles as they ran*
>   *That their children were all gone,*
> *Their houses down and door-key hid*
>   *Beneath the golden stone.*

The most serious employment was taking their fathers'
dinners to the hayfield and refilling the empty water-bottles
at one of the springs. Then they ran off behind the loaded
hay-wain "just for the joy of riding back again."

Their games were those that have not grown old or stale
from the time when the boys of Ancient Greece played
them until now—leap-frog, hare-and-hounds, ducks-and-
drakes, nine-peg Morris "nicked upon the green," hopscotch,
and

> Chucking up the bouncing ball
> By bee-haunted cottage wall.

Langley Bush, formerly the meeting-place of the old hundred
court of Nassaburgh, was a special rendezvous for fun.
Round it the boys played clink-and-bandy and chock-and-
taw. When cowslip-time came, they went off with baskets
to gather the flowers for tea and for wine, and garlanded
the village street on feast-days with the blossoms.

There were few clouds over Clare's early childhood ; he
always remembered these jubilant days with regret, could
not recall them often or vividly enough.

> Time writes them with a golden pen,
> But never lives them back again.

Yet, even as early as this, gleams of that rarer fancy which
was to be his comfort and his torment for so many years are
evident. Like most children, he believed in fairies ; but when,
with most, the very sympathy with these beliefs is fading,
Clare was remembering

> Acres of little yellow weeds,
> The wheat-fields' constant blooms
> That ripen into prickly seeds
> For fairy curry-combs,
> To comb and clean the little things
> That draw their nightly wain,
> And so they scrub the beetle's wings
> Till he can fly again.

The grey lichens among the creeping thyme at Swordy Well
for him as a boy were fairy forests : like the maturer Blake,
he saw the little folks' footmarks in the dark rings among the
mole-hills, "where ploughshares never come to hurt the
things antiquity hath charge of ";

> *And flannel felt for the beds of the queen*
> *From the soft inside of the shell of the bean,*
> *Where the gipsies down in the lonely dells*
> *Had littered and left the plundered shells.*

Although he kept his fancies to himself, he believed all these
hints of færie more literally than most boys. And, in such an
unlettered spot as Helpston was a hundred and thirty years
ago, when the existence of witches, will-o'-the-wisps, and
fairies was an open question in the minds of most of the
grown-ups, there was plenty of this kind of goblin-food for
a child's imagination.

"The sallow palms were called, when I was a boy, geese-
and-goslings and cats-and-kitlings. I asked an old cow-
woman or herd-woman the reason, and she said it might be
from their being known to belong to the fairies, who changed
them into wild geese and goslings and cats and kitlings at
their pleasure, or anything else, when they feasted on the
rings in the pasture on summer nights."

He often listened to the tales of other old dames, as they
sat down on summer noons to take their snuff. Stories of
Hickathrift and Jack the Giant-killer filled him with "fearful
ecstasy." His mother, too, knew all the superstitions of the
village, about the ghosts that haunted the spot where, in her
youth, the gibbet stood, about all the will-o'-the-wisps and
the witches. On winter evenings she regaled them with these
tales till the silent children trembled. Then she would break
off, promising to finish her stories the next night.

> *The children steal away to bed,*
> *And up the ladder softly tread;*

Scarce daring—from their fearful joys—
To look behind or make a noise;

.   .   .   .   .

While yet, to fancy's sleepless eye,
Witches on sheep-trays gallop by. . .

The minds of Parker and Ann Clare were uncorrupted by
that evil that was creeping upon the minds of the adult poor
about this time as a result of the industrial system—the
exploitation of children. The Clares did not regard their
son as a means of making money. If Ann believed the higher
learning to be witchcraft, she still respected it. She was
anxious that John should have the best education that the
village and their circumstances could give. Parker, always
the kindliest of fathers, backed her ambition loyally against
great odds. Never less than three months out of the twelve
were spared for schooling. The child went first to a dame-
school in the village, where he learnt to spell a little and to
read from the Bible. From the age of about seven to twelve
he attended, but still intermittently, a school at Glinton.
To obtain money for this, he helped his father at threshing,
and worked for the farmers himself, tending sheep and cows,
and bird-scaring in the fields; the wages for eight weeks'
work paid for one month's schooling. His sister Sophy, too,
may have gone to school, since in 1820 she wrote a very fair
hand. At Glinton, under a master named Seaton, Clare
learned to read and write and to understand the rudiments
of arithmetic. At first he had a boy's usual attitude to school,
hating the one o'clock bell which called him from play,
disliking the imprisonment, and mourning for liberty over
his old thumb-soiled horn book. A boy who loved his meadow
playground as dearly as Clare did could not be expected
to find the restraint anything but irksome. In time, though,
the cottage table of an evening became littered with pens
and paper. Ann, at her wheel, regarded them with awe and
secret delight.

Still Clare had not yet that high seriousness with which
he later regarded his studies. There were occasions when
he played truant from school, fishing for struttle and

gudgeon, seeking the "painted pooties" by the dyke-sides, or following the landrail's wandering voice for hours in the vain hope of finding her nest.

But in school, under Seaton, the children were awed and still. He was an old man, white-haired already, and he died before Clare reached the age of twelve; his peeled wand hung always over the smoke-stained chimney-piece. His school was held in the vestry of the church; the graveyard was the children's playground. The day-school was perhaps the same room as that in which the Sunday-school was held, to which Clare went as well, both his parents belonging to the Church of England. At the day-school, when he had mastered the "Three R's," Seaton encouraged him to go further, with the hope of qualifying himself for the position of usher in a village school. Sometimes the boy received from the master as much as threepence a week, reward for well-learnt work; once he earned sixpence for repeating, from memory, the third chapter of Job. Inspired by Seaton's praise, he tried to master the further intricacies of mathematics and spelling from such books as Bonnycastle and Fenning, and a love of learning was beginning to set him a little apart from the other boys.

Yet, in spite of what he tells us later, that he "had little relish for the pastimes of youth," Clare had, up to the age of eleven or twelve at least, a great pleasure in most of the enjoyments which his village life had to offer; and, when he was not at school or at work, he found time for all possible fun. Helpston prided itself on the upkeep of its feast-days. At Martinmas, neighbours met together to drink warm, nutmegged ale, to roast apples, and to play games till the old cottages rang with merriment. One was bid to shut his eyes and open his mouth to taste what gifts were sent him—when he received, amid peals of laughter, a handful of ashes on his tongue. Hodge was often baited with tricks, and that none too gently; he was invited to sit between two maids on a sheet thrown over a tub of water, but as he sat they rose and "let him swearing in." Then fortunes were told, while " poor beguilèd Kate," silent in her corner, listened eagerly, and hoped for the sweetheart whom by her lapse she had forfeited. When they were tired of " fortunes," the revellers made music with warming-pans and muffled combs, and danced till they were tired. About midnight they all went home, with lanterns gleaming along the snow.

Weddings and house-warmings and harvest-homes were great occasions for festivities; but Statute-time, the labourers' holiday week, when they spent all their past year's savings and hired themselves to new masters for the coming twelve months, was to the hard-working villagers of Helpston the most uproarious good time of all. At this May fair the country people came from all the surrounding villages and amused themselves with such rustic sports as hunting a "soapt and larded " pig, badger-baiting and cock-fighting, racing and wrestling:

> *Where wrestlers join to tug each other down,*
> *And thrust and kick with hard, revengeful toe.*

It is true that Clare, even though his father had local fame in this pastime, could not bear to look on at the rougher games. Indeed, though he loved to watch many of the sports, he perhaps did not often care to join in the "rude revelry." In the evening there was dancing to the tune of the gipsy's fiddle, when the maids, cotton drabs and worsted hose put away, enjoyed themselves to the full; or there was ale-drinking in the public-houses, where the rattling tongue of the landlady could barely keep peace among the brawlers, especially if there happened to be a sergeant or two recruiting for the Militia: these would ogle the girls from their lovers, and rouse the mettle of the men till they either fought among themselves or enlisted to fight shoulder to shoulder against Napoleon.

Still, for all his slight frame and acknowledged diffidence, Clare was by no means lacking in prowess at climbing trees or jumping fences and streams. When competing in this way with other boys of the village, he had one or two rather risky adventures:

"What a many heedless escapes from death doth a boy's heedless life meet with ! I met with many in mine. Once, when wading in the meadow-pits with a lot of cow-tending boys, we bid to do each other's tasks. We had gone several times and it was my turn to attempt again, when I unconsciously got beside a gravel ledge into deep water. My heels slipt up and I siled down to the bottom. I felt the water choke me and the thunder in my ears, and I thought all was past. But some of the boys could swim and so I escaped. Another time we were swimming on bundles of bulrushes, when, getting to one end, mine suddenly bounced from under me like a cork and I made shift to struggle to a sallow-bush. Catching hold of the branches of it, I managed to get out, but how I did it I know not, for the water was very deep. Yet we had dabbled there Sunday after Sunday without the least fear of danger.

" Once, when bird-nesting in the woods, of which I was very fond, we found a large tree on which was a buzzard's nest. It was a very hard tree to climb ; there was no twigs to take hold of and it was too thick to swarm. So we consulted for a while, some proposing one thing and some another, till it was decided that a hook tied to the end of a long pole that would reach to the collar of the tree would be the best to get up by. In taking hold of it and swarming, several attempted to no purpose, and at last I tried, though I was rather loath to make the experiment. I succeeded in getting up to the collar, which swelled in such a projection from the tree that I could not make a landing without hazarding the dangerous attempt of clinging with my hands to the grain, and flinging my feet over it. I attempted it and failed; so there I hung with my hands, and my feet dangling in the air. I expected every moment to drop and be pashed to pieces, for I was a great height: but some of my companions below (while some ran away) had the shrewdness to put the pole under me, and by that means I got on the grain just in time before I was exhausted."

With work and school, rural pleasures and boyish escapes such as these, Clare's early years were occupied. He enjoyed most of the fun, but he was beginning to be solitary, preferring one intimate companion, or a book:

"But there used to be [one game], 'crookhorn,' in those days, I used to like, and 'duck under water' on May Eve, or to toss the cowslip balls over the garland that hung from chimney to chimney across the street. And there was going to Eastwell on a Sunday to drink sugar and water at the spring-head; but Enclosure came and drove these from the village. I used to be very fond of fishing and of a Sunday morning I have been out before the sun, delving for worms on some old weed-blanketed dunghill, and sliving off across the wet grass that overhung the narrow path. Then I used to stop to wring my wet trouser-bottoms now and then, and off again, beating the heavy drops off the grass with my pole-end, till I came to the flood-washed meadow stream. My tackle was easily fastened on, and my heart would thrill with hopes of success as I saw a sizeable gudgeon twinkle round the glossy pebbles, or a fish leap after a fly, or a floating something on the deeper water. Where is the angler that hath not felt these delights in his young days? And where is the angler that doth not feel taken with their memory when he is old?

"I used to be very fond of poking about the hedges in spring to hunt pooties, and I was no less fond of robbing the poor birds' nests, or searching among the prickly furze on the heath, poking sticks into the rabbit-holes and carefully observing when I took it out if there was down at the end, which was a sign of a nest with young. Then in went the arm up to the shoulder; and then fear came upon us that a snake might be concealed in the hole. Our bloods ran cold within us and started us off to other sports. We used to chase the squirrels in the woods from grain to grain, that would sit washing their faces on the other side and then peep at us again. We used to get boughs from the trees to beat a wasps' nest, till some of us were stung, and then we ran away to other amusements.

"The year used to be crowned with its holidays as thick as the boughs on a harvest-home. There was the long-wished-for Christmas, the celebrated week with two Sundays, when we used to watch the clerk return with his bundle of ever-greens and run for our bunch to stick [in] the windows and empty candlesticks hanging in the corner, or hasten to the woods to get ivy branches with their chocolate berries which our parents used to colour with [whiting] and the blue-bag, sticking the branches behind the pictures on the walls.

"Then came Valentine. Though young, we were not without loves. We had our favourites in the village, and we listened the expected noises of creeping feet and the tinkling latch as eagerly as upgrown loves; whether they came or not, it made no matter; disappointment was nothing in those matters. Then, the pleasure was all. Then came the first of April. O! how we talked and hoiped of it ere it came! of how we would make April fools of others and take care not to be caught ourselves, when, as soon as the day came, we were the first to be taken in by running on errands for pigeons' milk and glass-eyed needles or some such April fool. When we were undeceived, we blushed for shame and took care not to be taken in again, till the day returned, when the old deceptions were so far forgotten as to deceive us again.

"Then there was the first of May. We were too young to be claimants in the upgrown sports, but we joined our little interferences with them and ran under the extended hand-kerchiefs with the rest, unmolested. Then came the Feast,⁵ when the Cross was thronged round with stalls of toys and many-coloured sugar-plums and sweets, horses on wheels with their flowing manes, lambs with their red necklaces, and box-cuckoos. We looked on these fineries till the imagination almost coaxed our itching fingers to steal and seemed to upbraid our fears for not daring to do it. The sweetmeats were unbounded; there was barley-sugar, candied lemon, candied horehound, and candied peppermint, with swarms of coloured sugar plums and tins of lollipops. Our mouths watered at such luxuries; we had our penny, but we knew not how to lay it out; there were gingerbread coaches and gingerbread milkmaids, and, to gratify two propensities, the taste and the fancy together, we bought one of these gilded toys and thought we had husbanded our pennies well till they were gone; and then we went away to coax our parents for more, thinking of making better bargains when we got money again.

"Then came the sheep-shearing, where we were sure of frumity from the old shepherds, if we sought the clipping-pens. And lastly came the harvest-home and its cross-skittles. Ah, what a paradise begins with life, and what a wilderness the knowledge of the world discloses! Surely the Garden of Eden was nothing more than our first parents' entrance upon life, and the loss of it their knowledge of the world."

II

A HAPPY AND A LONELY BOY
1805–1809

He ne'er is crown'd
With immortality who fears to follow
Where airy voices lead.

CLARE CLAIRMONT'S DIARY.

FROM the age of about ten, in spite of the many social
recreations of his village life, Clare's liking for rambles
with one intimate companion became marked. His first friendship was with Richard Turnill, a school companion and the
younger son of a neighbouring farmer for whom Parker
Clare sometimes worked.

"Among all the friendships I have made in life, those of
school-friends and childish acquaintances are the sweetest
to remember. There is no deception among them; there is
no regret in them but the loss; they are the fairest, sunniest
pages memory ever doubles down in the checkered volume of
life to refer to; there are no blotches upon them; they are
not found[ed], like bargains, on matters of interest, nor
broken for selfish ends. . . . One of my first friendships was
with Richard, the brother of John Turnill. . . . What number-
less hopes of successes did we whisper over, as we hunted
among the short, snubby bushes of the heath or hedgerows,
or crept among the blackthorn sprays after the nest of the
nightingale! What happy discourses of planning pleasures
did we talk over, as we lay on the soft summer grass, gazing
into the blue sky, shaping the passing clouds to things
familiar with our memories, dreaming of the days to come
when we should mix with the world and be men."

The sympathy and affection which thus sprang up between
Clare and Richard was unfortunately soon broken. Richard

died of typhus fever. He was a gentle boy, very much after Clare's own heart; Clare thought him "all goodness centred in one piece," and grieved for him in at least three poems many years afterwards:

> The grass, all dropping wet with dew,
>   Low bent its tiny spears;
> The lowly daisy bended too,
>   More lowly with my tears.
>
> O Turnill, Turnill, dear should[st] thou
>   To this fond mourner be,
> By being so much troubled now,
>   From just a-naming thee!

His regret for this earliest friend and their careless joys is perhaps reflected, too, in one of his unfinished prose tales, "The Two Soldiers," where one character reminds his companion: "These days, Richard, are all over, and our happiness gone after them, for some other boys to pick up and lose again as we did."

Although his affection for, and the death of, Richard Turnill laid deep hold of Clare's childish emotions, yet there was begun about this time another friendship which was destined to have a far greater influence on him. This was with Mary, the blue-eyed daughter of James Joyce, a Glinton farmer; it began only as a preference among schoolmates. Mary Joyce, four years younger than he, was born in January 1797, and towards the end of his year under Seaton, perhaps after Turnill's death, Clare and Mary worked and played together. He now loved the old church school under "the spire where pellitory dangled and grew" too well to play truant:

"I was a lover very early in life; my first attachment, being a schoolboy affection, was for Mary, who was beloved with a romantic or Platonic sort of feeling. If I could but gaze on her face or fancy a smile on her countenance, it was sufficient; I went away satisfied. We played with each other, but named nothing of love; yet I fancied her eyes told me her

CJ

affections. We walked together as school-companions in leisure hours, but our talk was of play, and our actions the wanton nonsense of children. Yet, young as my heart was, it would turn chill when I touched her hand, and tremble, and I fancied her feelings were the same; for as I gazed earnestly in her face, a tear would hang in her smiling eye and she would turn to wipe it away. Her heart was as tender as a bird's. . . . I cannot forget her little playful fairy form and witching smile even now.

"I remember an accident that roused my best intentions, and hurt my affection into the rude feelings of imaginary cruelty. When playing one day in the churchyard I threw a green walnut that hit her on the eye. She wept, and I hid my sorrow and my affection together under the shame of not showing regret, lest others might laugh it into love."

Sometimes, as he says, this "clownish, silent boy," in his patched coat, and the daughter of the well-to-do farmer wandered together among the fields. Then he

> *Loved to watch her wistful look*
> *Following white moths down the brook;*
> *And thrilled to mark her beaming eyes*
> *Bright'ning in pleasure and surprise,*
> *To meet the wild mysterious things*
> *That evening's soothing presence brings.*

Here too was a companion after Clare's own heart.

He was all this time becoming more and more attached to nature, to "woodland peace and privacy," longing for spring and the first primrose, now shunning the gangs of lads and their unpleasing play. The gossips began to think him "half a ninny," and prophesied no good for him:

"In fact I grew so fond of being alone at last that my mother was fain to force me into company; for the neighbours had assured her mind into the fact that I was no better than crazy. . . ."

He was reading eagerly the few books that came his way:

"The first books I got hold of, beside the Bible and the Prayer-Book, were an old book of Essays with no title, another large one on Farming, *Robin Hood's Garland*, and *The*

Scotch Rogue. The old book of Farming, and Essays, belonged
to old Mr. Gee. He had had a good bringing up and was a
decent scholar, and he was always pleased to lend me them,
even before I could read. . . . I became acquainted with
Robinson Crusoe very early in life, having borrowed it of a
boy in Glinton school, of the name of Stimson, who only
dare lend it to me for a few days for fear of his uncle's
knowing of it, to whom it belonged. Yet I had it a sufficient
time to fill my fancies."

There were also the "sixpenny romances" sold by the
hawkers.

About now, too, this boy who could spend hours creeping
among the matted thorn-bushes to watch the nightingale
feed her young began to be stirred by poetry. He spent the
winter evenings on his corner stool beside the hearth,
"reading poems not too long." Wordsworth's "We are
Seven," hawked about among the villages as a penny
ballad, was a favourite; and "Jessie, the Flower o' Dumb-
lane," one of the most popular, if not one of the best, achievements of the Scottish song-writer, Robert Tannahill, was
also sold on penny sheets, and was among the first he
read. Years after his childhood, Clare recalled his father's
reading him some stanzas from Pomfret's "Love Triumphant
over Reason," a poem then well known among the poor
folk. That rhythm haunted him often. And his father and
mother, who whiled away the long nights with singing
traditional ballads such as "Fare Thee Well," "Barbara
Allen,"and "Peggy Band," set him musing with their songs.

But Parker Clare was earning less and less money by his
labour, and the idea of John's qualifying for the post of usher
in a school became merely a castle in the air. He was now
thought learned enough for his "intended trade, which was,
to be a shoemaker"; so he was taken away from Seaton's
day-school, but, on the exhortation of the master, he was to
continue his studies at a night-school at Glinton. For
some time after his leaving the day-school there was no
suitable work at hand. He was slight of frame, because of
under-nourishment rather than from an inherited lack of

constitution, and thus he was not particularly suited to out-door work. In place of something better, he continued to work for the neighbouring farmers as he had done to earn the money for his education up to now; and in the winter he attended the night-school at Glinton kept by a Mr. Merri-shaw. Seaton died in 1805 or 1806, so that Merrishaw was perhaps both day- and evening-school master by this time.

Somehow Clare's cypher-book, with dates for 1803 and 1806, has escaped the demolitions of time. It contains sums in addition, multiplication, and rule-of-three, worked in his boyish figuring.

Like Seaton, this master was an old, white-haired man. He died in November, 1809, but not before he had so fostered Clare's love of reading that no lack of books afterwards could kill the boy's enthusiasm. While Merrishaw lived, Clare had the run of his small library, and years afterwards, in 1822, he found and visited his master's neglected grave, when he paid tribute to the old man's memory in a long poem of gratitude. James Merrishaw, a true scholar, died poor and lonely.

But meanwhile Clare had become team-leader, probably on the farm of Mr. Turnill, for whom he worked at weeding-time and haytime. Here, one day, when he saw the loader fall from the top of his wagon and break his neck, he was so affected that for some years afterwards he was taken with fits every spring and autumn. He tells how, at the time of the accident:

"The ghastly paleness of death struck such a terror on me that I could not forget it for years, and my dreams were constantly wanderings in churchyards, digging graves, seeing spirits in charnel-houses, etc., etc.

"In my fits I swooned away without a struggle, and felt nothing more than if I'd been in a dreamless sleep after I came to myself; but I was always warn'd of their coming by a chillness and dithering, that seemed to creep from one's toes till it got up to one's head, when I turned senseless and fell. . . . These fits were stopt by a Mr. Arnold, M.D., of Stamford. . . ."

Clare's work, his night-schooling, and his solitary musing, went on as before. Moreover, since Richard Turnill was dead, and Clare's leaving day-school had separated him for the time from Mary Joyce, he made two new confidants. One was John, the elder brother of Richard Turnill, a boy who had been educated at a boarding-school and was now at home working for his father and carrying on his studies energetically by himself. Clare's great ambition at the moment was to write "copper-plate" and to continue with his mathematics. John Turnill's interests were very varied indeed.

"John's acquaintance began with learning me, on winter nights, to write and sum. He was of a studious musing turn of mind, and fond of books, always carrying one of some sort in his pocket to read between toils, at leisure hours. They were sometimes sixpenny books of stories and at other times the books which he used at school; for he had been [to a] boarding-school and read in books there that are unknown in a village school.

"But in the midst of all his inventions and thirst after knowledge, a cousin came down from London who had a power of getting him a place in the Excise, his present occupation. So his friends' hopes were ripened and he was sent to school and then to the Excise; and all his hopes, anxieties, and crowds of schemes were left unfinished behind, to make room for new ones."

There is a family tradition that the vastness of the night sky seen through Turnill's telescope sent Clare home troubled and frightened. But, whether that is true or not, the departure of this friend left him without congenial companionship again. It deprived him, too, of a great source of books and information; for John Turnill spared neither time nor patience to teach the younger boy all he himself knew. The two kept in touch with each other until at least 1822. In September of that year Turnill wrote him a long rhyming letter from Manchester, but, though it expresses appreciation of Clare, it is without detail and contains no news.

Among Clare's manuscripts there are two poems to this
friend, the better of which is already printed.

> *Turnill, we toiled together all the day,*
> *And lived like hermits from the boys at play* . . .

Remarkably enough, Clare managed to find in this
remote place, where, he afterwards wrote, " useless Ignorance slumbers life away," yet another boy who was interested in books and flowers and insects, as he himself was.
So his spare time was once more occupied to his own delight:

"I found another boy-acquaintance, which grew up with
few breaks in it to manhood, with Tom Porter, who lives in
a lone cottage on Ashton Green. He had a fondness for
flowers and gardens, and possessed a few old books. . . .
Two which I used to be most pleased with were Sandys'
Travels and Parkinson's *Herbal*, and I used often to make
Sunday visits to read them. His fondness for books [was for]
those of gardening, and he bought, and buys still, the second-
hand ones that treat upon that subject, which chance lays
his hands on. We used to go out on Sundays to hunt curious
wild flowers such as the orchids."

Although George Sandys, Gibbon's "judicious traveller,"
had become a well-known writer, yet it is nevertheless an
inspiration and a revelation to find these "peasant" boys of
the early nineteenth century turning with delight to such
authors as Sandys and Parkinson for their recreation. Up
to now Clare had not, beyond his school-books, a single
volume of his own. In this year, 1806, when he was thirteen,
he managed to acquire two of note. One was a copy of
Watts's *Hymns and Spiritual Songs*, purchased of "J. T.
Drakard, Printer, Bookseller, Stationer, Binder, Music
Seller, Dealer in genuine Patent Medicines, Perfumery,
Umbrellas, Hat Cases, Bonnet Boxes, Trinkets, etc.," of
Stamford. The book contains a neat signature and the date
1806, but it is not certain whether he bought it with his own
money or not. The next book he bought he undoubtedly paid
for himself. In this same year either Tom Porter or another

young man in the village showed him Thomson's *Seasons*.
During the day he had time to dip into the book a good
deal, by stealth, when he ought to have been working.
Thomson's book had been so popular that its fame had
penetrated into almost every obscure country alehouse. Its
author could, as Coleridge said, "carry his fellow-men
along with him into nature." *The Seasons* so impressed Clare
that he managed to "tease" one and sixpence out of his
father, and to walk to Stamford the next Sunday morning
intending to buy the book for himself. This tale of him is
well known. The Stamford shop was shut. He had to give
one of his companions twopence to tend his horses for him,
while he stole away again to Stamford one day in the following week. This time he got his book, and for sixpence less
than he anticipated. As he came home, he says, through the
grove of limes in Burghley Park, his "itching after rhyme,"
an instinct that would not be still, which up to this time had
shown itself only in scribbled stanzas in his exercise-books,
expressed itself in what he afterwards said was his first
poem. This was "The Morning Walk." Even if he touched
it up later, this still-unpublished fragment deserves a hearing
at this point in his life. Though *The Seasons* had urged him
to take up his pen, he used a rhyming stanza, and his contact
with nature was direct; it was not got through Thomson.

> *Come, lovely Lucy, let's away,*
> *Sweet morning calls and we'll obey;*
> *Look yonder! see, the rising sun*
> *His daily course has just begun;*
> *Let's lightly beat the dewy grass*
> *And mark each object as we pass;*
> *There the unheeded daisy grows;*
> *There the golden kingcup blows;*
> *There the stinking bryony weaves*
> *Round the hazel her scallopt leaves:*
> *Here the woodbine and the rose*
> *All their blushing sweets disclose:*
> *Ah, lovely Lucy, to describe*
> *The different flow'rets, tribe by tribe,*

Would be too much for me or you,
Or any shepherd lad to do;
Nay, had I Darwin's prying thought,
Or all the learning Ray has taught,
How soon description would exhaust,
And in sweet Flora's lap be lost . . .

The metre might be copied directly from Watts's hymns, and
the poem reminds us of Parnell's " Hymn to Contentment,"
yet "Darwin's prying thought" and the bryony's "scallopt
leaves" throw us a hint of what this boy of thirteen might
become as a poet of the future.

Poetry now had the power to give him

joy in most delicious ways,
And rest my spirits after weary days.

As he worked in the fields, he watched with glee when the
south grew black with rain. Then he liked to hasten home
"to feed on books"; but for the time he kept his own attempts
at poetry a secret from his parents. He told his aspirations
to the older boy, Tom Porter, but Porter discouragingly
placed greater value on grammar and learning than on
verses. Borrowing a book from him, Clare battled with
spelling and syntax, only to come at last to the wise conclusion that if he made himself understood he might do
without grammar; so he discarded the spelling-book and
went on with his rhyming alone.

"I cannot say what led me to dabble in rhyme. I made a
many things before I ventured to commit them to writing;
for I felt ashamed to expose them on paper, and after I
ventured to write them down my second thoughts blushed
over them. I burnt them for a long time, but as my feelings
grew into song, I felt a desire to preserve some, and used to
correct them over and over until the last copy had lost all
kindred to the first, even in the title. I went on for some years
in this way, wearing it in my memory as a secret to all;
though my parents used to know that my leisure was

occupied in writing, yet they had no knowledge of what I could be doing; for they never dreamed of me writing poetry.

"At length I ventured to divulge the secret a little by reading imitations of some popular song floating among the vulgar at the markets and fairs till they were common to all ; but these imitations they always laughed at, and told me I need never hope to make songs like them. This mortified me often, and almost made me desist; for I knew that the excelling such doggerel would be but a poor fame if I could do nothing better. But I hit upon a harmless deception by repeating my poems over a book as though I was reading it. This had the desired effect. They often praised them and said if I could write as good I should do. I hugged myself over this deception and often repeated it, and those which they praised as superior to others I tried to preserve in a hole in the wall; but my mother found out the hoard and unconsciously took them for kettle-holders and fire-lighters whenever she wanted paper, not knowing that they were anything further than attempts at learning to write; for they were written upon shop-paper of all colours, between the lines of old copy-books, and on any paper I could get at; for I was often wanting, though I saved almost every penny I had given me on Sundays and holidays to buy it instead oi sweetmeats and fruit. I used to feel a little mortified after I discovered it, but I dare not reveal my secret by owning to it and wishing her to desist; for I feared if I did she would have shown them to someone to judge of their value, which would have put me to shame. So I kept the secret disappointment to myself and wrote on, suffering her to destroy them as she pleased; but when I wrote anything which I imagined better than others, I preserved it in my pocket, till the paper was chafed through and destroyed."

His parents had naturally little regard at first for their son's poetic efforts, and he used their criticisms to improve his style. They were patient with his inaptitude for any kind of trade, but they distrusted his rhyming. Ann Clare is reported to have said

" When he was fourteen or fifteen, he would shew me a piece of paper, printed sometimes on one side, and scrawled all over on the other, and he would say, Mother, this is

worth *so* much; and I used to say to him, Aye, boy, it looks
as if it warr!—but I thought he was wasting his time."[1]

But, in spite of her seeming hostility, she indulged his
fancy as far as her poverty allowed her:

"My mother bought me a pictured pocket-handkerchief
from Deeping May fair, as a fairing, on which was a picture
of Chatterton and his verses on Resignation.[2] She was mentioning the singular circumstance to me yesterday, by asking
me whether I remembered it, and saying that she little
thought I should be a poet then. Chatterton's name was
clouded in melancholy memories, while his extraordinary
genius was scarcely known. The common people knew he
was a poet and that was all. They know the name of Shakespeare as one, but the ballad-mongers who supply hawkers
with their ware are poets with them, and they imagine one
as great as the other. So much for that envied eminence of
common fame! I was fond of imitating everything I met with,
and therefore it was impossible to resist the opportunity
which this beautiful poem gave me."

The verses which he wrote concerning Chatterton were
composed a little later than this. Chatterton's tragic story
was often depicted on handkerchiefs, as well as extracts from
his poems, and the story was an inspiration to Clare among
the hardships of his own verse-making. He first came to
know Shakespeare as "a great playwright" through seeing
his name on the bills of the strolling players who visited the
village in his boyhood.

Thus he continued for some months, threshing with his
father or cow-tending for John Turnill's father and other
farmers, still attending Merrishaw's night-school at Glinton,
and using his spare time in writing verse or reading. What
he wrote about this time, and destroyed, was mostly "descriptive of local spots about the Lordship[3] and favourite
trees and flowers." "The Fate of Amy," later printed in his
first volume of poems in 1820, was begun when he was
fourteen. It was a true and tragic village story which he put
into stanzas under the influence of David Mallet's true and

tragic "Ballad of Edwin and Emma," which John Turnill had read to him while they were weeding.

Clare was encouraged to begin his own writing, as so many greater and less than he have been at the outset, because of some similarity between his own experience and another man's work that he had read and admired. But his sensitive perception of bird and insect, flower and plant, gave him his initial inspiration and his real bent. "The Lost Greyhound," another very early poem, was made, he says, when "I saw one lie quaking under a haystack in the snow." "Evening," also published in his first volume of poems, although "altered from a very early one of great length," is perhaps the first poem in which he freely but exactly translated his delighted sense of the *life* in creatures of nature into appropriate words:

> . . . *The heedless beetle bangs*
> *Against the cow-boy's dinner-tin,*
> *That o'er his shoulder hangs.*
>
> *The owls mope out, and scouting bats*
> *Begin their giddy round;*
> *While countless swarms of dancing gnats*
> *Each water-pudge surround.*

At this moment Clare was simply translating his appreciation of the bat's flight into the most accurate words he knew; he was sure that the result would be poetry, because of the intensity of his own feelings about the bat. This was as far as he had advanced, by the age of about fourteen or fifteen, in his ideas about poetry.

Meanwhile, in lighter moods, he could still throw up his hat when he saw the "scouting" creature in the dusk, and bawl, "Bat, bat, come under my hat, and I'll give you a slice of bacon." He and Tom Porter made long expeditions after the rarer orchises of the district; bee and spider orchis were to be found in Ashton Stone Pits, one of the disused quarries of the neighbourhood, and also on Wittering Heath, farther away. They prized the moth mullein and the pasque flowers. They were not yet too grown-up to creep among the blackthorn thickets and down the hedge-sides on hands and knees, seeking the snail shells, as soon as the sun looked warm on the hedges. They now tried to classify them according to colours.

A boy who sought the nest of the wryneck and rejoiced to find her hissing over no less than seventeen eggs was sure to have pets. But Clare's method with his was a little unusual for a boy who lived in days before field naturalists like W. H. Hudson. He heard sorrow in the song of the caged linnet and redcap, and not joy; he believed that he could learn more intimately the daily habits of birds without confining them:

"I kept a tamed cock sparrow three years. It was so tame that it would come when called, and flew where it pleased. When I first had the sparrow, I was fearful of the cat's killing it, so I used to hold the bird in my hand towards her, and when she attempted to smell of it I beat her. She at last would take no notice of it, and I ventured to let it loose in the house. They were both very shy at each other at first, and when the sparrow ventured to chirp the cat would brighten up as if she intended to seize it; but she went no further than a look or smell. At length she had kittens, and when they were taken away she grew so fond of the sparrow as to attempt to caress it. The sparrow was startled at first, but came to by degrees and ventured so far at last [as] to perch upon her back. Puss would call for it when out of her sight like a kitten, and would lay mice before it the same as she would for her own young; and they always lived in harmony; so much so [that] the sparrow would often take away bits of bread from under the cat's nose and even put itself in a posture of resistance, when offended, as if it reckoned her nothing more than one of its kind. In winter, when we could not bear the doors open to let the sparrow come out and in, I was allowed to take a pane out of the window; but in the spring of the third year my poor Tom Sparrow—for that was the name he was called by—went out and never returned. I went day after day, calling out for Tom, and eagerly eyeing every sparrow on the house; but none answered the name; for he would come down in a moment to the call, and perch upon my hand to be fed. I gave it out that some cat which it mistook for its old favourite betrayed its confidence and destroyed it."

There was also a robin which Clare tamed so that it would perch on his finger and eat from his hand; but

"it would never stay in the house at night, though it would attempt to perch on the chair-spindles, clean its bill, ruffle its feathers, and put its head under its wing as if it had made up its mind to stay; but something or other always molested it, when it suddenly sought its old broken pane and departed. It was sure to be the first riser in the morning."

Though Clare might labour with zeal and ardour to excel John Turnill in writing, and although he had written, secretly, verses of merit, yet the problem of a trade for him was becoming acute. There was talk of shoemaking for him, as there had been for Linnæus, not because Clare was considered a dunce, as the great naturalist was thought to be, but rather because of his unfitness for heavier work. The task was a difficult one, and the boy showed no willingness nor special leaning which might have rewarded his parents' patience with him. By this time he was fourteen, and had probably, under stress of poverty, ceased to attend the night-school.

"After I had done with going to school it was proposed that I should be bound apprentice to a shoe-maker; but I rather disliked this bondage. My scholarship was to extend no further than to qualify me for the business of a shoe-maker or stone-mason, so I learnt cross-multiplication for the one and bills of account for the other; but I was not to be either at last. A man of the name of Mowbray, of Glinton, would have taken me for a trifle, and another at home was desirous of taking me merely out of kindness to my father, but the trifle they wanted could not be found. I did not much relish the confinement of apprenticeship.

"This Will Farrow [the shoe-maker] was a village wit, a very droll fellow, a sort of Æsop. His shop used to be a place of amusement for the young ploughmen and labourers on winter evenings. He was famous for a joke and a droll story, and had a peculiar knack at making up laughable anecdotes on any curious 'bull' which offered in the village, and a satirical turn for applying nicknames to people, who were almost sure to be called by the one given till the day they died, and remembered by it afterwards when their own was forgotten. . . . He had a brother living who was a sailor twenty-one years and who kept a journal of his life, which he got me to copy out.

"George Shelton, too, a stone-mason, would have taken me, but I disliked this too, and shied off with the excuse of not liking to climb, though I had clomb trees in rapture after the nests of kites and magpies. This fondness for climbing trees after birds' nests went against me, but I whimpered and turned a sullen eye upon every occasion till they gave me my will. My parents' hopes were almost gone, as they thought I had been born with a dislike to work, and a view to have my liberty and remain idle. But the fact was I felt timid and fearful of undertaking the first trial in everything. They would not urge me to anything against my will, so I lived on at home taking work as it fell.

"I went weeding wheat in the spring with old women, listening to their songs and stories, which shortened the day. In summer I joined the haymakers in the meadow, or helped upon the stacks. When I was out of work, I went to the woods gathering rotten sticks or picking up dried cow-dung in the pasture, which we call cazons, for firing."

For a time, evidently, he was happy enough with such mean employment as this. In the days before the old village organisation was swept away by Enclosure, the pleasures of shepherds and herdboys had an innocent gaiety that was lost for ever a few years later. Sundays especially Clare remembered afterwards for their quiet enjoyment. He no longer cared for church-going, and when the bells rang from the "steeples shining round," and the farmers were nodding over their prayer-books, he and other shepherds sat on the heath and mused over the landscape in true country fashion: or

in snug nooks their huts beside,
The gipsy blazes they provide;

Shaking the rotten from the trees,
While some sit round and shell the peas,
Or pick from hedges pilfer-wood
To boil on props their stolen food:

.   .   .   .

While one within his scrip contains
A shattered Bible's thumbed remains,

.   .   .   .

And oft he'll read it to the rest,
Whose ignorance in every mood
Pays more regard to Robin Hood,
And Giant Bluebeard, and such tales,
That live like flowers in rural vales.

"Nature's niggard hand" is not discernible over this scene: nor does Clare, a peasant himself, often mention in his later writings the "boobies' broil" which Crabbe observed to be so often the end of the pleasures of the poor. Though Crabbe's pictures were needed to dispel the Arcadian illusion of his time and to show up the misery and degradation of the lower classes, they were, perhaps because of that very need, bound to be grim and unrelieved; his description of a cottage is, as Hazlitt says, like that of a "person sent there to distrain for rent." Clare, coming later, seeing from within and not from without, does not unduly stress the miseries of poverty, nor the shames of ignorance. His descriptions, both in prose and verse, of the life of the agricultural poor of his day give an almost perfectly balanced account of the innocence and the ignorance of village life in the early nineteenth century.

But meanwhile he is still a boy, and has begun to long for something better than this irregular work at home. His own narrative continues:

"Thus I lived for a season, spending the intervals of play along with shepherders or herdboys in lone spots out of sight; for I had grown big enough to be ashamed of it, and I felt a sort of hopeless prospect around me of not being able to meet manhood as I could wish. I always had that feeling of ambition about me that wishes to gain notice, or to rise above its fellows.

"After I had been left to my idle leisures awhile, doing jobs as I could catch them, I was then sent for to drive plough at Woodcroft Castle, of Oliver Cromwell memory. ' Though Mrs. Bellars, the mistress, is a kind, good woman, and though the place was a very good one for living, my mind was set against it from the first, and I was uneasily at rest. One of the disagreeable things was getting up so soon in the morning, as they are much earlier in some places than in others; and another was getting wetshod in my feet every morning and night; for in wet weather the moat used to overflow the causeway that led to the porch, and as there was but one way to the house, we were obliged to wade up to the knees to go in and out, excepting when the headman carried the boys over on his back, as he sometimes would. I stayed here one month, and then, on coming home to my parents, they could not persuade me to return. They now gave up all hopes of doing any good with me, and fancied I should make nothing but a soldier."

Here was an opportunity lost. Mrs. Bellars, however, overlooking this childish defaulting, later became a good friend who lightened the burden of poverty in the Clare household with occasional gifts. But almost at once there was hope of a situation for Clare which fostered his ambitions to be something different from his fellows. His uncle, Morris Stimson, was footman for a lawyer named Bellamy at Wisbech. There was a vacancy in Bellamy's office for a writer, or clerk, and Morris Stimson promised to do his best to get the boy the place. He was certain that Clare was "scholar good enough," but, though his father and mother were "full as certain," Clare himself was timid and shy and doubted his abilities very strongly. Counsellor Bellamy wished to see the aspirant for the post, at Wisbech. To get there, Clare would have to walk the seven miles to Peterborough, and then go, as Hazlitt went in *his* youth to see the farm where his mother was born, down the river Nen by one of the two packet-boats. Peterborough, in those days before the railways a small city of about five thousand inhabitants, depended a great deal for its communications on its river. The city stood on rising ground above the Nen,

which, at this point, separates the county from Huntingdon-
shire. The more important town of Stamford had the only
local newspaper of the time, the *Stamford Mercury*, and on
Stamford Peterborough depended for the coach to London.
In his walk Clare would go down the narrow street to the
fairground and the old Peterborough Brig, beside which
the packet lay. He would "hear the hoarse murmur of the
bargemen . . . come up from the willowy stream, sounding
low and underground like the voice of the bittern"; see,
from the rising ground above the Brig, "the fresh marshes
stretching out in endless level perspective, (as if Paul Potter
had painted them,) with the cattle, the windmills, and the
red-tiled cottages, gleaming in the sun to the very verge of
the horizon."[5]

Clare himself describes his feelings during this first journey
of his life:

"I started for Wisbech with a timid sort of pleasure, and
when I got to Glinton turnpike I turned back to look on the
old church as if I was going into another country. Wisbech
was a foreign land to me; for I had never been above eight
miles from home in my life. I could not fancy England much
larger than the part I knew. At Peterborough Brig I got
into the boat that carries passengers to Wisbech once a
week, and returns the third day, a distance of twenty-one
miles for eighteenpence. I kept thinking all the way in the
boat what answers I should make to the questions asked,
and then put questions to myself and shaped proper replies
as I thought would succeed; and then my heart burnt within
me at the hopes of success. I thought of the figure I should
make afterwards when I went to see my friends, dressed up
as a writer in a lawyer's office. I could scarcely contain
myself at times, and even broke out into a tittering laugh;
but I was damped quickly when I thought of the impos-
sibilities of success; for I had no prepossessing appearance
to win favours for such a place. My mother trimmed me up
as smart as she could. She had found me a white neckcloth,
and got me a pair of gloves to hide my coarse hands, but I
had outgrown my coat and almost left the sleeves at the
elbows; and all my other garments betrayed too old an
acquaintance with me to make me as genteel as could have

DJ

been wished. But I had got my father's and mother's blessings and encouragements, and my own hopes in the bargain made me altogether stout in the dreams of success.

"At length the end of my journey approached. When the passengers looked out to see Wisbech Brig that stretches over the river in one arch, my heart swooned within me at the near approach of my destiny. 'To be or not to be'; I kept working my wits up how to make the best use of my tongue while the boatmen were steering for the shore, and when I was landed my thoughts were so busy that I had almost forgot the method of finding out the house by enquiring for Counsellor Bellamy. People stared at me and paused before they pointed down the street, as if they thought I was mistaken in the name. 'And are you sure it is Counsellor Bellamy you want?' said another. 'I am sure of it,' I said; and they showed me the house in a reluctant way. When I got up to the house I was puzzled, as I often have been, in finding but one entrance, where a fine garden gate with a 'Ring the bell' seemed to frown upon me as upon one too mean to be admitted. I paused, and felt fearful to ring."

It was not likely that a diffident, nervous boy such as this would do himself justice in an interview on which his ambition had founded such hopes. Clare continues the story of Bellamy's very natural rejection of him in another account:

"I was puzzled what to do, and wished myself a thousand times in my old corner at home. At length my hand trembled and pulled the bell. It rang, and to my great satisfaction my uncle came, being the only man-servant, and bade me welcome. 'I have told Master about your coming,' said he. 'You must not hang your head, but look up boldly and tell him what you can do.' So I went into the kitchen as boldly as I could and sat down to tea. But I ate nothing; I had filled my stomach with thoughts by the way. At length the Counsellor appeared, and I held up my head as well as I could; but it was like my hat, almost under my arm. ' Aye, aye, so this is your nephew, Morris, is he," said the Counsellor. 'Yes, Sir,' said my uncle. 'Aye, aye, so this is your nephew,' repeated the Counsellor, rubbing his hands as he left the room. 'Well, I shall see him again.' But he never

saw me again to this day. I felt happily mortified, for the
trial was over. I was not much disappointed, for I thought
all the way that I cut but a poor figure for a lawyer's clerk.
So far, it seems, I was right. The next morning my uncle
said that his mistress had bade him to make me welcome,
and to keep me till Sunday morning, when the boat returned
to Peterborough. So I spent Saturday looking about the
town after amusements. . . .

"On Sunday my uncle saw me to the boat, and I left
Wisbech and my disappointment behind, with an earnest
though melancholy feeling of satisfaction. I made up for my
lost ambition by the thought of once more seeing home and
its snug fireside. My parents welcomed me home with a
melancholy smile that bespoke their feelings of disappointment, as I sat on a corner stool and related my adventures."

Soon after this rebuff, however, Parker and Ann's patience
with their son was rewarded. Francis Gregory, the proprietor of the Blue Bell, an inn a few yards away from the
cottage, offered to hire the boy for one year. Gregory, an
ageing man, over sixty, and in poor health, lived unmarried,
with his mother as housekeeper. He was, says Clare:

"fond of amusement, and a singer, though his notes were
not more varied than those of the cuckoo. He had but two
songs for all companies, one called 'The Milking Pail' and
the other 'Jack with his Broom.' His jokes, too, were like a
pack of cards; they were always the same, but told in a
different form."

Gregory kept a horse and a cow or two, and needed a boy
to attend to these and to plough his six or eight acres of
land. Chastened perhaps after his visit to Wisbech, Clare
regarded his offer with favour:

"I was glad and readily agreed. It was a good place.
They treated me more like a son than a servant, and I
believe this place was the nursery for that lonely and solitary
musing which ended in rhyme. I used to be generally
left alone to my toils, for the master was a very weak
man and always ailing. My labours were not very burthen-
some, being horse- or cow-tending, weeding, etc., when I

made up for the loss of company by talking to myself and engaging my thoughts with any subject that came uppermost in my mind.

"One of my worst labours was a journey to a distant village named Maxey, to fetch flour, once, and sometimes twice, every week. In these journeys I had haunted spots to pass, and as the often-heard tales of ghosts and hobgoblins had made me very fearful to pass such places at night, it being often nearly dark ere I got there, I used to employ my mind as well as I was able to put them out of my head. So I used to imagine tales and mutter them over as I went, making myself the hero; sometimes making myself a soldier and tracing the valorous history onwards through various successes till I became a great man; sometimes it was a love-story, not fraught with many incidents of knight-errantry, but full of successes as uncommon and out-of-the-way as a romance; travelling about in foreign lands and indulging in a variety of adventures, till a fair lady was found with a great fortune that made me a gentleman. My mind would be so bent on the reveries sometimes that I have often got to the town unawares, and felt a sort of disappointment in not being able to finish my story, though I was glad of the escape from the haunted places. . . . These journeys and my toiling in the fields by myself gave me such a habit that I never forgot it, and I always muttered and talked to myself afterwards. I have often felt ashamed at being overheard by people that overtook me. It made my thoughts so active that they became troublesome to me in company, and I felt the most happy to be alone."

If Francis Gregory hired Clare in May 1809, the boy would now be nearly sixteen. When the superstitions that enfolded a village community of the last century are remembered, his terrors along the road to Maxey, his invention of a tale "without a ghost in it," his fear of will-o'-the-wisps and of the "midnight-morris," are not surprising. When he reached manhood, his reason and common sense won him over to a disbelief in goblins and ghosts; but even then his nerves were always ready to betray him. His mother's tales had made a lasting impression; these dark walks, his solitary toils for Gregory, while they strengthened his imagination

and made him a much more sensitive observer, had a
correspondingly bad effect in heightening his nervous fears.
He hated to take the animals to graze on the heath in the
spring dusk, because of the "horrible squealing noise" from
badger or vixen. But perhaps the development of his poetic
imagination could for him in his circumstances only be
gained at the expense of these morbid fears. He continues
the story of his night-terrors with an account of how intensely
every creature and individual plant in nature began to
affect him at this time:

"On Sundays I used to feel a pleasure to hide in the woods
instead of going to church; to rustle among the leaves, and
lie upon a mossy bank where the fir-like fern its under-
forest keeps 'in a strange stillness'; watching for hours
the little insects climb up and down the tall stems of the
wood-grass, or the smooth plantain leaf, a spacious plain;
or reading the often-thumbed books which I possessed,
till fancy 'made them living things.' I loved the mossy
nooks in the fields and woods. My favourite spots had
lasting places in my memory . . . before Enclosure destroyed
them all. . . . The woodpecker sweeing away in its ups and
downs, the jaybird chattering by the woodside its restless
warnings of passing clowns, the travels of insects where the
black-beetle mumbled along, and the opening of field-
flowers, gave me the greatest of pleasures. But I could not
account for the reason why they did so. A lonely nook, a
rude bridge or woodland stile with ivy growing round the
posts, delighted me and made lasting impressions on my
feelings. But I knew nothing of poetry then; yet I noticed
everything anxiously. . . . I loved the gypsies for the beauties
which they added to the landscape. I heard the cuckoo's
'wandering voice' and the restless song of the nightingale,
and was delighted when I paused and [it] muttered its
sweet 'jug-jug' as I passed its blackthorn bower. I often
pulled my hat over my eyes to watch the rising of the lark,
or to see the hawk hang in the summer sky and the kite take
its circles round the wood. I often lingered a minute on
the woodland stile to hear the woodpigeons clapping their
wings among the dark oaks. I hunted curious flowers in
rapture and muttered thoughts in their praise. I loved the

pasture with its rushes and thistles and sheep-tracks. I
adored the wild, marshy fen with its solitary heronshaw
sweeing along in its melancholy sky. I wandered the heath
in raptures among the rabbit burrows and golden-blossomed
furze. I dropt down on a thymy molehill or mossy eminence
to survey the summer landscape. . . . I marked the various
colours in flat, spreading fields, checkered into closes of
different-tinctured grain like the colours of a map; the
copper-tinted clover in blossom; the sun-tanned green of the
ripening hay; the lighter hues of wheat and barley inter-
mixed with the sunny glare of the yellow charlock and the
sunset imitation of the scarlet headaches; the blue corn-
bottles crowding their splendid colours in large sheets over
the land and troubling the cornfields with destroying beauty;
the different greens of the woodland trees, the dark oak, the
paler ash, the mellow lime, the white poplars peeping above
the rest like leafy steeples, the grey willow shining chilly in
the sun, as if the morning mist still lingered on its cool
green. I loved the meadow lake with its flags and long
purples crowding the water's edge. I listened with delight
to hear the wind whisper among the feather-topt reeds,
to see the taper bulrush nodding in gentle curves to the
rippling water; and I watched with delight on haymaking
evenings the setting sun drop behind the Brigs and peep
again through the half-circle of the arches as if he longed
to stay.

"I felt the beauty of all these with eager delight: the gad-
fly's noonday hum, the fainter murmur of the bee-fly
spinning in the evening ray, the dragon-flies in their spangled
coats darting like winged arrows down the stream . . . the
shepherd hiding from a thunder-shower in a hollow dotterel,
the wild geese scudding along and making all the letters of
the alphabet as they flew, the motley clouds, the whispering
wind that muttered to the leaves and summer grass, as it
fluttered among them.

"I observed all this with the same rapture as I have done
since. But I knew nothing of poetry. It was felt and not
uttered."

These last two sentences are, of course, not quite true
concerning the time of which he is speaking. He had certainly written "The Morning Walk" and "The Evening

Walk"; he had begun "The Fate of Amy" and "Helpstone"
– though he did not complete these till some years later;
he had tried the sonnet form in "The Gipsy's Evening
Blaze," and (if we are to believe Gilchrist in the *Quarterly*
article) in "The Primrose." Besides these there were other
verses on village stories and his home scenes, which had been
destroyed. Evidence of quotation and the imitation of
metre in the poem "Noon," which was probably written in
1808, may mean that he had already read some of the
"Pastorals" of John Cunningham, and had liked the
occasional exactitudes of description which he found there.
He had perhaps read a little of *The Deserted Village*, or seen
it in extract. *The Seasons* we know he possessed, and had read
many times. Some unnamed friend had presented him
with Milton's poems and Percy's ballads "for keeping Sunday well and going to church." This gift must have been
made before the time of the defaulting he has already told of.
Chatterton's well-known story and his "Resignation" to
fate before the tragic 24th of August, 1770, had impressed
and inspired him more than any of the poet's other work
which he may have read; with his present opportunities for
leisure, he wrote the lines "(supposed to be) Written by the
Unfortunate Chatterton just before he took the deadly
Draught that put a Period to his Existence." These lines,
which are the first instance of those imitations which Clare
afterwards more deliberately practised, displayed more
realisation of Chatterton's loneliness and anguish than poetic
merit of Clare's. Chatterton's high resolve and indomitable
will helped Clare at this time. He had not, and could not
have, in the environment into which he was born, Chatterton's pride and challenge. He found his parents' continued
discouragement and the villagers' ridicule hard to support.
At this time, except for Francis Gregory's fatherly indulgence in the matter of his studies, there was not a single
person with whom he could discuss his ambition to write
poetry. John Turnill had left the village, and Tom Porter
offered no sympathy on the subject of authorship. Thus,
even in these early days of his apprenticeship to poetry,

he began to feel that mental loneliness which was always one of his sorrows. His poems were at present set down with timidity, and his muse very uncertain of her title, yet he went on secretly and quietly, with the utmost resolution. Other poems of this date are "To a Violet," published later in his second volume, *The Village Minstrel*, "The Robin," no doubt in praise of the pet he had had, "Reflection in Autumn," and "The Universal Epitaph." Other and still unpublished verses are "The Lodge House," a long narrative of midnight mystery concerning an old ruin where "the wild cat used to hide and raise its kittens," and a collection of verses, which he recast later, on Dobbin, "an old cart-horse [which] was in great fame in the village for his gentleness and strength and readiness for all sorts of jobs." About this time, too, Clare had enough spare money to buy another volume to add to his small store, from the book-shop at Stamford – Izaak Walton's *Angler*.

But one thing is clear. His books, much as he treasured them and gained from them ideas for work of his own, remained rather the encouragement of his inspiration than the inspiration itself. From the beginning it was nature which was the very source and meaning of his poetry. Again and again he tells how "I grew so much into the quiet love of nature['s] presence, that I was never easy but when I was in the fields."

III

SONS OF POVERTY
1809–1813

Maie Selynesse on erthes boundes bee hadde?
May yt adyght yn human shape bee founde?

ROWLEY'S POEMS, 1777.

WHILE Clare was still at Francis Gregory's, perhaps in the autumn of that year, something happened which gave a new stimulus to his poetry. The acquaintance with Mary Joyce, broken off when Clare left the day-school at Glinton, was suddenly renewed with deeper feelings. If what he himself says in an early poem is fact and not fancy, they met again at a village party on Martinmas night, when Mary, by some token during the games of cards or forfeits, betrayed her preference for him. After that she blushed, but "paid with joy a kiss for every fine."

So the childish companionship ripened suddenly into an idyllic love. How long it prospered is not clear. They met each other frequently during the winter of 1809 and the early spring of 1810, and they renewed their enthusiasm for flowers and fields. Clare's mind, already rich in love and observation, expanded happily under the new charm. Perhaps they parted in the following May-time, which would account for Clare's restlessness then, and his refusal to re-hire himself with Gregory for a second year. Perhaps it was only after Clare had been absent from the village at his next situation, from which he returned penniless, that they became estranged. The blame for separating the boy and girl lovers has hitherto rested with the father of Mary. There is no evidence in any of Clare's known writings for this condemnation of him. It was Mary herself who realised the difference between her position and that of the poor labourer's son who had no prospects. Clare says it was the world which

> *choked the hopes I had of thee,*
> *And made thee haughty, Mary;*

and he was evidently too sensitive about his poverty to make any attempt to overcome the world's baleful influence.

"She felt her station above mine; at least I felt that she thought so; for her parents were farmers, and farmers had great pretensions to something then. . . . I felt the disparagement in [my] situation, and, fearing to meet a denial, I carried it on in my own fancies to every extreme, writing songs in her praise, and making her mine with every indulgence of the fancy."

Before he even declared his love they parted, but during the years which followed, before the publication of his first book, he kept the half-smothered hope in his heart that he would one day be her equal and his dreams become reality.

Meanwhile the term of his hiring with Francis Gregory was up, and he was no nearer permanent employ than he had been a year ago.

"I left with the restless hope of being something better than a ploughman. My little ambitions kept burning about me every now and then to make a better figure in the world. I knew not what to be at.

"A bragging fellow named Manton from Market Deeping used to frequent the public-house when I lived there. He was a stone-cutter and sign-painter. He used to pretend to discover something in me deserving encouragement, and wanted to take me apprentice to learn the mysteries of his art. But then he wanted the trifle with me that had disappointed my former prosperities. He used to talk of his abilities in sculpture and painting over his beer, till I was almost mad with anxiety to be a sign-painter and stone-cutter. But it was useless; and such things made my mind restless."

There now came, in the guise of good luck, another chance of a situation. Clare heard from Tom Porter, whom he still visited on Sundays, that the head gardener of the Marquis of Exeter at Burghley House needed an apprentice. His health, no more robust than it had been, decided his mother and father that he would never be fitted for hard land-work. An opportunity at such a place seemed the very thing.

The "fretted Gothic windows" of Burghley House looked across a spacious, wooded park towards the many spires of Stamford. And Stamford, one of the centres of mediæval learning, honoured by Saxon, Dane, and Norman, and the scene of much Cecil pomp in Elizabeth's time, was perhaps at its most prosperous in these days just before the coming of the railways. Mentioned by Mr. E. V. Lucas as possibly the original home of Charles Lamb's family, it lay on the Great North Road, a day's posting journey from London. Coaches rattled down its streets, and its inns were always full of travellers. Though after the making of the railroads it settled down into the sleepy respectability of an ordinary market-town and watched Peterborough rapidly outstrip it in importance, in these days Clare would think of it as of a metropolis and excitedly imagine his life so near it in the beautiful gardens of Burghley.

When they heard of the vacant apprenticeship, Clare and his father lost no time in going to see the head gardener.

"So off my father took me. It was a fine Sabbath morning, and when we arrived, he, mistaking everyone for gentlemen that wore white stockings, pulled off his hat to the gardener as if it had been the Marquis himself. I often thought afterwards how the fellow felt his consequence at the sight, for he was an ignorant, proud fellow. He took me, and I was to stop three years. My work, for the time I stayed on, was taking vegetables and fruit down to the Hall twice a day as required. .... The Marquis was then a boy. I have him in my mind's eye, in his jean jerkin and trousers, shooting in the Park or fishing in the river.

"After a few weeks I saved my money to purchase Abercrombie's *Gardening*,[1] which became my chief study. The gardens were very large and I remember finding some curious flowers which I had never seen before, growing wild among the vegetables. One was a yellow headache, perennial, and another was a blue one, annual."

But this peaceful work and reading of Abercrombie did not last long. The head gardener, Clare says, "was of so harsh a temper that none liked him." He was evidently a drunkard, too.

"I was often sent to Stamford at all hours in the night for one thing or another, sometimes for liquors and sometimes to seek him by the mistress's orders. As I was of a timid disposition, I [was] very often fearful of going, and instead of seeking him I used to lie down under a tree in the Park, and fall asleep ; and in the autumn night the rime used to fall and cover me on one side like a sheet, which affected my side with a numbness. I have felt it ever since at spring and fall, and I oftentimes think that the illness which oppresses me now while I write this narrative proceeds from the like cause."

When the head gardener was this kind of a man, it was not likely that the behaviour of his staff would be quiet and orderly. Their ways had naturally some effect upon Clare, the youngest among them:

"I learnt irregular habits at this place which I had been a stranger to had I kept at home. Though I had no money to spend, yet my elder companions would treat me. We were far from a town; yet confinement sweetens liberty, and we stole every opportunity to get over to Stamford on summer evenings. When I had no money to spend, my elder companions used to offer to treat me for my company there and back again, to keep me from divulging the secret to my master by making me a partner in their midnight revels.

"We used to get out of the windows and climb over the high wall of the extensive gardens; for we slept in the garden-house, and were locked in every night to keep us from robbing the fruit, I expect. Our place of rendezvous was a public-house called the Hole in the Wall, famous for strong ale and midnight merriment, kept by a hearty sort of fellow called Tant Baker (I suppose the short name for Antony). He had formerly been a servant at Burghley, and his house was consequently a favourite place with the Burghley servants always. I wrote a long poem in praise of his ale in the favourite Scotch metre of Ramsay and Burns; it was not good, but there are parts of it worthy, I think, of a better fate than being utterly lost."

Writing in 1823, Clare does not mean that his long poem on "Tant" Baker's ale was composed while he was at Burghley. It was more probably written later, in 1814 or 1815, about the time when he used Allan Ramsay's metre for his "Address to a Lark." His judgment on "Ale" is right; it is not a very good poem. Where Burns's lines on "Scotch Drink" are national, Clare's on "Ale" are local and even personal. Yet for this they are valuable. He praises ale as a kill-care for the labourer because of his "water-porridge fate," for himself because of his "damps" or melancholy. But for both only a tenpenny quart at a time, at feast or inn. More is "brutish."

During the nine months of his apprenticeship in the gardens of the Marquis of Exeter he was not in the mood for poetry, and he soon grew to dislike the situation which had seemed so advantageous at first. The only one among the gardening staff with whom he had anything in common was the foreman, George Cousins, who had introduced Abercrombie's *Gardening* to him. Cousins was a man of the "most simple mind," inoffensive and credulous of everything he heard. His culture extended beyond Abercrombie to the Bible, from which he could repeat whole chapters by heart. Like Clare, he was weary of the place, but their agreements prevented them from leaving openly:

"So we got up early one morning in the autumn and started for Grantham, which we reached the first night, a distance of twenty-one miles; and I thought, to be sure, I was out of the world. We slept at an alehouse called The Crown and Anchor, and I wished myself at home often enough before morning; but it was too late then.

"Our enquiries not meeting work there, we travelled on to Newark-on-Trent, and there we got work at a nurseryman's of the name of Withers. We lodged at a lame man's house of the name of Brown, whose son was a carpenter celebrated for making fiddles. I felt quite lost when I was here, though it was a very lively town; we did not stay long; for the master did not give us wages sufficient, paying us one part and promising us the rest if we suited him by a further trial."

It was early autumn when Clare and Cousins arrived at Newark, and the ground was baked hard with the summer sun. Clare found the heavy digging and hoeing too much for his strength, though the strength of his companion was "stubborn enough for any toil." Moreover, his mind, like his body, was "strange and unfit with the world," so that he grew restless and unhappy.

They seem to have stayed some months at Newark; while they were there, Clare made his first attempt to join the Militia. This was, in these years, brief and cursory enough in its methods of obtaining recruits. He and Cousins went to the village feast at Baldwick, there "got fresh," and Clare, though only seventeen, offered himself for service. Fortunately for him, as he himself felt afterwards, he was found "too short" when he went to Nottingham to be sworn in.

. All this was done without the knowledge of Withers the nurseryman; although they were heartily tired of his dalliance with wages, they were still in his service. In the winter, however,

"We got up earlier than usual one morning, and as we were not burthened with luggage, we easily stole away undetected and left our credit with our host, [being] ninepence-halfpenny in debt. We travelled from Newark to Stamford the same night, but dare not show ourselves in a public-house. So we went through and lay under a tree in the Park. The rime fell thick and we were covered as white as a sheet when we got up."

Clare does not record the dismay with which his parents received him back again at Helpston, penniless and out of work once more. Doubtless they bore their troubles with that "dangerous patience" which men and women often have who work in the peace of the country. In the spring of 1811 the boy was nearly eighteen, but there was now far less chance of work for him than there had been before. In 1809, even before he left the village to work in the gardens of Burghley, an Act of Parliament had been passed "for enclosing lands in the parishes of Maxey with Deepingate, Northborough, Glinton with Peakirk, Etton, and Helpstone";² and, although the Award of Land bears the date 1820, already in 1811 those changes were afoot which altered the very structure of the village, obliterated its long-established customs, swept away the independence and freedom of the old community, and put an end to the "innocent pleasures of the old days." Before this, Helpston, like many another village before 1800, was largely under the open field system. Barbarous and unpleasing as the common heaths had become to the eye of the eighteenth century, Clare could see only loveliness in these scenes of all the dear delights of his youth. He looked on this disturbance with distaste and rebellion. His indignation and regrets are neverending.

> There once were springs, where daisies' silver studs
> Like sheets of snow on every pasture spread;
> There once were summers, when the crow-flower buds
> Like golden sunbeams brightest lustre shed;
> And trees grew once that sheltered Lubin's head;
> There once were brooks sweet whimpering down the vale:
> The brook's no more – kingcup and daisy fled;
> Their last fall'n tree the naked moors bewail,
> And scarce a bush is left to tell the mournful tale.

He makes Swordy Well, whose flowers people came for miles to praise, speak and tell the tale of its desolation:

> And save his Lordship's woods, that past
>   The day of danger dwell,
> Of all the fields I am the last
>   That my own face can tell;
> Yet, what with stone-pits' delving holes,
>   And strife to buy and sell,
> My name will quickly be the whole
>   That's left of Swordy Well.

In these years of his early manhood, ploughs destroyed the Green at Helpston, Cowper Green was levelled to a desert, and the very moles were hung for traitors. Even the brooks were injured and made sadly different from what they had been before. Nearly all the hollow trees which had made his favourite seats were cut down; Round Oak, above the ancient spring, and Lee Close Oak were gone. He tells how his fond attachment was broken with the

"old ivied oak in Oxey Wood, where I twisted a sallow stoven into an arbour which grew in the cramped way in which I had made it. . . . All my favourite places have met with misfortunes. The old ivied tree was cut down when the wood was cut down, and my tower was destroyed. The woodman fancied it a resort for robbers, and some thought the cramped way in which the thing grew were witch-knots, and that the spot was a haunt where witches met. . . . Lee Close Oak was cut down in the Enclosure and Langley Bush was broken up by some wanton fellows while kindling furze on the Heath. The carpenter that bought Lee Close Oak, hearing it was a favourite tree of mine, made me two rulers and sent me; and I preserved a piece of the old ivy, the thickest I have ever seen."

Whatever of ultimate good the land received through Enclosure, Clare himself could see none of it. He regarded the countryside as the habitation and the birthright of the rustic, and he rejoiced in it for the home of creatures and the garden that it was. The villages and cottages were part of it, but the "stately homes" possessed, for him, a very doubtful, certainly an alien, beauty. Everyone had been free to wander in the country, to gather sticks, and to cut furze on the common: these were rights they had had since any could remember. When game-preserving was begun and these freedoms denied to the villager, Clare, with many more, resented the insolence of the upstart game-keepers who warned men out of their old haunts, the woods.

From the obscurity that has closed round the records of

the poor in those days, Clare's voice rises to reveal their despair. In spite of the growth of luxury among farmers and the better classes after this alteration in the land, the class to which Clare belonged sunk deeper and deeper into poverty and distress. The whole movement can be examined later, when the total change had taken place. At the present moment it is sufficient to say that, at a time when so many farm labourers lost their strips of land, and even their privilege of keeping a cow, what the Clares lost was the chance of near and permanent work for father and son. Farmers bought up land from those who could not afford to keep it, enclosed their farms, and hired bailiffs to work them as economically as possible. While the labourer lost his independence and his cow, at the same time he frequently lost his work as well. Since there was not enough labour for all the villagers, " catch-work " men, under gang masters, congregated and tramped to any farmer, near or distant, who required them.

Clare does not say whether his father resorted to these gangs to help him towards employment at this period or not, nor does he mention whether his father had yet become totally incapacitated by his rheumatism. As for himself, his return to the village in 1811 marked the beginning of a great change in his outlook. Though it is important to re- member that the results of Enclosure were seen only very gradually, yet, when he came back, he found himself irre- vocably cut off from his happy boyhood. It was the shepherd- boy who had played on the heaths and sat in his wattled shelter, " piping as though he should never be old," sud- denly thrust out of youth. Probably, since land was being enclosed, not only in the immediate vicinity of Helpston by the Act of 1809, but also in other parts of the district, he drifted into one of the " catch-work " gangs before many months had passed. There was no more listening to the tales of old cow-tending women, and no more quiet Sunday pastimes with shepherds and herdboys while he waited for better employ. The familiar figures of pinder and hayward were gone from the village. In the general disruption, morals

EJ

were loosened and self-respect lost. Clare himself put aside
his poetry and forgot his reading :

"My fondness for study began to decline on mixing more
into company [with] young chaps of loose habits, that began
by force, and, growing into a custom, was continued by
choice till it became wild and irregular. Poetry was for a
season thrown by. These habits were gotten when the fields
were enclosed, mixing among a motley set of labourers that
always follow the news of such employments. I used to work
at setting down fencing and planting quick lines, with
partners whose whole study was continual striving how to get
beer ; and the bottle was the general theme from week-end
to week-end. Such as had got drunk the oftenest fancied
themselves the best fellows and made a boast of it as a fame ;
but I was not such a drinker as to make a boast of it. Though
I joined my sixpence towards the bottle as often as the rest,
I often missed the tot that was handed round, for my constitution would not have borne it.

"Saturday nights used to be what they called randy
nights, which was [when] all met together at the public-
house to drink and sing ; and every new beginner had to
spend a larger portion than the rest, which they called
'colting,' a thing common in all sorts of labour.

"Once in these midnight revels we escaped a great danger
very narrowly. On going for ale at the dancing a quarrel
ensued, when one of the party determined on cheating the
others by running off with the beer. I was [with him], and
we got into an old barn which had been open to the weather
for years, and had been falling a long time. We saw no danger
and hugged ourselves over our bottle till we had finished it,
when we started. The next day, when I passed, the gable-
end we had sat under was down, a heap of rubbish."

Despite this renegade behaviour, there is just a hint that
"nature in all her shows and forms" did not cease even now
to engage Clare's deeper attention. Copied up years later,
in 1828 perhaps, there is a jotting for July 2nd, 1811:
"Found a snake with a large frog in the belly of it"; there are
other entries made on the same sheet concerning a "rathe
primrose" of January and a blackbird in that month "singing as earnest as if it was April"; but whether these notes

refer to the January of 1812 cannot be told, because the year
is not given. Though he was at Helpston in 1811, he was probably not at home very long. There was little present hope
of permanent employ for the rough gangs of labourers. So
to his restlessness the Militia offered a solution a second time.
Under Castlereagh's reforms, each infantry regiment of the
line was attached to one of the counties. It consisted of two
battalions, the first for the line itself, the second, or Regular
Militia, for defence at home. These second battalions, to be
raised by annual ballot for a term of service of seven years,
were the local Militia. They were to be balloted from a
foundation, or Army of Reserve, of two hundred thousand
men between the ages of eighteen and thirty, who were to be
called up and trained for one month every year. It was under
this national training scheme for the local Militia that Clare
enlisted. In spite of his short stature,³ he was sworn in at
Peterborough. Thence he was marched to Oundle, where at
that time the Northamptonshire Militia was stationed; his
own story tells what a rough regiment of roysterers, village
Lotharios, runaway youths, and unemployed labourers like
himself, had been attracted by the lavish bounty then
given:

"When the country was chin-deep in the fears of invasion
and every mouth was filled with the terrors which Bonaparte
had spread in other countries, a national scheme was set on
foot to raise a raw army of volunteers; and to make the
matter plausible a letter was circulated said to be written by
the Prince Regent. I forget how many were demanded from
our parish, but I remember the panic which it created was
very great. No great name rises in the world without creat-
ing a crowd of little mimics that glitter in borrowed rays;
and no great lie was ever yet put in circulation with[out] a
herd of little lies multiply[ing] by instinct, as it were, and
crowding under its wings. The papers that were circulated
assured the people of England that the French were on the
eve of invading it, and that it was deemed necessary by the
Regent that an army from eighteen to forty-five should be
raised immediately. This was the great lie; and the little lies
were soon at its heels, which assured the people of Helpstone

that the French had invaded and got to London. And some of those little lies had the impudence to swear that the French had even reached Northampton. The people got at their doors in the evening to talk over the rebellion of '45 when the rebels reached Derby and even listened at intervals to fancy the French 'rebels' at Northampton, knocking it down with their cannon. I never gave much credit to popular stories of any sort; so I felt no concern at these stories, though I could not say much for my valour if the tale had proved true.

"We had a cross-grained sort of choice left us – which was to be fined, to be drawn, and go for nothing, or take on as volunteers for a bounty of two guineas. I accepted the latter and went with a neighbour's son, W. Clarke, to Peterborough to be sworn on, and prepared to join the regiment at Oundle. The morning we left home our mothers parted with us as if we were going to Botany Bay, and people got at their doors to bid us farewell and greet us with a Job's comfort that they doubted we should see Helpstone no more. I confess I wished myself out of the matter.

"When we got to Oundle, the place of quartering, we were drawn out into the field, and a more motley multitude of lawless fellows was never seen in Oundle before, and hardly out of it. There were 1,300 of us. We were drawn up into a line and sorted out into companies. I was one of the shortest and therefore my station is evident. I was in that mixed multitude called the battalion, which they nicknamed 'bum-tools,' for what reason I cannot tell; the light company was called 'light-bobs,' and the grenadiers 'bacon-bolters.' These were names given to each other, who felt as great an enmity against each other as ever they all felt for the French.

"Our company was the 5th and the Captain was a good sort of fellow, using his authority in the language of a friend advising our ignorance, when wrong, of what we ought to do to be right, and not in the severity of a petty tyrant who is fond of abusing those beneath him merely for the sake of showing authority. I was never wonderful clean in my dress – at least, not clean enough for a soldier, for I thought I took more than necessary pains to be so – and I was not very apt at learning my exercise, for then I was a rhymer, and my thoughts were often absent when the word of command was given. For this fault I was terribly teased by a little louse-looking corporal, who took a delight in finding fault with me

and loading me with bad jests on my awkwardness as a
soldier, as if he had been a soldier all his life. I felt very
vexed at this scurrilous coxcomb and retorted; which only
added more authority in his language. He found fault with
me when it belonged to others, merely to vex me, and if
I ventured to tamper with his mistake, he would threaten
me with the awkward squad for speaking. I grew so mad
at last with this fool that I really think I should have felt
satisfaction in shooting him, and I was almost fit to desert
home. Then again I thought my companions would laugh
at me, so I screwed up my resolution to the point at last
and determined, if he accused me wrongfully for the time
to come, I would certainly fall out of the ranks and address
him, be the consequence what it would. I had no great heart
to boxing, but I saw little fear in him ; for he was much less
in strength than I was, and the dread of the dark hole or
awkward squad was but little in comparison to the teasing
insults which this fellow daily inflicted. So I determined to
act up to my vengeance, be the consequence what it might,
and I soon found an opportunity, for he was presently at
his pert jests and sneering meddling again. Madness flushed
my cheeks in a moment ; and when he saw it, he rapped me
over my knees in a sneering sort of way, and said he would
learn me how such fellows as I were dealt with by soldiers.
I could stand it no longer, but threw my gun aside, and
seizing him by the throat I hurled him down and kicked him
when he was down—which got the fellow fame ; for those
that had been against him before lifted him up and called
him a good fellow and me a coward.

"I was threatened with the black hole by one, and even
the tying up to the halberd by others, who said that drum-
mers were exercising themselves and very able to use the
whip for punishment. . . . I thought I possessed common-
sense in a superior degree . . . to feel fear at threatened
surmises of any sort ; for I had always looked on such things
as mere trumpery for children ; but I confess my common-
sense was overcome, and I felt fearful that something was
in the wind till it blew over and got too stale. The Captain
enquired into the fray, and the black hole was dispensed
with, I serving an addition[al] . . . guard in its stead. The
fellow threw a mortified eye on me ever after, and never
found his tongue to tell me of a fault, even when I was in
one . . . ."

Clare was evidently not balloted for the local Militia ; he went home again and was, he says, called up a second time. On this last occasion he took a further bounty for service abroad. Five shillings of this was paid him on the spot, and the rest was to be handed over when he was wanted. But he heard no further about it ; for soon after the peace declaration in May 1814 the Northamptonshire Militia was disbanded.

IV

ITCHING AFTER RHYME
1813–1816

Oh, where be now those sports
And infant play-games? Where the joyous troops
Of children, and the haunts I did so love?

CHARLES LAMB.

CLARE was at home again in the changed village in May, 1813; on the same sheet as the jotting for 1811, he has an entry for May of the later year :

"Some men digging stone on Copper Green[1] found several bones of the human species lying all their length in one grave." The incident recorded here was the one that furnished him with some fragments of verse afterwards gathered into the long poem published in the *Rural Muse*, "On Seeing a Skull on Cowper Green."

Wert thou a Poet, who in fancy's dream
Saw Immortality throw by her veil,
And all thy labours in Fame's temple gleam
In the proud glory of an after-tale?

Whether or not in his own dreams Immortality had already disclosed her face to him, he was hard at it, as soon as he was at home from the Militia, writing verses again. Almost twenty years old by this, he was thin and slight and not much taller than Keats or Hartley Coleridge.[2] His eyes were light-blue, small and keen; his hair, a pale chestnut, waved over a wide brow. Though he had a reputation locally as a scholar, he had no better prospect before him in his manhood than occasional labour in the fields. There are some verses written on his twentieth birthday, in the July of this year, which disclose his hopelessness:

Luckless day: the sorriest tiding
   Thy last folded pages tell;
Youth from manhood thou'rt dividing,
   Youth and pleasure, fare thee well!

Twenty year, and this thy blessing!
   Much did hopes on manhood dwell;
Much to-morrow was expecting,
   Better prospects, fare ye well!

.   .   .   .

He might write despondently, in this review of his affairs
on the threshold of his manhood, but he did not throw aside
his studies a second time. On the contrary, he resumed them
with greater seriousness and vigour on his return from the
Militia; so that in 1814 he went to a bookseller named
Henson, of Market Deeping, and bought a book for copying
up those of his verses which he thought worthy of preservation. Into this folio volume he began to copy the best of what
had escaped his mother's fire. Up to now his reading and
writing had been chiefly of poetry, and his inability to write
"a common letter" did not please him. "I never saw a book
in grammar before I was twenty, or knew anything of the
proper construction of sentences." Books were an almost
inexcusable luxury while work was intermittent; "yet," he
adds, "I was so far benefitted from reading an old newspaper
now and then as to write pretty correctly, and never any
otherwise than to be intelligible." A later unaddressed letter
testifies that someone, perhaps Henson, allowed him to have
books on credit, "when no-one else would have trusted me
for a half-penny ballad."

So, though youth was over and circumstances as obdurate
as ever, Clare's ambitions and "green dreams" remained.
Since farm labour was not forthcoming except in haytime
and harvest, he used his experience at Burghley and Newark
to get him employment:

"I now followed gardening for a while in the farmers'
gardens about the village, and worked in the fields when I

had no other employment to go to. Poetry was a trouble-somely pleasant companion, annoying and cheering me at my toils. I could not stop my thoughts and often failed to keep them till night; so when I fancied I had hit upon a good image or natural description, I used to steal into a corner of the garden and clap it down. But the appearance of my employers often put my fancies to flight, and made me lose the thought altogether; for I always felt anxious to conceal my scribbling, and would as lief have confessed to be a robber as a rhymer.

"When I worked in the fields I had more opportunities to set down my thoughts and for this reason I liked to work in the fields. By and by I forsook gardening altogether till I resumed it at Casterton. I used to drop down behind a hedge, bush, or dyke, and write down my things upon the crown of my hat, and when I was more in a shape for[3] thinking than usual I used to stop later at night to make up my lost time in the day. Thus I went on, writing my thoughts down and correcting them at leisure, spending my Sundays in the woods or fields to be alone for that purpose; and I got a bad name among the weekly church-goers, forsaking the church-going bell and seeking the religion of the fields, though I did it for no dislike to church, for I felt uncomfortable very often. But my heart burnt over the pleasures of solitude and the restless revels of rhyme that were so continually sapping my memories, like the summer sun over the tinkling brook, till it one day should leave them dry and unconscious of the thrilling joys, burning anxieties, and restlessness, which it had created. I knew nothing of the poet's experience then.

"Though I was not known as a poet, my odd habits did not escape notice. They fancied I kept aloof from company for some sort of study; others believed me crazed; and some put more criminal interpretations to my rambles and said I was night-walking, associating with the gipsies, robbing the woods of the hares and pheasants, because I was often in their company: and I must confess I found them far more honest than their calumniators."

The dates of events in these years from 1814 to 1817 are vague. Clare probably tried gardening for the Helpston farmers in 1814 and 1815, and then gave it up until he went to Casterton in the spring of 1817. His acquaintance with the gipsies extended over the whole of this period, and his preference for their society became more marked the further he fell into disrepute among the farmers. He had friends in the village; but to the average mind which

> *Views new knowledge with suspicious eyes,*
> *And thinks it blasphemy to be so wise,*

he was suspect. Though he might stay at night and make up his time lost through writing, still his employers came readily to believe that since he was a dreamer and a poet he was no good for manual labour.

That corner of Helpston Heath round Langley Bush was the traditional camping-ground of the gipsies. The scene is desolate of the ancient whitethorn now; "its scarred trunk and grey mossy bough" were first struck by lightning, and then finally demolished by furze-burners. During Clare's childhood the gipsies were frequent visitors, seen at every village feast and merrymaking. He thought that the "quiet, pilfering, unprotected race" graced the landscape with their camps. Their liberty and their disregard of "parson's fetters" attracted him; their neighbours, the hare and the fox, he would have liked for his neighbours.

> *No matter where they go or where they dwell*
> *They dally with the winds and laugh at hell.*

As a child he had pitied the gipsies for the blame they often had to take for thefts which they had not committed. He loved to listen to their "gibberish talk" as they smoked the tainted flesh of "purloined cat" for their meal. Sometimes he had wealth and good fortune predicted him by the sibyl; but as he grew more sensible and refused her a coin she told him something nearer the truth; that he should

> *Of not a hoarded farthing be posses't,*
> *And when all's done, be shov'd to hell at last.*

The distrust of his own neighbours sent him in these years to seek the gipsies' company. He knew best the Boswells, whose name is well known with the Romany, and who were then a popular tribe famous for their fiddlers. On summer evenings and Sundays they taught him to fiddle by ear, a pastime which for some years afforded him great enjoyment. Like Lamb's friend, George Dyer, he wished to know more of the language and life of these wandering people, and he was often tempted, when they told him of the money to be made by fiddling at fairs and on the Kentish hop-fields, to join them for good. He does not seem to have aroused the hatred of any of them, as George Borrow aroused that of old Mrs. Herne. On the contrary, both the Boswells and the Smiths allowed him to join in their talk and amusements, so that he became "as ready as themselves" to converse in their language. He has left a long account of the humour and habits of this cunning, "untamable animal," and, from his more intimate knowledge, awards the gipsy a fairer name than he is given by common repute:

"I had often heard of the mystic language and black arts which the gipsies possessed, but on familiar acquaintance with them, I found that their mystic language was nothing more than things called by slang names like village provincialisms, and that no two tribes spoke the same dialect exactly. Their black arts were nothing more of witchcraft than the knowledge of village gossips and the petty deceptions played off on believing ignorance. . . . In fortune-telling they pretended to great skill both by cards and plants and by the lines in the hand and moles and interpretations of dreams; the credulous readily believed them, and they extorted money by another method of muttering over the power of revenge which fright[ed] the huswife into charity. I have heard them laugh over their evening fire at the dupes they have made . . . trying each other's wits to see who could make a tale that might succeed best the next day.

"But everything that is bad is thrown upon the gipsies; their name has grown into an ill omen, and when any of the tribe are guilty of a petty theft, the odium is thrown upon the whole tribe. An ignorant, iron-hearted Justice of the Peace at——Sessions, whose name may perish with his cruelty, sitting in absence of a wise and kinder associate, mixed up this malicious sentence in his condemnation of two gipsies for horse-stealing: "This atrocious tribe of wandering vagabonds ought to be made outlaws in every civilized kingdom and exterminated from the face of the earth!" And this persecuting, unfeeling man was a clergyman!

"I never met with a scholar amongst them, nor with anyone who had a reflecting mind. They are susceptible to insult, and even fall into sudden passions without a seeming cause. Their friendships are warm and their passions of short duration; but their closest friendships are not to be relied on. They are loose in their intercourse, delighting to run over smutty ribaldries; but the women have not lost the modesty that belongs to them so far as to sit and hear it without blushing. The young girls are reserved and silent-seeming in the company of men, and their love affections are cold and careless of return. They sometimes marry with the villagers, but it is very rarely, and if they do so they often take to their wandering courses again. Village clowns are oftener known to go away with the gipsy-girls, which happens very frequently.

"They are deceitful generally and have a strong propensity to lying. Yet they are not such dangerous characters as some in civilized life. One hardly ever hears of a gipsy committing murder. Their common thefts are trifling depredations, taking anything that huswifes forget to secure at night, killing game in the woods with their dogs. But some are honest.

"They eat the flesh of badgers and hedgehogs, which are far from bad food, for I have eaten of it in my evening merrymakings with them. They never eat dead meat but in times of scarcity, which they cut into thin slices and throw on a brisk fire till it is scorched black, when it loses its putrid smell and does very well for a makeshift. When they can afford it they wash the meat in vinegar, which takes the smell out of it and makes it eat as well as fresh meat. They are more fond of vegetables than meat, and seldom miss having tea in an afternoon, when they can afford it. They are fond of smoking to excess, both men and women. Their common talk is of horses, asses, dogs, and sport.

"In my first acquaintance with them I had often noticed that the men had a crooked finger on one hand; nor would they satisfy my enquiries till confidence made them more familiar; then I found that the secret was that their parents disabled the finger of every male child in war-time to keep them from being drawn for Militia or sent for soldiers, for any petty theft they might commit, which would invariably be the case if they had been able men when taken before a magistrate, as they lay under the lash of the law with the curse of a bad name. . . .

"There [are] not so many of them with us as there used to be. The Enclosure has left nothing but narrow lanes where they are ill-provided with a lodging."

Clare might have found, among the dark people, a lass to go a-gipsying with, but he had not their iron health, impervious to the severest weather, nor yet their restless longing after change of scene. His partiality for their society naturally did not put him in better odour with the majority of his neighbours and employers. His sympathy might, in time, have marked him in the eyes of authority; for his tale of the harshness of the J.P. is of a piece with what is known of the local tyranny of that official of the Crown, who, since the passing of the old manor courts, had acquired so much power in rural districts.

Clare made other friends as well during this period who were not calculated to put him in the highest repute either. At the wakes and fairs where he had met the gipsies, he tells that he now lost that lonely feeling which had been his in later childhood and most of boyhood; he "grew dissipated."

"I have often made the fields a bed when I have been at merrymakings, and stopped out when all were a-bed. And at other times when I had taken too much 'Sir John Barleycorn' and could get no further."

So, in the winter-time, when gipsy company was not available, he spent his evenings and Sundays with these other friends,

"at a neighbour's house of the name of Billings. It was a sort of meeting-house for the young fellows of the town, where they used to join for ale and tobacco and sing and drink the night away. The occupiers were two bachelors, and the cottage was called 'Bachelors' Hall.' It is an old,

ruinous hut and has needed repairs ever since I knew it; for
they neither mend up the walls nor thatch the roof, being
negligent men, but quiet and inoffensive neighbours. I still
frequent their house; it has more the appearance of a deserted hermitage than an inhabited dwelling. I have sat
talking of witch and ghost stories over our cups on winter
nights till I felt fearful of going home.

"We used to go often to the woods to pill oaks and some
times to shoot crows in the winter evenings, or, in fact,
anything chance started; and once we went on a Sabbath
day. There were three of us, and James Billings was the
gunner; for I had no eyes to kill anything even if I was close
to it, though my will perhaps was as good as the rest. On
rustling about among the bushes we started a hare, which
hopped on a little way and stood to listen, when my companion lifted his old gun to take aim, and a sudden shock
tingled in my ears like the sound of broken glasses. We were
astounded and looked on each other's faces with vacancy.
The gun had burst and all the barrel was carried away
to the lock, and part of the lock likewise. We saw danger
in each other's faces and dare not make enquiry what was
the matter, as all of us expected we were wounded; but
as soon as the fright was over we found none of us was hurt.
What became of the gun we could not tell, for we could not
find a fragment but that which he held in his hand. Was not
this an alarm to tell our consciences that we were doing
wrong? And whether it was chance or providence that
interfered, it was a narrow escape. I felt the warning for
me and never was caught on the same errand again.

"John Billings, the elder, had a very haunted mind,
and had scarce been out on a journey with the night without
seeing a ghost or will-o'-wisp or some such shadowy mystery.
Such recollections of midnight wanderings furnished him
with stories for a whole wintry fireside. . . . [He] was an inoffensive man. He believed everything that he saw in print
as true, and had a cupboard full of penny books, *The King
and the Cobbler, The Seven Sleepers*, accounts of people being
buried so many days and then dug up alive, of bells in
churches ringing in the middle of the night, of spirits warning men when they were to die. . . . He had never read
Thomson or Cowper or Wordsworth, or perhaps heard of
their names; yet nature gives everyone a natural simplicity
of heart to read her language, and the gross interferences

of the world adulterate them. He used often to carry a curious old book called *The Pleasant Wit* [Art?] *of Money-Catching*, and another whose title was *Laugh and be Fat*; there was a tale of *Juggler Percy and the Butcher's Dog*, several rules and receipts for saving and cheap living, a collection of proverbs, and a long poem of forty or fifty verses. I fancied some of the verses good, and I think they were written by a poet, perhaps Randolph . . . . He felt as happy over these, as we whiled away the impatience of a day's bad fishing under a green willow or an old thorn, as I did over Thomson, Cowper, and Walton, which I often took in my pocket to read.

" He is fond of getting 'cuckoos,' bluebells, primroses, and any favourite flowers from the fields and woods, to set in his garden. His Sunday's best leisure is, when the weather and season permit him, to ramble by the river-sides a-fishing, and we have spent many Sundays together in that diversion."

At a time when the fierce ruthlessness of game-preserving permitted laws of such severity that one of them, at least, as Romilly, the philanthropic law-reformer, said, had no parallel in any country in the world, Clare was wise when he decided to go no more to the woods with firearms. Once, while sitting writing in some secret nook, more than half a day's journey from home, he was nearly discovered by the keepers of the Marquis of Exeter, and he sat hidden in great fear of being taken for a poacher. But among all his records there is no further indication than the incident just recounted that he ever permitted himself a little "harmless" poaching, so easy for a man who spent a great deal of time alone in the woods. Even Isaac Bawcombe, that "good shepherd" and most admirable of men, eked out his poverty in this way and held himself innocent. Clare's dislike of violence grew stronger as he grew older. He had a contract with the boys of the village to bring all birds which they caught to him. He purchased them for some trifle, and, courting ridicule perhaps, gave to the boys

> *a fee*
> *To buy the captive sparrow's liberty.*

Poaching with sticks and snares, which, in spite or because of all its attendant dangers, still held a fascination as a sport among many men, was not likely to attract him.

On another occasion he records a nasty experience of a different kind in the woods. He does not say whether his companions this time were the Billings brothers or not. While he was gathering acorns, the branch on which he was sitting broke with him, and he fell fourteen or fifteen feet to the ground. The fragment which describes his sensations, though brief, is worth its place:

". . . On coming to myself I crawled up and saw that the large grain had lodged above me. I could not catch my breath unless by deep groans ; but I got over that."

" Bachelors' Hall," for some years to come, provided Clare with entertainment, with occasional solace for his loneliness, and comfort for his melancholy. Once he had been drunk he drank again, he says, to stifle self-reproach over the folly that was past. Besides, he could keep his talents and his learning to himself no longer; since, as he admits, "I had no tongue to brag with till I was inspired with ale," conviviality at "Bachelors' Hall" became an outlet for him. There, at least, was some appreciation of his powers:

"I had got the fame of being a good scholar, and, in fact, I had vanity enough to fancy I was far from a bad one myself. I could puzzle the village schoolmasters over my quart, with solving algebra questions; for I had once struggled hard to get fame in that crabbed wilderness, but my brain was not made for it and would not reach it. Though it was a mystery scarcely half unveiled to my capacity, yet I made enough of it to astonish their ignorance. For a village schoolmaster is one of the most pretending and most ignorant of men, and their fame is often of the sort which that droll genius 'Peter Pindar' describes."

There are drinking songs referring to this period which show a very different Clare from the solitary youth, half naturalist, half poet, that he had been till lately :

Away with your songs and your glasses
  That laud foreign wines to the sky;
Though they please your gay lords and rich lasses,
  They are nought to such topers as I;
Class me with a hedger and ditcher,
  Or a beggar that carries his horn;
Such spirits aye make me the richer,
  That love nought but "John Barleycorn."

Give me any crone of a fellow
  That loves to drink ale in a horn,
And loves to sing songs when he's mellow
  That topers sang ere he was born;—
For such a friend fate shall be thankèd,
  And we should want nothing but brass,
And we'd soak up ale from a blanket
  Ere we should be shamed with a glass.

· · · · · · · ·

Like Lamb, Clare could carry but little ale. At any time, a quart was enough to loosen his tongue and unsteady his legs. But that did not prevent him from spending a good deal of time in the congenial company at the Billings's house, where for the moment his anxieties and responsibilities were lightened, and his serious ambitions took on a fairer prospect.

Yet, as Clare has already related, he and John Billings, the elder brother, had more tastes in common than carousing. They took long walks to seek the country flowers and transplant them to their gardens. Probably from John Billings Clare acquired the habit, which he kept ever after, of socialising his aristocratic garden blooms by setting them beside wild blossoms from the woods. Not that he preferred the "retired flowers" to those which pranked the garden in open splendour. The catholicity of his love set one beside the other without precedence.

But sometime in these three or four years before 1817, another interest appeared which drew him a little from the society at "Bachelors' Hall" and from the company of the gipsies. Clare fell in love a second time. We do not know

FJ

when he first met Elizabeth Newbon. A definite date during
this period, when his time was divided among work, fiddling
with the gipsies, drinking at the Billings's house, and courting
Elizabeth, would be welcome; but there is none. Apparently
Elizabeth revealed her affections in rustic fashion one
Sunday by writing "an unfinished sentence with chalk on
the table in an old ruined cottage where young people used
to meet." Remembering Mary, Clare wrote of Elizabeth
without glamour:

"She was no beauty, but I fancied she was everything,
and our courtship was a long one. I used to meet her on
Sundays at a lodge-house on Ashton Green at first and then
went to her home. Her father was a wheelwright and an
old man who professed to be learned in the Bible. He was
always trying my wisdom, where such and such passages
might be found. My silence generally spoke my lack of
religion, and he shook his head at my ignorance. He thought
that religion consisted in learning such scraps as a sort of
necessity by heart. He knew the book in the Bible in which
God was not once mentioned; it was *Ezra*; and he knew the
name of the mountain where Noah's ark rested, and other
Bible curiosities. He read it to search for these and to be
able to talk about them. He thought himself a religious man
though he never went to Church; and he was so, for he was
happy and harmless. He possessed a large Bible with notes,
which he took in numbers when he was a young man. It
was Wright's Bible and he often spoke of the pleasure he
felt in reading the first number one Sunday night in a
terrible thunderstorm. He had another book on which he
set great value; it was Lord Napier's Key to the *Revelations*.
He believed the explanations there given as the essence of
truth. . . . He believed in Moore's Almanack, too, with great
reverence, and unlocked its mystical hieroglyphics with his
Revelations Key yearly; though it was not so mutable a key
as Moore's, who waited the events of the year and explained
[them] afterwards."

If we may judge from the space which Clare devotes to his
recollections of Elizabeth's father, it seems to have been he
as much as his daughter who attracted Clare to their cottage

at Ashton. He has no more to say of his courtship of Elizabeth than that it "went on for years with petty jealousies on both sides. At length, giving ear to the world, she charged me with sins of changing affection." Events between them were not closed till some time near 1817, when Clare had hopes of Mary Joyce again. The lines "To a Cold Beauty," in *Poems Descriptive*, probably refer to Elizabeth. But he pays a much higher tribute to old Mr. Newbon; the far better poem "The Cottager," first printed in the *Stamford Bee*, was surely inspired by him:

> *The "Pilgrim's Progress" and the "Death of Abel"*
> *Are seldom missing from his Sunday table,*
> *And prime old Tusser in his homely trim,*
> *The first of bards in all the world with him,*
> *And only poet which his leisure knows. . . .*

Elizabeth's jealousies and accusations about Clare's rambling affections were perhaps justified. But there were causes. He was restless, and for more reasons than one. His father's rheumatism had gradually grown worse, till he was, by 1815 or 1816, almost a cripple. Certainly he was unable to work anything like regularly, even if the work were there. For some years now, he had earned five shillings a week by working on the roads. In some way Lord Milton,¹ eldest son of Earl Fitzwilliam of Milton, had heard of his illness and difficulties, and had sent him to the Sea-bathing Infirmary at Scarborough. The treatment there gave him relief, but, to save expense, he made part of the journey home on foot, so aggravating his disease that he became worse than before. Ann Clare, troubled with dropsy, could do no extra work to supply the deficiency of money caused by her husband's illness. The whole responsibility of providing for his father, mother, and sister, now fell on John, and, by a poem "Address'd to my Lame Father," we realise how bitterly he felt his helplessness to give any of the comforts so badly needed at home. Parker Clare was now forced from his independence for the first time, and he had to ask for the hated "parish bounty."

These considerations were enough to make Clare restless
and dissatisfied with himself. But, besides this, he knew himself capable of something better than casual labour in the
fields. By "frequent trials" his verses were now much better
than they had been; "I always wrote my poems in great
haste," he notes, "and . . . what corrections I made I always
made them while writing the poems, and could never do
anything with them afterwards." Their numbers grew
steadily. Schemes began to form in his mind as to what he
might do with them. His friends at "Bachelors' Hall"
fostered his ambitions. They urged him to try for something
better than agricultural work:

"The neighbours, believing my learning to be great,
thought it a folly in me to continue at hard work when they
fancied I might easily better myself by my learning; and, as
Lord Milton was a great friend of my father, they persuaded
me to go to Milton to see what he would do for me. The
parish clerk, a man of busy merits, who taught the Sunday-
school, offered to go with me, as he knew his Lordship better
than I did, by seeing him at his Sunday-school often. I
accepted the proposal and started once more upon ambition's
hitherto fruitless errands. I remember the morning; we saw
two crows as soon as we got into the fields, and harped on
good luck and success, and my companion gave me advice
with the authority of a patron as well as a friend. As soon as
we got there, on making the necessary enquiries, we were
told that his lordship would see us by and by. Hour passed
after hour till night came and told us we were disappointed.
The porter comforted us by saying we should call again
to-morrow, but my friend the clerk had more wit in the way
and we met his Lordship the next day at the Heath Farm
near home, which he was in the habit of visiting often. As
soon as we came up to his Lordship, my companion began to
descant on my merits in a way that made me hang my head,
and begged his Lordship to do something for me. But I found
he had a double errand, for before he had finished his tale of
my [learning] he pulled an antique box out of his pocket,
which he had found in levelling some headlands near Eastwell
Spring, a spot famous for summer Sunday revels. It was in
the form of an apple-pie and contained several farthings of
King Charles the Second's reign. His Lordship reached and

took it and gave him a good exchange for his curiosity, which raised the clerk's voice in the conclusion of his story of me. When he [Lord Milton] heard to whom I belonged he promised to do something for me; but such trifling things are soon shoved out of the memory of such people, who have plenty of other things to think of. I heard no more of it and worked on at my employment as usual."

Clare was not particularly disturbed by Lord Milton's failure to keep his promise. His dreams and plans continued. Indeed, his whole life began to centre round his poetry and his studies. He was no longer ashamed of his rhyming before anyone; and, though his methods had not yet become consciously formulated in his mind, his aim is clear enough. An invocation to the "Muse of youth's fairy themes" reveals something of his hopes after fame:

> . . . *Look on thy votary like the clouds of even,*
> *And let a portion of thy spell be given,*
> *If one so mean as I may merit aught of heaven.*

His methods were the same as they had been from the beginning. Although he wrote the following long after his poetic theory was complete and articulate, it is valuable as a memory of part of its emergence.

"I used to drop down under a bush and scribble the fresh thoughts on the crown of my hat. . . . As I found nature then, so I made her. If an old pond with its pendant sallows fringing its mossy sides happened to be in the pleasant nook where I sat concealed among the blackthorns drawing its picture, I called it a pond. . . . And so my feelings were stirred into praise, and my praises were muttered in prose or rhyme as the mood might suit at the moment. Then these moods, often repeated, grew unperceived into quantity on paper; and then I indulged my fancy in thinking how they would look in print. I selected what I thought best, and hid the others out of shame's way, as laughing-stocks for the crowd who think it a child's occupation to indulge in such feelings, and inexcusable in a man."

The poems completed and copied fair during this period are numerous, but definite dates for any of them are scarce.

He tried his hand at satire, and wrote the " Elegy on the Death of a Quack" on a certain "Doctor Touch" who came to Deeping and gave out that he could cure diseases by laying his hands on the sufferers. People, credulous then as now, flocked to him, and Parker Clare was taken too, in hopes of having his rheumatism cured. But, says Clare, "the fellow did not cure them by touch, but by blisters, which he laid on in unmerciful sizes at half a guinea a blister." When Parker heard that the "Doctor" required his fee to be paid down before he did his work, his faith was shaken and he returned home as he had gone. His recital of the story and "Doctor Touch's" decamping in the night stirred Clare to the first of his satirical poems.

There is, however, one date belonging to this period. He wrote "The Village Funeral" in 1815. In it there is a surety of phrase and a dignity of thought which was not in his poetry before.

> Now from the low, mud cottage on the moor,
>   By two and two sad bend the weeping train;
> The coffin, ready near the propt-up door,
>   Now slow proceeds along the wayward lane:
>
> While, as nearer draw in solemn state,
>   The village neighbours are assembled round
> And seem with fond anxiety to wait
>   The sad procession in the burial ground.
>
> There the lank nettles sicken as they seed,
>   Where from old trees eve's cordial vainly falls
> To raise or comfort each dejected weed,
>   While pattering drops decay the crumbling walls.
>
> Here stand, far distant from the pomp of Pride,
>   Mean little stones, thin scatter'd here and there;
> By the scant means of Poverty applied,
>   The fond memorial of her friends to bear.
>
> .   .   .   .

At this time his reading of subjects other than poetry was various rather than finite in any one branch :

"As to my learning I am not wonderfully deep in science, nor so wonderfully ignorant as many may have fancied. . . . I puzzled over everything in my hours of leisure . . . with a restless curiosity that was ever on the enquiry and never satisfied. When I got set fast in one thing I did not tire, but tried at another, though with the same success in the end. Yet it never sickened me; I still pursued knowledge in a new path, and, though I never came off victorious, I was never conquered."

He had "gotten together by savings a quantity of old books of motley merits." Among these were books on mathematics, on land-surveying, on astrology, on electricity, on travel, and on botany. To "Sir" John Hill's *British Herbal* he acknowledged a deep debt for much of his wild flower lore. Lee's *Introduction to Botany* confused him.

"I have puzzled wasted hours over Lee's *Botany* to understand a shadow of the system so as to be able to class the wild flowers peculiar to my own neighbourhood; for I find it would require a second Adam to find names for them in my way and a second Solomon to understand them in Linnæus's system. Modern works are so mystified by systematic symbols that one cannot understand them till the wrong end of one's lifetime; and when one turns to the works of Ray, Parkinson, and Gerard, where there is more of nature and less of art, it is like meeting the fresh air and balmy summer of a dewy morning after the troubled dreams of a nightmare."

Although he had just bought Lee's *Botany* second-hand, he soon abandoned his attempts at Linnæan classification, and all his life he preferred the old herbalists to the "modern" botanists. As he says, his habits of study at this time were "anxious and restless," increasing into a "multiplicity of things." Sometimes this desultory reading of his, depending as it did so largely on the books he happened to come across, dissatisfied and annoyed him:

"I always had a thirst after knowledge in everything, and by that restless desire have only acquired a very superficial knowledge of many things that serves no other purpose than to make me feel my real ignorance of everything so much the more."

Poetry always had the first place in his reading. His knowledge of it was detailed, and carefully, if unmethodically, gathered. It must be here again remembered how dependent he was on a chance book in an out-of-the-way bookshop and on his own sacrifice or the sacrifice of his parents to find the requisite shilling or so with which to buy the book when he saw it. (Had not his father once given more than a day's wage to buy his most treasured of books, *The Seasons*?) Among the books he possessed at this time (most of which he sold later to a Stamford bookseller), there are some very obscure names and some very well-known ones. Besides Cobb's, Fawkes's, Broome's, and Mrs. Hoole's poems, there are Cowley's works, Milton's *Paradise Lost*, Samuel Wesley's *Maggots*, Waller's, Parnell's, and Carew's poems ; and of course there are his great favourites, Walton's prose-poem and Bloomfield's poems. For some years now Bloomfield's example and his many-editioned *Farmer's Boy* had been a constant encouragement to Clare. Among his prose, too, there are books now unfamiliar; Sturm's *Reflections*, *The Female Shipwright*, and *The Father's Legacy*, are side by side with L'Estrange's *Fables of Aesop*, *Tom Jones*, and the story which "charmed all Europe," *The Vicar of Wakefield*.

He was dissatisfied with his mode of reading, but he could not change it:

"I cannot and never could plod through every book in a regular mechanical way as I met with [it]. I dip into it here and there, and if it does not suit I lay it down and seldom take it up again; but in the same manner I read Thomson's *Seasons* and Milton's *Paradise Lost* through when I was a boy, and they are the only books of poetry that I have regularly read through. . . . Yet in novels my taste is very limited, *Tom Jones* and *The Vicar of Wakefield* are all that I am acquainted with. They are old acquaintances and I care not to make new ones. . . . I read *The Vicar of Wakefield* over every winter and am delighted, though I always feel disappointed at the end of it."

He complains of his lack of historical knowledge, but he had already introduced himself to some of the classical authors, though only, of course, in translation.

About the end of 1816 he last saw Mary Joyce. Although she did not die till 1838, and they lived only a few miles from each other for many years yet, he did not meet her again. Even on this occasion, Mary herself gave Elizabeth Newbon little cause for jealousy. She had no word of kindness for Clare. He may have had hopes in his heart and poems in his pocket; but neither, even in the sounding years immediately ahead, gave him Mary. From this time onward he had to content himself with the memory of how at sunset they had once hastened with eager feet to each other; and that memory changed curiously as the years passed, "such tricks hath strong imagination." Now, in 1816, while he did not know it, the last link with his happy boyhood broke, and the dreary burdens of his maturity began to accumulate:

" There is nothing but poetry about the existence of childhood, real, simple, soul-moving poetry, laughter and joy of poetry, and not its philosophy. And there is nothing of poetry about manhood but the reflection and the remembrance of what has been.

" Surely our play-prolonging moon on spring evenings shed a richer lustre than the mid-day sun that surrounds us now in manhood; for its poetical sunshine hath left us, and we have learned to know that. For, when boys, every new day brought a new sun. We knew no better, and we were happy in our ignorance. There is nothing of that new and refreshing sunshine upon the picture now. It shines from the heavens upon real matter-of-fact existences and weary occupations."

The experiences of his manhood always appeared to him thus; but he discovered a way out of the alien world in which he now found himself. He revisited—relived almost— again and again, in memory, his happy, lost childhood. Much more than that, his fraternity with beast and flower, his ability to consider the lilies, that wisdom which worldly calculation may assail with scorn but never quite subdue, kept him in the innocency of a child till the end of his long life.

V

A POET IN HIS JOY
1817

Yes, thus the Muses sing of happy swains,
Because the Muses never knew their pains:
They boast their peasants' pipes; but peasants now
Resign their pipes and plod behind the plough;
And few, amid the rural tribe, have time
To number syllables and play with rhyme;

CRABBE, "The Village."

IN the spring of 1817 Clare was nearly twenty-four. When he was a child, nothing in the world of plant and creature was too simple for him to admire; now he expressed in poetry all his admiration, and again, nothing was too simple or too trivial to be praised—a prettily shaped stone, a shell, a little path. Probably not even in his own mind had he yet allowed his dreams about publication and fame to assume much likeness to reality; but he was beginning to have very decided opinions on poetry in general. He wrote an excellent hand when he was paying heed and copying his poems carefully. At other times it was strong and bold. By disposition he was thoughtful and silent, rarely expanding into talk except after his quart of ale. An acute knowledge of what he called his own failings led him often into self-condemnation that was perhaps over-sensitive.

Neither in gardening nor field-labour had Helpston enough employment to offer him, and wages were imperative. Therefore he and the brother of a friend called Gordon obtained work, in the spring of this year, as lime-burners for a man named Wilders at Bridge Casterton, in Rutlandshire. Clare has left a description of the quiet village, the peace of which was broken only by the rattle of the daily stage along Ermine Street. Amid these "dear vallies" he wrote and read with an impatient energy during the next two years.

" It was a pleasant, lively town, consisting of a row of houses on each side the turnpike, about a furlong long. The river Gwash ran its crooked courses at the back of them on the south side, and washed the foot of the gardens till it crossed the turnpike under a modern-looking bridge and wound along a sloping meadow northward, losing its name and its waters [among] stranger stones. There are some beautiful spots on its banks towards the little village of Tickencote southward, where the bank on the field side rises very stunt in some places from the edge of the river, and may, by a fancy used to a flat country, be easily imagined into mountains. The whole prospect is diversified by gently-swelling slopes and easy-swimming valleys."

The reaches of the rivulet, the Gwash, gave him shelter for contemplation, and inspiration to write. But during the first few weeks he worked long hours at the lime-kiln to cover the expenses which a change of situation always involves.

"We worked at first from light to dark, (and in some emergencies all night,) to get some money to appear a little decent in a strange place, having arrived penniless, with but a shabby appearance in[to] the bargain. We got lodgings at a house of scant fame, a professional lodging-house, kept by a man and his wife, of the name of Cole. We were troubled at night with treble fares in each bed, an inconvenience which I had never been used to; they took in men of all descriptions, the more the merrier for their profits. When they were all assembled round the evening fire, the motley countenances of many characters looked like an assemblage of robbers in the rude hut dimly and mysteriously lighted by the domestic savings of a farthing taper.

" When we first went we worked hard to save money, and I got about fifty shillings in about six weeks, with which I intended to purchase a new olive-green coat, a colour which I had long aimed at, and for which I was measured already ere I left home."

Clare's employer, Wilders, who kept the New Inn at Casterton, had a kiln in that village, another at the neighbouring village of Ryhall, and was about to open a third at the more distant village of Pickworth, about four miles away. Clare had not been employed at the Casterton kiln very long when Wilders, hearing that he had worked in the gardens of Burghley, offered him work in his own garden at the New Inn. Here the work was easier, but temptation nearer. In the autumn Clare went, with his companion, Stephen Gordon, to burn lime at the Pickworth kiln. The village of Pickworth he calls "a place of other days," and adds that the piece of ground where they "dug the kiln was full of foundations and human bones."

Here Clare wrote the " Elegy on the Ruins of Pickworth." He preferred, although lime-burning was more laborious than gardening, to work out there rather than at the inn, because he was more alone. Not that, in these days, he invariably chose solitude. On Sundays he and his companions took long walks in field and lane, usually ending up at the Flower-Pot public-house at Tickencote. Beyond Tickencote and the Gwash again, there were valleys and ancient woods, which pleased his eye and inspired his pen. Accustomed as he was to the flat fen almost at his doorstep, his joy in this rolling country all round Casterton and Pickworth kept him writing feverishly. A favourite walk was round to Pickworth and back to Tickencote or Casterton across the fields by Walkherd Lodge. The Lodge, a stone cottage with barn at one end, two large draughty rooms above, and two below, is there to-day. It stands high enough to command a prospect of some miles all round. To the west of it the woods then crept up almost to the cottage wall. Clare has left more than one description of this favourite scene:

> Here steeple tops, and there a misty town
> [Are] stretching through each opening to be seen,
> And woodlands melting from their gloomy hues
> To sprout in freshness, while the heath-hills lean

In triumph to the eyes; their blooming gorse
Wild nature's brightest ornament, as now,
Speckt o'er with sheep and beast and nibbling horse
That still roams free from the long-lazy plough.

The farmer who lived at Walkherd Lodge was William
Turner. His daughter Martha, or Patty, dark-haired and
rosy-cheeked, was, in the autumn of 1817, in her eighteenth
year. Clare, out of sight of Glinton's taper spire,[1] and lately
jilted by Elizabeth Newbon, was ready enough to fall in
love again. He first saw Patty Turner on one of his Sunday
"excursions" to Tickencote,

"going across the fields toward her home. I was in love at
first sight, and, not knowing who she was or where she
came from, I felt very ill at rest. I clomb on the top of a
dotterel to see which way she went till she was out of sight;
but chance quickly threw her again in my way a few weeks
after when I was going to fiddle at Stamford. I then ventured
to speak to her and succeeded so far as to have the liberty
to go home with her to her cottage about four miles off,
and it became the introduction to some of the happiest
and unhappiest days my life has met with.
  " After I left her to return home I had taken such a
heedless observance of the way that led over a cow-pasture
with its thousand paths, and dallied so long over pleasant
shapings of the future, that twilight with its doubtful guidance overtook my musings and led me down a wrong track
in crossing the Common. As I could not correct myself, I
got over a hedge and sat down on a baulk between a wheat-
field. When the moon got up I started again, and, on trying
to get over the same hedge again, (as I thought,) to cross
the Common, I saw something shine very bright on the
other side. I fancied it to be some bare ground beaten
by the sheep and cows in hot weather, but doubting, I
stooped down to feel, and to my terrored surprise I found
it was water. While in that stooping posture I saw by the
lengthy silver line that stretched from me that it was the
river! I was frighted and sat under the hedge till daylight."

The courtship was the more fervent because, although
Patty favoured Clare, a rival was there before him. " When

John came," she would recall long afterwards, "I'd run
and get my gingham dress from the hedge where it was
airing, and put it on whether dry or not." But her parents,
who had known better days, and whose friends still enjoyed
comparative prosperity, considered a lime-burner a very
unfitting match for their daughter, and did their utmost
to encourage Clare's rival. He records how

"a young shoemaker paid his addresses to her, whose visits
were approved of more by her parents than herself. When I
had disinherited him of [her] affections they encouraged
him to come on, and urged and tried to win her mind over
to his and their wishes. Such was the tide that bore strongly
against us on our first acquaintance."

Still, since Patty returned his love, neither her parents
nor the shoemaker proved much of a hindrance. He rejoiced
in the seclusion round the place where she lived, and, when
he was not with her, he was rambling there to write, or to
watch the creatures of the woods and meadows:

"Casterton cow-pasture, where I used to pass on my
visits to Patty, was a very favourite spot, and I planned and
wrote some of the best poems in my first volume among its
solitudes. My love-rambles then made me acquainted with
many of the privacies of night which she seemed wishing to
keep as secrets. I was then the companion of the evening,
and very often the morning, star. Patty's Lodge stood in a
lone spot, and the very path seemed to lose itself in the
solitudes and was glad to take the direction of rabbit-tracks
ere it led one to the door. Nature revelled in security.
"I used to go on evenings in the week and every Sunday
to the Lodge, not at all times on love-errands merely, but
to get out of the way; for the lodging-house was generally
cumbered with inmates and the Inn was continually
troubling one with new jobs. The solitude round the Lodge
was plentiful, and there were places where the foot of man
had not printed for years perhaps . . . where beautiful heaths
and woods swelled their wild and free varieties to the edges
of the vision. I used to wander about them with my artless
and interesting companion in more than happiness. A large

wood in summer used to be covered with lilies-of-the-valley, of which she used to gather handfuls for her flower-pots, and I helped her to gather them."

But meanwhile events of another nature were stirring about him, and to recount these fully the story must turn back a little way in a new chapter.

VI

THE STRUGGLES YOUNG AMBITION MADE
1817-1819

And so it cheered me while I lay
Among their beautiful array
To think that I in humble dress
Might have a right to happiness
And sing as well as greater men;
And then I strung the lyre again
And heartened up o'er toil and fear
And lived with rapture everywhere,
Till dayshine to my themes did come.

JOHN CLARE, "The Progress of Rhyme."

THE dayshine that came to Clare's themes in 1820 had first glimmered faintly in 1814, when he purchased the manuscript book from Henson, of Market Deeping, in order to preserve the poems hitherto jotted down on odd scraps of paper. This book cost eight shillings, and was paid for in instalments. Its first page reveals Clare's secret ambition, for on it is neatly printed, in imitation of the title-page of a book, *A Rustic's Pastime In Leisure Hours: Helpston* 1814.

J. B. Henson "was a religious man belonging to the congregational dissenters or Independents," whom Clare had met at the chapel at Helpston, where he was fond of hearing the Independents at that time. At the time of Clare's acquaintance with him, he was doing tolerably well as a bookseller and printer in a small way, but eventually his business declined; he "did some dirty doings with Satan, was turned off from his profession of clerk to the Independents," and left Deeping in search of better fortune.

Clare's purchase of the book aroused Henson's curiosity. "He urged many side-wind enquiries . . . but I had kept the secret too long to be so easily persuaded to let it go." The name of poet was still

> *A title that I dared not claim,*
> *I hid it like a private shame.*

However, one fair-day, when flushed with ale, Clare let slip some hints about dabbling in rhyme, and later showed Henson some of his earliest poems, one of which, "On the Death of Chatterton," "he wanted to print in a penny book to sell to hawkers, but I was very doubtful of its merits and not covetous of such fame." But when Henson proposed that a volume of poems should be published by subscription, Clare agreed. The printing was to begin as soon as a hundred subscribers were found, and Henson offered to print three hundred prospectuses for a pound.

Clare was working at Pickworth toward the end of 1817, and his meeting with Patty had quickened his ambition to better his fortunes; for "a poor man's meeting with a wife is reckoned but little improvement to his condition, and particularly with the embarrassments I laboured under at that time." So at Pickworth

"by hard working nearly day and night I at last got my pound saved for the printing of the proposals, which I never lost sight of; and getting a many more poems written, as excited by a change of Scenery, and from being over head and ears in love, above all the most urgent propensity to scribbling, I fancied myself more qualified for the undertaking, considering the latter materials much better than what I had done, which no doubt was the case. So I wrote a letter from this place immediately to Henson, of Market Deeping, wishing him to begin the proposals and address the public himself, urging he could do it far better than myself; but his answer was that I must do it.

"After this I made some attempts, but having not a fit place for doing any thing of that kind, lodging at a public house, and pestered with many other inconveniences, I could not suit myself by doing it in a hurry; so it kept passing from time to time, till at last I determined, good or bad, to produce something. And as we had another lime kiln at Ryhall,

GJ

about three miles from Pickworth, I often went there to work by myself; where I had leisure to study over such things on my journeys of going and returning to and from. And on these walks morning and night I have dropped down five or six times to plan this troublesome task of An Address, &c. ; in one of these musings, my prosing thoughts lost themselves in rhyme, in taking a view, as I sat beneath the shelter of a woodland hedge, of my parents' distresses at home, and of my labouring so hard and so vainly to get out of debt, and of my still added perplexities of ill-timed love.

"Striving to remedy all, and all to no purpose, I burst out into an exclamation of distress, "What is Life!" and instantly recollecting such a subject would be a good one for a poem, I hastily scratted down the two first verses of it, as it stands, as a beginning of the plan which I intended to adopt; and continued my journey to work. But when at the kiln, I could not work for thinking about what I had so long been trying at; so I sat me down on a lime scuttle, and out with my pencil for an address of some sort, which, good or bad, I determined to send off that day. And for that purpose when finished, I accordingly started to Stamford, about three miles from me.

"Still along the road, I was in a hundred minds whether I should throw all thoughts up about the matter, or stay while a fitting opportunity to have the advice of some friend or other; but on turning it over in one's mind again, a second thought soon informed me that I had none. I was turned adrift on the broad ocean of life, and must either sink or swim. So I weighed matters on both sides and fancied, let what bad would come, they could but balance with the former. If my hopes of the Poems failed, I should be not a pin the worse than usual,—I could but work then, as I did already,—nay, I considered I should reap benefit from disappointment. Their downfall would free my mind from all foolish hopes, and let me know that I had nothing to trust to but work. So with this favourable idea, I pursued my intention—dropping down on a stoneheap before I got in the town, to give it a second reading, and correct what I thought amiss. . . . I felt as I went on as if everybody knew my errand and my face reddened at the gaze of a passer-by."

This letter, which Clare sealed with pitch, and for which he could not produce the penny demanded as late-postage fee, contained his "Proposals for publishing by Subscription, a Collection of Original Trifles, on miscellaneous Subjects, religious and moral, in Verse, by John Clare, of Helpstone." A quotation from Ramsay was followed by the conditions of publication; the book was to cost three shillings and sixpence, and be printed "on a superfine yellow wove foolscap paper, in octavo size," as soon as three hundred subscribers had promised to buy it. Then came the Address to the Public:

"The Public are requested to observe, that the Trifles humbly offered for their candid perusal can lay no claim to eloquence of poetical composition, (whoever thinks so will be deceived,) the greater part of them being *Juvenile* productions; and those of a later date offsprings of those leisure intervals which the short remittance from hard and manual labour sparingly afforded to compose them. It is hoped that the humble situation which distinguishes their author will be some excuse in their favour, and serve to make an atonement for the many inaccuracies and imperfections that will be found in them. The least touch from the iron hand of *Criticism* is able to crush them to nothing, and sink them at once to utter oblivion. May they be allowed to live their little day, and give satisfaction to those who may choose to honour them with a perusal, they will gain the end for which they were designed, and their author's wishes will be gratified. Meeting with this encouragement, it will induce him to publish a similar collection, of which this is offered as a specimen."

This specimen poem was the "Sonnet to the Setting Sun," one of his earliest. Soon a letter arrived from Henson, arranging to meet Clare at the Dolphin Inn at Stamford. "I accordingly went and for the first time saw a sonnet of mine in print and I scarcely knew it in its new dress and felt a prouder confidence than I had hitherto done, thinking it got merit by its dress." He found Henson less enthusiastic about the scheme and demanding five or six shillings more than the sum agreed upon. As they were drinking together, "a dull-looking fellow in a genteelish dress" came in, and Henson gave him one of the papers; "but the fellow just threw his eyes over it, then looked at me and walked out of the room without saying a word." However, the next arrival restored Clare's confidence. He read the paper, praised the sonnet, asked Clare to drink with him, wished him success, and bade Henson set his name down as a subscriber. " This gave me heart and did me more good than all I ever met with before or after. I felt it deeply and never forgot the name of the Rev. Mr. Mounsey." Clare's first subscriber, Thomas Moun-sey, was second master, which meant acting headmaster, of the Stamford Free Grammar School, where he taught "the Greek and Latin Languages and every branch of Commercial and Mathematical Learning."

For a while the hopes aroused by this first success seemed likely to be realised. Clare wrote to Henson enclosing a list of subscribers, one of whom was a baronet. "Good God, how great are my Expectations! What hopes do I cherish! as great as the unfortunate Chatterton's were, on his first entrance into London, which is now pictured in my mind; and undoubtedly, like him, I may be building 'Castles in the Air'; but Time will prove it." He urged Henson to pro-cure subscribers, and considered that the printing might begin when a hundred names had been obtained. But the hundred subscribers did not respond to the invitation. Clare's first efforts procured seven, and when all his papers were distributed the number was still seven. Soon all his hopes seemed lost.

" I knew not what course to take. I had got no work to go to and I hardly dare show my face to seek for any. Everybody seemed to jeer me at my foolish pretensions, and I felt ashamed as I went down the street scarcely daring to look anyone in the face; for the prospectuses had filled everybody's mouth with my name and prospects. Enquiry stood on tiptoe with questions, go where I would, and I hated to hear them. I evaded them as well as I could. I felt uncommonly uneasy and knew not what to do. I sometimes thought of running away and leaving home, where I might be at peace among strangers, for my disappointment was fast growing into a byword. I went to Stamford twice to enlist in the artillery which was recruiting there, but my variety of minds pre-vented me; besides, my love matters were a strong tether that I could not easily break. I went so far at one time as to take the money for a recruit, but the sergeant was a better man than such usually are, and said he took no advantage of a man in liquor—for I was fresh at the time—and let me off with paying the expenses of the drink. But I was wanting in height, which might be a better plea than the sergeant's honesty."

Despite the uncertainty which inspired this, his third, attempt to enlist, Clare went on preparing poems for the proposed volume. But Henson now wanted £15 before he would begin printing them, and as Clare could not borrow even fifteen shillings, his hopes sank still lower. Soon, his lack of fifteen shillings involved him in worse difficulty; he received a bill for that sum from Thompson, a Stamford bookseller, with a demand for immediate payment. Clare wrote a brief explanation of his situation, promising to pay the bill as soon as he was able, and his old, once-sceptical friend, Tom Porter of Ashton, took the letter with a few prospectuses to Thompson's shop. The bookseller treated the letter with contempt and abused the messenger. But at this black moment in Clare's fortunes, chance not only brought him relief from his temporary difficulty, but opened the way to a fulfilment of the hopes he had almost relinquished. It brought Ned Drury into Thompson's shop before Tom Porter departed with the rejected prospectuses. Drury read one of them, became interested, and paid the fifteen shillings for Clare, with a promise to enquire further about him.

Edward Bell Drury prided himself on being a descendant of the famous Elizabethan family in whose honour Drury Lane was named. He was the son of John Drury, a Lincoln printer, whose sister was the mother of John Taylor, the London bookseller and publisher. Edward Drury, having served his apprenticeship, came to Stamford in 1818, took a shop opposite the post-office, and became a bookseller and "agent for Twining's Tea and Antiscorbutic Drops." He was a keen young business man, and perceived in his discovery of Clare a possibility of making use of his connection with a London publisher. He lost no time; in December 1818, accompanied by his friend, Robert Newcomb, proprietor of the *Stamford Mercury*, he visited a farmer named Clark to enquire about Clare's character and merits as a poet.

"The former," wrote Clare, "was open to every meddler, but the latter was a secret, so they came to enquire more about it with me. I was at a neighbour's house when they came (at Billings's, the "Bachelors' Hall"), and my sister ran for me; and on telling me two gentlemen wanted to see me, I felt hopeful and hurriedly went home, where I found them talking to my parents. Drury said little or nothing, but Newcomb asked some questions as to how my writings were disposed of. When I told him that I had made proposals for Henson to print them, he said they did not wish to take them out of his hands, but that instead of desiring money to print them they would let me have money for my necessities. So I thought the difference of advantage a good one and readily engaged to get my MSS. from Henson. Mr. Newcomb invited me to dine with him on the Monday as he prepared to start, but cautiously opened the door again to remind me that unless I brought the MSS. I need not come. I felt insulted with his kindness and never accepted the invitation, though I took some of them the next day, when Drury looked over them and gave me a guinea as a sort of earnest, I suppose, and promised to pay my debts. I remained with him the whole day, and he gave me a poem in my hands to read of Lord Byron's—I think it was "The Giaour"—the first time I had ever seen any of them."

Clare's next concern was to retrieve the poems he had sent to Henson, who now became anxious to retain them, holding that Clare had incurred responsibility by agreeing to let him publish them. Clare replied that he considered the engagement broken by the request for £15 which he could not obtain, and asked him to give up the poems. This Henson did with some reluctance, and Clare took them to Stamford, Drury stating that he was prepared either to purchase them or to conclude an agreement which would leave Clare independent of his proceedings.

Drury now desired to obtain an estimate of the literary value of his find, so he showed the poems to "the Revd.

Mr. Twopenny, of Little Casterton; who sent them back with a cold note stating that he had no objection to assist in raising the poor man a small subscription, though the poems appeared to him to possess no merit." Clare took the criticism to heart.

"As I fancied all men in a station superior to mine as learned and more wise, especially parsons, I felt my fortunes as lost and my hopes gone. . . . I felt dejected a long time and almost carried it too far. After prosperity shone out upon me, I remembered it keenly, and wrote the following lines on his name, and a letter, which I never sent :

> *Twopenny his wisdom is, and Twopenny his fame is,*
> *Twopenny his merit is, and Twopenny his name is,*
> *And as Twopence is a trifle, I will do without him;*
> *I'll sing in spite of Twopences and not care Twopence*
>   *about him."*

However, Drury soon found a more friendly critic in Sir John English Dolben,[1] who liked the poems and left his name as a subscriber. Clare took heart again and went on with his rhyming in peace. During this winter, 1818–1819, at home and out of work, he wrote many new poems, and completed and corrected others, some of which had been begun as early as 1807.

With the spring of 1819 Clare returned to Casterton to work in Wilder's garden at the New Inn; but his life there was widened by his new prospects.

"I used to seize the leisure that every wet day brought me to go to Drury's shop to read books and to get new tunes for my fiddle. . . . Whenever I wrote a new thing I used to take it to Drury, very often on Sunday morning to breakfast with him. In one of these visits I got acquainted with Dr. Bell, a man of odd taste, but a pleasant acquaintance. He was fond of books and had edited a droll one entitled *The Banisher of the Blue Devils*, a jest book. He used to cut all the curious and odd paragraphs out of the newspapers and paste them on sheets of pasteboard. He had a great many of these things which he had collected for many years. He had

been a doctor in the army, and in the East or West Indies
became acquainted with 'Peter Pindar,' then in the same
capacity, some of whose early poems he possessed, which had
never been published."

While at Casterton, Clare first had to endure those attentions from curious visitors which his acute shyness turned
into a misery that he never outgrew. "My mistress wished
to see some of my pieces and used to be anxious to introduce
me to strangers whom she would talk to about me and who
would express a curiosity to see me. But I used to get out of
the way whenever I could."

There were worse troubles than this. His return to Casterton and his better prospects had brought about a renewal of
his acquaintance with Patty Turner, which ripened with
the year into a deep affection. Patty's relatives and friends,
whose opposition to her connection with a poor lime-burner
had hitherto harassed the lovers, now began to look more
favourably upon the match, and even courted Clare's
company. But he was not disposed to trim his sails so suddenly to their favourable wind, for his pride had been
touched, and he "neglected to go, or but slightly heeded
their urgent invitations." Nor was this the only rapid in the
course of his love for Patty. He has left this record of his
feelings in the autumn of 1819 :

"While I was at home in the winter, I renewed my acquaintance with a former love and had made a foolish
confidence with a young girl at Southorpe; and though it
began in a heedless [frolic] at Stamford Fair, from accom-
panying her home it grew up into an affection that made my
heart ache to think it must be broken. For Patty was then
in a situation that marriage only could remedy. I felt awkwardly situated and knew not which way to proceed. I had
a variety of minds about me and all of them unsettled. My
long-smothered affections for Mary revived with my hopes,
and as I expected to be on a level with her by and by, I
thought then I might have a chance of success in reviving
my former affection. In these delays Patty's emergency
became urgent. She had revealed her situation to her parents

when she was unable to conceal it any longer, who upbraided her with not heeding their advice and told her as she had made her bed hard she should lie on it. . . . When she complained of their harshness, I could stand out no longer and promised that my prosperity should make me her friend; and to prove that I was in earnest, I gave her money till we should be married. This behaviour pacified them and left her at peace."

Some of the poems written during these months enable us to glimpse the conflicting emotions behind this dispassionate chronicle. The girl of Southorpe, whom Clare met at Stamford Fair, was Betty Sell. She was sixteen years old and worked in the fields; Clare wrote several songs to her, some even as late as 1835, commemorating her black ringlets and hazel eyes and the freshness of the mornings when they met.

His poems to Patty bear clear traces of the events of this year. In "The Adieu" he bids farewell to his "Stain'd Rose-bud," though by a poetic licence he appears to attribute the stain to her dealings with some rival lover. In a verse-letter, "To Patty under a Cloud," he deplores the storm that is brewing around his rose-bud, and the beauties "all despoiled by luckless amorous Johnny." Again he assures her of his love, despite his "many failings" and her "injured merit."

But it is in some verses entitled "An After-Repentance" that Clare's perturbations find most characteristic utterance.

> *I seek the shop that's full of noise,*
> *Where signs in gay temptation hing,*
> *And join the ranting roaring boys*
> *To blunt old memory's hornet sting.*
> *Past is the scene of love's delights,*
> *Curst bitter dregs the sweet succeed,*
> *Gone are my honey-mooning nights,*
> *How hard love's sweets should prove a deed!*
>
> *But parsons' lessons fools deceive,*
> *Their pocket-fees their preachings suit;*
> *Without we wed they make's believe*
> *To taste of love's forbidden fruit.*

Good Lord! I tremble at the crime,
A sinful, sad, unruly lout;
I quake, I quake at gossip time
Whose tongue blabs every secret out.

These months also saw the earliest of Clare's many poems about Mary Joyce. They are simple love-poems, often touched with a quiet regret for hopes which cannot be realised, but not yet quickened by the intense yearning and despair of later days, nor etherealised by the mystic emotion of the asylum lyrics. There are songs in praise of Mary's charms, valentines, invitations to ramble with him to his favourite nooks. He employs his regret for Mary's lost love to point the familiar theme of autumnal melancholy and winter dearth, or pleads that with the sanction of Saint Valentine he may call her his lover for that one day only. In another mood he accepts the fate that has parted them, and regards their love as a thing of the dead past. Yet in that mood of resignation was the hint of a "sea-change" which was before long to transform his early love for Mary "into something rich and strange."

VII

TRAVEL INTO DAY
1819–1820

*John Clare uncovered infinite worth
In a cold worm, a common weed.*

ALAN PORTER, "The Cosmopolitan."

THE autumn of 1819, despite these troubles, brought many compensations to Clare.

"Drury told me now that my poems were crowned with the utmost success I could wish for, as they were in the hands and met the favourable opinion of a gentleman who could and would do them justice; but he would not tell me his name. A painter of profiles was in the town, whom he engaged to take my likeness. These things were trifles to remember, but they were great at their beginnings; they made me all life and spirits, and nothing but hope and prosperity was before me."

The "person of talent" who was superintending the printing of the poems in London was Drury's cousin, John Taylor, of the firm of Taylor and Hessey. But Drury continued to write as if he were in full control of the publishing. Clare sent Drury all his poems as he wrote them, and received in return various small sums of money to pay his debts or buy necessities. Drury wrote frequently in this vein : "I consider myself to be the purchaser of your MSS. and to sustain all risks . . . you will receive from me every encouragement to induce you to dispose of future productions to me." Clare took the precaution of obtaining the opinion of a trusted friend upon his new acquaintance, Drury. Isaac Knowles Holland, a Nonconformist minister of Deeping—

Whose tongue did ne'er belie its good intent,
Preacher, as well in practice, as in trade—[1]

had given Clare encouragement and criticism at a time when there was no one else to perform that friendly office; he remained a sympathetic adviser until he left Deeping for St. Ives. In October, 1819, he called on Drury, and wrote to Clare after the visit that, as far as he could judge, Drury was his friend and would promote his interests.

In November, Clare finally ceased working for Wilders at Casterton, and returned home.

"I worked on at the New Inn till the winter and then returned home on a disagreement on the wages. He promised me nine shillings a week the year round and then wished to put me off with seven. He was an odd man but a good master, and the place, on the whole, was one of the best I ever met with. I left it with regret and rather wished to return, as I like the town, and the fields and solitudes were wild and far better than the fenny flats that I had been used to. I left Casterton on the Bullring Day at Stamford,[2] and on calling on Drury I fell in with John Taylor, whom I found was the Editor of my poems, then in the press and nearly ready for publishing. He was visiting at Mr. Gilchrist's, and in the evening they sent one of the servant-maids to Drury's to invite me to go. I felt loath, but on his persuasion I started and he showed me the door. I read an account of Woodcroft Castle from Wood's *History* and Taylor talked over some sayings and doings of the living authors."

John Taylor, born in 1781 at Retford, was the son of a publisher of Scottish extraction. He went to London in 1803, and, after some years in the service, first of Lackington at the famous "Temple of the Muses," then of Vernor and Hood, he formed a partnership with James Augustus Hessey to open a publishing and bookselling business at 93, Fleet Street. By 1819 they had built up a sound and progressive business; not content merely to meet the demands of the general reading public, they had already published for Keats, Hazlitt, Cary, and Reynolds, and were soon to add

Lamb, De Quincey, and Landor to the list. By their honesty and liberality the firm had gained the respect of all who had dealings with them; the tale of their friendship and generosity toward Keats is well known. Taylor was himself a writer and scholar of strange tastes. "For a man of very thoughtful and quiet temperament," wrote his friend Augustus De Morgan, "he had a curious turn for vexed questions. But he reflected very long and very patiently before he published: and all his works are valuable for their accurate learning . . . ." The identification of Junius with Sir Philip Francis, first made by him in 1813, is still considered the best solution of the problem. Taylor was also an authority on currency and in later years became a student of theology and evolved theories about the Great Pyramid. According to his friends, the ruling features of his mind were "order, precision, exactness, and fact."

Clare's poetry, and the circumstances under which it had been written, had aroused considerable interest in the publisher and champion of Keats. He realised that the story of the "peasant-poet" would be an excellent advertisement for the poems, and he did everything he could to ensure a favourable reception of Clare's first book by the critics and the public. In this he found a useful ally in Octavius Graham Gilchrist, for among his friends was one who was no friend of Taylor's, William Gifford. So it came about that the *Quarterly*, which had damned Keats, gave its hearty and influential blessing to Clare. Gilchrist, who was fourteen years older than Clare, owned a grocery business at Stamford. In his leisure time he indulged his tastes for scholarship and criticism; he had published a volume of verses in 1805, edited Bishop Corbet's poems in 1807, was an authority on the Elizabethan dramatists, and contributed freely to Leigh Hunt's *Reflector*, the *Quarterly Review*, and other periodicals. He was a man of catholic tastes and lively humour, no shirker of controversy, whether political or literary. Clare's visit was the first of many, for Gilchrist's house soon became a regular port of call, where Clare could always be sure of a hearty meal, cheerful company, good advice, music, and poetry, usually followed by a visit to the theatre.

The review of Clare's poems in the *Quarterly* for May, 1820, was not the only outcome of Gilchrist's influence and advocacy. A more immediate result of the meeting at Stamford was his article in the *London Magazine* for January, 1820, the first number of that famous journal and Clare's introduction to the literary world. John Scott, the editor of the *London*, was another of Gilchrist's friends; Scott had edited the *Stamford News*, which he took to town in 1813 as *Drakard's London Paper*, later re-named the *Champion*. In the *London* article Gilchrist described Clare's visit to his house:

"Clare announced his arrival by a hesitating knock at the door—'between a single and a double rap,'—and immediately upon his introduction he dropped into a chair. Nothing could exceed the meekness and simplicity and diffidence with which he answered the various inquiries concerning his life and habits, which we mingled with subjects calculated or designed to put him much at his ease. Nothing, certainly, could less resemble splendour than the room into which Clare was shown; but there was a carpet, upon which it is likely he never previously set foot; and wine, of which assuredly he had never tasted before. Of music he expressed himself passionately fond, and had learned to play a little on the violin, in the humble hope of obtaining a trifle at the annual feasts in the neighbourhood, and at Christmas."

Clare's music-books suggest that he was no mean fiddler. He collected there some hundred and fifty tunes, chiefly old country-dances and folk-songs, with annotations for the dances themselves—eighteenth-century hornpipes and jigs, and a sprinkling of waltzes, polkas, marches, and songs by Dibdin.

Back at home again in the December of 1819, Clare needed all his hopes for the success of his book; for the family fortunes were at a very low ebb. Parker Clare, now entirely disabled by rheumatism and quite unable to work, had depended for some time on an allowance of five shillings a week from the parish. When Drury found Clare, two years' rent was owing. So the cottage was to be given up and Clare's parents were to move to a parish house; the town officer had already branded the paupers' goods and set them down in the parish books, an indignity which Clare never forgot and which earned the officer a place in his satire " The Parish." The dawn of better days in January, 1820, gleamed the brighter for this darkest hour before it; nothing gave Clare more happiness in his prosperity than being able to keep on the old house and remove from his parents' lives the shadow of pauperdom.

The new year found Clare preparing a second volume of poems and cheered by the promise of better days; nor had he to wait long for a fulfilment which exceeded his wildest dreams. *"Poems Descriptive of Rural Life and Scenery*, by John Clare, A Northamptonshire Peasant," was published by Taylor and Hessey, and E. Drury on January 16th, 1820. The book was an immediate success; a second edition of a thousand copies was soon called for, and in May a third followed it; before the end of the year a fourth was printed. The first news of his success was brought to Clare by his good friend Holland. "He came over as soon as the book was published and before I was aware of its fate; but I instantly read success on his countenance, for he opened the door eagerly and laughed as he shook me by the hand, saying, 'Well, am I not a good prophet?' "

This news heralded a new era in Clare's life; he found himself suddenly whirled from a quiet backwater into a turbulent mid-stream. In the months which followed, events crowded upon him, each one a strange and disturbing experience to a man accustomed to the obscurity of poverty and the solitude of his native fields. Thus in February he was requested to present himself to the neighbouring nobility at Milton and Burghley, places which he had visited in earlier days in very different circumstances. On the publication of *Poems Descriptive*, Clare sent a copy by his mother to Milton, and she returned with a request for ten copies and an invitation to Clare. Drury sent one of his own shirts, and advised Clare not to pay the visit in his Sunday clothes, "which are more suitable to a Squire of high degree than humble John Clare."

"On the following Sunday I went, and after sitting awhile in the servants' hall where I could eat or drink nothing for thought, his Lordship sent for me, and instantly explained the reason why he did not answer my letter, in a quiet, unaffected manner which set me at rest. He told me he had heard of my poems by Parson Mossop [Vicar of Helpston], who, I have heard, took hold of every opportunity to speak against my success or poetical ability before the book was published, and then when it came out and others praised it, instantly turned round to the other side. Lady Milton also asked me several questions and wished me to name any book that was a favourite, expressing at the same time a desire to give me one; but I was confounded and could think of nothing, and so lost the present. In fact I did not like to pick out a book for fear of seeming over-reaching on her kindness, or else Shakespeare lay at my tongue's end. Lord Fitzwilliam, and Lady Fitzwilliam too, talked to me and noticed me kindly, and his Lordship gave me some advice which I had done well perhaps to have noticed better than I have. He bade me beware of book-sellers and warned me not to be fed with promises. On my departure they gave me a handful of money, the most that I had ever possessed in my life together, and I felt almost sure I should be poor no more; there was seventeen pounds."

Clare sent the good news of his kind reception at Milton to all his friends, one of whom passed on the story to the *Morning Post*, which was assiduously booming the "peasant-poet" at this time.

Some weeks later the Hon. Henry Manvers Pierrepont* brought an invitation for Clare to visit Burghley on the following Sunday.

" But when Sunday came it began to snow too unmerci-fully for a traveller ever to venture thus far. So I declined going, though it was not the weather prevented me. I felt fearful that my shoes would be in a dirty condition for so fine a place. When I got there the porter asked me the

reason why I did not come before, and when I spoke of the
weather he said, 'They expected you, and you should stand
for no weathers, though it rained knives and forks with
the tynes downward. We have been suspected of sending you
away.' This was a lesson which I afterwards took care to
remember. After awhile his Lordship sent for me. I went
upstairs and through winding passages after the footman
as fast as I could hobble, almost fit to quarrel with my
hard-nailed shoes at the noise they made on the marble
and boarded floors, and cursing them to myself as I set
my feet down in the lightest steps I was able to utter. His
Lordship received me kindly, asked me some questions, and
requested to look at the MSS. which Mr. Pierrepoint wished
me to bring in my pocket. He expressed a regret that Lady
Sophia, his sister, could not see me, being very ill and having
sat up too long the day before on expecting my coming. I
felt vexed I did not go but it was no use. Her Ladyship
gave me the *Pleasures of Hope*. After I had been about half
an hour eyeing the door and now and then looking at my
dirty shoes and wishing myself out of danger of soiling such
grandeur, he saw my embarrassment, as I suspect, and said
I should lose my dinner in the servants' hall and had better
go. But it was no use starting, for I was lost, and could not
stir a foot. I told his Lordship, and he kindly opened the
door and showed me the way ; when he suddenly made a
stop in one of the long passages and told me that he had no
room in his gardens for work at present, but that he would
allow me 15 guineas a year for life."

Meanwhile the publicity given to Clare by magazines
and newspapers had brought upon him the vanguard of a
host of visitors and correspondents, some moved by a desire
to help and befriend, others by a passing curiosity to know
more of the "peasant-poet." Among the former was Mrs.
Emmerson, of 4, Berners Street, London, who began her
long friendship with Clare in a letter of February 7th,
praising his poems and sending a copy of Young's *Night
Thoughts*. On the 12th, Taylor enclosed a letter from Lord
Radstock with a copy of Blair's *Sermons*. Admiral the Hon.
William Waldegrave, second son of the third Earl Waldegrave, became the first Baron Radstock after an active and

HJ

successful career in the Navy. He had been a friend of
Nelson's, and as Naval Governor of Newfoundland quelled
a mutiny on board H.M.S. Latona at the time of the mutiny
of the Nore, nicely mingling his threats to blow the ship out
of the water with exhortations to prayer and repentance.
"This fire-eating old Admiral was most sincerely religious
and in private life the kindest and most benevolent of men;
he looked carefully after the food and comfort of the soldiers
and sailors, and organized a society for the relief of the poor
in St. John's."⁴ The titles of two books by Lord Radstock
sufficiently reveal his dominant interests: "*The Cottager's
Friend*, or a word in Season to him who is so fortunate as to
possess a Bible or New Testament and a Book of Common
Prayer," which was in its twentieth edition in 1816; and
"*The British Flag Triumphant* . . . being copies of the London
Gazette containing the accounts of the victories . . . of the
British Fleets during the last and present war." Having
made enquiries of Taylor and written to the Vicar of Helpston about Clare, Radstock was satisfied that he deserved
help, and took up his cause with characteristic energy.

The first letter of congratulation Clare received was from
Dawson Turner, botanist and antiquary, and friend of
J. S. Cotman. He saw in Clare the herald of a cultivated
peasantry, and warned him against any temptation to escape
from his humble station. Another correspondent was
Captain M. E. Sherwill, who knew Walter Scott and brought
Clare's poems to his notice. He hoped to do something
more when Scott came to London in March.

The zeal of Lord Radstock won two more friends for
Clare nearer home—Herbert Marsh, Bishop of Peterborough, that fiery controversialist, and his wife Marianne.
In spite of his official pugnacity, in private life Bishop Marsh
was a benevolent man, and Clare saw only the amiable side
of his character. Marianne Marsh, a German by birth, was a
woman of kindliness and tact, and her notes to Clare, accom-
panying comforts, medicine, books, or invitations to the
palace, were entirely free from any hint of patronage. She
came to see him for the first time early in the spring.

But not all his visitors were as tactful or as welcome as Marianne Marsh.

"The first publication of my poems brought many visitors to my house, out of a mere curiosity, I expect, to know whether I really was the son of a thresher and a labouring rustic, as had been stated; and when they found it really was so, they looked at each other as a matter of satisfied surprise, asked some gossiping questions, and on finding me a vulgar fellow that mimicked at no pretensions but spoke in the rough way of a thorough-bred clown, they soon turned to the door, and dropping their heads in a good-morning attitude, they departed. I was often annoyed by such visits, and got out of the way whenever I could. . . .

"I was now wearing into the sunshine, and the villagers saw carriages now and then come to the house filled with gossiping gentry that were tempted by curiosity more than anything else to seek me. From these I got invitations to correspond and was swarmed with promises of books till my mother was troubled and fancied that the house would not hold them. But her trouble was soon set aside, for the books never came."

Or letters would arrive,

"worded with extravagant praise, wanting a quick reply. I replied warmly and there the matter ended. I had nothing but my disappointment in return; but I soon felt experience growing over these deceptions, and when such matters were palmed on me again I never answered them. I had two or three of these, nay more, from parsons."

Clare was troubled by the disparagement of some of his neighbours no less then by this tactless appreciation of strangers. There were those who suspected a Bacon hiding behind their local Shakespeare, who could not even display "small Latin and less Greek." Clare wrote of this under the heading, "A Prophet is nothing in his own Country":

"Envy was up at my success with all the lies it could muster. Some said that I never wrote the poems and that Drury gave me money to father them with my name. Others said that I had stolen them out of books and that Parson this and Squire t'other knew the books from which they were stolen. Pretending scholars said that I had never been to a Grammar School, and therefore it was impossible for me to write anything. Our parson industriously found out the wonderful discovery that I could not spell, and of course his opinion was busily distributed in all companies which he visited, that I was but a middling promise of success; but his opinion got its knuckles rapped, and then he excused the mistake by saying he did not read poetry and consequently knew little about it; there he was right."

Yet Clare made some new friends near home who did much to compensate for the envy of his neighbours. For he received another invitation to visit Milton Hall, not this time from Lord Milton, but from his servants.

"They were the first rate of the house, well-informed men, not unacquainted with books, and I never met with a party of more happy and heartier fellows in my life.

"There was Artis, up to the neck in the old Norman coins and broken pots of the Romans; and Henderson, never wearied with hunting after the emperor butterfly and the hornet sphinx in the Hanglands Wood, and the orchises on the Heath; and West, an upright, honest man, though his delight in reading extended little further than the prices that fat sheep and bullocks fetched, and the rise of corn each week—'the man's the man for a' that'; and Roberts, who, seeing a song of Moore's, admired his poetry as cleverly and stoutly as most amateurs; and 'Grill' the cook. He was a Frenchman and possessed a fund of patient good-humour and a countenance unmatchable in England. His visage was a caricature in good earnest and would heartily repay Cruikshank a journey from London to take it. . . . And there was Hague, the wine butler, whose library consisted of one solitary book, Brown's *Reflections on a Summer Day*. He was an odd, good sort of fellow. There were two young maidens, Mrs. Procter and Mrs. Byron, who had not the womanly affectation about them of even attempting to show some affinity of kindred in the coincidences of their names with two popular poets. They were above pardonable vanities, and one of them was a lover of poetry."

With Henderson, the naturalist, and Artis, the archæologist, Clare enjoyed many a country excursion during the
years at Helpston; his friendship with these men of kindred
tastes and ready sympathies often relieved him when the
burden of loneliness and isolation grew intolerable.

To account for that sudden popularity of Clare's first
volume of poems, which sold three thousand copies within a year and made him a nine days' wonder, we must
look beyond the book itself. In his able and sympathetic
Introduction, John Taylor gave the reviewers a cue: "The
following poems will probably attract some notice by their
intrinsic merit; but they are also entitled to attention from
the circumstances under which they were written." So he
went on to give some account of this poet, "the least favoured
by circumstances, and the most destitute of friends, of any
that ever existed." Having aroused interest and sympathy
thus, he proceeded cleverly to disarm criticism of the poems.
Clare, he suggested, was in the position of the early poets
who had no traditions to guide them. His innovations
followed "that rational mode of procedure, by which all
languages have been formed and perfected." Many of these
unfamiliar expressions were indeed not new, but some of
the oldest in the language, preserved by oral tradition.
Then he extolled Clare as a child of nature: "No poet has
more completely devoted himself to her service, studied her
more closely, or exhibited so many sketches of her under new
and interesting appearances." Concluding with a renewed
appeal for sympathy, Taylor quoted from one of Clare's
letters: "If my hopes don't succeed, the hazard is not of
much consequence: if I fall, I am advanced at no great
distance from my low condition: if I sink for want of friends,
my old friend Necessity is ready to help me as before. It
was never my fortune as yet to meet advancement from
friendship: my fate has ever been hard labour among the
most vulgar and lowest conditions of men; and very small
is the pittance hard labour allows me, though I always
toil'd even beyond my strength to obtain it."

Most of the reviewers gladly followed this lead. The article in the *Quarterly* for May, 1820, prepared by Gilchrist but rounded off by Gifford himself, gave generous praise to the poems and the poet. Considering the discouraging circumstances under which most of the poems were written, the writers were astonished "that so few examples should be found of querulousness and impatience, none of envy or despair." The *London Magazine* printed a second article in March, with a further account of the poet and a full review of the poems. The *Gentleman's Magazine*, the *New Monthly* and the *Monthly Magazine* gave Clare kindly welcome, and were willing to pass over the "vulgarisms." A reviewer in the April number of the *Eclectic Review*, the organ of the pro-testant dissenters, saw some danger in the general attitude toward him. "If, instead of thinking them 'very clever considering they are by a day-labourer,' our readers agree with us in conceding to them a high degree of poetical merit quite independent of the circumstances of their author, they will be prepared to enter with the requisite sympathy into the details of his history." Clare was also honoured by the *Annual Register* for 1820. The newspapers followed suit; in the *Morning Post*, poems, news of Clare, and letters from admirers, appeared almost daily for some time. His fame spread even to America, where the *Analectic Magazine* of Philadelphia reviewed his book.

The story of the "peasant-poet," thus broadcast by most of the influential periodicals of the day, was sympathetically received by their readers. Some, no doubt, were more inter-ested in the story than in the poetry; yet there did exist in 1820 a considerable poetry-reading public. During fifty years of rapidly changing social conditions, a new reading public among the middle classes had grown steadily, nourished by a wider system of education, by circulating libraries, book-clubs, and debating-societies, and encouraged by enterprising publishers such as Harrison, Bell, Cooke, and Lackington, who provided cheap books of all kinds. Then the genius of Scott and Byron captured the popular imagination, and the genius of Constable and Murray exploited it to the full. In the flush of that popularity astonishing prices were given for copyrights, a host of periodicals appeared to guide the public, a new era began for the profession of letters, poetry became a fashion and a rage, and a popular poet was the hero of the day. Clare wrote of the London public: "I heard one literary friend say that a popular name had need to hold his head or they would have it. A word cannot be spoken, a remark cannot be made, or a jest returned, without the hazard of seeing them in print the next day."

It is not surprising that this demand for poetry should be erratic and limited. It gave Scott and Byron full measure of praise and reward; but it failed to recognise some greater than they, and it applauded many less. Taylor wrote to Clare in August, 1820, of Keats's *Lamia* volume, " We have some trouble to get through 500 copies of his work, though it is highly spoken of in the periodical works." Shelley's circle of admirers was lamentably small. The five hundred copies of Wordsworth's *Excursion*, 1814, were not sold out until 1820. Southey said he would be surprised if the five hundred copies of his *Curse of Kehama* sold within seven years. Yet many beside Scott, Byron, Moore, and Campbell reaped rich rewards. Murray could give Crabbe £3,000 for his copyrights in 1819; ten thousand copies of Rogers's *Pleasures of Memory* sold between 1801 and 1816; Bloomfield's and Kirke White's poems ran into many editions ; Milman had five hundred guineas for his *Fall of Jerusalem*. "In 1822," wrote R. P. Gillies, with some justice, "the fortunes of literary men from high to low wore *couleur de rose* . . . even minor authors were paid and encouraged then."

Clare's own correspondence testifies to the widespread and active interest in poetry in 1820. He had letters from men of all ranks and conditions, who, inspired by his success, hoped to win fame or money by their verses. The success of *Poems Descriptive* was largely due to this widespread interest in poetry among the middle and lower classes of society. Unfortunately for Clare, the book appeared toward the end of that first flush of enthusiasm when poetry of all kinds and degrees of excellence was read with avidity. As Cyrus Redding shrewdly noted, "Clare's first works were read because they were published about the culminating point of the true and false in the popular taste." The financial failures among publishers in 1825 marked the end of the boom. During the next decade the popular taste rose little higher than the album verses of the annuals, and the best of the popular poets were James Montgomery, Bernard Barton, L.E.L., and Barry Cornwall. Clare had found his public only to lose it, and those who applauded *Poems Descriptive* in 1820 had no ear for the *Shepherd's Calendar* in 1827.

The poems of Clare's first book were arranged in three sections: forty descriptive and narrative poems, twelve songs and ballads, and twenty-one sonnets. The earliest had been written in 1806, when he was thirteen, the latest in 1819, when he was twenty-six, so that the book represents, though by no means entirely, the achievements of the poet's apprenticeship. In this period of a poet's life we usually find traces of indebtedness to other poets, and, although Clare's early life had afforded few facilities for wide reading, imitation, and experiment, he had made the most of the books which came into his hands. He had browsed over Thomson, Goldsmith, Walton, Cowper, Milton, John Cunningham, Bloomfield, and Ramsay; he had used Hill, Parkinson, and Ray as guides in his flower-hunting. "Helpstone," the first poem in the book and one of the earliest, was intended, says Clare, for a poem in the manner of Goldsmith. It was left unfinished until 1819, when he sent it to Drury with a note:

"I hinted to you that I had seen the *Deserted Village*. You may think I imitated it. I saw it as I have seen a many, dipping in it here and there. I perhaps may have read a hundred lines; the Parish Priest was what struck me. Therefore to clear this and let you see I am not a plagiarist, I beg you to compare them together, and then the difference will be seen. My imitations I may be proud of; I have never taken a single line or sentence from any but what I owned to."

The influence of the older poets on Clare's early writing was often of this kind. Goldsmith's poem suggested the idea and form of "Helpstone," but the subject was already so familiar to Clare, the decline of the social life of a village so nearly concerned him, that the finished poem was no mere imitation. It was the story of his own boyhood. Some of the critics spoke of Clare's imitations of Burns in such poems as "Address to a Lark" and "Familiar Epistle." Here the indebtedness was more direct and obvious, but not, said Clare, to Burns. "The fact is that when my first poems were written I knew nothing of Burns, not even by name, for the fens are not a literary part of England. . . . I had an odd volume of Ramsay a long while, and if I imitated any it should be him to which I am ready to acknowledge a great deal."

Clare's early reading was chiefly among the eighteenth-century poets, and, of these, the poet whose influence is most clearly discernible in *Poems Descriptive* was John Cunningham. In Cunningham's pastorals, with their delicate scene-painting and quiet, meditative mood, he found much to his taste and purpose. As the *Deserted Village* suggested "Helpstone," so Cunningham's "Morning," "Noon," "Evening," "An Elegy on a Pile of Ruins," seem to have inspired Clare's "Summer Morning," "Noon," "Evening," "Elegy on the Ruins of Pickworth." There is more than a similarity of subject, as may be seen by placing a verse from "Summer Morning"—

> *As slow the hazy mists retire,*
> *Crampt circle's more distinctly seen;*
> *Thin scatter'd huts, and neighbouring spire—*
> *Drop in to stretch the bounded scene.*

beside the last verse of Cunningham's "Landscape"—

> *Hamlets—villages and spires,*
> *Scatter'd on the Landscape lie,*
> *Till the distant scene retires,*
> *Closing in an azure sky.*

Moreover, in the poem "Noon" we find a quotation, from Cunningham's "Evening"—the line "Verges in successive rings." Cunningham's songs, and his miscellaneous stanzas, epigrams, and fables, also gave Clare suggestions for the numerous poems of a similar kind to be found in the manuscripts of his apprentice period.

In writing these verses he became familiar with a great variety of stanza forms and conventions, yet from the first his devotion to his first love, nature, guided him in his experiments. He had seen poetry in nature before he read it in books, and that early vision shone before him in his wanderings among the poets, and revealed the path wherein his native genius lay. That path he was to pursue steadily, and often against the advice of his friends, who urged him to write of other things and court popularity by following the fashion of the moment. But Clare was never persuaded, as were Stephen Duck and Robert Bloomfield, to forsake his own style and the subjects he knew so intimately. Nor was his allegiance to his creed merely instinctive; his remarks on poetry show clearly enough that he knew what he was about. He wrote in one of his letters on natural history:

"To look on nature with a poetic eye magnifies the pleasure, she herself being the essence and soul of Poesy." In another letter he expressed the corollary to that creed: "I think an able essay on objects in nature that would beautify descriptive poetry might be entertaining and useful to form a right taste in pastoral poems, that are full of nothing but the old threadbare epithets of 'sweet-singing cuckoo,' 'love-lorn nightingale,' 'fond turtles,' 'sparkling brooks,' 'green meadows,' 'leafy woods.' These make up the creation of pastoral and descriptive poetry, and everything else is reckoned low and vulgar. In fact they are too rustic for the fashionable or prevailing system of rhyme, till some bold innovating genius rises with a real love for nature, and then they will no doubt be considered as great beauties, which they really are."

These two aims, to regard all nature with the eye of a poet, and poetry with the eye of a field naturalist, understood in their essential relationship, define Clare's original contribution to English nature poetry. Like Wordsworth, he was in revolt against the outworn conventions which cut off poetry

from its source in nature; and, if Wordsworth expressed the
new vision more richly and with wider apprehension than
Clare, he could not do it more clearly or more directly. Nor did
Clare ever forget, in emphasizing that poetry must be brought
to the touchstone of reality, that the reality in question must
be a poetic reality, nature illuminated by the poetic vision.
The very simplicity and directness of Clare's insight prevented it from fading with the years; unlike that of the
greater poet, it grew ever keener, more penetrating, throughout his whole life.

Clare's first book is to be chiefly valued for the many
glimpses of that world which he had discovered in the happy
rambles of his boyhood, and which he now desired to claim
for the realm of poesy. In the descriptive poems he had already travelled far from the pastorals which inspired them.
The themes and forms are similar, but a new eye regards
the scene and a fresh voice describes what the eye sees;
the old forms are quickened by the poet's intimate knowledge of the rural world, acquired by years of patient and
detailed observation. Instead of the soft tones and careful
grouping of the pastoral water-colour, here are the vigorous
lines and minute detailing of an etching. Clare seldom
lingers to paint the rounded scene, but, after a swift glance
round, he explores with delight the underworld of plant and
insect life, noting the adventures of heedless beetle, slowly-
pacing snail, dancing gnat, and chirruping cricket. He
translates directly into words the sights and sounds of a busy
harvest morning:

> *His scythe the mower o'er his shoulder leans,*
> *And whetting, jars with sharp and tinkling sounds;*
> *Then sweeps again 'mong corn and crackling beans,*
> *And swath by swath flops lengthening o'er the ground.*

Frugality in the use of epithets, vigour and originality in the
use of verbs, give strength and directness to Clare's utterance.
It is significant that among the dialect words in the glossary
of *Poems Descriptive* verbs outnumber adjectives by more than
three to one. Clare's attitude at this time toward provincial

and coined words is expressed in the following notes, sent to his publishers with a list of instructions about the editing of his text:

" 'Eggs on' in the 'Address to the Lark'—whether provincial or what I cannot tell; but it is common with the vulgar, (I am of that class,) and I heartily desire no word of mine to be altered.

"The word 'twit-a-twit,' (if a word it may be called,) you will undoubtedly smile at, but I wish you to print it as it is; for it is the Language of Nature, and that can never be disgusting."

Clare is not so much concerned with the pictorial or decorative value of natural objects as with their inner life and individuality. It is the characteristic movement of plants, no less than of insects and birds, that catches his eye:

> the sedge
> Ramping in the woodland hedge.
>
> Drowking lies the meadow-sweet,
> Flopping down beneath one's feet.
>
> The meadow-sweet taunts high its snowy wreath,
> And sweet the quaking-grasses hide beneath.
>
> Flowers now sleep within their hoods;
> Daisies button into buds.
>
> The flowers, reviving from the ground,
> Perk up again and peep.

There are many happy descriptions of insect life from the same vital point of view. But when he greeted the inhabitants of his native fields and woods, he was lover as well as naturalist. Many a tree and bush he numbered among his earliest friends, and he grieved when his old favourites were destroyed.

> Nay e'en a post, old standard, or a stone
> Moss'd o'er by Age, and branded as her own,
> Would in my mind a strong attachment gain. . . .

From this respect for the individual being of every living thing sprang Clare's hatred of cruelty, especially that inflicted by man upon other creatures. In the poem " On Cruelty" he grieved for Dobbin beaten, for dumb, cringing dogs, burthened asses, even for trapped flies, mice, and sparrows. His instinctive dislike of violence was strengthened by conclusions based upon his observations as a naturalist. He saw that man's destruction of so-called vermin was often unnecessary and perverse, and he deplored the blindness of "Stupidity Street":

> *Hardy clowns! grudge not the wheat*
> *Which hunger forces birds to eat:*
> *Your blinded eyes, worst foes to you,*
> *Can't see the good which sparrows do.*
> *Did not poor birds with watching rounds*
> *Pick up the insects from your grounds,*
> *Did they not tend the rising grain,*
> *You then might sow to reap in vain.*

The sonnets of *Poems Descriptive* have more originality than the songs, where the poet's prentice hand is most in evidence. He adapted the sonnet form to his own needs in a way which will be discussed more fully later; but he had already realised its value for expressing his moods of quiet contemplation, touched with melancholy, or to sketch one of his "native Scenes, for ever, ever dear."

Thus in Clare's first book, among the imitations and experiments of a young poet's workshop, there was abundant promise of later achievement; even before *Poems Descriptive* issued from the press that promise had already been amply fulfilled.

SUMMER

VIII

PUBLIC PRAISE'S HUE AND CRY
1820

I think when young you blushed among
  The gay town's curious eyes;
How tripped the truth from beauty's tongue,
  "A noble in disguise!"

EDMUND BLUNDEN, "The Death-mask of John Clare."

THE crowding excitements of the new year culminated in
Clare's first visit to London early in March. He left
Stamford at six in the morning in company with Octavius
Gilchrist, travelling by the Regent coach, which conveyed
passengers to the George and Blue Boar, Holborn, within
fourteen hours. Clare's account of this journey reveals his
emotions as he realized that a new life was opening before
him:

"Mr. Gilchrist often asked me if I should like to see London, and as I felt an anxiety he said I should go up with him
the next time he went, which was early in March. I started
in the old Stamford coach but I felt very awkward in my
dress. My mind was full of expectations all the way about
the wonders of the town, which I had often heard my
parents tell stories about by the winter fire. When I turned
to the recollections of the past, by seeing people at my old
occupations of ploughboy and ditching in the fields by the
road-side, while I was lolling in a coach, the novelty created
such strange feelings that I could almost fancy that my identity as well as my occupations had changed; that I was not
the same John Clare, but that some stranger soul had
jumped into my skin. When we passed through Huntingdon,
Mr. G. showed me the house at this end of the town, where
Oliver Cromwell was born, and the parsonage with its
melancholy-looking garden at the other, where Cowper had

lived. As we glided along in the heavy, sweeing coach, I amused myself with catching the varying features of scenery. I remember the road about Royston was very dreary; the white, chalk-like hills opened all round the circle and not a tree was to be seen; one melancholy thornbush by the road-side with a bench beneath it was all that my eye caught for miles. As we approached nearer London . . . the roads were lined with lamps that diminished in the distance to stars. 'This is London!' I exclaimed. He laughed at my ignorance and only increased my wonder by saying we were yet several miles from it. . . . On the night we got into London it was announced in the Play Bills that a song of mine was to be sung at Covent Garden by Madame Vestris, and we were to have gone but it was too late. I felt uncommonly pleased at the circumstance. We took a walk in the town by moon-light and went to Westminster Bridge to see the River Thames. I had heard large wonders about its width of water, but I was disappointed, thinking I should have seen a freshwater sea, when I saw it was less in my eye than Whittlesey Mere. I was uncommonly astonished to see so many ladies, as I thought them, walking about the streets. I expressed my surprise and was told they were girls of the town, as a modest woman rarely ventured out by herself at nightfall. . . . The next morning everything was so uncom-mon to what I had been used to that the excess of novelty confounded my instinct. Everything hung round my con-fused imagination like riddles unsolved. While I was there I rarely knew what I was seeing, and when I got home my remembrance of objects seemed in a mass, one mingled in another like the mosaic squares in a Roman pavement."

The song which Madame Vestris sang was "The Meeting," set to music by Haydn Corri, and the success of this venture led to quite a demand for Clare's songs by the music-setters. Clare stayed, during his visit, with Gilchrist's brother-in-law, a jeweller named Burkhardt. They took him round sight-seeing, and his impressions reveal both naïvety and native shrewdness:

"Octave took [me] to see most of the curiosities. We went to Westminster Abbey to see the poets' corner, and to both Playhouses, where I saw Kean and Macready and Knight

and Munden and Emery. The two latter pleased me most
of all, but the plays were bad ones. [1] . . . Burkhardt took me
to Vauxhall and made me shut my eyes till I got in the midst
of the place, and when I opened them I almost fancied myself in a fairy land; but the repetition of the roundabout walk
soon put the romance out of my head and made it a faded
reality. These were the scenes that he delighted in, and he
wished to take me sometime to see the Beggars' Opera, [2] a
public house so called, the resort of [   ]; but we had no
time. I had had a romantic sort of notion about authors and
had an anxious desire to see them, fancying they were beings
different to other men; but the spell was soon broken when
I became acquainted with them."

Clare cannot have been sorry to lose some of these romantic notions, for he had brought a full pack of them to town
with him. He has an amusing note about the solemn warnings given him by one of his neighbours concerning the
awful dangers which beset the innocent countryman in
London, so that he fancied every lady he met a decoy and
every gentleman a pickpocket.

A shopping expedition gave Clare justification for some of
his less lurid apprehensions and an opportunity of exempli-
fying one of his favourite themes, the prevalence of hypocrisy
in political life.

"On my first visit to London I wanted to take something
home for Patty, and thinking that Waithman [3] had been a
great stickler for freedom and fair dealing among the citizens,
his newspaper notoriety recommended me to his shop at the
corner of Bridge Street, in the hope that I might come in for
a fair bargain. But here I was more deceived than ever, for
they kept the best articles aside and recommended the worst
as soon as they found out their customer was from the
country. When I took the things home, I found they were a
bad bargain still and a great deal dearer than they might
have been bought for at home. So much for patrons of
liberty and newspaper proprietors for honest men!"

During his week in London, Clare dined several times at
John Taylor's, where, as the publisher wrote to his brother,

he "pleased us all by his simple, manly, and sensible conduct and conversation." Here he first met Lord Radstock,
of whom he has left this description:

"Lord Radstock at first sight appears to be of a stern and
haughty character, but the moment he speaks his countenance kindles up into a free, blunt, good-hearted manner, –
one whom you expect to hear speak exactly as he thinks.
He has no notion of either offending or pleasing by his talk
and cares as little for the consequences of either. There is a
good deal of bluntness and openheartedness about him, and
there is nothing of pride or fashion. He is as plain in manner
and dress as the old country squire. A stranger would never
guess that he was speaking to a Lord, though his is one of
the oldest families in England. . . . His Lordship is a large
man of a commanding figure."

Radstock's interest in Clare was strengthened by their
meeting, and soon revealed itself in practical form in various
schemes to better the poet's condition. Meanwhile, through
him Clare met another friend and benefactor:

"Lord Radstock introduced me to Mrs. Emmerson. She
has been, and is, a warm, kind friend, of tastes, feelings, and
manners almost romantic. She has been a very pretty
woman and is not amiss still, and a woman's pretty face is
often very dangerous to her common sense; for the notice
she received in her young days threw affections about her
feelings which she has not got shut of yet; for she fancies that
her friends are admirers of her person as a matter of course
and acts accordingly, which appears in the eyes of a stranger
ridiculous enough. But the grotesque wears off on becoming
acquainted with better qualities, and better qualities she
certainly has to counterbalance them. She, at one word, is
the best friend I found, and my expectations are looking no
further. Her correspondence with me began early in my
public life and grew pretty thick as it went on. I fancied it
a fine thing to correspond with a lady, and by degrees grew
up into an admirer, sometimes writing as I felt, sometimes
as I fancied, and sometimes foolishly, when I could not account for why I did it."

Unfortunately Clare's letters to Mrs. Emmerson have not come to light, although she kept them carefully, intending to publish them. Her letters to him, to the number of three hundred, are preserved among the Clare correspondence in the British Museum Library. The opinion of them expressed by J. L. Cherry, editor of Clare's *Life and Remains*, cannot be bettered: "The Editor, having read the whole of them, feels constrained, a different version of the relationship having been given, to state his conviction that no poor struggling genius was ever blessed with a tenderer or a truer friend. No man of feeling could rise from the perusal of them without the deepest respect and admiration for the writer. The style is effusive, and the language in which the lady writes of Clare's poetry is occasionally eulogistic to the point of extravagance, and was to that extent injudicious; but all the blemishes are forgotten in the presence of overwhelming evidences of pure and disinterested friendship."

The friendship lasted for more than fifteen years, and was shared by her husband, Thomas Emmerson, who was always ready to help in such business matters as Clare's distance from London made it difficult for him to transact. They spread his fame and copies of his books among all their friends. Mrs. Emmerson had indeed a large circle of literary acquaintances, and befriended several young writers beside Clare. She herself contributed frequently to the periodicals, and her letters are thickly sprinkled with her own fluent verses. She also best understood that much of Clare's illness was of nervous origin; for she herself was delicate, and suffered in the same way. Her advice was therefore inspired by sympathy and, on occasion, frankly worded. Nor was her friendship limited to advice and encouragement; gifts of money, clothing, and books, for Clare and his family, frequently accompanied her letters.

Clare also became acquainted with Taylor's partner, J. A. Hessey, whom Keats used to call "Mistessy," and whom J. H. Reynolds remembered as "a very respectable person." Most of the other writers who mention Hessey seem to have agreed with Reynolds, and were content to leave it at that. We find no account of him among Clare's papers. Expressing surprise at his failure in business in 1829, Clare remarked that he had always thought of him as "a sort of miserly, cautious, and monied man." In this paucity of information, John Taylor's pen-portrait of Hessey, written in the early days of their partnership, is very welcome:

"James Augustus Hessey is thin, dresses principally in black, his face is round and good-humoured when he does not frown – when he does, *it has the contrary expression*. He is about 22, but retains a boyish appearance about the head. His application is good – his Conversation and manners lively. He has a readiness of droll quotation, and humorous allusion – is somewhat witty but had rather be considered a man of strong sense. His enunciation is not very distinct, but rapid, and when he wishes to utter his opinion in a serious manner, he hesitates or stutters a little, as if in doubt what words to select next. His reading has been various, but not *very* deep nor extensive. He can speak with propriety on all subjects because his good sense teaches him how far he is qualified to speak. He is a great favourite wherever he goes, particularly with young ladies, who like him for his cheerfulness, and because he sings a little, plays a little, and dances well. . . ."

Hessey's first letter to Clare on March 14th was accompanied by the gift of a violin of some value, which he himself used to play; the last phrase suggests that Hessey, now married, had renounced those youthful gaieties which won him favour with the young ladies. Indeed, we find in his many letters to Clare little of the lively wit and humorous allusion with which Taylor credited him, but much of the earnest good sense.

Other friendships with men whom Clare came to know well on his second and longer visit had their beginnings at Taylor's house during this week. H. F. Cary, the translator of Dante, wrote to his brother-in-law, Thomas Price, on March 8th, asking him to review *Poems Descriptive*, "which, remember that you have told me, you find *surprising* and *beautiful*. . . . I spent an evening lately with him [Clare] at

our common bookseller's. . . . He has the appearance rather
of a big boy who has never been used to company, than of a
clown, though his dialect is clownish enough; and like *all
true geniuses*, he was longing to be at home again, and is now
there." The second edition of Cary's translation had been
published by Taylor and Hessey in 1819, and Cary had been
agreeably surprised by the liberality of the firm, and pleased
by Taylor's keen interest in the work. Clare and he did not
begin to correspond until after the second visit to London.

Clare also made the acquaintance of J. H. Reynolds, and
enjoyed both his jokes and his poetry; Taylor gave him a
copy of *The Naiad*, and, on the publication of *The Fancy* in
the summer of 1820, sent him a copy. We know from Clare's
journal that he read these books and *The Garden of Florence*,
1821, with critical attention.

Taylor's letter of the 16th of March is interesting for its
reference to a greater than Reynolds:

"Keats came to dine with me the Day before yesterday
for the first Time since his Illness—He was very sorry he did
not see you—When I read Solitude to him he observed that
the Description too much prevailed over the Sentiment—
But never mind that—it is a good fault."

Thus Clare seems to have missed his only opportunity of
meeting Keats, who left for Italy in the following September. It would have been an interesting meeting between these
two poets, to whom illness and neglect came in such different
guises.[4] No less different were their attitudes toward their
common loves, nature and poetry, as may be exemplified
by placing Clare's opinion of *Endymion* beside Keats's
criticism of "Solitude."

"Keats keeps up a constant allusion (or illusion) to the
Grecian mythology, and there I cannot follow: yet when he
speaks of woods, Dryads and Fauns and Satyrs are sure to
follow, and the brook looks alone without her Naiads to his
mind. Yet the frequency of such classical accompaniments
makes it wearisome to the reader, where behind every rose

bush he looks for a Venus and under every laurel a thrumming Apollo. In spite of all this his descriptions of scenery are often very fine. But, as it is the case with other inhabitants of great cities, he often described Nature as she appeared to his fancies, and not as he would have described her had he witnessed the things he described. Thus it is he has often undergone the stigma of Cockneyism, and what appears as beauties in the eyes of a pent-up citizen are looked upon as conceits by those who live in the country. These are merely errors, but even here they are the errors of poetry. He is often mystical, but such poetical licences have been looked on as beauties in Wordsworth and Shelley, and in Keats they may be forgiven."

In Taylor's company Clare visited the painter, William Hilton, and sat for his portrait. Hilton, elected R.A. in 1819, was more highly esteemed by the Academy, of which he became Keeper in 1826, than by the public. He suffered from ill health continually; according to his friend and fellow-student, Benjamin Haydon, "A more amiable creature never lived, nor a kinder heart; but there was an intellectual and physical feebleness in everything he did." The boisterous Haydon was not among those who considered Hilton "the first historical painter of the age."

His picture of Clare now keeps fitting company with his portrait of Keats in the National Portrait Gallery. It is a happily conceived and vivid impression of Clare in an inspired moment, "C in alt." The face, with its finely balanced features and fresh colouring, wears an eager and candid expression; far-seeing, blue eyes look out beneath the high forehead and light-brown wavy hair; the nose is delicately moulded, the mouth tranquil and sensitive, the cheeks rosy. Hilton sloughed away the peasant in Clare and left us the poet and "noble in disguise."

We do not know whether Clare appreciated Hilton's historical painting, but he was keenly interested in another branch of the art, and held decided views about it; and in Peter De Wint, the landscape painter, Hilton's brother-in-law, he recognised an artist who had achieved in his own

medium the very effects which Clare sought in his. De Wint's
Dutch ancestry made the level stretches of fen country
around Peterborough especially attractive to him, and in
his frequent visits to the district he painted Whittlesey Mere
and other scenes familiar to Clare. He was never so happy
as when in the fields, and loved to paint direct from nature;
his water-colours, faithful renderings of typical English
scenes, are notable for their realism, simplicity, and
breadth of light and shade. Clare's sensitive appreciation
of De Wint's work appears again and again, both in his
letters and in his rough notes for an "Essay on Landscape Painting," from which the following passages are
taken:

"In contemplating the scenery of De Wint's [pictures] we
see natural objects not placed for effect and set off by the
dictates of the painter's fancies, but there as they are, just as
nature placed them. Landscapes are ridiculous when loaded
with summer-houses, temples and fauns and satyrs, with
modern fish-ponds, and naiads. . . . There is no mere
trickery in disposing of lights and shadows to catch the eye
from object to object with excessive fractions of diminishing.
. . . De Wint has none of these minute gradations, these atom
stipplings by which beautiful, effective compositions are produced, but not paintings from Nature as they profess to be.
. . . Look at his sketches, his studies. There are the simplest
touches possible, giving the most natural possible effects.
The eye is led over the landscape as far as a sunbeam can
reach, and there sky and earth blend into a humanity of
greeting, a beautiful harmony and mystery of pleasant
imaginings. There is no harsh stoppage, no bounds to space,
nor any outline further than there is in nature. If we could
possibly walk into the picture, we fancy we might pursue the
landscape beyond those mysteries (not bounds) assigned to
it, as we can in the fields. . . . Look at them. There they are,
the very copies of nature! and she rewards the faith of her
worshippers by revealing such beauties in her settings [as
the] fanciful never meet with. . . . The dewy morning is not
more fresh in her features than the air and the sky and the
grass of the pictures. 'Tis summer; the very air breathes hot
in one's face. . . ."

The "Essay on Landscape Painting" was never published, probably never finished; but in a sonnet to De Wint, included in the *Rural Muse*, Clare paid as eloquent a tribute to the painter of "the sunny truth of Nature," whose pencil

> *worked such rich surprise,*
> *That rushy flats, befringed with willow tree,*
> *Rivalled the beauties of Italian skies.*

It is a pity that Clare had so few opportunities for studying examples of an art about which he could write with such insight and authority. His impressions of the work of Constable, John Crome, Cotman, and other painters of East Anglia, that home of landscape painting, would have been illuminating; for he is not the least of that group of poets whom East Anglia may claim as peculiarly her own – Crabbe, Bloomfield, Fitzgerald, and the Tennysons.

Clare returned home at the end of the first week in March, and on the 16th his marriage with Patty took place at Casterton Magna. His account of their troubled courtship ends with this comment: "I held out as long as I could and then married her at Casterton Church. Her uncle, John Turner, was father and gave us the wedding dinner." John Turner and Sophy Clare signed as witnesses, and Martha Turner made her mark, for though Patty could read she could not write. She did not leave Walkherd for some time after the marriage. There was no room for another family in the part of the cottage which the Clares then inhabited, and there was a scheme to provide a new home for John and his wife. Radstock had already written to Lord Milton to ask for a neat cottage and land, rent free for life. Gilchrist wrote on March 28th: "Surely Patty and you would be more 'snug and canny' in a room together, till the cottage was ready, than two counties asunder as at present."

The poem "Proposals for Building a Cottage," written at this time, describes the kind of dwelling Clare wanted. It was to be built beside a runnel, with a thatch which he might pull out here and there to make hiding-places for the sparrows,

THE COTTAGE AT HELPSTON

and with holes within the chimney-top for the swallows' nests. There were to be grass plots by the door and "a little garden, not too fine," with woodbines and spindling sedge and "old man's beard" in it; inside he wanted shelves and cupboards in all the corners for his books. In April, Lord Milton sent for Clare to meet him in the fields to choose a piece of ground; but they missed each other. Then Clare grew impatient, and wrote to Milton on his own account, against the advice of his friends; but nothing came of it. Finally, when the tenement next door to the Clares became vacant, John took it and brought Patty there. His later comments show that he was not sorry to remain under the old roof:

"I have often been urged and advised to leave it and get a more roomy and better-looking house by visitors who gave me no better encouragement than their words and whom I did not expect would be of any service to me in case their advice happened to lead me into greater inconvenience in the end. So I took no notice of them and lived on in the same house and in the same way as I had always done, following my old occupations and keeping my old neighbours as friends, without being troubled or disappointed with climbing ambitions, that, shine as fine as they may, only tempt the restless mind to climb so that he may be made dizzy with a mocking splendour and topple down headlong into a lower degradation than he left behind him."

This settlement in a house of his own did not take place until early summer; meanwhile he lived on with his parents, enjoying the sweet springtime of his good fortune. In the "Address to Plenty," written in December, 1817, Clare interrupted his passionate plea for the "Sad sons of Poverty," whose sufferings were then his own, to give a vivid picture of the life he would lead if Plenty smiled on him. He narrated with gusto how he would shut out the blast and take his ease before a roaring fire, a pitcher and barrel near at hand, his chimney corner well supplied with coal or wood, his cupboard lined with victuals. There he would loll in an elbow-chair, reading a page in a book, peeping at the news, or taking a nap. After his return from

London, and before he settled down with Patty, Clare came near to realising his dream, and revelled in the favours of his new friend, Plenty. The reviewers who hastened to urge Clare not to desert his field labours certainly meant well; their sympathy for his recent condition was sincere if imperfect. For the gulf fixed in those days between a pauper peasantry and the other classes of society was too vast to be bridged by a poem. Thus, while they wished to see Clare's poverty relieved, they were unable to sympathize with his expressed desire to escape from the estate to which a wise providence had called him; nor did they accept him as an advocate for his fellow-peasants. He must be helped, not because he was a peasant to whom, as such, the conditions of the time denied a livelihood, but because he was, by some miracle, a peasant-poet. The term represents the age's solution of a very awkward problem. As poet, Clare ought to be encouraged in his ambition; as peasant, clearly discouraged. So he became a " peasant-poet," and was half-helped.

But only the lightest shadow of difficulties to come yet rested upon his life. His letters to Gilchrist give glimpses of his enjoyment of the period of respite. He is reading Pope, Dryden, and Johnson's *Dictionary*, gifts from Lord Milton; he returns Wordsworth and asks for the loan of a Byron. He is writing, and requests "a good fair jar of ink"; he is quite set up now as to money matters, and will not be much friendly with work for a time. He must write an ode to the Marquis of Exeter as his Laureate. Flattering verses teem in upon him, accompanied by gifts of money, and he is busy answering them and writing anecdotes of his early life for Gilchrist. A guest from Trinity Hall, Cambridge, has paid him a special visit. The pitcher and barrel of the "Address to Plenty" also have their place in these celebrations, though he found them a less pure joy in reality than in dream. Gilchrist writes on the 28th of March: " Is not the headache the denunciation threatened in Scripture – 'Woe unto them that drink strong drink'? When will you leave off these sad doings, John Clare, John Clare?"

These unwonted excitements, suddenly succeeding years

of hardship and want, soon threatened more serious trouble than headaches. On the 22nd of April, Hessey wrote to Gilchrist in some alarm because Drury, who was in town, had heard that Clare had been attacked by "a fit on the 19th or 20th of a dangerous kind." Rumour had exaggerated; Clare's own letter of the 19th reported that he was indeed "worse in health than you can conjecture or than myself am aware of"; yet he was in good spirits still.

The visitor from Cambridge of whom Clare spoke was Chauncy Hare Townshend, then twenty years old and a student at Trinity Hall. In his account, written some years later, Clare mis-dated the visit; it took place in March.

"Chauncy Hare Townsend⁵ came to see me one evening in summer and asked me if John Clare lived there. I told him I was he, and he seemed surprised and asked again to be satisfied, for I was shabby and dirty. He asked freely and was disappointed, I dare say, at finding I had little or nothing to say, for I always had a natural depression of spirits in the presence of strangers that took from me all power of freedom or familiarity and made me dull or silent. For [when] I attempted to say anything, I could not recollect it and made so many hums and ha's in the story that I was obliged to leave it unfinished at last. I often tried to master this confusion by trying to talk over reasonings and arguments as I went about in my rambles, which I thought I did pretty well. But as soon as I got before anybody, I was as much to seek as ever. C. H. T. was a little affected with dandyism, and he mimicked a lisp in his speech which he owed to affectation rather than habit. Otherwise he was a feeling and sensible young man. He talked about poets and poetry and the fine scenery of the lakes and other matters for a good while, and when he left me he put a folded paper in my hand, which I found after he was gone was a sonnet and a pound bill. He promised and sent me Beattie's *Minstrel*. Some letters passed between us, and I sent him a present of my *Village Minstrel*, when I never heard of him afterwards. He has since published a Volume of Poems."

Townshend's sonnet to Clare was published in the *Morning Post;* he sent Beattie's *Minstrel* in April, and Clare's reply to his letter is interesting:

"The *Minstrel* is a sweet Poem, and as far as I have read many thoughts occur which are in my 'Peasant Boy.' I doubt the world will think them plagiarisms; therefore I must alter them or cut them out altogether; but nature is the same here at Helpstone as it is elsewhere. I am now employed in writing songs for a music-seller in Town. If I succeed it may perhaps be to my advancement; if I don't there is not much risk to run. So I am careless as to these matters. . . . I shall be happy to see you again at Helpstone likewise. Your first visit found me in a gloomy, desponding condition that often gets the sway, but when I have been inspired with a pint of 'John Barleycorn' and in one of my sunshiny moments, you would not know me. I am a new man and have too many tongues. Though your visit did not find it, still I can be cheery; but in my sullen fits I am defiled with the old silence of rusticity that always characterized me among my neighbours before I was known to the world. I was reckoned a 'glumpy half-sort-of-fool' amongst 'em. You will excuse all this; it is only to make excuse for the ill behaviour that might seem predominant at our first interview."

As late as 1865, after the publication of Martin's *Life of Clare*, Townshend recalled with pleasure his visit to Helpston, remembered the poet's "fine intellectual countenance, the paleness of which gave the impression of weak health," and criticized the absurd story which Martin concocted from Clare's account of the visit, where among other inventions Townshend is said to have mistaken Clare for a highwayman.

Early in April, Clare paid a visit to Holywell Hall, the seat of the Reynardson family, descendants of a Jacob Reynardson who was Lord Mayor of London in 1649 and suffered imprisonment for his adherence to the cause of Charles the First. This is Clare's story of the visit:

"It was a pleasant day for the season, and I found the scenery of Holywell very beautiful. . . . After looking about the gardens and the library, I was sent to dinner in the Servants' Hall. When it was over, the housekeeper invited me into her room, where the governess came and chatted in a free manner, and asking me to correspond with her gave me her address. The housekeeper wished me to write an address to her son, in imitation of Cowper's lines on his mother's picture. The governess was a pretty, impertinent girl and mischievously familiar to a mind less romantic than my own. I felt startled into sudden surprises at her manner, and in the evening on my return home I was more surprised still when, on getting out of the park into the fields, I found her lingering in my path, and on coming up to her she smiled and told me plainly she was waiting to go a little way home with me. I felt evil apprehensions as to her meaning, but I was clownish and slow in smiles and advantage to interpret it. She chatted about my poems and resumed the discourse of asking me to correspond with her, which I promised I would. When we came to the break of the heath that stands in view of Patty's cottage, I made a stop to get rid of her, but she lingered and chattered on till it grew very late; when a man on horseback suddenly came up and asked the road we had come from. She, thinking it was the General, hastily retreated, but on finding her mistake she returned and resumed her discourse till it grew between the late and early, when I wished her good night and abruptly started without using the courage of shaking her by the hand. I felt excessively awkward all the way home, and my mind was filled with guesses and imaginings at her strange manner and meanings. I wrote one letter to her and intended to be very warm and very gallant in it, but fancying that she only wanted me to write love letters to have the pleasure to talk about them and laugh at them, my second mind wrote a very cold one, in which I inserted the "Second Address to a Rosebud in Humble Life," in which I requested no answer nor hinted a second advance. So there the matter or mystery ended; for I never unriddled its meaning, though it was one of the oddest adventures my poetical life met with. It made me rather conceited as I fancied the young lady had fallen in love with me. She came from Birmingham; I shall not mention her name here."

Soon after this visit to Holywell there came definite news from London that Lord Radstock's efforts were bearing fruit. A subscription list had been opened for a fund to provide Clare with a settled income, and, by the end of April, Radstock had collected about £100. To this was added £100 which had been sent to Taylor by Earl Fitzwilliam in February, and a further £100 advanced by the publishers themselves. In a letter of April the 18th, Taylor called this last sum a gift, and as such it appeared in the subscription list. But the gift was taken back again out of the profits on *Poems Descriptive;* the policy of generosity for which the firm was at this time renowned underwent drastic changes in the next few years. On the 28th of April, £250 was invested in Navy 5 per cents., and on the 7th of June a further £125 was added. The investment was held in trust to Clare by Taylor, who took Richard Woodhouse as joint trustee in September, and the half-yearly dividend of £9 7s. 6d., which fell to £7 17s. 6d. in 1823, was paid through the publisher. Clare was not consulted in this transaction, but, if he had been, he was too amazed by his good fortune and too aware of his ignorance of business affairs to question the wisdom of his benefactors. In May came a further addition to his income through his friend Dr. Bell of Stamford, who had pleaded his cause with Earl Spencer. [6] The earl promised an annuity of £10, which was also paid through Taylor and Hessey. Thus, with the £15 from the Marquis of Exeter, Clare now had a yearly income of £43 15s. Relating these facts in the Introduction to the *Village Minstrel*, Taylor added, "His means of living, it is hoped, will be increased still further by the publication of the present work, and by the profit which may arise from the continued sale of his first production."

With his assured and regular income, and with every prospect of increasing it by an occupation which was no labour to him but his chiefest delight, Clare might well feel that the spring of 1820 had amply fulfilled the new year's promise.

BOOKS ARE OUT AND BOOKS ARE READ
1820–1822

*It is—however dishonouring to us as a nation—certain that, by
some fault in our commonwealth, the poor poet has not in these days,
nor has had for two hundred years, a dog's chance. . . . we may prate
of democracy, but actually a poor child in England has little more
hope than had the son of an Athenian slave to be emancipated into
that intellectual freedom of which great writings are born.*

QUILLER-COUCH, *The Practice of Writing.*

A s spring passed into summer, and Clare settled down in
the old cottage with Patty, he gradually became aware
of the importance of those profits of which Taylor spoke.
His new income, that "small fortune" which the bene-
volence of his patrons had assured to him, was in fact just
a little more than the £30 a year he might have earned by
full-time work as a day labourer. Now the earnings of a day
labourer in 1820, in view of the cost of living at that time,
were not sufficient for even the barest needs; from the first
Clare had to support his parents as well as his own family;
and the little more was swallowed by those necessary expenses, unknown to the peasant, which he incurred as a
writer. It is true that his patrons thought that he could easily
add to his income by part-time work at his old occupations;
his letters from London friends often contained idyllic
pictures of the happy life he was supposed to be leading in
his country retreat, composing poems or working in the fields
just as it pleased him, free from care. They do not seem to
have considered what employer would hire a labourer on
those terms. Clare did in fact work in the fields in the busy
harvest months whenever he was able; but at other times
there was little enough work for the full-time labourer.
Knowing from experience the difficulties and uncertainties

of the peasant's lot, Clare naturally turned his hopes toward
his new profession rather than his old. It was by his writing
that he trusted to win freedom from the bitter struggle with
poverty which had recently overshadowed his life; hence his
business relationship with his publishers becomes a matter
of first importance.

That relationship was complicated from the very beginning
by the fact that the poems had been published by Taylor
and Hessey in partnership with Drury, and the partnership
was not a happy one. Drury had discovered Clare, had
received and copied his poems, decided to publish them,
advanced money on them, and therefore considered himself
the prime mover in the affair. Taylor, with the experience
and resources which Drury lacked, had edited and published
the poems, introduced Clare to the literary world, and had
seen the venture crowned with success. So he was by no
means content to be regarded merely as his cousin's agent
in the business. Realising this, Drury had taken steps to
strengthen his claims before Clare visited London. Clare
made this memorandum in one of his note-books:

"Drury has persuaded me to write down in his account
book and under my accounts with him that I have sold him
my first Vol. for £20, which is to be deducted from my
account, as he only wishes to have a check against Taylor
and Hessey, who he strongly thinks will cheat him."

In the Introduction to the *Village Minstrel*, referring to
Poems Descriptive, Taylor wrote: "The present Publishers
gave Clare twenty pounds for his Poems." Yet in fact Clare
was neither given £20 by Taylor and Hessey nor was it
deducted from Drury's account, which was presented and
paid in full later; for it appears as an item in the expenses
for the publishing of *Poems Descriptive*, the account of which
Clare did not receive till 1829: "Cash paid Mr. Clare for
copyright p. Drury." To this Clare added a note: "How can
this be? I never sold the Poems for any price. What money
I had of Drury was given me on account of profits to be
received; but here it seems I have got nothing and am

brought in minus twenty pounds of which I never received a sixpence."

Drury was not satisfied with this claim on the copyright. He wanted an agreement; but he evidently feared that Clare's caution, even in his then ignorance of publishing matters, would defeat his plans. So he chose his opportunity thus:

"I once signed an agreement with Drury which allowed me a quarter profit. I was fresh at the time, but it got wind and others heard of it that knew better than I did, who called it a villainous trick. So he sent it up to London to be destroyed as they say. I know nothing; though I know that I have never signed an agreement of any kind since and never will."

It is not surprising, therefore, to find that by March the partnership between Drury and Taylor had become very strained; their letters to Clare show them skirmishing for position. "Have you any Letters of his wherein he Speaks of the Share I took in bringing out the Poems? or any later letters referring to the agreement?" inquired Taylor on the 28th. On the same date Drury wrote that he could not consent to give up the MS. book for which Clare had sent: "It is so importantly useful to me towards clearing up a mischievous misunderstanding between me and Mr. Jn. Taylor of London. . . ." This book contained Clare's receipt for the £20. In April, Drury commented on the "dilatory twaddling habits of J. T.," and announced his intention of going to London to clear up the disagreement between them. The result of that visit was the destruction of the agreement, which marked a temporary truce to their discord. Taylor explained what had been decided at that meeting:

"We have settled to give E. D., on condition that he sends up the agreement for us to destroy it, one half of whatever profit we may derive from the present or future Poems, retaining in our own Hands the sole management, and perfectly uncontrolled in what we think proper to give the Author. E. D. has been repaid the Copyright and all the other Expenses and I have charged nothing for my Trouble as Editor so far. . . . You shall have at least half of all the profits, and he shall sustain no loss by our advancing any sums we may deem right to you. These Things I state for your Information, for I have no Disguise."

For the moment affairs ran more smoothly. Drury continued to receive and copy poems for the new volume; but he was by no means satisfied with his position, and disapproved of Taylor's management of Clare's affairs. His letters later in the year were full of complaints about the publisher's reticence and reserve; he would give them no information about the profits on the first book or about the progress of the new one. Drury's view of the situation was very different from Taylor's. "However useful their services may have been both to you and myself, I humbly apprehend that, as they were volunteered, and, moreover, as Lord R. observes, they have been amply repaid—they have no title, no consideration nor any plea for monopolizing your Poems as they now do. . . . What moral or gentlemanly feeling can they possess?—if they continue thus to abuse the confidence I have reposed in them; in return for which they abstract entirely from my control or even approval the undertaking which to all intents and purposes is an affair entrusted by you to me alone—They are in the situation of individuals with whom I have associated in order to accomplish your views."

Edward Drury was not an unbiased judge, but he had a shrewd eye for his cousin's character. Taylor was indeed capable of exceptional reticence and procrastination in conducting his business affairs. But, to do him justice, we may add that in this instance he was deliberately limiting Drury's share in the business, and that during 1820 he was facing continual difficulties because of his generosity to John Keats. In September the firm was £130 out of pocket over *Endymion*, and *Lamia* had not yet paid the expenses of publishing. In an unsent letter to Keats, Taylor wrote: "If I were rich enough to do without the whole sum that you might want, I would gladly give it to you, but if I wanted it I know nobody who would let me have it." Here, no doubt, is the explanation of those gifts to Clare which

were later retracted by the firm. We think that he would
not have resented it had he known that, in effect, the profits
on his first book were being used to help a fellow-poet in
dire distress, especially when that poet was John Keats.

The dispute between Taylor and Drury, with its atmosphere of distrust and uncertainty, placed Clare in an unpleasant position. Both men appealed to his loyalty and
friendship; he was asked to choose between the publisher
upon whom depended the success of his books and the earlier
friend who had set his feet on the road to fame. There could
be little doubt about the issue, for Taylor had the stronger
hand, and played it skilfully; but Clare did his best to keep
both friends. A note, dated July, 1820, and scribbled in the
front of the MS. book *A Rustic's Pastime*, testifies clearly
enough that he was sensible of his debt to Drury: "These
lines of scribbling, that . . certainly would have been obliterated by the flames had not friendship's warm attachments
interposed to retrieve them from so just a fate, are left to
E. Drury as desired."

Thus, as the year wore on, Clare was discovering that the
problems and difficulties of the writer were no less real than
those of the peasant. Moreover, he had to consider not only
his publishers, but also his patrons, whose zeal on his behalf
sometimes led to unpleasant situations. When Walter Scott
came to London in April to be made a baronet, Captain
Sherwill, according to his promise, visited him and spoke
about Clare. The "spoils of his victory" were a copy of the
Lady of the Lake and £2 to be laid out in books. Clare chose
Currie's *Life of Burns*, Southey's *Life of Nelson*, and Chatterton's *Life and Works*. The *Lady of the Lake* was to be sent, at
Scott's own desire, from Scotland, but after three months'
delay it was forwarded by Sherwill himself with this comment: "All my endeavours, all my efforts of persuasion,
proved fruitless in the anxious desire I had expressed to
Him, that He would address a few lines to you in the blank
leaf. Sir W. seemed bound hand and head, not from any
disapprobation of your talent or taste, but occasioned by
the high path in which He strides in the literary field of the

present day." Clare's reply shows that he felt the rebuff: "I thought Sir Walter a different person; his omitting to write his name in the book shows a stiffness of pride too much affected with little things. There was a day when as a poet he shone little above his humble servant. He has patronized the 'Ettrick Shepherd' and some others, but— I was going on, but murmurs are useless."

It is possible that Scott disliked being importuned by Sherwill, who evidently expected some large benefit to accrue to Clare from this connection. As a leader of the new profession of letters, he may have disapproved, as did Dickens, of an attempt to revive the almost defunct system of patronage. For Radstock also had been urging him to use his influence with Lockhart for an article in *Blackwood's*. The article appeared, but it was not liberal, and recommended Clare to remain a happy peasant rather than become a mediocre poet.

In Lord Radstock, Clare had found a patron who was untiring in his efforts to improve the poet's circumstances and widen his reputation; but, with his autocratic character and decided views, the old admiral was not content to confine his energies to this. As early as February there were signs of friction between Clare's publisher and his chief patron. Taylor had written to his father on the 15th:

"Lord Radstock still exerts his utmost interest to sell the Book and did I not hate Patronage for its Selfishness (for such it is too frequently) I could not but admire the pains he takes. He is now proposing by broad Hints a better Bargain as he thinks for Clare's next Vol. viz. for us to publish and divide the Profits with the Author. This I would willingly consent to, if anybody would do the office of Editor *gratis*. It is amusing to think how different an Estimate would have been formed of these Poems in any other person's hands. I should be interested to see Gifford and Murray attempt to decypher and publish them, and should have no objection at all if the latter would make an offer of £500 or £1,000 for the next Volume."

About the same time Taylor informed Clare that Radstock

disapproved of some of the poems in the book, and wished
them to be omitted in the next edition. The poems were
"Dolly's Mistake," a rollicking ballad about a wake and
how the too-trusting Dolly was deceived by Young Ralph,
and "My Mary," a love poem of a refreshingly original
character. Mary, a rough, dirty, hard-working servant-girl,
is described with vigorous realism yet delicate sympathy;
this lover's eye does not, conventionally, see "Helen's beauty
in a brow of Egypt"; it accepts the brow of Egypt and
loves none the less. But it was not Lord Radstock's idea of
a love poem. There were other passages in the book which
aroused even greater disapproval; one in "Dawnings of
Genius," where Clare described the ploughman as

> *That necessary tool of wealth and pride;*

the other in "Helpstone":

> *Accursed Wealth! o'er-bounding human laws,*
> *Of every evil thou remain'st the cause.*
> *Victims of want, those wretches such as me,*
> *Too truly lay their wretchedness to thee:*
> *Thou art the bar that keeps from being fed,*
> *And thine our loss of labour and of bread;*
> *Thou art the cause that levels every tree,*
> *And woods bow down to clear a way for thee.*

In May, when the third edition was to be published,
Mrs. Emmerson wrote urging Clare to agree to the omission
of these "highly objectionable" passages, and quoting
Lord Radstock: "Tell Clare if he has still a recollection of
what I have done, and am still doing for him, he must
give me unquestionable *proofs* of being that Man I would
have him to be—he must expunge—expunge!" The lines
were held to contain "radical and ungrateful sentiments."

But Clare considered that the kindness shown to him had
not rescued the English peasantry from their evil plight;
nor had it absolved the promoters of Enclosure from all
responsibility for the disasters it brought on the poor. He
also resented the interference in a matter which concerned
himself and his publisher, and was for leaving the lines as

they stood. Taylor approved of Clare's feeling; he disliked
Radstock's encroachment into his own domain in this and
other matters. He wrote to his brother on the 31st of May:

"We have published the 3rd edition of Clare which
seems likely to go off with as much spirit as its predecessors.
I am much annoyed by Lord R.'s Puffing in the *Post* and
New Times and am determined to put an end to it, for I
cannot but think it is disgraceful to me and injurious to
Clare's fame as well as feelings . . . ."

However, he thought it best to give way for the moment
and the offending lines were omitted from the fourth edition.
Taylor gave this explanation to Clare: "Lord R. has expressed his Intentions of disowning you in such strong
terms . . . that I conceived it would be deemed improper
in me as your friend to hold out any longer. . . . . When the
Follies of the Day are past . . . we can restore the Poems
according to the earlier Editions." Clare did not write to
Radstock for some time; he had refused to have anything
to do with the alteration of the poems, and left the matter
in Taylor's hands. Since the subscription list was not yet
closed, and Radstock was still busy collecting money,
Taylor decided to propitiate him for the moment. But he
had not changed his views about patronage, and merely
awaited a more favourable opportunity to join issue with
Radstock for the control of Clare's affairs.

On the 1st or 2nd of June, Clare's first child, Anna Maria,
was born. He celebrated the occasion by writing verses in
the Burns stanza, "To an Infant Daughter," which Hessey
liked; but he added prudently, "There are Reasons why they
should not be made public just yet." According to Taylor,
Clare was finding Patty a termagant, but their lack of a home
and their unsettled condition in these early months were
unfavourable to harmony. The birth of the child, followed
by their settlement in the cottage at Helpston, relieved
the strain. Mrs. Emmerson wondered if Clare read her
letters aloud to "dear Patty," as she read his to her husband
and Lord Radstock. "I've ever addressed you in your own

very affectionate language—for we may unblushingly acknowledge ourselves lovers in poetry." She sent him a portrait of herself, and wished him to put it in a private drawer. If in the nature of things Patty could only claim the more domestic part of Clare's affection, it was not for Mrs. Emmerson that he reserved the rest, and they soon outgrew the mild literary flirtation of their early relationship.

In the summer, Clare returned to work in the fields, which he continued during the harvest months; he did not find the laborious employment very congenial after his burst of freedom, but he was short of money. The Fund-money brought him no dividend until December, and he received nothing directly in the way of profits on *Poems Descriptive*, of which the third edition was selling fast. Taylor had promised him half-profits, but as they were used to pay back the £100 which stood in the publishers' name in the subscription list, he got no benefit from them for the moment. So despite his good fortune, he lacked ready money when he most needed it.

This, besides sending him back to field labour, made him glad to fall in with Drury's scheme to gain a few pounds by having songs set to music. Clare's London friends all disapproved of this side-line, which, indeed, seems to have profited Drury more than Clare. His friendship with Drury was not affected by the discord between Drury and Taylor.

Clare continued to receive many visitors, and after his return to field labour he found their visits often untimely and troublesome. He was sometimes sent for several times a day to satisfy the curiosity of strangers, and Patty and his mother were occasionally caught with an untidy house, which annoyed them greatly. If many of these visitors were like one of whom he has left an account, his annoyance is not to be wondered at.

"Among the many that came to see me, there was a dandified gentleman of unconscious oddity of character, that not only bordered on the ridiculous but was absurdly mothered in it. He made pretensions to great learning and knew nothing. On his first coming he began in a very dry manner to examine the fruits of experience in books, and said he hoped I had a fondness for reading, as he wished to have the pleasure to make me a present of some. He then begged my walking stick, and after he had got it he wanted me to write my name on the crook. I really thought the fellow was mad. He then asked me insulting liberties respecting my first acquaintance with Patty, and said he understood that in this country the lower orders made their courtship in barns and pigsties, and asked me whether I did. I felt very vexed and said that it might be the custom of the high orders for aught I knew, as experience made fools wise in most matters; but I assured him he was very wrong respecting that custom among the lower orders here. His wife said he was fond of a joke, and hoped I should not be offended; but I saw naught of a joke in it and found afterwards that he was a scant remove from the low order himself, as his wife was a grocer's daughter. After he had gossiped an hour, he said, 'Well, I promised to give you a book, but after examining your library I don't see that you want anything, as you have a great many more than I expected to find. Still I should make you an offer of something. Have you got a Bible?' I said nothing, but it was exactly what my father had long wanted, and he instantly spoke for me and said, 'We have a Bible, Sir, but I cannot read it, the print is so small. So I should thank you for one.' The man looked very confused and explained by his manner that he had mentioned the very book which he thought we had, to escape giving it."

According to Drury, Clare's mind was also harassed and oppressed by the laborious correspondence which he was obliged to support against his inclinations. But, whatever his other occupations, he continued to write poems assiduously. In January, Taylor had suggested as a subject, "A Week in a Village," to consist of a story about village life for each day. Clare took up the suggestion, and the result appears in a bound quarto volume, entitled "Village Scenes and Subjects on Rural Occupations," dated August 21st, 1820. The volume contains sixteen poems, written in Clare's hastiest handwriting, but fairly legibly and evidently intended for the press. Six of them were included in the *Village Minstrel*, three in the *Shepherd's Calendar*, and the rest remained

unpublished. Of this series of bucolics Mr. Blunden has
written:

"The collection as a whole is a painting of life in an English
village a hundred years since in most of its common mani-
festations. The artist knew his theme, and was gifted with
extraordinary freshness of outlook upon the familiar spec-
tacle. In this respect he differed from many who like himself
were born tillers of the soil; the shrewd enthusiasm of the
best of them was not accompanied by his sweet intensity
and universality of feeling. What he saw, that he was. His
pity through all the delineation reminds one of Lamb's great
words, 'feeling, which seems to resolve itself into the elements
which it contemplates,' and his 'Princely Clare.' . . .

"Rustic in form these poems certainly are, and, judged by
the polish of other poets and by not a little of Clare's own
later work, they have many flaws. His conception of poetry,
at this time, appears on the title page of his *Village Minstrel*
in Spenser's verse, 'I play to please myself,' and that has
something to do with this raggedness. . . . He lacked form a
little, but what poet ever made up for that with greater
riches of material? Even these early writings display that
careless variety of rapture; and it is of course true that they
have a hardy energy which is not so clear in later work, as he
became aware of hues and tones at first unknown."

The writing and copying up of these poems fully occupied
Clare's leisure during the spring and summer months. In
July came a letter from Bloomfield, his "brother bard and
fellow-labourer," to whom Drury had sent a copy of *Poems
Descriptive*. The letters of both Taylor and Hessey frequently
contained news of Keats. Taylor had written on the 27th
of April, "I have got all Keats's MSS. in my hands now to
make a Selection out of them for another Volume, as I did
of yours; and I should like to write an Introduction too, as
Editor, to speak about the unfair Reception he has met with
from the Critics, & especially from the *Quarterly Review*;
but perhaps I had better not." During the preparation of
the *Lamia* volume, when Keats frequently visited Taylor to
correct proofs and make emendations, they sometimes talked
of Clare. There exists a postscript sheet torn from a letter of

Clare's to Taylor, dated June 5th, on which is written in Keats's writing a couplet of *Lamia*, an emendation of the earlier MS. reading.[1]

On the 6th of June, Taylor sent a number of extracts from *Lamia*, which was to appear in about three weeks. On the 27th, Hessey wrote that Keats was very ill again, and three days later he sent a copy of the book with further news: "A Blood Vessel in his Lungs broke last week and he has been under Dr. Darling's Care ever since. By copious bleedings and active medicines the evil is at present reduced, but the prospect of its return & the evidence it affords of the state of his Constitution make me feel the greatest concern for him. I think the simplicity of 'Isabella' will please you much. 'Hyperion' is full of the most sublime poetical Images & the small Poems delight me very much. . . ."

On the 19th of August, Taylor wrote that Keats would have to spend the winter in Italy. "You are now a richer Man than poor K. and how much more fortunate— We have some trouble to get through 500 Copies of his work, though it is highly spoken of in the periodical Works, but what is most against him, it has been thought necessary in the leading Review, the *Quarterly*, to damn his [Poems] for [imputed] political Opinions—Damn them [I say] who could act in so cruel a way to a young man of undoubted Genius— I hate Criticism at all Times except when it is of that enlarged kind that takes entire Surveys of a Subject, and conceiving old writers to be new and new ones to be old awards to each his proper Share of Commendation. Besides in Poetry I think Praise should be given where it is due, and that Silence is sufficient Dispraise—" On September the 27th, he told Clare that Keats was on the way to Italy. "If he recovers his Strength he will write to you. I think he wishes to say to you that your Images from Nature are too much introduced without being called for by a particular Sentiment— To meddle with this Subject is bad policy when I am in haste, but perhaps you conceive what it is he means: his remark is only applicable now and then when he feels as if the Description overlaid and stifled that which ought to be

the prevailing Idea—He likes your first pastoral which E. D.
copied and sent very much indeed."

Keats's criticism was pertinent enough; Clare's revolt
from poetry in which the images were so overlaid by the
sentiment that they lost their freshness and truth to nature
sometimes tempted him to the opposite extreme.

Impatient for the publication of his new book, Clare was
under the impression that the poems he had sent up were
ready for the press. He now heard from Sherwill that Taylor
had not yet begun to select them, and was going out of Town
shortly. He intended, he said, to visit Helpston and take
Clare back with him to help in the editing. In the meantime,
Clare turned to his Stamford friends for companionship.
During one of his visits in September an incident occurred
which caused him considerable perturbation at the time.
He wrote to Gilchrist about it:

"I went to Drury's again, and now comes the d——d
hobble that vexes me. After I had been there a few minutes,
a gentleman came in and asked me how I did. I very bluntly
answered, 'Very well, thank you, sir.' He stared [at] me very
hard and asked the prentice if it was not Clare and told me
that he came to hear if my book was out. 'No, sir,' (with my
hat on) was the answer. He went out without saying a word
more, and he had not gone two minutes when the disclosure
of the secret came out. D——n it!—'twas a thunderbolt to my
ignorance, and I stood gauping like an idiot to hear the man
say it was no worse a person than the marquis. What the
marquis will think of me I don't know but I wish very much
I had been the length of London out of the matter. But if
there is anything to disadvantage, the poor devil your humble
servant is sure to get head over ears in it."

Gilchrist informed Clare later that he had seen Mr.
Pierrepont and explained the mistake, so that the matter
was now set right.

Taylor's policy of reticence during the autumn of 1820
brought the truce between Lord Radstock and himself to an
end; by December a wordy conflict, into which Drury and

Mrs. Emmerson were drawn, was being waged for the control of Clare's affairs. Radstock's interest had not ceased with the closing of the subscription fund. He often sent messages through Mrs. Emmerson, and sometimes wrote himself, in an almost unreadable hand, letters of encouragement and admonition and concern for Clare's mental and spiritual development. He also sent books frequently, many of them on religious subjects, and among the others the works of Akenside, Beattie, Coleridge, and Cowper, volumes of the *Idler* and *Rambler*, and Johnson's *Lives of the Poets*.

In September we hear of a scheme of Radstock's whereby Clare was to visit a clergyman who would improve his external conduct and make it accord with his inner delicacy. November foreshadowed a crisis; Mrs. Emmerson passed on Radstock's complaints about Taylor's secrecy and lack of respect to him; he was going to look into the matter on his return to town. Then events moved quickly. Radstock wrote to Taylor, stressing the need for a written agreement between Clare and his publisher. In his reply, dated December 11th, Taylor stated that he was actually benefiting Clare more than he would have been bound to do under the terms of the obligation suggested by Radstock in a conversation of the previous April, namely, that the publishers should defray the expenses and share the profits with the author. "But my Lord, if you think your arbitration will be advantageous to Clare—I as a Publisher can have no objection to it; in the meantime I shall suspend those labours which are not within the province of a publisher." To this Radstock replied immediately. He did not doubt the publisher's goodwill, "but still I apprehend that in matters of real business, no man's word, however well established his integrity, would be considered sufficiently binding, unless accompanied by some written document. As the case now stands between you and Clare, I understand that no terms whatever have been offered, he would therefore I think be to blame to resign his manuscript to any Publisher whatever, without a specified security for his labours." As to the labours of editing, if "no Lord Radstock had stepped forth in support of the

Work, my own private opinion is, that a second edition of
the Poems would not yet have shewed itself. That your
labours were great respecting the little volume in question,
I most willingly allow, but that you were amply remunerated
I am equally convinced."

These remarks seem sensible and just enough; on Taylor's
own showing, he had no real objection to the proposed
written agreement. But he was not one of those who suffer
criticism gladly; his next move was to deliver an ultimatum
to Lord Radstock: "I will write to Clare to know whether
I am to treat with him or your Lordship for the Copyright
of his next Volume; and upon his answer will depend whether
I shall again have the Honour of addressing your Lordship."
Then he turned his attention to Clare. In a letter written
on the 16th of December he described Radstock's criticisms
as the meddling interferences of a patron anxious for
notoriety. "Unless you commission Lord R. to interfere in
this Matter I know of no Right that he has to write to me
on the Subject, and if he possessed ever so good a Right the
observations he has allowed himself to make on my Conduct
would disincline me to have any further Communication
with him. . . . I would resign the MSS. rather than acknowledge his agency after what he has said. . . ." If, however,
Clare wished to go on as heretofore, he must insist on an
agreement being executed between them on a basis of half
profits, as the only way to keep meddlers out. On the 17th,
Mrs. Emmerson wrote that Lord Radstock had broken with
Taylor, whose impetuosity had done Clare real injury. She
urged him to press for a written agreement, but advised him
not to withdraw his manuscripts, since that would delay
the new book and derange his affairs generally. This
consideration placed Taylor in a very strong position, as he
well realized. On the 24th of December he consolidated that
position by informing Clare that he was busy selecting poems,
and intended to publish two volumes under the title "Ways
of a Village." He also sent the first half-yearly dividend
several days before it was due—in the future it usually
arrived several days late—and suggested how pleasant it was

to receive £20 a year free from obligation to anyone. Of Radstock he said, "I fear he will not be content till he is acknowledged your supreme Friend, and pre-eminent Patron." Clare was to ask Drury to show him the story of Sinbad, who also had relations with "an old Gentleman who belonged to the Sea-service." Mrs. Emmerson wrote again on the 30th of December, very sensibly promising to do her best to smooth things over; she believed Taylor's intentions were honourable, but he had not been candid and liberal in his communications. Clare was to send up a copy of the agreement to Lord Radstock. Taylor's letter of the 1st of January marked his victory, won on his own terms, or lack of terms. Clare had expressed his confidence in his publishers; he was willing not only to sign an agreement for the forthcoming book, but one binding him for future publications. Taylor thanked him, but could not accept the latter proposal. "I know we cannot be more secure of your Goodwill than we are without any such Bond, and should a Difference arise between us . . . it would be unjust to tie you fast. . . . That foolish Lord R. has no Conception of such Sentiments as these; what a wretched world he moves in, to have learnt no better at his time of life than thus to estimate his Friends as he pretends to call them—" Clare felt that these last remarks were uncalled-for, and commented "very unjust" in the margin of the letter.

Meanwhile Drury had been carrying on a guerilla warfare on his own account. He expressed grave concern to Clare about Taylor's conduct, advising him to apply to Radstock to get an exact statement of his position, but warning him not to become too friendly with his patron. Then we hear that Radstock had written to Drury a "flaming appeal" about Taylor's reserved and disingenuous ways. Whereupon since "hawks mustn't peck out hawks' eyes," he wrote back to persuade Radstock he was mistaken about Taylor, setting his private dudgeon aside, and in the process taking some blame on himself and scattering a few spots on Clare. In his opinion, he explained to Radstock, the published and forthcoming works were entirely Clare's property, and he would be justified in demanding the whole profits on them if he felt inclined.

Here for the time the matter rested. The agreement, suggested by Radstock to save Clare from Taylor, then insisted upon by Taylor to save Clare from Radstock, then accepted by Clare but refused by Taylor to save Clare from himself, remained still unsigned. The publisher's intentions were honourable enough, but his business methods were peculiar, as Clare realized more fully in later years. Writing of this business then, he commented :

"Lord Radstock was my best friend. It was owing to him that the first Poems succeeded. He introduced them into all places where he had connections, got them noticed in newspapers and other [periodicals], and if it did nothing more it made them known. He kindly undertook to settle my affairs with my Publishers, which they kindly enough on their parts deferred, and it's not settled yet. He wrote Taylor a letter wishing him to draw up an agreement in 'black and white,' as his Lordship expressed it, as faiths in men were not to be trusted. Taylor pretended to be insulted at this and wrote his Lordship a genteel saucy one that settled the affair in the present confusion of no settling at all. Nay, they will neither publish my poems nor give them up."

Clare's indisposition during December and January was augmented, if not caused, by this conflict among his friends. He was troubled by "nervous fears" and "phantasies of the brain," and suffered great agitation of mind about the fate of his forthcoming book. At times he thought he would not recover, and received a will-form from Woodhouse. Meanwhile, the fourth edition of *Poems Descriptive* had been printed in December, and progress was made with the new volumes. On the 23rd of January, Taylor sent the first proofs, and proof correction went on steadily during February and March. The choice of a title gave some trouble. "Ways of a Village" had been dropped, and " The Village Minstrel" was finally chosen, but with some reluctance because of its resemblance to Beattie's *Minstrel*.

LJ

It was about this time that Clare, an innocent spectator, received a stray shot from the fierce Battle of the Pamphlets which had been raging for some years between the Rev. W. Lisle Bowles on the one side and Campbell, Gilchrist, and Byron on the other. It began in 1806, with Bowles's criticisms of Pope in his edition of that poet's *Works*, to which reference is made by Byron in *English Bards and Scotch Reviewers*. Ten years later, Campbell, in his *Essay on English Poetry*, championed Pope, and was answered by Bowles in a pamphlet. Then in the *Quarterly Review*, 1820, appeared an article supporting Campbell, ridiculing Bowles, and bringing Byron's name into the conflict. Byron took up the cudgels in Pope's defence, and wrote two *Letters to John Murray*, attacking Bowles, who replied in 1821 with two *Letters to Byron*. But Bowles had also replied to the *Quarterly* article of 1820, and, because he knew that Gilchrist had already defended Pope's character in the *London Magazine*, February 1820, and had written the review of Clare's poems in the *Quarterly*, he attributed to Gilchrist the *Quarterly* article on Pope, which was really from the pen of Isaac Disraeli. Thus, in his reply, Bowles assumed that his antagonist was the critic who had written about "certain productions of a 'poet of nature.' If so, his praise or blame may be held in equal contempt." Gilchrist joyfully made capital out of Bowles's mistake and his supposed slight on Clare, quoting two of Clare's sonnets to show that he was a better poet than Bowles in the only branch of the art in which the latter was noteworthy. In his next counterblast, Bowles made some amends to Clare and contended that his remarks applied only to the critic, "whose pompous and pedantic criticism rather injured than promoted the cause of him it was intended to serve." Byron took up this reply in his second *Letter*.

"In my humble opinion, the passage referred to both. . . . 'A certain poet of nature' is not the style of commendation. . . . Had he felt a spark of kindling kindness for John Clare, he would have named him. There is a sneer in the sentence as it stands. How a favourable review of a deserving poet can 'rather injure than promote his cause' is difficult to comprehend. The article denounced is able and amiable and it *has* 'served' the poet, as far as poetry can be served by judicious and honest criticism."

The lives of Clare and Byron did not touch more closely than in this incidental, though sincere, tribute; there could indeed be few greater contrasts than that between these two poets, as diverse in their births and fortunes as in their characters and poetry. Clare's first acquaintance with Byron's poetry had been made in 1819, but he had heard of Byron many years before that. In the reminiscences of his boyhood, Clare tells how he copied out the journal of one of the villagers who had been an able seaman on board the *Fox* cutter, when Lord Byron sailed in her. The sailor remembered him as an odd young man "of a resolute temper, fond of bathing in the sea and going ashore to see ruins in a rough sea when it required six hands to manage the boat. This teased the sailors so much that his name became a by-word in the ship for unnecessary trouble." After 1820 there is abundant evidence of Clare's interest in Byron, both as a man and as a poet, and the interest grew as each year increased the contrast between their fames and fortunes.

In February came news of an event which was to have a great influence on John Taylor's plans and bring Clare into close contact with some of the greatest writers of the day. John Scott, whose ability had placed the *London* among the foremost magazines of the time, had been shot in his unfortunate duel with Christie. In the same letter, Taylor said that he had just heard again of Keats, who could not live a fortnight longer. He thought of writing his life to do justice to his memory. On the 9th of March he wrote again: "We heard yesterday of Keats; he was still alive, though very weak—but calmer than he had been. It was not considered that he could last many Days longer—Probably at the very Time Scott died, he also died. In this last Letter we are told that Keats desires to have this Line put upon his Tombstone 'Here lies one whose name was writ on

Water.'" On the 26th of March he sent news of Keats's death, and suggested that Clare might write some lines to his memory. "Poor Keats, you know how I reverence him," wrote Clare in reply, with a tirade on the dead poet's critics. He treated this theme allegorically in one of his long poems, and a sonnet was written just in time to be included in the *Village Minstrel*.

> *When Rancour's aims have past in nought away,*
>   *Enlarging specks discern'd in more than thee,*
> *And beauties 'minishing which few display,—*
>   *When these are past, true child of Poesy,*
> *Thou shalt survive.*

Clare read the *Lamia* volume with keen delight and copied into one of his note-books a number of its finest lines and phrases. On his cottage wall hung a reproduction of one of the portraits of Keats; his children used to call it "the miserable man."

By the end of March, Clare was again restored to health. His nervous disorder had been accentuated by the threatened destruction of some elm-trees which had sheltered the cottage and murmured in the chimney-top long before his earliest memory. He wrote to Taylor:

"My two favourite elm-trees at the back of the hut are condemned to die—it shocks me to relate it but 'tis true. The savage who owns them thinks they have done their best, and now he wants to make use of the benefits he can get from selling them. O was this country Egypt, and was I but a caliph, the owner should lose his ears for his arrogant presumption; and the first wretch that buried his axe in their roots should hang on their branches as a terror to the rest. I have been several mornings to bid them farewell. Had I one hundred pounds to spare I would buy them reprieves—but they must die. Yet this mourning over trees is all foolishness—they feel no pains—they are but wood, cut up or not. A second thought tells me I am a fool: were people all to feel as I do, the world could not be carried on—a green would not be ploughed—a tree or bush would not be cut for firing or furniture, and everything they found

when boys would remain in that state till they died. This is
my indisposition, and you will laugh at it."

Clare's feeling for these friendly trees, and his fine anger
against the ruthless destruction which Enclosure brought,
were eloquently expressed in his poem "The Fallen Elm."
But for a time, through the intervention of Gilchrist and
Drury, the elms were spared.

About this time, Clare's visits to Stamford gave his
London friends some concern. Taylor was grieved to hear
of his "late fit of drinking," and wrote, "One of the very
very few poets of this day is gone—let another beware of
Stamford. I wish you may keep to your resolution of shunning
that Place for it will do you immense injury if you do not."
Drury, on the other hand, thought he would not get well
until he left Helpston and his " low-minded companions."

On the 7th of April, Taylor acknowledged the receipt
of some poems and an account of Clare's early life which
he was to use in his Introduction to the *Village Minstrel*.[2]
Taylor remarked that he had never had such strong proof
of what Clare was capable of producing in prose, and asked
him to send accounts of the origins of his poems, his opinions
of books, or passages from his novel of low life. Thus encouraged, Clare set himself to master the art of prose
expression, and his achievements in this, for him, much more
difficult art, though fragmentary, are by no means as
negligible as they have sometimes been represented to be. He
had already sent Taylor a long descriptive passage, "The
Woodman, or the Beauties of a Winter Forest," and the
publisher had been so surprised by its correctness that he
had enquired if it was all his own composition. Clare was
soon busy with a number of projects, some of which never
passed the experimental stage. In the next few years he
wrote stories, part of a novel, many essays on such subjects
as Pride, Industry, Popularity, Affectation, Happiness,
Friendship, Nothing, Fashion, and Pretension, sketches
of rural life and characters, criticisms of poetry and painting,
descriptions of scenes, further chapters of autobiography,

a journal, and a natural history of Helpston. In the essays
and stories, his lack of training in the orderly exposition
of ideas was an obstacle which he did not entirely overcome,
but in the descriptive and personal prose the gifts of exact
observation and clear expression notable in his poetry were
ample compensation. Drury also was impressed by Clare's
progress with his prose writing; he praised some "spirited
observations on Crabbe," and advised Clare to write for
some magazine, as Hogg did for *Blackwood's*. Then, on the
1st of May, Taylor wrote that he would like Clare to try his
hand at an article for the *London Magazine*, and would tell
him why in his next letter. The reason was that Taylor
was on the point of buying the *London* for his firm. Since
Scott's death in February, both Hazlitt and Cary had
been approached with regard to the editorship, and the
latter appears to have been quite willing to take the
post, should a definite offer be made. On the 11th of May
Taylor informed Clare that they had bought the *London* and
there would be a chance of his writing articles for it in prose
as well as poetry. There is little doubt that he had already
decided to edit it himself; he wrote to Cary on the 18th
asking for contributions, but making no mention of the
editorship. On the 31st he informed his family that his
editorial duties began that day; he looked forward to them
with confidence and enthusiasm. The new venture began
well; all the old contributors promised their support;
and Cary, who had just cause for complaint in Taylor's
treatment of the editorship problem, was won over.

With these new duties on his hands, Taylor could find no
time for the *Village Minstrel*; yet delay was serious. The season
was slipping by; within a month, wrote Mrs. Emmerson,
all the families of consequence who had patronized the
first book would be out of Town. In the midst of Clare's
anxiety for the fate of his book came a family trouble. A
second daughter was born on the 2nd of June, but died
soon after. On the 23rd, Hessey wrote apologizing for the
delay; the book was now ready except for the Introduction,
which Taylor was too busy to write. On the 5th of July,

Hessey sent three copies for the Marquis of Exeter, lacking
the Introduction, which was still unfinished. It had been
decided to omit a print of Clare's cottage from a drawing
by De Wint, intended as a frontispiece to the second volume;
the drawing was unsatisfactory. On the 7th of August,
Taylor found time to write; he was still attempting to
complete the Introduction. He thought that as the season
was now past it was of little consequence whether the book
came out then or a month later. On the 29th he wrote that
the Introduction was at last completed. It had taken him
four months to write it. "I am overworked, and have much
more reason than you to think of dying," he commented.
He wanted to delay publication until November, but, in
view of Clare's distress, decided to issue the book at once.
He dwelt on the difficulties of the work; he would have given
£100 to anyone who would have taken the editing off his
hands. He bade Clare be satisfied: "You have now £45 a
year, and reckoning one page monthly in the *London*, £57."
Two poems had already been printed in the July and
August numbers, and Clare was to have a guinea a page for
them. Altogether thirty poems appeared in the *London* in
the next three years; but there was no sign of the promised
guineas. Clare made a note some time later in his memorandum book: "This year I commenced writing for the
London Magazine and was to have £12 in addition to my
income, but I have not had anything allowed me as yet."
In fact, Taylor entirely forgot his promise. There was no
mention of this money in the accounts presented in 1829,
and Clare had to call Taylor's attention to the omission.
The publisher was already finding his new duties a too
heavy burden; yet he might have remembered that the
publication of the *Village Minstrel* was a prior obligation;
it was indeed practically ready for issue before Taylor
bought the magazine.

To the busy publisher the delay of a few months appeared
a small matter; but it seemed a very long time to Clare,
isolated at Helpston and longing to follow up his first success.
Had he known that his third book would suffer a delay of as

many years as his second had months, he might not have shown the restraint which marks his letter of the 20th of August:

"Your cousin D. fancies, I believe, that you and I are confederate in dark mysteries about the publication, for he grumbled like a bear with a sore head last Friday when I called on him, and seemed discomforted. I told him I was going to write for the *London* a short while before, and I dare say that's what gravels him. At all events it will be as beneficial as writing his songs, for I've got nought yet either by dedications or music save a small sum which I borrowed at times with the intention of never paying again. I will begin a series of 'Village Sketches' for the Mag. as Hessey hinted a while back, and you may insert those you have got when you please upon that head.

"Your delay makes me swear cursedly at times—that is, grumbling to oneself—for I say little elsewhere. Still I am yours sincerely and affectionately and ever shall be."

During the summer months Clare had been busy as usual with his harvesting work, but there were occasional respites. Bishop and Mrs. Marsh paid him a visit in July, and in August he visited Whittlebury Forest as the guest of Joseph Bunney, Lieutenant, K.O.S.M., of Silverstone. At last, on September the 22nd, he received a dozen copies of the *Village Minstrel*. "The season is sadly against the sale," wrote Mrs. Emmerson. Taylor had printed 2,000 copies; by December, 800 had been sold. In March, 1822, Hessey wrote, "I am happy to tell you that the *Village Minstrel* continues to sell as well as we could expect"; but Taylor was less cheerful: "It is certain that the last work does not take like the first."

It was natural enough that those who had been attracted in 1820 chiefly by the novelty of a peasant-poet should be less interested in Clare now that he was "possessed of a small fortune," "passing rich with forty pounds a year," as one reviewer quoted, forgetting that Goldsmith's preacher would have been much less rich in 1820. Yet the sale of 800 copies in three months—Keats's last book had sold only 500 in eighteen months—seems to indicate that Clare had a public genuinely interested in his poetry; had Taylor been able to publish books as often as Clare could write them, he might well have established himself with his own public, as Wordsworth did with his between 1820 and 1830. The *Village Minstrel* was less widely reviewed than *Poems Descriptive*, but the reviews were favourable enough, if more critical. It was recognised by all that Clare had more than fulfilled his promise and had improved on his first book. Reviews appeared in the *New Monthly, Literary Chronicle, Literary Gazette, Gentleman's Magazine, European Magazine*, and *Eclectic Review*. The adverse criticism was chiefly of the poet's use of provincialisms and "low and insignificant" words. The *Literary Gazette* also thought that the kind of scenery Clare described—"the rushes, sedges, willow groves and sluggish rivulets of Northamptonshire"—would not excite general interest, and advised him to turn his attention to "landscape of a more sublime and beautiful order."

As an example of a critical reader's opinion of the *Village Minstrel* in 1821, a review which was intended for the *London Magazine* but rejected by Taylor may be noticed here. Taylor sent the manuscript to Clare, saying that he had thought that the genius and taste of the poet to whom he had entrusted the task would have had better results. He did not name the writer, but the handwriting and style suggest Allan Cunningham. He found much that was extraordinary and beautiful in the book, but noted obscurity and wordiness in some of the poems, and thought the imagery too confined. He disliked the glossary, assuming that the words in it were the poet's coinings, and suggesting that Burns and Ramsay furnished no excuse, for they were using their native tongue. He was evidently unaware that Clare was doing the same thing. He wished to see in Clare's poetry more human situations and events, more pruning and selection, more action and incident, greater elegance and wider use of the established language of poetry.

At the end of this manuscript Clare has written an interesting comment, which reveals his ability to distinguish between sound criticism and irrelevant.

"There are a many just faults found in this Criticism among some trifling. The censures are generally just, and the praises, in one or two instances, more than I dare or can believe I deserve. His observation that Poets should conform their thoughts or style to the taste of the country, by which he means fashion, is humbug, and shows that he has no foundation of judgment for a critic that might be relied on. His lights lead astray."

Taylor's Introduction to the *Village Minstrel* was ably written. He quoted freely from Clare's own story of the events which led to the publication of the first book and the raising of the subscription fund, adding, "Money is still a desirable accompaniment, and for want of it our Poet's finances are somewhat too much straitened to support his family with comfort." He also gave Clare's notes on some of the old country sports and customs mentioned in the poems. He put forward a plea for fair criticism rather than indulgence: "the critic is not the poet's superior, though he often affects to be so, on the strength of having had, probably, a better education." There followed a guarded reference to Keats: "Clare has created more of these never-dying forms, in the personification of things inanimate and abstract—he has scattered them more profusely about our paths, than perhaps any poet of the age except one." He explained this in a letter: "I will alter that mention of Keats, for I am not very certain whether it be correct, but if not of him it is not of anyone—[we] will say 'except one,' and leave every man to [suppose] it means his own peculiar favourite." Taylor went on to deplore the illiberal spirit of criticism in late years, which had "let slip the dogs of war in the flowery fields of poesy."

Of the title-poem, begun in the autumn of 1819, Clare has left the following note:

"The encouragement my first volume met with lifted me up into heartsome feelings, and rhyming was continually with me night and day. I began the "Village Minstrel" a long while before, attempting to describe my own feelings and love of rural objects. I then began in good earnest with it after the trial of my first poems was made, and completed it . . . but I was still unsatisfied with it. I am now, and often feel sorry that I did not withhold it a little longer for revision. The reason why I dislike it is that it does not describe the feelings of a rhyming peasant strongly or locally enough. . . .''

Though Clare himself was not satisfied with the vigilance of his eye and the vigour of his descriptions, this long poem on the pleasures, trials, and aspirations of the poetically inclined village boy betrays few of the faults which he found with it in these respects. The whole of this second book was written chiefly "to please myself," as Clare indicated on the title-page. He was definitely concerned with the development of his art, as well as with making some money. Contemptuous of conventional phrasing and vain pen-flourishings, he was ardently concerned to use only the "genuine word," enforced by keen and truthful observation, reinforced by passionate necessity to speak. More than once in the "Village Minstrel," the word he used was so genuine that his editor winced at it, and changed it to one less startling for the age and more vague.

Compared with James Beattie's *Minstrel*, with its rhetorical flow and its moral and philosophical undertones, Clare's poem is remarkable for these very characteristics which he was not satisfied about—strength of local colouring, truth of observation in country custom and landscape, and simplicity of emotional description. There were suggestions that he copied Beattie, but, excepting that he used the Spenserian stanza, as Beattie did, there is nothing in the two poems to compare. Clare's poetic aim in his "Village Minstrel" was deliberate, and his own.

But his creed was not yet entire. Among the shorter poems of the book there are reminders of John Dyer's "Grongar Hill," of Kirke White's "Solitude," echoes of Samuel Wesley's metres and of Smart's translations of the Psalms, which had been reviewed side by side with Clare's *Poems Descriptive* in the *London Magazine*. Many of these poems were written before his first book was published, and belong to his apprenticeship period.

Among the poems of the second volume of the *Village Minstrel* are sixty sonnets. We may fall foul of the scholar by using the term here. Clare knew nothing of octave and sestet, presentation and application of idea, pause and continuity. In these sixty sonnets he used thirty-six different rhyme-schemes, ranging from rhymed couplets through the Spenserian and Shakespearian forms to combinations as intricate as the Petrarchian model. He did not always insist even upon the fourteen lines; some of his later "sonnets" had twelve or sixteen. So Clare's sonnets often lack "adequacy of sonnet-motive," as William Sharp noted in his *Sonnets of this Century*. Sharp did not, however, trouble to seek the best of Clare's sonnets, where there is this adequacy.

Clare was not using the sonnet form chiefly for its principle of emotional compression. He was experimenting with fourteen lines, linked into a stanza by some system of rhyme which served as a frame for a scene-painting—of "Hillywood," "Summer Tints," "A Lair at Noon," "Pleasures Past," or "A Wild Nosegay." He was using the stanza pictorially; yet it would be misleading to say that the pictures have no emotional significance. In the best of these sonnets there are penpaintings, finished and richly coloured, but emotionally conceived and given with impassioned selection and clarity for our "most innocent enjoyment."

While Clare was trying his hand at these sonnet experiments, or at a kind of poem which Smart had composed almost inimitably before him, he was working out another part of his contribution toward the poetry of his day. Besides the characteristics already mentioned concerning the poem, the "Village Minstrel," there glows in all the poems in this volume a delight in every hour, however commonplace to the countryman's mind, however gloomy to the townsman's, in the four seasons. A new world, crowded with creature-loves and full of new sources of joy, was revealed to the reader; cowslips are "bowing adorers of the gale"; habits of a butterfly are described with the tenderness of a Skelton:

> Oft I've seen thy little leg,
> Soft as glass o'er velvet slides,
> Smoothen down thy silken sides.

Even Burns and Thomson and Cowper had not seen the thousand and one things that Clare saw. He was now determined that neither conceit in his art nor any artifice should stand between his vision and his reader. The "brave new world" he had loved as a child and introduced to the poetry-reading public in his first book was now more accurately and more deliberately disclosed in the *Village Minstrel*.

While Clare was eagerly awaiting news of the fate of his new book, he was busy in the harvest field. In October he received a visitor; John Taylor, returning to London after a visit to his family, spent a day with Clare at Helpston. Taylor wrote an account of this visit for the November *London Magazine*, in the form of a letter to the editor, headed Wansford, October 12th, 1821. He combined a picture of Clare at home and some interesting observations on his character with a notice of the *Village Minstrel*, from which he quoted extensively.

Taylor tells how he met Clare, who was not aware of his coming, on King Street, about a mile from the village. He was going with Patty and her sister to a Michaelmas re-union of the Turner family at Casterton, intending to call first at Burghley House for his quarter's salary. Clare turned back with his guest, but, before returning to the village, they paid a visit to Lolham Bridges, where King Street crosses the flood-meadows and marshes of the Welland. Taylor was interested to look on the scene of the poem "The Last of March," and noted with wonder what Clare's eye and imagination had revealed in this "dull line of ponds, or rather one continued marsh, over which a succession of arches carries the narrow highway." Retracing their steps, they saw in the distance Langley Bush, that ancient landmark which had sheltered so many generations of shepherds and gipsies. Referring to Clare's poem on this old whitethorn, Taylor wrote:

"The discretion which makes Clare hesitate to receive as canonical all the accounts he has heard of the former honours of Langley Bush, is in singular contrast with the enthusiasm of his poetical faith. As a man, he cannot bear to be imposed upon—his good sense revolts at the least attempt to abuse it;—but as a poet, he surrenders his imagination with most happy ease to the illusions which crowd upon it from stories of fairies and ghosts. The effect of this distinction is soon felt in a conversation with him. From not considering it, many persons express their surprise that Clare should be so weak on some topics and so wise on others. But a willing indulgence of what they term weakness is the evidence of a strong mind. He feels safe there, and luxuriates in the abandonment of his sober sense for a time, to be the sport of all the tricks and fantasies that have been attributed to preternatural agency. Let them address him on other subjects, and unless they entrench themselves in forms of language to which he is unaccustomed, or take no pains to understand him according to the sense rather than the letter of his speech, they will confess, that to keep fairly on a level with him in the depth and tenour of their remarks, is an exercise requiring more than common effort. He may not have read the books which they are familiar with, but let them try him on such as he has read, (and the number is not few, especially of the modern poets,) and they will find no reason to undervalue his judgement. His language, it is true, is provincial, and his choice of words in ordinary conversation is indifferent, because Clare is an unpretending man, and he speaks in the idiom of his neighbours, who would ridicule and despise him for using more or better terms than they are familiar with. But the philosophic mind will strive to read his thoughts, rather than catch at the manner of their utterance; and will delight to trace the native nobleness, strength, and beauty of his conceptions, under the tattered garb of what may, perhaps, be deemed uncouth and scanty expressions."

There follows a reasonable and eloquent defence of Clare's use of his native idioms; but we must press on to the cottage. On the white-washed wall of the living-room Taylor noticed the water-colour of Clare's portrait by Hilton which the artist had copied and sent as a present to Parker Clare. Parker was in the garden, hobbling about on his two sticks, too crippled by his rheumatism to kneel or stoop. While Taylor talked to him, Clare prepared a meal of bread and cheese, with capital beer from the Blue Bell.

"In the midst of our operations, his little girl awoke, a fine lively pretty creature, with a forehead like her father's, of ample promise. She tottered along the floor and . . . her father looked after her with the fondest affection, and with a careful twitch of his eyebrow when she seemed in danger."

They next examined Clare's library, where Taylor noticed the works of Burns, Cowper, Wordsworth, Coleridge, Keats, Crabbe, and about twenty of Cooke's poets. Most of them were presentation volumes, and their handsome bindings and gilded letters made a brave show in that poor cottage, which "except in cleanliness" was "no whit superior to the habitations of the poorest of the peasantry."

Then Taylor and Clare walked together as far as Barnack, pausing on the way before several of the scenes described in the *Village Minstrel*. They parted at the top of Barnack Hill, Clare proceeding thence to Casterton and Taylor to Wansford to await the London coach.

Early in November, Taylor sent news of some of the *Londoners*—Cary, Reynolds, and Allan Cunningham. Cunningham was one of Taylor's closest friends at this time, but Clare had not yet met him. Following the custom of Murray, Blackwood, and other publishers of the day, Taylor had already instituted those famous dinner-parties at which the contributors of the *London Magazine* talked and jested together. Richard Woodhouse, in his "Notes of Conversations with Thomas De Quincey," mentions dinners at Taylor's and De Wint's in November and December, attended by De Quincey, Reynolds, Lamb, Cunningham, Rice, Hood, Wainewright, Talfourd, Dr. Darling, and others. On the 8th of December, Taylor read to his visitors part of a letter from Clare, to whom he had sent Wordworth's poems. "I like Wordsworth better than Crabbe," wrote Clare. "I can read the one a second time over with added pleasure, but I am disgusted with the other after it has been once read. Still Wordsworth's nursery ballads inspire me with an uncontrollable itch of parodying them; I did ease myself by burlesquing one, which you shall have in my next." De Quincey wondered at the comparison between Wordsworth

and Crabbe, who had nothing in common; Crabbe was
no poet at all, and Wordsworth's apparent simplicity was
subtle, deep insight. Clare referred to his itch for parody
in a later letter:

"Do you mistake my imitation of W. W. as a serious
attempt in his manner? 'Twas written in ridicule of his
affectations of simplicity, and I had thoughts of imitating
the styles of all the living poets as I got hold of them to
read them, nor has the thought left me yet. Southey and
Crabbe I fancy I can do to a tittle; the one's affectation
in mouthing over big words and the other's tedious prosing
about trifles often border on the ridiculous, though they are
both great men and geniuses I venerate and esteem."

Toward the end of the year Clare found himself in
straitened circumstances, and asked Taylor if he could
advance his dividend money. After some delay, Taylor
sent the £10 on the 17th of December, and promised Earl
Spencer's £5 and 6 guineas for the magazine poems in a few
days. The former arrived on the 30th of January, the latter
not at all. The comparative failure of the *Village Minstrel*
was now apparent enough; the news merely stirred Clare
to renewed activity; he was "determined in the teeth of vexation to surmount disappointment by unwearied struggles."
"I am all madness for writing," he wrote in January, "but
how long it's to last I don't know." He was then busy with
a love-tale in the measure of Spenser, a novel of village life,
a dramatic pastoral, and several long poems for the *Magazine*.

Clare continued to feel the need for congenial company
as a relief from his writing and his solitary rambles. He
sometimes went over to Stamford, where the Gilchrists
were always glad to see him. He also visited the Simpson
family, Mrs. Gilchrist's relatives, and became very friendly
with her nephews, Frank and Octavius Simpson, both
young art students at this time. Clare did not go to Drury's as
often as formerly. In January he spent three pleasant days
with Artis at Milton, inspecting the remains of a Roman bath
and pavement which he had recently unearthed. These
visits relieved somewhat, but could not entirely compensate

for, the lack of congenial society at Helpston; Clare's isolation had become much more marked since his success. "I live here among the ignorant like a lost man; in fact, like one whom the rest seems careless of having anything to do with. They hardly dare talk in my company for fear I should mention them in my writings, and I find more pleasure in wandering the field than in mixing among my silent neighbours, who are insensible to everything but toiling and talking of it and that to no purpose." We hear of one occasion on which he had evidently tried to break down the barriers between himself and his neighbours, with not very happy results. Mrs. Emmerson wrote: "You tell me by an act of inebriety you have made yourself 'ridiculous and have been suffering for it this week past.' Why suffer the goodness of your heart to mislead your understanding by taking you into society no longer suited to your situation and pursuits in life? Why not, (if they were your once fellow-labourers), give them a trifle to enjoy themselves in their own way—they would feel equally grateful to you for it." Clare had certainly realised by this time that an overdose of John Barleycorn was a poor remedy for an overdose of solitude. The rare occasions upon which he sought this remedy were followed by fits of remorse, which, like Bunyan's, were out of all proportion to the gravity of the offence. There is a glimpse of the effect of such a mood on Clare's imagination in the poem "The Dream," written for the February *London* and included later in the *Shepherd's Calendar*. It gives a vivid picture of the world dissolving into chaos amid the fury of the elements, and of the poet's terror as hell yawned for his damned soul.

Clare's extraordinary literary activity during December and January was partly inspired by his desire to raise some money to help his old acquaintances, the jovial brothers Billings, who had fallen on evil times. They had had to mortgage their property, the "Bachelors' Hall" with its seven-acre farm, to a Jew, and they could not pay the interest. Clare wanted to take over the mortgage and set up a "Poet's Hall." He could not use his Fund money for

MJ

the purpose, so he proposed to sell his interest in his poems for five years for £200. Taylor refused the offer, and wisely pointed out the risky nature of the proposed transaction, which could benefit Clare little at the best. Clare's disappointment was eased when Lord Milton came to the rescue and lent £20 to pay off the interest.

The urgent need of his old friends and the excitement of a creative mood had tempted Clare to overwork himself. With the passing of the mood he suffered from the inevitable reaction. "I must do no more terrible things yet," he wrote in February, referring to "The Dream"; "they stir me up to such a pitch that leaves a disrelish for my old accustomed wanderings after nature . . . the Muse is a fickle Hussy with me; she sometimes stilts me up to madness and then leaves me as a beggar by the wayside with no more life than what's mortal and that nearly extinguished by melancholy forebodings." This mood persisted throughout February and March, and his dissatisfaction at his idleness did not improve it. On the 16th of March he wrote of the "confounded lethargy of low spirits that presses on me to such a degree that at times makes me feel as if my senses had a mind to leave me. Spring and Fall such feelings it seems are doomed to be my companions, but it shall not overpower me as formerly with such weak and terrible dread and fears of dropping off. When death comes he will come, and while life's mine I'll make the best of it."

Clare realised that he needed a change of scene and company as well as a rest; he wished that London were nearer. In April Mrs. Emmerson wrote entreating him to pay them a visit; she had recently moved to a house in Stratford Place, and he should have "the most elevated spot in the house"—his "sky-chamber," as they later called it. Clare was only too eager to accept, and, when Hessey also wrote assuring him that they would be glad to see him, and enclosing £5 for his expenses, the last difficulty was removed, and in May Clare set out on his second visit to London.

X

THE WITS
1822–1824

Streets, streets, streets, markets, theatres, churches, Covent Gardens, shops sparkling with pretty faces of industrious milliners, neat sempstresses, ladies cheapening, gentlemen behind counters lying, authors in the street with spectacles . . . lamps lit at night, pastry-cooks' and silver-smiths' shops . . . noise of coaches, drowsy cry of mechanic watchmen at night, with bucks reeling home drunk; if you happen to wake at midnight, cries of Fire and Stop thief; inns of court, with their learned air, and halls, and butteries, just like Cambridge colleges; old book-stalls, Jeremy Taylors, Burtons on Melancholy, and Religio Medicis on every stall. These are thy pleasures, O London with-the-many-sins.

CHARLES LAMB, Letter to Manning.

CLARE arrived in London toward the end of the third week in May. He travelled up alone, for Gilchrist had been ill for some time and could not accompany him. Clare's first visit had been too brief to give him assurance in the whirl of the metropolis and allay his country suspicions; on arriving in London, he is said to have denied himself to the messenger sent by Taylor to conduct him to Fleet Street. Here he remained for the first few days, and became more familiar with his surroundings.

"On my second visit, things became more distinct or separate on the memory and one of my greatest wonders then was the continual stream of life passing up and down the principal streets all the day long and even the night. One of my most entertaining amusements was to sit by Taylor's window in Fleet Street to see the constant successions throng this way and that way."

Further acquaintance with the methods of London tradesmen did not allay his suspicions of them, but he evolved a plan to counter their wiles.

"I observed it was always a custom in most shops that when you went in to ask for an article the thing they first shewed you was always put on one side and another recommended as superior; which I found was always to the contrary. So experience taught me always in future to take the one thing they did not recommend."

Clare did not forget to send home presents for the family, including some dress material for Patty and Sophy, "two very difficult creatures on that point, as I have before experienced." "Remember to take care of the Doves," he added in his letter. When Gilchrist was well enough to join him in London, they went visiting together.

" He took me to see Gifford, who the first time we went up was too ill to see us, but this time he was rather getting near neighbour to health and gave me welcome with a hearty shake of the hand and congratulated me on my last poems, ... which he said were far better than my first. He also bade me beware of the booksellers and repeated it several times. He was sitting on his sofa, surrounded with books and papers of all sorts. He chatted awhile to Gilchrist about books and Authors and Pope, and lent him a New Satire to read, called *The Mohawks*, in which he said he was mentioned. He supposed Lady Morgan was the Author, and after Gilchrist had dipped into it here and there he pronounced it worthless. The next day we went to call on Murray in Albemarle Street, who flattered me with some compliments on my success and hoped that I would always call on him whenever I came to London. He is a very pleasant man. He showed us the *English Bards and Scotch Reviewers*, illustrated with Portraits, which we turned over, and departed. As we got at the door, Gifford's carriage drove up, and on leaving the shop he gave each of us a copy of his *Translations of Persius*."

Gifford's warning about booksellers was no doubt directed against Taylor in particular; there was no love lost between the editor of the *Quarterly* and the publisher of Keats's poems.
When Clare had been at Fleet Street a few days, he heard from Mrs. Emmerson, who begged him to go and stay with

her, adding that Rippingille was there. Edward Villiers
Rippingille was a native of King's Lynn, the son of a farmer,
and a self-taught artist. His pictures of rural and domestic
life, "Scene in a Gaming House," "Country Post Office,"
"Going to the Fair," "The Recruiting Party," brought him
some renown as a reward for his early struggles. Mrs. Emmerson had met him in Bristol, where he resided at this time,
and he had visited her in 1821. She could not persuade him
at first that Clare's poetry was as worthy of admiration as
that of Burns. Then he had been won over, and sought all
over London for a book to send to Clare, the *Remains of Nithsdale and Galloway Song*, for which Allan Cunningham had been
partly responsible. Clare had, in fact, seen some of Rippingille's pictures years before. In his account of his visit to
Wisbech, he tells how he found a shop-window full of the
pictures of a painter who was then teaching drawing in that
town. "I little thought when I was looking at these things
that I should be a poet and become a familiar acquaintance
with that painter who had blinded the windows with his
attempts for fame."

Clare and Rippingille soon struck up a friendship, and on
this, as on the next visit to London, they spent some time in
each other's company, exploring the lighter side of London
life. They visited playhouses, inns, and boxing-booths, as
well as the picture galleries and houses of Rippingille's fellow-
artists. Clare liked the man for his lively and generous temperament, was amused by his affectations as the artist and
man-about-town, and admired his paintings.

"He is a rattling sort of odd fellow, with a desire to be
thought one, and often affects to be so for the sake of sin-
gularity. He is a man of great genius as a painter, (I understand a man of great faults as a colourist,) and what is better,
he has not been puffed into notice like the thousands of
farthing rush lights (like myself perhaps) in all professions,
that have glimmered their day and are dead. I spent many
pleasant hours with him while in London. He is a pleasant
fellow over the bottle and a strong dealer in puns. What a
many jokes have we cracked together and what a many of

life's farces have we acted over together in London ! We
once spent a whole night at Offley's, the Burton Ale house,
and sat till morning. He has some pretensions to rhyme and
wrote an 'Address to Echo' which was inserted in the *London
Mag.*[1] Most of his Trifles in that way are satirical. I was to
have gone over to Bristol to see him but illness prevented me.
He affected to be little ta'en with worldly applause and was
always fishing for it. He was very careless of money and
squandered it away as a thing of no other use but to spend."

Clare several times couples Rippingille's name with
De Wint's in his esteem of their painting, praising the
"grouping of peasantry" of the one and the landscape of the
other for their realism. "Nobody has such a true English
conception of real pastoral life and reality of English manners
and English beauty as Rippingille, and the poesy of painting
is breathing in every story he shadows on the canvass."

They corresponded for some years; Rippingille's lively,
fly-away letters are typical of the man. He lectured and wrote
on art in later years, started the *Artists' and Amateurs' Magazine*
in 1843, and became a champion of orthodoxy against
Pre-Raphaelitism and the author of *Modern Painters*.

When Clare could not find a conductor, his excursions
were necessarily more limited.

"I did not know the way to any place for a long time but
the Royal Academy, and here I used to go almost every day,
as Rippingille the painter had told the ticket keeper who I
was and he let me come in whenever I liked; which I often
made use of from necessity, although I had conquered the
old notion of kidnappers or mensteuers being common."

But the most memorable events of his stay in London were
his meetings with "those former wonders of Poets, Painters,
and Authors of all denominations," many of whom were
contributors to the *London Magazine*. The early months of
1822 marked the zenith of the *Magazine* under Taylor's
editorship. Foremost among the regular contributors were
Lamb, Hazlitt, Cary, Allan Cunningham, Thomas Hood,
Hartley Coleridge, C. A. Elton, and Clare himself. There

were also occasional poems or essays by J. H. Reynolds, B. W. Procter, T. N. Talfourd, James Montgomery, and John Taylor. Of the more famous names we miss only De Quincey's; his first contribution for the year was in December.

Most of these contributors attended the monthly dinners given by the firm at Waterloo Place, where, as Barry Cornwall has chronicled, "all the fences and restraints of authorship were cast off, and the natural human being was disclosed." Clare, of course, was one of the guests when he was in London, and he met some of his fellow-contributors on other occasions. He visited Hilton and Lamb, dined at Wainewright's, and spent two days with Cary at Chiswick; there were doubtless other visits which have not been recorded. After his third visit in 1824, Clare jotted down his impressions of the *Londoners* he had met, and these jottings, rough and fragmentary as they are, give vivid and intimate pictures of some of that band of brilliant writers who talked and jested together round the dining-table at Waterloo Place.

"One of my greatest amusements while in London was reading the booksellers' windows—I was always fond of this from a boy—and my next greatest amusement was the curiosity of seeing literary men. Of these . . . I shall give a few pictures just as they struck me at the time. Some of them I went purposely to see, others I met in literary parties, that is, the confused contributors' dinners at Taylor and Hessey's. I had no means of meeting the constellations of Genius in one mass. They were mingled parties. Some few were fixed stars in the world's hemisphere, others glimmered every month in the *Magazine*. Some were little vapours that were content to shine by the light of others—I mean dabbling critics who cut monthly morsels from genius, whose works are on the waters, free for all to catch at that choose. These, by the by, I could observe had a self-satisfaction about them that magnified molehills to mountains: I mean that little self was in its own eye a giant and that every other object was mere nothing. I shall not mention names here, but it is evident I do not allude to friends."

This introduction is followed by a description of J. H. Reynolds, who, despite his prudent but oft-regretted "Farewell to the Muses" in 1818, continued to express his versatile genius in verse and prose. Clare's richly detailed picture may be compared with those of other observers. Barry Cornwall recorded that his "good temper and vivacity were like condiments at the feast," and Keats's friend Woodhouse wrote, "Reynolds when in fine cue, and amongst friends, is equally ready and lavish in his wit, sporting it extempore on every subject and with astonishing good humour and freedom from acrimony and personality."

"Reynolds was always the soul of these dinner parties at Taylor and Hessey's. He was the most good-natured fellow I ever met with. His face was the three-in-one of fun, wit and punning personified. He would punch you with his puns very keenly without ever hurting your feelings, for if you looked in his face you could not be offended: and you might retort as you pleased—nothing could put him out of humour either with himself or others. If all his jokes and puns and witticisms were written down which were uttered at two or three of these dinner parties, they would make one of the best 'Joe Millers' that have ever passed under that title. He sits as a careless listener at table, looking on with quick knapping sort of eye, that turns towards you as quick as lightning when he has a pun, joke or story to give you. They are never made-up or studied; they are the flashes of the moment and mostly happy. He is a slim sort of make, something (as you may conceive) of an unpretending sort of fashionable fellow without the desire of being one. He has a plump, round face, a nose something puggish, and a forehead that betrays more of fun than poetry. His teeth are always looking through a laugh that sits as easy on his unpuckered lips as if he were born laughing. He is a man of genius, and if his talents were properly applied I believe he would do something. I verily believe that he might win the favours of fame with a pun— but be as it will, whether she is inclined to smile or frown upon him, he is quite at home with content: the present is all with him. He carries none of the Author about him. A hearty laugh (which there is no resisting, at his jokes and puns) seems to be more recompense than he expected, and he seems startled into wonder at it, and muses a moment as if he turned the joke over again in his mind to find the 'merry thought' which made the laughter. They drop as it were spontaneously from his mouth, and turn again upon him before he has had time to consider whether they are good or bad. He sits in a sort of surprise till another joke drops and makes him himself again. . . . He is one of the best fellows living, and ought to be a poet of the first order—himself is his only hindrance at present."

Reynolds's impression of Clare was written with a sonnet in a copy of the *Rural Muse*, which he gave to a niece in 1843:

"I knew Clare well, and from the first hour of his escape from oppression, poverty and ignorance (except through the inspiration and observation of nature) he was a quiet and worthy yet enthusiastic man; . . . a guileless yet suspicious man; . . . a true observer of nature in her generous earth-work and water-work, but a man alive to more . . . than town apprehensions . . ."

Clare also had his place in that pleasant quip of Reynolds's, "The Literary Police Office, Bow Street," which appeared as an "Edward Herbert" letter in the *London* for February, 1823. Notable writers of the day were described as appearing before the magistrates, charged with various extravagant offences:

"John Clare (a comely country-looking man, in a smock frock, and a face to match) appeared to resist an order of filiation, made on the affidavit of one of the Muses with whom he had kept company, and who appeared to have been too liberal of her favours to him. The oath being persisted in, his innocence stood him in no stead; and he was ordered to set apart half-a-crown, out of sixpence a day, to support the child. He pleaded poverty; but the magistrates explained to him that a poor soldier had been known to have managed such an allowance, and therefore they resisted his plea. Clare is said to have a wife, and ten little children all under the age of four years, which makes his case more repre-hensible."

Clare's friend, Gilchrist, was also in court and " gave information of having been shot at while playing a game at Bowles, in his garden at Stamford.''

Struck by the contrast between the two men, Clare followed his account of Reynolds with a sketch of Hazlitt, who must have attended one of the dinners during Clare's visit. He was in London for a week toward the end of May, correcting the second volume of *Table Talk* for the press; his habitual shyness and his silence at the dinners, noted by Barry Cornwall, may well have been accentuated by the distressing experiences he was passing through at this period.

"Hazlitt is the very reverse of this. He sits a silent picture of severity. If you were to watch his face for a month you would not catch a smile there. His eyes are always turned towards the ground except when one is turned up now and then with a sneer that cuts a bad pun or a young author's maiden table-talk to atoms, wherever it is directed. I look upon it that it carries the conviction with it of a look to the wise and a nod to the foolish. He seems full of the author too, and I verily believe that his pockets are crammed with it. He seems to look upon Mr. This or Mr. T'other—names that are only living on Cards of Morning Calls and Dinner Invitations, as upon empty chairs; as the guests in 'Macbeth' did on the vacancy where Banquo's ghost presided. They appear in his eye as nothings, too thin for sight; and when he enters a room he comes stooping, with his eyes in his hand as it were, throwing under-gazes round at every corner as if he smelt a dun or thief ready to seize him by the collar and demand his money or his life. He is a middle-sized, dark-looking man, and his face is deeply lined with a satirical character. His eyes are bright, but they are rather buried under his brows. He is a walking satire, and you would wonder where his poetry came from, that is scattered so thickly over his writings. For the blood of me I could not find him out: that is, I should have had no guess at him, of his ever being a scribbler, much more a genius. They say she is an odd lady, and sure enough in him her oddities are strongly personified.''

Leaving this enigma of Hazlitt, Clare passed, by way of another contrast, to a *Londoner* with whom he felt much more at ease. 1822 was a busy year for Charles Lamb; it was the last of the three years which produced such a remarkable harvest of essays. Lamb was beginning to tire and to think seriously of leaving the India House, yet the essays continued to grace the pages of the *London*. At the time of Clare's visit, Charles and Mary were on the eve of their journey to France, which Lamb mentions in his charming letter to Clare. They saw each other several times during the month; meetings at Taylor's, Wainewright's, Cary's, and Lamb's are recorded. [2]

"Then there is Charles Lamb, a long remove from his friend Hazlitt in ways and manners. He is very fond of snuff, which seems to sharpen up his wit every time he dips his plentiful fingers into his large bronze-coloured box, and then he sharpens up his head, throws himself backwards on his chair, and stammers at a joke or pun with an inward sort of utterance ere he can give it speech, till his tongue becomes a sort of packman's [3] strop turning it over and over till at last it cames out whetted as keen as a razor: and expectation, when she knows him, wakens into a sort of danger as bad as cutting your throat. But he is a good sort of fellow, and if he offends it is innocently done. Who is not acquainted with Elia, and who would believe him otherwise? As soon as the cloth is drawn, the wine and he become comfortable: his talk now doubles and trebles into a combination, a repetition, urging the same thing over and over again, till at last he leaves off with scarcely a 'goodnight' in his mouth, and disappears, leaving his memory like a pleasant ghost hanging about his vacant chair. And there is his sister Bridget, a good sort of woman, though her kind cautions and tender admonitions are nearly lost upon Charles, who, like an undermined river bank, leans carelessly over his jollity, and receives the gentle lappings of the waves of woman's tongue unheedingly till it ebbs; and then in the same careless posture sits and receives it again. Though it is all lost upon Charles she is a good woman and her cautions are very commendable: for the New River runs very near his house, and the path for a dark night is but very precarious, to make the best of it; and he, hearty fellow, is not always blind to dangers; so I hope the advice of his sister

Bridget will be often taken in time to retire with the cloth
and see home by daylight."

It is clear from Clare's last remarks that he had his third
visit to London in mind: the Lambs did not move from
Great Russell Street to Colebrooke Cottage until 1823.
Lamb and Clare certainly enjoyed each other's company;
Thomas Hood has left a lively picture of them hobnobbing
at a *Magazine* dinner:

"On the right hand of the Editor sits Elia, of the pleasant
smile, and the quick eyes—Procter said of them that 'they
looked as if they could pick up pins and needles,—and a wit
as quick as his eyes, and sure, as Hazlitt described, to stam-
mer out the best pun and the best remark in the course of
the evening. Next to him, shining verdantly out from the
grave-coloured suits of the literati, like a patch of turnips
amidst stubble and fallow, behold our Jack i' the Green—
John Clare! In his bright, grass-coloured coat, and yellow
waistcoat (there are greenish stalks too, under the table),
he looks a very Cowslip, and blooms amongst us as Goldsmith must have done in his peach-blossom. No wonder the
door-keeper of the Soho-bazaar, seeing that *very countrified*
suit, linked arm-in-arm with the Editorial sables, made
a boggle at admitting them into his repository, having seen,
perchance, such a made up Peasant 'playing at playing,'
at thimble-rig about the Square. No wonder the gentleman's
gentleman, in the drab coat and sealing-wax smalls, at
W—'s [Wainewright's] was for cutting off our Green Man,
who was modestly the last in ascending the stairs, as an
interloper, though he made amends afterwards by waiting
almost exclusively on the Peasant, perfectly convinced that
he was some eccentric Notable of the Corinthian order,
disguised in Rustic. Little wonder either, that in wending
homewards on the same occasion through the strand, the
Peasant and Elia, *Sylvanus et Urban*, linked comfortably
together; there arose the frequent cry of 'Look at Tom and
Jerry— there goes Tom and Jerry!' For truly, Clare in his
square-cut green coat, and Lamb in his black, were not a
little suggestive of Hawthorn and Logic in the plates to
'Life in London.'

"But to return to the table. Elia—much more of House

Lamb than of Grass Lamb—avowedly caring little or
nothing for Pastoral; cottons, nevertheless, very kindly to
the Northamptonshire Poet, and still more to his ale,
pledging him again and again as 'Clarissimus,'and 'Princely
Clare,' and sometimes so lustily, as to make the latter cast
an anxious glance into his tankard. By his bright happy
looks the Helpstone Visitor is inwardly contrasting the
unlettered country company of Clod, and Hodge and Podge,
with the delights of 'London' society Elia, and Barry, and
Herbert, and Mr. 'Table Talk,' *cum multis aliis*—i.e. a multiplicity of all.

"But besides the tankard, the two 'drouthie neebors'
discuss Poetry in general and Montgomery's 'Common
Lot' in particular, Lamb insisting on the beauty of the
tangental sharp turn at 'O! She was fair!' thinking, mayhap,
of his own Alice W——, and Clare swearing 'Dal!' (a
clarified damn) 'Dal! if it isn't like a Dead Man preaching
out of his coffin!' Anon the Humourist begins to banter the
Peasant on certain 'Clare-obscurities' in his own verses,
originating in a contempt for the rules of Priscian, whereupon
the accused, thinking with Burns,

> *What ser'es their grammars?*
> *They'd better ta'en up spades and shools,*
> *Or knappin hammers,*

vehemently denounces all Philology as nothing but a sort
of man-trap for authors, and heartily 'dals' Lindley Murray
for 'inventing it.'

"It must have been at such a time when Hilton *conceived*
his clever portrait of C——, when he was 'C in alt.' He was
hardy, rough, and clumsy enough to look truly rustic—
like an Ingram's rustic chair. There was a slightness about
his frame, with a delicacy of features and complexion, that
associated him more with the Garden than the Field, and
made him look the Peasant of a Ferme Ornée. In this respect
he was as much beneath the genuine stalwart bronzed
Plough-poet, Burns, as above the Farmer's Boy, whom I
remember to have seen in my childhood. . . . There was
much about Clare for a Quaker to like; he was tender-
hearted and averse to violence. How he recoiled once,
bodily taking his chair with him—from a young surgeon,
or surgeon's friend, who let drop, somewhat abruptly, that

he was just come 'from seeing a child skinned!'—Clare, from his look of horror, evidently thought that the poor infant, like Marsyas, had been flayed *alive*! He was both gentle and simple . . ."

Lamb's interest in Clare's poetry went beyond these dinner-table banterings; Clare sent him copies of his two books, which Lamb acknowledged in the following letter:

"INDIA HOUSE, 31 *Aug.* 1822.

"DEAR CLARE,—I thank you heartily for your present. I am an inveterate old Londoner, but while I am among your choice collections, I seem to be native to them, and free of the country. The quantity of your observation has astonished me. What have most pleased me have been Recollections after a Ramble, and those Grongar Hill kind of pieces in eight syllable lines, my favourite measure, such as Cowper Hill and Solitude. In some of your story telling Ballads the provincial phrases sometimes startle me. I think you are too profuse with them. In poetry *slang* of every kind is to be avoided. There is a rustick Cockneyism, as little pleasing as ours of London. Transplant Arcadia to Helpstone. The true rustic style, the Arcadian English, I think is to be found in Shenstone. Would his Schoolmistress, the prettiest of poems, have been better, if he had used quite the Goody's own language? Now and then a home rusticism is fresh & startling, but where nothing is gained in expression, it is out of tenor. It may make folks smile and stare, but the ungenial coalition of barbarous with refined phrases will prevent you in the end from being so generally tasted as you deserve to be. Excuse my freedom, and take the same liberty with my *puns*.

" I send you two little volumes of my spare hours. They are of all sorts, there is a methodist hymn for Sundays, and a farce for Saturday night. Pray give them a place on your shelf. Pray accept a little volume, of which I have duplicate, that I may return in equal number to your welcome presents—

"I think I am indebted to you for a sonnet in the London for August.

"Since I saw you I have been in France, and have eaten frogs. The nicest little rabbity things you ever tasted. Do look about for them. Make Mrs. Clare pick off the hind

quarters, boil them plain, with parsly and butter. The fore-
quarters are not so good. She may let them hop off by themselves. Yours sincerely, CHAS. LAMB."

Criticism of the provincialisms in the *Village Minstrel* had
been expressed by others, but by none so sensitively and
wisely. It is true that Clare had a wider aim than the trans-
planting of Arcadia to Helpston, but the advice to use native
words only when they added force to the line was essentially
sound, and Clare took it. His later books needed no glossary,
and his use of dialect became more sparing and forceful.

The two little volumes mentioned by Lamb were those of
the 1818 edition of his *Works*, and bore the inscription, "For
Mr. Clare, with C. Lamb's kindest remembrances." The
third volume was *Tracts by Sir Thomas Browne, Knight, M.D.*,
an edition of 1822 containing "Hydriotaphia," "that obscure
but gorgeous prose composition." The *Essays*, published in
1823 by Taylor and Hessey, Clare received "with Elia's regards" probably on his third visit, but he was already familiar
with them in the pages of the *London*. "Lamb's best poetry
is in Elia," wrote Clare in his journal; the sonnet mentioned
in Lamb's letter expands this thought and gives the measure
of Clare's appreciation. It is a fine tribute to the author of
"New Year's Eve," "Witches and Other Night Fears,"
"Mackery End," and "Dream Children," from one who
wrote so often in verse and prose of the poetry of childhood.

> *Elia, thy reveries and visioned themes*
> *To Care's lorn heart a luscious pleasure proves,*
> *Wild as the mystery of delightful dreams,*
> *Soft as the anguish of remembered loves;*
> *Like records of past days their memory dances*
> *'Mid the cool feelings manhood's reason brings,*
> *As the unearthly visions of romances*
> *Peopled with sweet and uncreated things,*
> *And yet thy themes thy gentle worth enhances;*
> *Then wake again thy wild harp's tenderest strings,*
> *Sing on, sweet bard, let fairy loves again*
> *Smile in thy dreams with angel extasies;*
> *Bright o'er our minds will break the witching strain*
> *Through the dull gloom of earth's realities.*

"Dream Children" had appeared in the January *London Magazine*, and Clare's Mary Joyce was as surely lost to him as Lamb's Alice W——n. In the "records of past days" and "anguish of remembered loves," the inner lives of these two men touched most closely. But there was another point of contact which was also the subject of a sonnet by Clare. First printed in *Hone's Year Book*, November 18th, 1831, and revised for the *Rural Muse*, it praises Lamb for his devotion to "our old by-gone bards with their warm homely phrase." Lamb's devotion to the "Elizabethan poets of glorious memory" needs no comment; Clare's, and the strange form it took, will claim our attention later.

Next to Lamb in Clare's portrait gallery appears H. F. Cary, whose life, like Clare's, was to be overshadowed, as Lamb's had already been, by the dark clouds of mental disease. Renewing their former acquaintance, Clare saw a good deal of the shy clergyman during this visit. Lamb's "model of a country Parson, lean (as a curate ought to be), modest, sensible," Procter's "mildest and most amiable of men," Hood's "mild and modest Cary," was yet as ready as the rest for the riotous jesting of the *Magazine* dinners. Besides meeting at their publishers', Clare and Cary were both present at Wainewright's dinner on the 27th of May; then Clare spent two days with Cary at Chiswick. On one of these occasions occurred an incident referred to by Thomas Bennion, Taylor's porter, in a letter to Clare after his return home. Bennion had met Mrs. Emmerson:

"she commenced her conversation in the usall Theatrical Manner respecting you, first by enquiring if you had not disgraced yourself very much the night you dine with the contributors of the London Mag and if you had not given great offence to the Revd. Mr. C—— by saying you wished the churches were all in ashes and the parson's sent to beg their bread, i told her i did not hear you say it, and if you did some excuse was to be made for you as you might be a little fresh, i told her that Mr. C—— was on very good terms with you so i was sure that he was not offended she said she heard you was very D—— i told her it was not so you was

very merry. She said she had heard all this from a friend that
you had told, and that she was very sorry to think you was
so strong a deist i told her you was but a little way inclined
to deisem I found out who this friend was before I left her
its Mr. R—— you'll know who i mean so you'll be on your
guard if you write to him of what you say as it's sure to go
to her. . . ."

Rippingille might have taken lessons in discretion from
the diplomatic Bennion. But Cary was not the man to take
offence at an outspoken opinion, whether it was inspired by
ale or not. According to the *Memoir of H. F. Cary*, written
by his son, a contributors' dinner was held at Chiswick;
Lamb, Clare, and James Kenney the farce-writer, were
among those present, and the writer comments on the
"strange mixture of learning, wit, and puns, bad and good."
Clare, the most interesting of the party to a looker-on, was
dressed in a labourer's holiday suit, and divided his attention
between his host and "a jug of prime ale, imported for the
especial use of Clare."

According to Mr. King, Cary's biographer, Clare's description "is the best verbal likeness extant, and is fully
confirmed by the existing portraits."

"And there sits Cary, the translator of Dante, one of the
most quiet, amiable and unassuming of men. He will look
round the table in a peaceful silence on all the merry faces,
in all the vacant unconcernment imaginable, and then he
will brighten up and look smilingly on you and me and our
next-hand neighbour, as if he knew not which to address
first—and then perhaps he drops a few words like a chorus
that serve all together. His eyes are not long on a face. He
looks you into a sort of expectation of discoursing and starts
your tongue on tiptoe to be ready in answering what he
may have to start upon, when suddenly he turns from you to
throw the same good-natured cheat of a look on others. He
is a tallish, spare man, with a longish face and a good forehead; his eyes are the heavy-lidded sort whose earnest look
seems to meet you half closed. His authorship and his priest-
hood sit upon him very meekly. He is one of those men
NJ

which have my best opinions and of whom I feel happy with every opportunity to praise. On my second visit to London I spent 2 very happy days with him at Chiswick (I was then in good health). His wife is a good sort of person and of so young a look in his company that I mistook her a long while for his daughter. He lives [in] the house once occupied by Thornhill the painter, and he showed me the window through which Miss Thornhill eloped with Hogarth and over the chimney piece were some heads sketched on the wall by Hogarth; but the servants, being left to themselves to whitewash the room in Mr. Cary's absence from home, utterly defaced this precious relic and he greatly regretted the loss when he told me. . . ."

They went to Richmond to visit the grave of James Thomson, poet of the *Seasons*. After Clare's return home, they began a correspondence which was kept up for some ten years. In his first letter Clare wrote, "The two days spent at Chiswick have left pleasant remembrances behind them of friendship and hospitality." Cary also recalled the visit in a later letter: "I often think of you in that walk we took here together, and which I take almost every day, generally alone, sometimes musing of absent friends and at others putting into English Prose old French verses. . . ."

Allan Cunningham, who had written most of the supposed old Scottish ballads in the *Remains of Nithsdale and Galloway Song* which Rippingille had sent Clare, and whose *Traditional Tales of the English and Scottish Peasantry* was published in 1822 by Taylor and Hessey, had transferred his allegiance from *Blackwood's* to the *London*. Hood calls him "the grenadier of our corps," De Quincey speaks of his "dark flashing guerilla eye," Procter notes that he is "very Scotch in aspect, but ready to do a good turn to any one," and to Lamb he is "the large-hearted Scot." Clare's sketch hints at some imperfect sympathies between Cunningham and the rest, for a hater of puns must often have had occasion to keep his head down at the *Magazine* dinners.

"Then there is Allan Cunningham (Reynolds calls him the Dwarf), comes stalking in like one of [his own] black knights: but his countenance is open and his look is hearty. He hates puns and is fond of Scotch Ballads, Scotch Poets and everything Scottish, down – no doubt – as far as Scotch snuff. Well, he is a good fellow, and a good poet: and when the company's talk is of poetry, he is ready to talk two ways at once, but when puns are up, his head is down over his glass, musing and silent – and nothing but poetry is the game to start him into hilarity again."

On the 24th of May, T. G. Wainewright wrote to H. F. Cary, inviting him to dinner on the 27th.

"On this next Monday several friends have agreed to eat their dinner with me, at half-past six *precisely*. Their names are Chas. Lamb, Taylor and Hessey, Cunningham, Clare and the Ode to Dr. Kitchener [Thomas Hood]."

The last-named writer has already given us a glimpse of this dinner-party; here is Clare's account of his host:

"Wainewright is a very comical sort of chap. He is about 27, and wears a quizzing-glass, and makes an excuse for the ornament by complaining of bad eyes. He is the Van Vinkbooms, Janus Weathercock, etc., of the Magazine. He had a picture in the exhibition of 'Paris in the Chamber of Helen,' and the last time I was in London he had one there of 'The Milkmaid' from Walton's Angler – both in my opinion very middling performances, but my opinion is but of itself a middling one in such matters, so I may be mistaken. He is a clever writer and some of his papers in the Magazine are very entertaining, and some very good, particularly the beginnings of one, a description of a Churchyard." [4]

We may gladly forget the "prince of poisoners" and recall with Clare the friend of Lamb and Cary, writer of the lively and often discerning, if extravagant, articles in the *London*, one of the few who then recognised Blake's genius and bought his books, Lamb's "light, and warm-as-light hearted, Janus." He and Clare were more familiar with Cary than were the other *Londoners* in 1822. Writing in the *Magazine* for June, 1820, Wainewright thanks him who "introduced us to the Sylvan Muse of John Clare." In December, 1821, he praised Hilton's "natural and characteristic" portrait.

In January, 1823, appeared "Janus Weatherbound, or the Weathercock Steadfast for Lack of Oil," an article in which he took his leave of the *London* with entertaining addresses to the contributors, particularly Lamb, Cary, and Clare.

"And first, then, for JOHN CLARE; for *first* doth he stand in the sixth volume. 'Princely Clare,' as Elia would call thee, some three hours after the cloth was drawn – Alas! good Clare, never again shall thou and he engage in those high combats, those wit-fights ! Never shall his companionable draught cause thee an after-look of anxiety into the tankard! – no more shall he, pleasantly-malicious, make thy ears tingle, and thy cheeks glow, with the sound of that per-plexing constrainment! that conventional gagging-bill! – that Grammar!! till in the bitterness of thy heart thou cursedst Lindley Murray by all the stars. – Not once again shall thy sweetly-simple Doric phrase and accent beget the odious *pun*. Thou mayest imbibe thy ale in peace, and defy Priscian unchecked, – Elia is gone! – Little didst thou think that evening would be the last, when thou and I, and two or three more, Messer Brunetto, Dugdale Redivivus, T—— that anthery Cicero, parted with the humanity-loving-Elia be-neath the chaste beams of the watery moon, warmed with his hearty cheer – the fragrant steam of his ' *great plant*,' – his savoury conversation, and the genuine good nature of his cousin Bridget gilding all. There was something solemn in the manner of our clasping palms, – it was first ' hands round,' then 'hands across.' – That same party shall never meet again! . . .

"One word at parting, John Clare ! and if a strange one, as a stranger give it welcome. I have known jovial nights – felt deeply the virtues of the grape and the barley-corn – I have co-operated in 'the sweet wicked catches,' 'bout the chimes at twelve, yet I say to thee – visit London seldom – shutting close thy ears in the abounding company of empty scoffers, – ever holding it in thy inmost soul, that love and perfect trust, not doubt, is the germ of *true* poetry. Thy hand, friend Clare! others may speak thee fairer, but none wish thee solider welfare than Janus."

Clare undoubtedly wrote down his impressions of Thomas Hood, assistant editor of the *London* from 1821, in which capacity, says Hessey, "he first amused himself by concocting humorous notices and answers to correspondents in the "Lion's Head." The success of these quips led to his collaboration with that other jester, Reynolds, whose sister, Jane, he married in 1824. Procter describes him as "almost silent" at the dinners, "except when he shot out some irresistible pun, and disturbed the gravity of the company." As the vivid pen-pictures in his *Literary Reminiscences* bear witness, he made good use of his silences. Clare also has his niche in the "Ode to W. Kitchener, M.D.," author of the Cook's Oracle:

> *Then came John Clare, the poet, nor forbore*
> *Thy* Patties. . . .

Unfortunately, all that survives of Clare's sketch of Hood is a line or two on a torn page. Clare, like posterity, seems to have appreciated the irresistible punster better than his graver companion, author of "Lycus the Centaur" ; in a letter to Hood he candidly confessed that he could not understand a word of that poem, a confession which, says Hessey, caused Hood much amusement.

In his memoir of Charles Lamb, B. W. Procter makes mention of Clare in connection with the *London* dinners:

"John Clare, a peasant from Northamptonshire, and a better poet than Bloomfield, was one of the visitors. He was thoroughly rustic; dressed in conspicuously country fashion, and was as simple as a daisy. His delight at the wonders of London formed the staple of his talk. This was often stimulated into extravagance by the facetious fictions of Reynolds. Poor fellow, he died insane."

He seems to be recalling a definite occasion, and it would be strange if Clare overlooked Barry Cornwall, "candid and affectionate as his own poetry," who, with *Marcian Colonna* in 1820 and *A Sicilian Story* in 1821, had become one of the popular poets of the day. However, no description of him has come to light, nor were any of his books in Clare's library.

It is probable that Clare did not meet De Quincey in 1822. His account of him gives no clue as to the date, but De Quincey's recollection of Clare in *London Reminiscences* clearly refers to 1824; as he did not contribute to the *Magazine* during the spring and summer of 1822, it is unlikely that he attended the dinners in May and June. We know that he was not very popular with his fellow-guests, and his re-appearance as a contributor helped to sever the connection of some of them with the *Magazine*.

The account of the *London Magazine* in 1822 would not be complete without some picture of John Taylor, its editor. References to him by the *Londoners* are few and scanty; many of them merely express disapproval of his policy. De Quincey, in his *London Reminiscences*, remembered the publishers as "both hospitable and friendly men," and noted that Taylor professed himself a religious dissenter and a blind admirer of Locke. Clare's sketch of Taylor is therefore most valuable. It was written some years after 1822, and the events of those years revealed traits in Taylor's character which were not apparent on the occasion of Clare's second visit.

"Taylor is a man of very pleasant address, and works himself into the good opinions of people in a moment; but it is not lasting, for he grows into a studied carelessness and neglect that he carries into a system, till the purpose for so doing becomes transparent and reflects its own picture while it would hide it. He is a very pleasant talker and is excessive fluent on paper currency and such politics. He can talk on matters with a superficial knowledge of them very dexterously, and is very fond of arguing about the Latin and Greek poets with the Reverends and the Cambridge [wits] that drop in to his Waterloo House. He assumes a feeling and fondness for poetry and reads it well—not in the fashionable growl of mouthing spouters but in a sort of whine. . . . His manner is that of a cautious fellow who shows his sunny side to strangers. . . .

"He never asks a direct question or gives a direct reply, but continually saps your information by a secret passage, coming at it as it were by working a mine – like a lawyer examining a witness; and he uses this sort of caution even in his common discourse till it becomes tedious to listen or reply. He sifts a theory of truth, either true or false, with much ingenuity and subtlety of argument, and his whole table talk is a sort of 'Junius Identified.' But his patience carries it to such lengths in seeming consistency till the first end of the ravelled skein which he winds up at the beginning is lost again and unwound in looking for the other. To sum up his character, he is a clever fellow and a man of genius and his 'Junius Identified' is the best argument on circumstantial evidence that ever was written."

In taking leave of the *London Magazine* in the brief heyday of its fame, we may quote from a letter written by Taylor to his father on the 19th of June. The glimpse of Clare taking his place as an equal among the *Londoners* is a valuable corrective to the oft-drawn picture of him as the simple country visitor, overawed by high company. The casual observer noted his rustic dress and manners, his naïve delight and wonder at the strange new world about him; but those who knew him better recognised, as Taylor had already done, that his intellectual qualities were no less remarkable than the keen observation and nervous sensibility which made him a poet. The letter also indicates Clare's attitude toward his publisher in 1822:

"I have just lost my visitor Clare . . . he was excellent company while he staid, but a little too much elated with a Glass of Ale if you indulged him in it – he saw all our literary Acquaintance, and kept his Ground with all of them. He could not pun, but then he had such a Fund of Good Sense & so many shrewd Remarks to make on whatever anyone said, – besides his Judgement of Books was so very sound, – that let what would be the Subject of Conversation he was always well worth listening to. – Gilchrist came to Town & carried him to Gifford's & to Murray's – he much likes Gifford, who was particularly friendly in his Conduct, & gave him the strongest encouragement, & much excellent advice – but Murray he set down as 'a mere craftsman.' I was not much afraid of his being spirited away from us, – if it could have been done Lord Radstock would have accomplished it. . . .

"I entertain no Resentment, because I have no need to feel anything but Pity for this weak-headed old gentleman –"

Events at Helpston led Clare to cut short his visit and return home hurriedly without seeing the Emmersons again. Bennion and he drowned their regrets at parting in a last drink together on Sunday night, June 16th, just before Clare left town. On his arrival at Helpston, he found that a daughter had been born on the 16th. She was called Eliza Louisa, after her godmother, Mrs. Emmerson, who sent a silver cup and other gifts and later paid for the child's schooling. Lord Radstock sent a gown for Patty, with regrets that he had not had Clare under his roof during the visit. It was but natural that Clare should find Helpston somewhat dull after the excitement and good company of London, but he consoled himself with his books and with letters to and from his friends.

Charles Lamb's letter of August 31st has already been quoted. On the 23rd Clare wrote to Cary, recalling the pleasant days spent at Chiswick. He sent a poem which he had written the day before, on going out again after an attack of fever which had been "raging from house to house in our fenny villages like a plague." He told how he looked forward to Cary's "Lives of the Poets" in the *London*, but thought that some of the other contributors were writing themselves out. In his reply of September 1st, Cary promised to give his opinion of Clare's poems, and recommended him to read Bacon's *Essays* rather than Knox's – Lord Radstock had sent Clare *Essays Moral and Literary*. "I was very glad to hear that your appetite for reading has come again, as I think you said, when I had the pleasure of your company here, that you had in great measure lost it. I have found a fondness for books one of the chief comforts through life."

Hessey wrote on the 30th of August about Clare's sonnets which they were inserting in the *London*. In the September and October numbers, six sonnets appeared, of which only one was signed, the publishers thinking it best not to let Clare's name appear too often. They give us glimpses of his

moods during this summer. He is frequenting his old
"secret nooks," musing there on distant friends, reading in
his favourite books, recalling his happy childhood and early
loves, finding new joys in contemplation of the simple
weeds:

> *Star-pointed thistle, with its ruddy flowers;*
> *Wind-waving rush, left to bewildered ways,*
> *Shunning the scene which culture's toil devours.*

These were the "old familiar faces" whose passing Clare
deplored more poignantly each year as Enclosure and fen-
drainage progressed.

In the same letter Hessey sent news that Woodhouse had
been very seriously ill and had gone to the sea. He suffered
from the same weakness as his friend Keats, and succumbed
to tuberculosis in 1834, at the age of forty-six. There was
also news of Hood and Cunningham, and an enthusiastic
note about Reynolds's long-delayed marriage to Miss
Drewe.

Mrs. Emmerson wrote in September with news of a "new
and delightful correspondent." This was Derwent Coleridge,
younger brother of Hartley, then studying at St. John's
College, Cambridge, and contributing to *Knight's Quarterly
Magazine* above the pen-name "Davenant Cecil." Mrs.
Emmerson became acquainted with him through his aunts,
Martha and Eliza Fricker, whom she had met in Bath. She
found Derwent an "amiable and kind creature – poet in all
his doings and sayings." He visited her several times in the
years before the young poet of promise was lost in the
schoolmaster and the divine; later he became the first
Principal of St. Mark's College, Chelsea.

Clare also heard from friends nearer home. Drury, now at
Lincoln, invited Clare to visit him. Gilchrist wrote in October; he was very ill, but cheerful as ever. December brought
a letter from Frank Simpson of Stamford; he had been en-
deavouring to get something inserted in the *London*, but with
no success; he was busy making sketches of Gothic crosses.

Clare evidently tried to help his friends at home by introducing them to his friends in London.

During this autumn it became more apparent than ever that Clare's publishers had too many irons in the fire, a policy which was to have serious consequences for Clare. Taylor's preoccupation with the *London* had already led to the delay in the appearance of the *Village Minstrel*. Clare was now given other causes for dissatisfaction with his publishers' conduct of his affairs. The first of these is trivial enough in itself, but it is of interest in view of the oft-repeated charge that Clare had no aptitude for business affairs. From 1820 onwards he kept a careful account of all money sent by Taylor and Hessey; but he was finding it difficult to do this to his satisfaction, because they did not always state the source of the money sent. He also noted once more that he had received nothing for his *Magazine* poems. With the new year he had a more irksome negligence to complain of – the delay in sending him his dividend, which was due on the 1st of January. Mrs. Emmerson thought it unpardonable, since they knew his limited means. On the 5th of February Hessey wrote: " The enclosed £10 note has been lying on my desk for you for some time."

On the 13th of January came a letter from Thomas Bennion, in which mention is made of a visit to Milton to see Henderson and Artis. "Was it a trial of strength between your old friend John Barleycorn and you?" asked Bennion. "i am sorry to hear you are so troubled with the blue devils i have only to say i wish it was in my power to relieve you of them and to send them to oblivion for ever as for myself i no nothing of this infernal tribe." Clare had dedicated to him a sonnet intended for the *London*; Bennion, whom Hood classed among the contributors because of his valiant struggles with the English language, records sadly that his own literary offspring died in infancy. "i can never satisfy myself with what i doo, so that i commit them to the fire in their young days."

Clare was writing poems for his next book, but Taylor had been too busy to deal with them, and he was now ill through overwork. "I am anxious to hear," Clare wrote to Hessey, "but you take no notice in the world about it. Men of business and poets are the worst correspondents that can come together. I am sorry Taylor is ill but I am very poorly myself. I have had a regular sickness every morning as soon as I got up for this three weeks." A second issue of the *Village Minstrel* was being prepared, and Clare wanted some copies to present to London friends, Cunningham, Reynolds, Hood, and Hilton. He asked for Cunningham's *Sir Marmaduke Maxwell* and a copy of the *Opium Eater*. "If you will give an opinion of my poetry you shall have 'The Parish,' but if you will not I am determined I will send no more for your criticism at present."

He was no doubt acting on Mrs. Emmerson's advice to withhold his manuscript until he obtained more satisfaction. She condoled with him on his "mental depressions," due to the silence and apathy of Taylor and Hessey, and mentioned the possibility of finding new publishers. Her counsels were usually for moderation and peace; evidently something was afoot to make her take this line. Clare's depression must have been so apparent in his letters that she felt something must be done. On the 14th of March, Lord Radstock came into action again with a flourish of trumpets.

"We have formed plans in our minds concerning you, but these, unless manfully and steadily pursued by yourself, can avail nothing. . . . You have long known my opinion of T——. The more I hear of him, the more am I convinced that that opinion was well founded – in a word that it is his determined resolution to keep you in *Bondage* and *obscurity* so long as he has the power of so doing – Now if these vile and ignominious chains be not speedily broken the fault will not be mine . . . therefore he shall learn, I trust, to his *cost* that I clearly see through all his . . . duplicity."

On the 31st of March, Hessey wrote that copies of the "second edition" of the *Village Minstrel* would follow in a few days. This "second edition" consisted of the second thousand copies of the first edition, which had not been bound; so there were no changes in the text, but a sketch of Clare's cottage by Cowen was engraved as a prefix to the second volume. Hessey eventually sent the promised books on the 6th of May, with apologies for the delay. "I know how tantalising it is to wait beyond the time when one has reason to expect a pleasant thing . . . but I have been pestered to death almost with such variety of matters that I have not been able to write before." Taylor was too busy with his editing to attend to anything else. Clare did not hear from him until August.

Lord Radstock and Mrs. Emmerson had another score against Taylor. The Rev. W. Allen had written a critique of Clare's poetry in the form of four letters to Lord Radstock, dated February 1823. They wanted Taylor to publish them in the *London*, but he declined; and when they decided to have them published in book form, he would not even mention the book in his list of new publications. The *Four Letters* contained detailed comments on the poems in Clare's two books, with frequent reference to the earlier poets, sound criticism, and discerning praise. Allen had a wide acquaintance with the highways and byways of English poetry, and his comparisons and contrasts are illuminating; but he also had a keen eye for what was new in tone or treatment, and his critique is the best and fullest contemporary account of Clare's poetry.

On the 12th of April, Cary wrote in answer to a letter in which Clare had voiced his discontent with Helpston society. "Do not wish for a residence near London," wrote Cary; "you would ere long have cause to wish yourself away again. Be contented with seeing the 'freckled fair one,' as I think Cowper calls it, now and then." Clare had also mentioned his intention of visiting Cowper's haunts. Cary had just met Wordsworth, and found in him "much frankness and fervour. The first impression his countenance gave me was one which I did not receive from Chantrey's bust of him, that of his being a very benevolent man. Have you seen Barry Cornwall's new volume ? [5] He is one of the last writers of blank verse we have; but I think blank verse is not much in

favour with you. The rhyme that is now in fashion runs rather
too wild to please me. It seems to want pruning & nailing
up. A sonnet like a rose-tree may be allow'd to grow straggling. But a long poem should be train'd into some order."

A sonnet of Clare's which appeared in the *London* in July
under the pen-name "Percy Green" was greatly admired by
Cary before he discovered its authorship. "Percy Green" was
a little joke of Clare's. He had written a letter to Taylor in
October, 1822, signed by that name, offering to send a
small collection of poems for perusal. He enclosed a ballad as
a specimen of his abilities, and his postscript ran thus: "I
have heard it affirmed that your predilection for the Northamptonshire Peasant's poetry has made you blind to the
more high and refined style. Be as it will, I have made the
attempt, whether it be attended with success or not." There
was some earnest behind the jest; Clare had never been
enamoured of the rôle of "peasant poet," and his anxiety to
know whether his poems were appreciated for their own sake
showed itself again and again. Cary's notice of the poem
pleased him greatly. Three of the *London* sonnets in 1823
were attributed to "Percy Green."

Through the *Magazine* poems we can trace some of Clare's
moods during this year. He is still preoccupied with the contrast of present and past, with change and decay. He muses
upon "a venerable tree, pining away to nothingness and
dust"; or, in the sonnet which Cary liked, greets an old
friend in "Round-Oak Spring," whom also change has not
spared:

> *Sweet brook! life's glories once were thine and mine,*
> *Shades clothed thy spring that now doth naked lie;*
> *On thy white boiling sand the sweet woodbine*
> *Darkened, and dipt its flowers:*

or, as in "Antiquity," he plunges into a remoter past and
marks the grassy mound, the grave of one of those Roman
camps which he sometimes helped his friend Artis to explore.

There are also three poems to Mary, and they mark the
third stage in the strange pilgrimage of his love for her. He

had loved her in youth's happy day; then fate parted them, and he bade farewell. Now, when life is revealing that it holds no happiness like that which is past, his thoughts return to his love for Mary as the epitome of that early joy. He addresses to her the valentine which was printed in the May *London*, " from one who loves thee still." Yet, he seems to ask himself, what kind of love is this? For the past is for ever dead, and "With me thy love's a withered joy." He concludes that it is but a shadow love, haunting the memory.

In two sonnets published in the August *London*, we find that this idea has found fertile soil and begun to germinate. Since change and decay is a rule of life, and "The flower that's gathered beauty soon forsakes," perchance this re-membered love is better than the reality itself, being beyond time and change.

> *I met thee like the morning, though more fair,*
> *And hopes 'gan travel for a glorious day;*
> *And though night met them ere they were aware,*
> *Leading the joyous pilgrims all astray –*
> *Yet know I not, though they did miss their way*
> *That joy'd so much to meet thee, if they are*
> *To blame or bless the fate that bade such be.*
> *Thou seem'dst an angel when I met thee first,*
> *Nor has aught made thee otherwise with me:*
> *Possession has not cloyed my love, nor curst*
> *Fancy's wild visions with reality.*
> *Thou art an angel still; and Hope, awoke*
> *From the fond spell that early raptures nurst,*
> *Still feels a joy to think that spell ne'er broke.*

This feeling, that in losing Mary he had really won her, was prophetic.

In July, Octavius Gilchrist died, after a long illness, at the age of forty-four. Clare felt deeply the loss of this good friend and jovial companion. Now, with Gilchrist dead and Drury at Lincoln, there was little incentive for Clare to visit Stamford, although he was always welcomed by Mrs. Gilchrist and the Simpsons.

On the 1st of August, Taylor wrote at last with good news for Clare:

"I shall be very agreeable to the Publication of another Volume this ensuing Winter & what with the Magazine Poems & some long & good ones you have besides I doubt not a very creditable Volume may be completed without any great Difficulty. Talking the other day with Hessey it occurred to me that a good title for another book would be – 'The Shepherd's Calendar.' "

Thus Taylor once more effectively countered Lord Radstock's challenge; for, so long as Taylor was willing to go on publishing his poems, Clare had no desire to part company with a man who had done much for him. Had he known that the *Shepherd's Calendar* promised for the next winter was destined to remain on the publishers' stocks for nearly four years, he might have taken other counsel.

During September, Clare was further cheered by an unexpected gift. Sir Michael Benignus Clare, M.D., a rich West Indian, sent him five guineas for his name's sake. Hessey thought optimistically that he was "in all probability a Relation (who knows but you may be his heir!)."

In the letter which contained this news, Hessey spoke of the death of Bloomfield and of the unhappiness of his later days. Bloomfield and Clare had never met, but they corresponded and exchanged books, and Clare had intended to visit Shefford on his way back from London. On May 3rd, 1822, Bloomfield had sent his *May-day with the Muses*, with a note to "Neighbour John."

In March, 1825, Joseph Weston, then engaged on a life of Bloomfield, wrote to Clare for permission to publish his letters to the Farmer's Boy. In his reply Clare said:

"I sincerely loved the man and admired his Genius and had a strong anxiety to make a journey to spend a day with him on my second visit to London. . . . He died ripe for immortality and had he written nothing else but 'Richard and Kate,' that fine picture of Rural life were sufficient to establish his name as the English Theocritus and the first of Rural Bards in this country."

Clare also sent three sonnets which he had written "in a melancholy feeling" after Bloomfield's death; the best of them was included in the *Rural Muse*. In a "pretty, unaffected letter," added to Weston's reply, Bloomfield's daughter Hannah spoke of her father's regard for Clare, and his regret that they had never met. Many years later Hannah Bloomfield visited Clare in the asylum, and he wrote some verses to commemorate the visit.

At harvest-time Clare found work in the fields again, but he continued to send up poems for his next book. Hessey complained because they were too much like what he had written before, and he could find none suitable for the *London*. After the two sonnets to Mary in August, 1823, no poem from Clare's pen was published in the *Magazine* until July, 1824, and the sonnet in that number was the last.

Toward the end of 1823 appeared the first symptoms of an illness more severe than any Clare had yet experienced; he had little respite for two years. The symptoms took the form of acute mental distress. Mrs. Emmerson wrote in November asking the reason for his two months' silence; in her next letter she had heard from him and wrote sympathetically of his "abiding shadow of misery," his "fiery torments," wondering what could be the cause. In her Christmas letter she asked him to send particulars of his present means of support, since Lord Radstock meant to discover what Taylor held on Clare's behalf in his accounts. Radstock had also written again to Lord Milton soliciting a cottage and a piece of ground for Clare.

On the 5th of January, 1824, Clare's first son was born; he was christened Frederick. Cary wrote again on the 3rd, misdating his letter 1823:

"I am glad to see a New Shepherd's Calendar advertised with your name. You will no doubt bring before us many objects in nature that we have often seen in her but never

before in books; & that in verse of a very musical construction. These are the two things, I mean description of
natural objects taken from the life, & a sweet melodious
versification, that particularly please me in poetry; and these
two you can command if you chuse. Of sentiment I do not
reck so much. Your admiration of poets I felt most strongly,
earlier in life, & have still a good deal of it left, but time
deadens that as well as many of our other pleasantest feelings."

In January also we first hear of W. Sharpe, who paid a
visit to Helpston; Clare and he met at Lolham Bridges,
where they both had a fit of the "blue devils." Sharpe, who
worked in the Dead Letter Office, did Clare good service
later by acting as his representative in certain business
matters.

The correspondence during the first quarter of the year
has many references to Clare's illness. Hessey sent him pills
from Dr. Darling, who had a wide practice among literary
men and artists. He had doctored Keats, Hazlitt, J. Scott,
Wilkie, and Haydon; Clare met him in 1822 at the *London*
dinners. Taylor suggested a visit to town to consult Dr. Darling. Meanwhile Lady Milton had sent her own physician,
Dr. Walker of Peterborough, and he had assured Clare that
he would soon recover. Taylor also wrote to Dr. Arnold
asking him to attend Clare. From Mrs. Emmerson's letters
we gather something of his symptoms, which were chiefly
nervous and mental; his "mind was dead," he had spoken
of "loss of memory," of "being nearly blind," of "wandering pains" and "cold chills." She thought he was
suffering from " high nervous debility, which is of all diseases
the most painful to the poor patient," and she sympathised
the more because she had suffered from it herself. " It is
the mind's disease, and the body only suffers in sympathy."
But she assured him that his mind was as sound as ever.
Clare needed the assurance, for he was certain that he was
dying. In this belief he determined to make his will. He wrote
to Hessey, who handed his letter to Richard Woodhouse,
who was a solicitor. Woodhouse sent him a long and

Oj

sympathetic letter, with a will form to fill up. Clare left £10 to his sister, Sophy Kettle, four shillings a week to his parents out of the copyright of his works, and the interest from the Fund-money to his wife and family. Taylor was to publish his books and edit his Remains: "he was one of the first friends I met, and I wish to leave him one of my last."

Casting about for the cause of his illness, Clare further troubled his mind with regrets for past follies; in repentant mood, he decided to turn his back on John Barleycorn. He also sought for some solace in religion, and contemplated joining the Ranters. "I do not wonder at the feelings you describe," wrote Hessey, "nor am I sorry that you experience them – a broken heart and a contrite spirit are much more welcome in the sight of God than undue presumption."

By the end of April, as his health had not improved, Clare had decided to take Taylor's advice and consult Dr. Darling in London. He spent the first weeks of May in preparation for his third visit.

XI

CROWDS AND CITIES PASS AWAY
1824

What is this world with London in its lap?
  Mogg's Map.
The Thames that ebbs and flows in its broad channel?
  A tidy kennel.
The bridges stretching from its banks?
  Stone planks.
Oh me! hence could I read an admonition
  To mad Ambition!
T. HOOD, "Moral Reflections on the Cross of St. Paul's."

CLARE arrived in London toward the end of May. It was after his return from this visit that he began to record his impressions of his three visits, and the following passage served as a general introduction to his reminiscences:

"A journey for pleasure is a precarious sympathy, soon robbed of its enjoyment by unforeseen disasters, but a journey for the improvement of ill-health, undertaken by that smiling encourager hope, hath little to make it palatable, though the joys of the one are as much to be relied on as the other. Upon this last matter my journey to London was made. I went for the benefit of advice to a celebrated Scotch physician, Dr. Darling. The complaint lay in my head and chest. I was very ill when I first went, but I gradually received benefit. Some recollections of this visit shall be the subject of this chapter; they are observations of men and things thrown together in a miscellaneous manner. This was the third time I had been up, so the vast magnitude of that human ant-hill that strikes every stranger with wonder had lost its novelty."

After recording some general impressions of his previous visits, Clare continued:

"On this my last visit, I amused my illness by catching the most beautiful women faces in the crowd as I passed on in it; till I was satiated, as it were, with the variety and the multitude and my mind lost its memory in the eternity of beauty's successions and was glad to glide on in vacancy with the living stream."

After resting for some days at Fleet Street, Clare visited the Emmersons; Mrs. Emmerson wrote to Patty on the 31st of May that she had seen Clare that morning for the first time, and that his health had gradually improved since his arrival in London. Thereafter he divided his time between Stratford Place and Fleet Street, as on his second visit. Under Dr. Darling's treatment his bodily health improved considerably, but his mental distresses were more stubborn. He found that his demons were as much at home in London as at Helpston.

"When I used to go anywhere by myself, especially Mrs. E's, I used to sit at night till very late because I was loath to start, not for the sake of leaving the company but for fear of meeting with supernatural [agents] even in the busy paths of London. Though I was a stubborn disbeliever of such things in the daytime, yet at night their terrors came upon me tenfold, and my head was as full of the terrible as a gossip's. Thin, death-like shadows and goblins with saucer eyes were continually shaping on the darkness from my haunted imagination; and when I saw anyone of a spare figure in the dark, passing or going on by my side, my blood has curdled cold at the foolish apprehensions of his being a supernatural agent, whose errand might be to carry me away at the first dark alley we came to. . . .

"I could not bear to go down the dark narrow street of Chancery Lane. It was as bad as a haunted place to pass; and one dark night I resolved to venture the risk of being lost rather than go down, though I tried all my courage to go down to no purpose. For I could not get it out of my head but that I should be sure to meet death or the devil if I did. So I passed it and tried to find Fleet Street by another road; but I soon got lost, and the more I tried to find the way, the more I got wrong. So I offered a watchman a shilling to show me the way thither; but he said he would not go for that and asked a half-a-crown, which I readily gave him."

Clare attributed these night fears to an incident in his youth, when he was terribly frightened in a lonely lane one summer evening. He did not venture far abroad unless he could find a companion.

"I used to go with Thomas Bennion, Taylor's clerk or head porter, about the city when he went on errands. We often went into each curiosity that came our way, claptraps to ease the pocket of its burthen. I remember going into the Bullock's Mexico[1] with the editor's ticket that Taylor gave me, and the fellows at their several posts for money-catching, fancying, I daresay, that I was the criticising editor, looked with much surprise at my odd, clownish appearance and asked me so many pumping questions that I was glad to get out again without paying much attention to the wonders of the show. Tom was very fond of introducing me to the book-sellers where he had business, who were too busy occupied in their own concerns to take much heed of me."

On another occasion, Hessey was his conductor.

"I went with Hessey to visit a very odd sort of character at the corner of St. Paul's Churchyard. He was a very simple, good sort of man with a troublesome sort of fondness for poetry, which was continually uppermost. He wrote rhymes himself, which he thrust into anyone's notice as readily as if they were another's. He had two daughters who seemed to be very amiable girls, one of which kept an album in which her father's productions were very prominent. He was a friend and acquaintance to Miss Williams,[2] to whom he had sent a copy of my poems. At his house I met with Etty the painter. He was a man of a reserved appearance and felt as awkwardly situated, I daresay, as myself when Mr. Vowler proposed healths and expected fine speeches in reply. For though Etty replied, he did it very shortly, and when mine was drunk I said nothing; and though the company's eyes were expecting for some minutes, I could not say a word, though I thought of some several times, and they were wishes that I was out of the house."

William Etty, fellow-student of Hilton and Haydon, had at last won fame as a "historic" painter, after years of patient endeavour. He became an A.R.A. in this same year and an R.A. in 1828, competing for that honour with Constable, whom he was one of the few to appreciate at that time.

At the Fleet Street shop Clare renewed his acquaintance with several of the contributors to the *London*, and made some new friends. Since his last visit, the *Magazine* had passed from high summer to the verge of winter. Dissatisfied with the editor's conduct of affairs, many of the contributors had fallen away, among them Hazlitt, Wainewright, Hood, and Procter. Lamb felt like the last rat lingering among the creaking rafters, and only his sense of loyalty kept him contributing. Taylor was overworked, and the business suffered with his health. He favoured some of his team unduly – De Quincey certainly had more than his share of the space at this time – and he affronted others by withholding or curtailing their contributions. There were also complaints about delay in payment. However, Cary, Cunningham, and Elton still appeared regularly, and there were newcomers since 1822 whom Clare now met for the first time.

The falling off of the contributors had been noted by Thomas Bennion when he wrote to Clare in March:

"The Dinner, that was given to the Contributors of the L. Mag. this last time was attended by only two of the old Contributors, that you know, the one was Reynolds and the other Mr. C. Phillips those two where the chief sport of the party indeed i may say the verry life and soul of it after dinner, and you was mentioned twice or thrice during the night. Your old friend Elia was prevented from being one of the party thro being ill but he is better, but there wanted him and you and then there would have been more mirth among them."

The contributors present on that occasion were "Van Dyk, H. Taylor, G. Darley, C. Phillips, Dr. Darling, Revd. Mr. Percival, Reynolds, Taylor, and Hessey."

Charles Phillips, barrister and miscellaneous writer, Clare had evidently met in 1822. Van Dyk and Darley he now met for the first time, and formed friendships with them which lasted for several years.

George Darley, that "sometimes glorious poet," had come from Dublin to London in 1821 "to conquer the literary world with a volume of poems in his pocket." Beddoes saw him in 1824 as "a tallish, slender, pale, light-eyebrowed, gentle-looking baldpate, in a brown surtout with a duodecimo under his arm – stammering to a most provoking degree...." Darley did not become intimate with Cary and Lamb till 1827, but the friendship he made with John Taylor, his publisher, long outlasted the *London* days.

Yet not *Errors of Ecstasie* in 1822, nor *Labours of Idleness* in 1826, nor *Sylvia* in 1827, conquered the literary world for him. *Letters to the Dramatists of the Day*, begun in the *London* of July, 1823, where he could never help, as he wrote to Clare, "cutting, slashing, pinking, and carbonadoing" the rest of the brotherhood, only earned for the gentle spirit the appellation of "the bloody John Lacy"; while Palgrave knew so little of him in 1861 that he placed his "Ryghte Pythie Songe," "It is not beautie I demande," between poems by Milton and Carew. Yet that was its spiritual home; and it is significant that immediately after this visit Clare began writing his "imitations" of those same poets from whom Darley drew his inspiration. He certainly recognised in Clare's poetry that "musical singing note" which he held was the mark of the true poet. Clare was also interested in Darley the mathematician, and praised those popular text-books in geometry, trigonometry, algebra, and astronomy, by writing which Darley soothed a sensitive conscience on the subject of his life's devotion to literature.

In 1824, Harry Stoe Van Dyk was a young man of leisure to whom literature was a hobby rather than a profession; but on the failure of his estate in the West Indies he was driven to depend upon his pen for a livelihood, and thereafter his story is a sad one of declining hopes, poverty, and ill health, closed by his death in 1828 at an early age. Clare found in him a congenial companion, and left this brief account of him among his reminiscences:

"I got acquainted this time with Van Dyk, a young man whose literary matters sat very quietly about him. He was of a very timid and retreating disposition before strangers, but to a friend he was very warm-hearted. He published a little volume of Poems called *Theatrical Portraits*.[3] He was very ready at writing an impromptu, which he would often do very happily. He went back with me to Mrs. E's where we met with Lord R. who was very friendly to him."

Soon after Clare's return home, Van Dyk offered to prepare the poems for the *Shepherd's Calendar*. Busied with his other affairs, Taylor was glad to accept the offer, and Van Dyk acted as editor for about a year.

Mrs. Emmerson wrote to Patty on June the 14th with news that Clare's health was still improving, though slowly. He was now getting about the town much more, visited the Emmersons frequently, and picnicked with them on Hampstead Heath. Then Rippingille came up from Bristol, and Clare had a round of sight-seeing with his old friend. They were accompanied on some of these jaunts by Charles Abraham Elton, who had come with Rippingille from Bristol. Elton, elegant Greek scholar and translator of Hesiod and Propertius, supplied the *London* with poems, translations, and articles, under the pen-name "Olen." Clare and Elton met frequently during this visit, and enjoyed each other's company. After their return home, Elton sent Clare a letter in verse, with a copy of *The Brothers*, 1820. "The Idler's Epistle to J. Clare," which was printed in the *London* for August, is of interest, not only as a record of their friendship and common tastes, but for its character-sketch of Clare and its references to the other *Londoners*.[4]

> So loth, friend John, to quit the town?
> 'Twas in the dales thou won'st renown:
> I would not, John for half-a-crown
> Have left thee there;
> Taking my lonely journey down
> To rural air.

What thou hast been the world may see,
But guess not what thou still may'st be;
Some in thy lines a Goldsmith see,
  Or Dyer's tone:
They praise thy worst; the best of thee
  Is still unknown.

Some grievously suspect thee, Clare!
They want to know thy form of prayer;
Thou dost not cant, and so they stare
  And smell free-thinking;
They bid thee of the devil beware,
  And vote thee sinking.

  .   .   .   .

I would not have a mind like thine
Thy artless childhood tastes resign,
Jostle in mobs, or sup and dine
  Its powers away,
And after noisy pleasures pine
  Some distant day.

And, John! though you may mildly scoff,
That curst confounded churchyard cough
Gives pretty plain advice, be off!
  While yet you can;
It is not time yet, John! to doff
  Your outward man.

  .   .   .   .

Does Agnus[5] *fling his crotchets wild,*
"In wit a man," in heart a child?
Has Lepus'[6] *sense thine ear beguiled*
  With easy strain?
Or hast thou nodded blithe and smiled
  At Herbert's[7] *vein?*

Does Nalla,[8] *that mild giant, bow*
His dark and melancholy brow;
Or are his lips distending now
  With roaring glee,
That tells the heart is in a glow,
  The spirit free?

Or does the Opium-eater quell
Thy wondering sprite with placid spell?
⁹Read'st thou the dreams of murkiest hell
    In that mild mien?
Or dost thou doubt, (yet fear to tell,)
    Such e'er have been?

And while around the board the wine
Lights up the glancing eye-ball's shine,
Seest thou in elbow'd thought recline
    The poet true⁹
Who in Colonna seems divine
    To me and you?

But, Clare the birds will soon be flown;
Our Cambridge wit resumes his gown:
Our English Petrarch¹⁰ trundles down
    To Devon's valley:
Why, when the Mag is out of town,
    Stand shilly-shally?

    .   .   .   .   .   .

And Rip Van Winkel¹¹ shall awake
From his loved idlesse for thy sake;
In earnest stretch himself, and take
    Pallet on thumb;
Nor now his brains for subjects rake;
    John Clare is come.

His touch will, hue by hue, combine
The thoughtful eyes that steady shine,
The temples of Shakespearian line,
    The quiet smile,
The sense and shrewdness which are thine,
    Withouten guile.

To return to Clare's story of his sight-seeing with Rippingille:

"After I had been in London a while Rippingille came
down from Bristol with Mr. Elton, and as I was much
improved in health under Dr. Darling, I indulged in some
of the town amusements with my old comrade; for he was

fond of seeking after curiosity and traversing about the town. He was always for thinking that last exercise, taking all weathers rough and smooth as they came, was the best physic for a sick man, and a glass of Scotch Ale only served to strengthen his notions. The first jaunt that we took together was to see 'The art of Self-defence' practised at the Fives Court. It was for the benefit of Oliver, and I caught the mania so much from Rip for such things that I soon became far more eager for the Fancy than himself. I watched the appearance of every new hero on the stage with as eager curiosity to see what sort of fellow he was as I had before done the poets. I left the place with one wish strongly uppermost and that was that I was but a Lord to patronise Jones the Sailor Boy, who took my fancy as being the finest fellow in the Ring."

Tom Oliver was one of the "old ones" in 1824, and as such entitled to an annual benefit. Jones the Sailor Boy provided some of the "prime sparring" at several such benefits. Clare's memories of these scenes sank deep into his mind, to reappear in strange guise later, when many rounds had been added in his long struggle with adversity. It was Jack Randall whom he remembered then, and in whose name he issued his "Challenge to All the World," the Prime Irish Lad, the Nonpareil of Reynolds's sonnet, "Good with both hands and only ten stone four," whose fight with Ned Turner Keats had witnessed in 1818, the Out and Outer, whose deeds were celebrated in many verses and in the pages of *Boxiana*. In 1824 he kept the Hole in the Wall at 45, Chancery Lane, which Clare must have visited.

Clare next tells how, in the company of Rippingille and Elton, he went to see Deville, the phrenologist from Paris, who had a shop in the Strand where he entertained the many visitors who came to have their "phrenological developments" explained and to see his collection of plaster casts of the heads of noted people. Clare allowed a cast to be made, and found the operation very stifling. He has left a full account of the methods of this high-priest of phrenology who pronounced Coventry Patmore's adolescent "bumps" to be those of a poet, and whom Thomas Hood mentions in

his poem "Craneology," where he pokes fun at this fashionable craze. Deville's plaster cast of Blake's head may be
seen in the National Portrait Gallery.

"He is a kind, simple-hearted, good-humoured man.
Phrenology is with him something more than a System; it
seems the life and soul of his speculations. He is never weary
of talking about it or giving Lectures on heads. Strangers of
all descriptions – poets, philosophers, mathematicians, and
humble, unknown beings that with the world have no name
– are all welcomed up the stairs and led to his matchless
head-gallery, while he with smiling politeness satisfies every
eager enquiry as readily as it is asked for. They have only to
pull off their hats and drop half-hints, and then the lecture
on heads commences. He mostly begins with, 'Why, Sir, I
should say here's order very strong (or, vice versa, the want
of it); here's plenty of constructiveness; I should say you're
fond of mathematics. And here's ideality; I should say that
you had a talent for poetry. I don't say that you are a poet,
but that you have a talent for it, if applied. Here's the order
of colour very strong; I should say that you are very fond
of fine colours (or vice versa, where there's the organ of
form without colour, nothing showy is liked). Here is be-
nevolence very prominent; I should say you seldom pass a
beggar or street-sweeper without dropping a coin. Here's
veneration very high; I should say you are religious. (The
head perhaps is worldly minded and remains silent.) I don't
say you're a Christian, mind, but you have a veneration for
the Deity; that's sufficient for our system. Here's combative-
ness very large; I should say you are not slow at avenging
an insult, particularly if it be offered to a female; for the
amorous propensities are large also. I should say you have
a love for the fair sex, but not so as to make it troublesome.
Aye, aye, sir, now I look again, here's order very strong, sure
enough; I should say that things being out of order dis-
pleases you very much and that you are often tempted while
at table to put a spoon or knife and fork in its place. I should
say it's the most likely thing to create disturbances in your
family. Here's form very strong; I should say you are a
painter, or that you have talents for painting, if applied. . . .
Are you a poet, sir? (Yes.) Aye, aye, the system's right, but I
should not venture so far as to decide upon that, as many

heads develop poetry very strongly where it has never been applied. Well, sir, you see the system is correct.' He then in smiling silence waits your decision of his remarkable prophecy; and hard and earthlike is that soul who can return an harsh and unbelieving opinion on the system. But I believe he is seldom paid so unkindly for his good-natured trouble. His predictions are so cautiously uttered, with so many causes for the likelihood of failures in nice points, that even failings themselves in his lectures strike as convictions. . . . Deville then leads your eye to his collection, points out on particular heads the most convincing proofs of his system in the characteristics of murderers, poets, painters, mathematicians and little actors of all work, where his vice versas become very frequent. He then takes you below where the apparatus is always ready to bury you in plaster if you choose, and of literary men and artists he politely hints that he should like a cast. They cannot do less than comply, and the satisfaction of adding fresh materials to his gallery doubly repays him for all his trouble."

We next hear of a visit to Sir Thomas Lawrence's:

"Rippingille also introduced me to Sir T. L., who was a very polite, courteous and kind man, which made the other matters sit very agreeably about him. Just as we got up to the door, Prince Leopold was going in to sit for his picture, and we took a turn up the Square for a while and did not offer to venture till we saw him depart. Rip sent in his card and we were instantly sent up into his painting gallery, where we amused ourselves till he came and kindly shook me by the hand and made several enquiries about me. He paid Rip several fine compliments about his picture of the Breakfast at an Inn, and told him of his faults in a free, undisguised manner but with the greatest kindness. After he had showed us about the painting-room and chatted a considerable time, we proffered to start, when he followed us and said he could not let me go without showing me a brother poet, and took us into another room where a fine head of Walter Scott stood before us. I left his house with the satisfied impression that I had never met with a kinder and better man than Sir T. L. and I daresay Rip was highly gratified with the praise he had received; for Sir T. told him that the

Royal family at a private view of the Exhibition before it
opened to the public took more notice of his picture than all
the rest. But Rip would not own it, for he affects a false
appearance in such matters."

Other acquaintances made in Rippingille's company were
Frank Howard, the painter, remembered for his series of
clever outline plates, "The Spirit and the Plays of Shakespeare," and the genial and witty T. K. Hervey, critic of
art and literature, who edited the *Athenæum* from 1846 to
1853.

It was one of Rippingille's foibles to affect an
interest in things of which he understood little. "With this
feeling," Clare continues, "we went 2 or 3 times to the
French Playhouse somewhere in Tottenham Court Road.
None of us understood a word of French and yet we fancied
ourselves delighted, for there was a very beautiful actress
that took our fancies. Rip drew a sketch of her in pencilling
for me, which was something like her, though he stole none
of her beauty to grace it. We also went to Astley's Theatre[12]
where we saw morts of tumbling."

As we have already seen, Clare's account of Charles
Lamb was written when the memory of his visits to Islington
in 1824 was fresh in his mind. We are indebted to Crabb
Robinson for a record of one of these occasions. He wrote in
his diary for July 6th:

"Took tea with Lamb –   There were Hessey and Taylor,
Clare the shepherd poet, Bowering, and Elton the translator
from the classicks. Clare looks like a weak man but he was
ill –   Elton a sturdy fellow more like a huntsman than a
scholar."

"Bowering" was John Bowring, master of some fifteen
languages and an authority on their literature; his translations frequently enriched the pages of the *London* at this time.
He prepared numerous anthologies, was a friend of Jeremy
Bentham and Cobden, and eventually won fame and a
knighthood for his political services at home and abroad.
He had lately published his successful *Specimens of the Russian*

Poets, Ancient Poetry and Romances of Spain, and a volume of
devotional verse called *Matins and Vespers.*

Clare also met Lamb at Taylor's, along with other old
acquaintances and some new ones. Elton referred to one of
these gatherings in a letter to Clare on the 8th of September:

"I went down to Islington and dined and smoked a pipe
in the evening with Lamb: he got a little into the romps as
he did at Taylor's: but was very entertaining. The capital
paper on the old country house was written at my instance:
though he chose the subject himself."

This paper was "Blakesmoor in H——shire," which appeared in the September *London,* the first contribution from
Lamb's pen for that year; he had been in indifferent health
and low spirits during the first half of 1824.

It was at Taylor's also that Clare met De Quincey, whose
Confessions of an Opium Eater was a favourite book of his.
This is Clare's impression of him:

"A little, artless, simple-seeming body, something of a
child overgrown, in a blue coat and black neckerchief, (for
his dress is singular,) with his hat in his hand, steals gently
among the company with a smile, turning timidly round the
room. It is De Quincey, the Opium Eater, and that abstruse
thinker in logic and metaphysic, X.Y.Z."

De Quincey's comments on Clare and his poetry were included in his *London Reminiscences:*

". . . His poems were not the mere reflexes of his reading.
He had studied for himself in the fields, and in the woods,
and by the side of the brooks. I very much doubt if there
could be found in his poems a single commonplace image,
or a description made up of hackneyed elements . . . in 1824,
perhaps upon some literary scheme, he came up to London,
where, by a few noble families and by his liberal publishers,
he was welcomed in a way that, I fear, from all I heard,
would but too much embitter the contrast with his own
humble opportunities of enjoyment in the country. . . . It
is singular that what most fascinated his rustic English eye

was not the gorgeous display of English beauty, but the French style of beauty, as he saw it amongst the French actresses in Tottenham Court Road. He seemed, however, oppressed by the glare and tumultuous existence of London; and, being ill at the time, from an affection of the liver, which did not, of course, tend to improve his spirits, he threw a weight of languor upon any attempt to draw him out into conversation. One thing, meantime, was very honourable to him, – that even in this season of dejection he would uniformly become animated when anybody spoke to him of Wordsworth – animated with the most hearty and almost rapturous spirit of admiration. As regarded his own poems, this admiration seemed to have an unhappy effect of depressing his confidence in himself. It is unfortunate, indeed, to gaze too closely upon models of colossal excellence. Compared with those of his own class, I feel satisfied that Clare will always maintain an honourable place."

There is other evidence that Clare's appreciation of Wordsworth had grown steadily since 1820. In a journal entry for October 29th, he gave a list of his favourite poems and told of his first discovery of Wordsworth's greatness. "Wordsworth bids fair to be as great in one way as Byron was in another," he wrote, also in 1824. "His having little share of living popularity is no proof to the contrary." But he was not so depressed by gazing upon "models of colossal excellence" as De Quincey imagined. His natural modesty could be misleading, and his admiration was never blind. In 1820, after praising Wordsworth's truth to nature, he wrote in a letter: "But after all I don't think I favour his affected Godliness. In some of his longer pieces, there's some past all bearing. Still, with his faults and abilities, he is a poet with whom for originality of description the present day has few, if any, equals."

The criticism is revealing; Clare fought shy of all men and all poetry that seemed to have, in Keats's phrase, "a palpable design" upon him. Godliness, unless it be unobtrusive, was suspect; nor was he happy with what he called Wordsworth's " mysteries." It was not because he was unable to see nature as Wordsworth saw it, but because that vision was so natural and spontaneous to Clare that he did not regard it as a mystery. "Wordsworth's vision came to him by flashes, therefore it seemed to him an abnormal and extraordinary visitation which needed to be related by thought and meditation to ordinary experience. If Wordsworth had seen a primrose as Clare saw it – and he did occasionally see things thus – he would have felt that he was seeing 'into the heart of things,' whereas Clare – who seems always to have seen in this way – felt that he was merely seeing things."[13]

We know less of Clare's opinion of Coleridge, though he coupled him with Wordsworth in 1820 as among his favourite poets. Coleridge was present at one of the gatherings during this third visit to London; unfortunately, Clare's sketch of him is fragmentary; half the page on which it is written has been torn off:

"There was Coleridge at one of the Parties. He was a man with a venerable white head; fluent of speech; not a 'silver-tongued Hamilton;' his words hung in their places at a quiet pace from a drawl, in good set marching order, so that you would suppose he had learnt what he intended to say before he came. It was a lecture, parts of which. . . ."

Then, at Mrs. Emmerson's, Clare met Coleridge's and Southey's sisters-in-law, Martha and Eliza Fricker. With them he talked of Southey and Wordsworth:

"I never met him [Southey] but I heard something about him by meeting in company two of his wife's sisters at Mrs. Emmerson's, those 'Pretty milliners of Bath' as Byron calls them; but I cannot say much for his judgement if these sisters are to be taken as a sample for the rest. They are sharp ready-witted girls, but rather plain. I learned from them that Southey was a lively sort of man, always in gay spirits, who wrote both in prose and verse with a great deal of ease; but the number of his publications would almost tell us that this is the fact. He writes amid the noise of his children and joins in their sport at intervals. Wordsworth on the contrary cannot bear a noise and composes with great

PJ

difficulty. I should imagine he prefers a mossy seat on the mountains to the closet for study; at least his poems would lead one to think so. Southey presents a copy of every work he publishes to his wife and he wrote a copy of *Roderic* on French green paper on purpose to present to her."

On Monday, the 14th of July, Byron's funeral *cortège* crossed London. It was at the bottom of Oxford Street that George Borrow, arrested by the gathering crowds, watched the passing of the hearse with the long train of empty carriages, and mused upon the dead poet and his fame. A similar chance found Clare in Oxford Street at that same hour, and he too has recorded what he saw and thought:

"While I was in London, the melancholy death of Lord Byron was announced in the public papers, and I saw his remains borne away out of the city on its last journey to that place where fame never comes. . . . His funeral was blazed in the papers with the usual parade that accompanies the death of great men. . . . I happened to see it by chance as I was wandering up Oxford Street on my way to Mrs. Emmerson's, when my eye was suddenly arrested by straggling groups of the common people collected together and talking about a funeral. I did as the rest did, though I could not get hold of what funeral it could be; but I knew it was not a common one by the curiosity that kept watch on every countenance. By and by the group collected into about a hundred or more, when the train of a funeral suddenly appeared, on which a young girl that stood beside me gave a deep sigh and uttered, 'Poor Lord Byron.' . . . I looked up at the young girl's face. It was dark and beautiful, and I could almost feel in love with her for the sigh she had uttered for the poet. It was worth all the newspaper puffs and magazine mournings that ever were paraded after the death of a poet. . . . The common people felt his merits and his power, and the common people of a country are the best feelings of a prophecy of futurity. They are the veins and arteries that feed and quicken the heart of living fame. The breathings of eternity and the soul of time are indicated in that prophecy. . . . They felt by a natural impulse that the mighty was fallen, and they moved in saddened silence. The streets were lined on each side as the procession passed, but they were all the commonest of the lower orders. . . .

The young girl that stood by me had counted the carriages in her mind as they passed and she told me there were sixty three or four in all. They were of all sorts and sizes and made up a motley show. The gilt ones that led the procession were empty. The hearse looked small and rather mean and the coach that followed carried his embers in an urn over which a pall was thrown. . . . I believe that his liberal principles in religion and politics did a great deal towards gaining the notice and affections of the lower orders. Be as it will, it is better to be beloved by those low and humble for undisguised honesty than flattered by the great for purchased and pensioned hypocrisies."

This visible proof of a poet's fame among the common people, the "grass eternal" of humanity, springing up "where castles stood and grandeur died," made a lasting impression on Clare's mind. It inspired his "Essay on Popularity," which was begun soon after his return home and contains a critical estimate of Byron. In September he began reading *Don Juan*, lent him by Henderson of Milton; he had already written his sonnet in memory of Byron, "A splendid sun hath set!" He returned to the same theme in prose; in a passage headed "Necessity for mercy in criticism rather than fault-finding," he concluded that Byron "won the applause of popularity less by his sterling merits as a poet than by his oddities as a man," that his exploits in Greece were those of an actor playing the part of hero, yet his infirmities were but as spots in the sun. "He is enrolled among the immortals and shines as the jewel in the crown of modern literature." Clare criticised alike the friends who "surround him with every virtue under heaven" and "every meddling hypocrite who professes to be a saint" and "utters his condemnation." "It is said that Byron is not to have a monument in Westminster Abbey. To him it is no injury. Time is his monument, on whose scroll the name of Byron shall be legible when the walls and tombs of Westminster Abbey shall have mingled with the refuse of ruins, and the sun, as in scorn, be left free again to smile upon the earth so long darkened with the pompous shadows of bigotry and intolerance."

On the 13th of July, Mrs. Emmerson wrote again to Patty, telling her not to worry because she had not heard from Clare; he was not sufficiently recovered to enable him to give a satisfactory account of himself. It is not strange that two months' treatment had failed to remove all traces of an illness which was due to some years of nervous strain; when the tonic results of the change had worn off, the symptoms reappeared. Dr. Darling desired to continue his treatment with the patient under his eye. Hessey wrote to Patty on the 31st of July that Clare had been anxious to return home for some weeks, and nothing but the positive orders of his doctor kept him in London. They did not keep him much longer; his mind was set upon home. On Friday, the 8th of August, he left Fleet Street for Helpston. He says that he hastened home to get ready some lectures on painting which Rippingille intended to give at the Bristol Institution.

A letter to Thomas Inskip, friend of Bloomfield, written soon after his return, reveals clearly enough that the chief object of his visit to London had not been achieved.

"I am sorry to acknowledge that I feel very little better. I have been in a terrible state of ill-health six months, gradually declining, and I verily believe it will upset me at last. I was taken in a sort of apoplectic fit and have never had the right use of my faculties since; a numbing pain lies constantly about my head and an aching void at the pit of my stomach keeps sinking me away weaker and weaker. . . . I shall only be at home for a few weeks to try the air. To be sure, if it improves my spirits I shall remain; if not, the next thing for me to try is salt water."

During August and September he continued to receive what treatment he could from Dr. Darling, who sent pills and prescriptions. According to Hessey, the situation of Clare's cottage was considered unhealthy, and there was some talk of obtaining another from the Marquis of Exeter. Hessey also suggested that pies and puddings, which had been forbidden by Darling, had disordered Clare's stomach. "I can do nothing with Sir John Barleycorn now," wrote

Clare to Inskip. There was an impression abroad in 1824, as a hundred years later, that most people ate too much; Clare's friends frequently suggested, with unconscious irony, that his ills must be due to over-eating. Strict dieting was the fashionable treatment of the day, though it had not ousted bleeding from its old pride of place, and we find both prescribed even for diseases like consumption. Clare was as little likely to benefit from such treatment as Keats, since he suffered from under- rather than over-nourishment. This, with the continual worry of trying to make ends meet and the suspense and disappointment that attended his literary work, seems to have been at the root of Clare's trouble. An examination of the symptoms of his illnesses suggests that the physical derangements were the results, not the causes, of his nervous distress. While the conditions that caused that distress persisted, it is not surprising that Clare found no cure, though he was attended by several local doctors besides Dr. Darling.

September brought letters from several friends. Rippingille wrote twice in his usual sprightly vein, asking if Clare had forgotten "the Delia fun" at the French Playhouse, and the "atmosphere of smoke, smocks, smirks, smells and smutty doings." He sent his "Echo" verses for the *London,* and urged Clare to come to Bristol, where Elton and he would be delighted to see him. Elton also wrote, repeating the invitation and inveighing against Catholics and Calvinists and "the superstitions and bigotry of this pretended liberal age." Cunningham wrote on the 23rd, thanking Clare for a letter of Bloomfield's which he had given him. " I am glad to hear that you are a little better – Keep up your heart and sing only when you feel the internal impulse and you will add something to our Poetry more lasting than any of the Peasant Bards of Old England have done yet." On the 18th, Clare had written to Cary, whom he had met again in London and visited at Chiswick.

"I am ill able to write or do anything else. I thought I was getting well once, but I've not a hope left me now. I have employed myself when able, since I came home, at writing my own life, which, if I live to finish it, I should like to trouble you to read it and give your opinion of it; for my own judgement in such matters is very often faulty."

Cary replied on the 22nd, sympathising with Clare, discussing his own Life of Chatterton which Clare had commended, and assuring him that he would read the autobiography with interest. On the 30th of December, Clare reported progress:

"I feel anxious to finish it and I feel also anxious that you should see it, and I shall be greatly obliged for your opinion of it, as I mean if I live to publish it. I have gotten 8 chapters done, and have carried it up to the publication of the 'Poems on Rural Life,' &c. I feel it rather awkward to mention names, as there are some that I cannot speak well of; that is, where I feel an objection I cannot flatter over it, and I would not willingly offend any one. I have made free with myself and exposed my faults and failings without a wish to hide them, neither do I care what is said about me; but if you should see anything that might be against me in speaking of others, I shall be thankful of your advice and also your remarks on the thing altogether; for it is written in a confused style and there will doubtless be found a deal of trifling in it, for I am far from a close reasoner in prose."

Cary renewed his promise in a letter of the 19th of February, 1825. The correspondence then lapsed until the end of 1827, so that the later history of Clare's autobiography is uncertain. If it was indeed finished and sent to Cary, it has vanished, and only the fragmentary drafts of several chapters remain.

During the months following his return home, despite severe illness, but also because of it, since he wished to make the most of what he thought might be the last days of his life, Clare's mind was extraordinarily active. He read widely among the poets, jotting down quotations and criticisms; he wrote many poems, some to be copied up by Van Dyk for the new book, some for magazines and annuals, some that were not published until 1835, and many others not printed at all in his lifetime. In prose, besides the autobiography, he wrote several essays, some literary criticism, and part of his natural history of Helpston in the form of letters to Hessey, who had suggested the idea; and, in addition to all these activities, he found time to set down in a journal a record of his daily thoughts and occupations.

XII

RURAL CHRONICLES
1824–1825

Nature, enchanting Nature, in whose form
And lineaments divine I trace a hand
That errs not, and find raptures still renew'd,
Is free to all men—universal prize.
Strange that so fair a creature should yet want
Admirers, and be destined to divide
With meaner objects even the few she finds!

COWPER, "The Task."

THE Journal, the best record possible for Clare's thoughts and doings from the 6th of September, 1824, to the 11th of the same month in the following year, needs little introduction. In it he sets down his opinions on the books he has just read, tells of his efforts to overcome his ill-health, records some of his observations in natural history, and notes his literary aims. From these pages only the least important entries have been omitted:

"*Mon. 6 Sept. 1824.* I have determined this day of beginning a sort of journal to give my opinion of things I may read or see, and set down any thoughts that may arise either in my reading at home or my musings in the fields. . . . This day must fill up a sort of introduction; for I have nothing else to set down. All I have read today is Moore's Almanack, for the account of the weather, which speaks of rain, though it's very hot and fine.

"*Tues.* I have read Fox's Book of Martyrs and finished it today; and the sum of my opinion is tyranny and cruelty appear to be the inseparable companions of religious power. The aphorism is not far from truth that says: 'All priests are the same.' The great moral precepts of a meek and unoffending teacher were: 'Do as ye would be done by,' and 'love those that hate you.' If religious opinion had done so, her history had been worthy praise.

"*Wed.* The rainy morning has kept me at home and I have amused myself heartily sitting under Walton's sycamore tree hearing him discourse of fish-ponds and fishing. What a delightful book it is!—the best English pastoral that can be written. The descriptions are nature unsullied by fashionable tastes of the times. They are simply true, and like the pastoral ballads of Bloomfield, breathe of the common air and the grass and the sky. One may almost hear the water of the river Lea ripple along and the grass and flags grow and rustle in the pages that speak of them. I have never read a happier poem in my time.

"*Thur.* Took a pleasant walk today in the fields, but felt too weak to keep out long. 'Tis the first day of shooting with the sportsmen, and the poor hares, partridges, and pheasants were flying in all directions panic-struck. They put me in mind of the inhabitants of a village flying before an invading enemy. The dogs run with their sleek, dappled sides rustling in the crackling stubbs and their noses close to the ground, as happy as their masters in the sport; though they only 'mumble the game they dare not bite,' as Pope says. I was forced to return home fearing I might be shot under the hedges. Wrote two letters, one to Cunningham.

"*Fri.* My health would permit me to do nothing more than take walks in the garden today. What a sadly pleasing appearance gardens have at this season! The tall gaudy hollyhock with its melancholy blooms stands bending to the wind and bidding the summer farewell, while the low asters, in their pied lustre of red, white, and blue, bend beneath in pensive silence, as though they mused over the days gone by and were sorrowful. The swallows are flocking together in the skies, ready for departing, and a crowd has dropt to rest on the walnut tree, where they twitter as if they were telling their young stories of their long journey, to cheer and check fears.

"*Sat.* Written an essay today on 'The Sexual System of Plants' and began one on 'The Fungus Tribe' and on 'Mildew, Blight, Etc.,' intended for 'A Natural History of Helpstone,' in a series of letters to Hessey, who will publish it when finished. I did not think it would cause me such trouble or

I should not have begun it. Received a kind letter from
C. A. Elton. Read the September number of the *London
Mag.* Only two good articles in it—'Blakesmoor in H——
shire,' by Elia, and 'Review of Goethe,' by De Quincey.
These are excellent and sufficient to make a bad number
interesting.

"*Sun.* A wet day. Wrote a letter to Rippingille and [one]
to H. F. Cary and finished another page of my Life,
which I intend to bring down to the present time, as
I did not keep a journal earlier. I have read the first
chapter of Genesis, the beginning of which is very fine;
but the sacred historian took a great deal upon credit
for this world when he imagines that God created the sun,
moon, and stars, those mysterious hosts of heaven, for no
other purpose than its use, 'the greater light to rule the day,
and the lesser light to rule the night,' and the stars also
'to give light upon the earth.' It is a harmless and universal
propensity to magnify consequences that appertain to
ourselves and would be a foolish thing to try the test of the
scriptures upon these groundless assertions; for it contains
the best poetry and the best morality in the world.

"*Mon. 13 Sept.* Wrote two or three more pages of my Life.
Read some of the sonnets of Shakespeare, which are great
favourites of mine, and looked into the Poems of Chatterton
to see what he says about flowers and have found that he
speaks of the lady-smock:

> *So have I seen the lady-smocks so white*
> *Bloom in the morning and mowed down at night,*

as well as my favourite line of

> *Like kingcups brasting with the morning dew.*

"*Tues.* Continued the reading of Chatterton in search
for extracts to insert in my Natural History. I was
struck with the many beautiful and remarkable passages
which I found in them. What a wonderful boy was this
unfortunate Chatterton! I hate the name of Walpole for
his behaviour to this genius and his sneering and cold-
blooded mention of him afterwards when his gossiping
trouble had discovered them to be forgeries. Why did he

not discover the genius of the author? no! because they surpassed his Leadenhall forgery of 'Otranto.'

"*Wed.* Finished the reading of Chatterton. Admire his tragedy of 'Ælla' and 'Battle of Hastings'; noticed a good description of a thunder-storm in the 'Balade of Charitie' and a beautiful one of a lady. Chatterton seems fond of taking his similes from nature. His favourite flower seems to be the 'kynge-cuppe' and his favourite bird the 'pied chelandrie.' The only trees he speaks of are the oak and elm.

"*Thur.* Had a visit from my friend Henderson of Milton, who brought *Don Juan* in his pocket. I was very ill and nursing my head in my hand, but he revived me and advised me to read *Don Juan.* We talked about books and flowers and butterflies till noon, and then he descanted on *Don Juan* which he admired very much. I think a good deal of his opinion, and shall read it when I am able.

"*Fri.* Began *Don Juan.* Two verses of the Shipwreck very fine and the character of Haidée the best I have yet met; it is very beautiful; the hero seems a fit partner for Tom and Jerry, fond of getting into scrapes and always finding means to get out again; forever in the company of ladies who seem to watch at night for every opportunity for everything but saying their prayers. Perhaps they are as good as their neighbours; nay, better; they do without that fashionable veil hypocrisy.

"*Sat.* Bought the *John Bull Magazine* out of curiosity to see if I was among the black sheep. It grows in dullness; that's one comfort to those that it nicknames 'Humbugs.' I have seen a boy grope in a sink [in] the hopes of finding a lost halfpenny, but I have been worse employed than that boy, for I have dabbled in filth and found nothing; abuse without wit is dullness double-distilled. The *John Bull News* is keen and witty and in consequence entertaining. Have writ five letters—T. Henderson, Rev. Mr. Cary, A. Cunningham, H. S. Van Dyk, and Hessey.

"*Sun.* I wish I had kept a journal sooner, not of facts only, but opinions of books. When one rises fresh from the reading, thoughts that may rise at the moment for such a collection would be an entertaining medley of the past, out of which, though there might be a many weeds, one might cull a few flowers, if not candidates for eternity, yet too good to be totally lost in the blank unreckonings of days gone by. Took a walk about the fields; a deep mist in the morning hid everything till noon. Returned and read snatches in several poets and the 'Song of Solomon.' Thought the supposed allusions in that luscious poem to our Saviour very over-strained, far-fetched, and conjectural; it appears to me an eastern love-poem and nothing further; but an over-heated religious fancy is strong enough to fancy anything. I fancy that the Bible is not illustrated by that supposition; though it is a very beautiful poem it seems nothing like a prophetic one as it is represented to be.

"*Mon. 20 Sept.* A very wet day. An occurrence has happened in the village though not very remarkable yet very singular, for I have not heard of a former one in my day. 'Tis a gipsies' wedding, Israel Smith and Lettyce Smith. What odd names these people have! They are more frequently from the Bible than the Testament, for what reason I know not, and more common from their own fancies than either. The fiddle accompanied them to Church and back. The rest of it was nothing different to village weddings—dancing and drinking. Wrote a song for them, being old friends.

"*Tues.* The Statute and a very wet day for it. The lasses do not lift up their gowns to show taper ankles and white stockings, but on the contrary drop them to hide dirty ones. Wrote a poem on the Statute last year; looked it over and think it a good one. Taylor is of another opinion and thinks it not, but it is true, like the 'Lodge House' and others he dislikes. I shall one day publish them and others he has in his possession under the title of 'A Living Poet's Remains.'

"*Wed.* Very ill and did nothing but ponder over a future existence and often brought up the lines to my memory, said to be uttered by an unfortunate nobleman when on the brink of it, ready to take the plunge:

> *In doubt I lived, in doubt I die,*
> *Nor shrink the dark abyss to try,*
> *But undismayed I meet eternity.*

The first line is natural enough, but the rest is a rash courage in such a situation.

"*Thur.* A wet day; did nothing but nurse my illness; could not have walked out had it been fine. Very disturbed

in conscience about the troubles of being forced to endure
life and die by inches, and the anguish of leaving my children,
and the dark porch of eternity whence none returns to
tell the tale of his reception.

"*Fri.* Tried to walk out and could not. Have read nothing
this week. My mind almost overweights me with its up-
braidings and miseries. My children very ill night and
morning with a fever makes me disconsolate; and yet how
happy must be the death of a child ! It bears its suffering
with an innocent patience that maketh man ashamed;
and with it the future is nothing but returning to sleep with
the thoughts, no doubt, of waking to be with its playthings
again.

"*Sat.* Read some of the Odes of Collins; think them
superior to Gray's; there is little pomp and much luscious
sweetness. I cannot describe the pleasure I feel in reading
them, neither can I possess discrimination enough in Criticism to distinguish the different merits of either. Both are
great favourites of mine, yet their perusal gives me different
pleasures. I find in the same volume odes by a poet of the
name of Ogilvie, 'full of sound and fury, signifying nothing.'
They appear to me bold intruders to claim company with
Gray and Collins.

"*Sun.* Took a walk in the fields; heard the harvest cricket
and shrew-mouse uttering their shrill, clicking songs among
the crackling stubbles. The latter makes a little ear-piercing
noise, not unlike a feeble imitation of the skylark. . . .
Came home and read a chapter or two in the New Testament.
I am convinced of its sacred origin and that its writers were
inspired by an almighty power to benefit the world by
their writings, that was growing deeper and deeper into
unfruitful ignorance, like bogs and mosses in neglected
countries for want of culture; but I am far from being
convinced that the desired end is or will be attained at
present while cant and hypocrisy are blasphemously allowed
to make a mask of religion and to pass as current characters.
I will not say that this is universal—God forbid!

"*Mon. 27 Sept.* Read in Milton; his account of his blindness is very pathetic and I am always affected to tears when
I read it. The opening and end of *Paradise Lost* I consider
sublime and just as the beginning and finish of an epic
poem should be. I never could read *Paradise Regained*

through, though I have heard it praised highly. 'Comus' and
'L'Allegro' and 'Il Penseroso' are those which I take up
oftenest. What beautiful description at the shut of evening
is this!

> *what time the laboured ox*
> *In his loose traces from the furrow came,*
> *And the swinked hedger at his supper sat.*

"*Tues*. Wrote another chapter of my Life. Read a little in
Gray's Letters—great favourites of mine; they are the best
letters I have seen and I consider Burns's very inferior to
all the collections I have met with; though they have gained
great praise they appear to me when I read them as the
letters of a man who was looking further than his correspondent and straining after something fine till he forgets
both. His boast of independence is so often dwelt upon that
it becomes tiresome and seems more like the despair of a
disappointed man than the content of a happy one.

"*Wed*. Took a walk in the fields. Saw an old wood stile
taken away from a favourite spot which it had occupied
all my life. The posts were overgrown with ivy and it
seemed so akin to nature and the spot where it stood, as
though it had taken it on lease for an undisturbed existence.
It hurt me to see it was gone, for my affections claim a
friendship with such things; but nothing is lasting in this
world. Last year Langley Bush was destroyed, an old
whitethorn that had stood for more than a century, full of
fame. The gipsies, shepherds, and herdmen, all had their
tales of its history and it will be long ere its memory is
forgotten.

"*Thur*. Looked over *The Human Heart*;[1] the title has little
connection with the contents; it displays the art of book
making in half-filled pages and fine paper. 'The Murderer's
Death-bed' is very poor—the worst thing in the *Newgate
Calendar* is as interesting. 'Thou shalt do no Evil, etc.' is a
new version of Colonel Kirk's Cruelty better told in history
than in prose-poetry. 'Amy Welton' is an imitation of the
Scotch novelists and of course inferior. 'The Lucrece of
France' is good.

"*Fri*. Had a new will made as the old one was not right,
proving nothing that I wished and everything contrary.

This I don't like. I leave C. Mossop, E. T. Artis, and J. A. Hessey, executors, and all moneys arising from book profits etc. in their trust, with that in the Funds and whatever may be put out to interest. The money in the Funds to be drawn out and shared equally among my children when the youngest is twenty-one . . . .

"*Sat.* Read the Poems of Conder over a second time; like some of them very much; there are a great many and unpretentious beauties among them. The imitations of the Psalms are good; the ode to the nightingale is good, but the expression 'Sir Nightingale' is bad and spoils it; the principal poem is, like many such attempts, poor. The best poems on religion are those found in the Scriptures which are inimitable and therefore all imitations cannot but be inferior. The first sonnet on autumn is a good one and the song 'Twas not when early flowers were springing' is beautiful. I am much pleased with many more which I shall read anon.

"*Sun.* Began to read again *The Garden of Florence* by Reynolds; it is a beautiful simple tale with few conceits. . . . 'The Romance of Youth' is too romantic; that is, the youth it describes is not a general character. Yet there are several beauties in it of true poesy; the redcap is a beautiful comparison—'Itself a feather'd flower'; the comparing the white stem of the birch to a serpent is bad taste, something like the serpents wreathing round the artificial trees in Vauxhall Gardens; verse thirty-two about the kingfisher turns on a conceit and verse sixty-six about the fairy's bodice is a worse conceit still; 'May, the rose of months the violet of the year' is very pretty; the volume is full of beauties of the best sort; the verse about the children is another addition to the many from Chantrey's monument. Let C. Mossop take my new will home with him for lawyer Taylor to alter. . . .

"*Tues. 5 Oct.* . . . In the *Times Telescope* they re-christened me Robert Clare; there went the left wing of my fame.

"*Wed.* Received the *London Magazine* by my friend Henderson who brought from town a very dull number. The worst of magazines is waste-paper repetition, for humbug is the editor of them all. In the June number De Quincey had a paper on 'False Distinctions' which contended quite right enough that women had an inferior genius to men. In July 'Surrey' put up a little clever petition[2] against it which read very well but proved nothing. In the 'Lion's Head' a little Unknown[3] stuck a letter to the Editor on the same side. In August another[4] popt a plea for female genius between the two opinions of middling stuff. In September 'Surrey' popt in another push for his opinion, and in October the middling middle one is pushing a go-between again. When will it end? The article on Byron carries ignorance on the face of it. Received a letter from Cary.

"*Thur.* Got a parcel from London, Elton's *Brothers* and Allen's *Grammar*[5] gifts of the authors, and Erskine's *Internal Evidences of Religion*,[6] the gift of Lord Radstock, one of my best friends. A very sensible book; this passage struck me [when] I first opened—'To walk without God in the world is to walk in sin and sin is the way of danger. Men have been told this by their own consciences and they have partially or occasionally believed it; but still they walked on.' Too true! Received three letters—from Van Dyk, Mrs. Emmerson, and Hessey. Done nothing.

"*Fri.* Very ill today and very unhappy. My three children are all unwell. Had a dismal dream of being in hell: this is the third time I have had such a dream. As I am more and more convinced that I cannot recover I will make a memorandum of my temporal concerns, for next to the spiritual they ought to come and be attended to for the sake of those left behind. . . . Neglect is the rust of life that eateth it away and layeth the best of minds fallow and maketh them desert. Done nothing.

"*Sat.* Observed today that the swallows are all gone. Where they went I know not. Saw them at the beginning of the week. A white one was seen this season by Mr. Clark in the fields while out shooting. Patty has been to Stamford and brought me a letter from Ned Drury, who came from Lincoln to the mayor's feast on Thursday. It revives old recollections. Poor fellow, he is an odd one, but still my recollections are inclined to his favour. What a long way to come to the mayor's feast! I would not go one mile after it to hear the din of knives and forks, and to see a throng of blank faces about me, chattering and stuffing, 'that boast no more expression than a muffin.'

"*Sun.* A wet day. Have finished the life of Savage in Johnson's *Lives of the Poets*. It is a very interesting piece of biography, but the criticisms are dictated by friendship that too often forgets judgement ought to be one of the company. To leave this and turn to the life of Gray, what a contrast! It almost makes the mind disbelieve Criticism and to fancy itself led astray by even the wisest of men. I never take up Johnson's *Lives* but I regret his beginning at the wrong end first and leaving out those beautiful minstrels of Elizabeth; had he forgot that there had been such poets as Spenser, Drayton, Suckling? But it was the booksellers' judgement that employed his pen and we know by experience that most of their judgements lie in their pockets; so the poets of Elizabeth are still in cobwebs and mystery. Read in the afternoon Erskine's *Evidence of Revealed Religion* and find in it some of the best reasoning in favour of its object I have ever read. . . .

"*Mon. 11 Oct.* I have been dipping into *The Miseries of Human Life*⁷ here and there. The petty troubles are whimsical enough and the thing a novel one, which is sufficient to ensure success now; and I understand it ran through a many editions and that the Authors made £1,500 by it, clear profit. So much for fashion! Collins's poems would not pay for the printing and the price Milton got for his *Paradise Lost* is well known. So fashion's taste is still the same; her outside only alters—out upon her foolery!

"*Tues.* Began to learn a poor lame boy the common rules of arithmetic and find him very apt and willing to learn. Began an enquiry into the life of Bloomfield with the intention of writing one and a criticism on his genius and writings. A fellow of the name of Weston pretended to know a great deal about him, but I must enquire into its authenticity. Capel Lofft did not improve on the account given by his brother George, by altering it. Editors often commit this fault.

"*Wed.* Feel rather worse. Looked over the Magazine for amusement, for magazines are the best things in Literature to pass away a melancholy hour. Their variety and the freshness of their subjects, whether good or bad, never fail of amusement to recommend them. *Blackwood's* have had a hard hit on Taylor; there are no more Editor Scotts at present to check them.

"The letter on Macadamizing⁸ is good. The review on *Walladmor* is thirty pages long; I wish De Quincey had better subjects for his genius, though there are some parts of the novel that seem alive with action.

QJ

"*Thur.* Wrote a letter to Lord Radstock. Read some passages in the Poems of Tannahill; some of his songs are beautiful, particularly 'Loudon's bonny woods and braes,' 'We'll meet beside the dusky glen,' and 'Jessie'; his poems are poor and appear as if they were written by another. The Scotch poets excel in song-writing because they take their images from common life where nature exists without affectation.

"*Fri.* Read in Elton's Poems; some passages in *The Brothers* are very good and appear to be the utterance of feeling; the small poems are middling; 'Rob Roy' and 'A Father's Reverie' are two of the best. . . . There is a pleasant sound lingers on the ear whilst reading these lines:

> *the bare trees with crashing boughs aloft*
> *Rock and re-echo, and at whiles are hush'd:*
> *I commune with my spirit and am still.*

"*Sat.* Wrote two more pages of my Life: find it not so easy as I at first imagined, as I am anxious to give an undisguised narrative of facts, good and bad. In the last sketch which I wrote for Taylor° I had little vanities about me to gloss over failings which I shall now take care to lay bare for readers, if they ever are published, to comment upon as they please. In my last four years I shall give my likes and dislikes of friends and acquaintances as free as I do of myself.

"*Sun.* . . . Looked into the poems of Coleridge, Lamb, and Lloyd; Coleridge's monody on Chatterton is beautiful, but his sonnets are not happy ones; they seem to be a labour after excellence which he did not reach. Some of those by his friend Lloyd are excellent and seem to have attained it without trouble; 'To Craig Millar Castle' and 'To November' are the best in my opinion. Lamb's best poetry is in *Elia*, though 'tis a sufficient fame in a late harvest. I wish he would write on.

"*Mon. 18 Oct.* Looked over *Don Juan*; like it better and feel a wish that the great poet had lived to finish it, though he appears to have lost his intended plan on setting out and to have continued it with any purpose that came uppermost; Don Juan's visit to England reads tiresome and one wishes at the end that he had met with another shipwreck on his voyage to have sent him elsewhere.

"*Tues.* Looked over a new vol. of provincial poems by a

neighbouring poet, Banton—*Excursions of Fancy*; and poor
fancies I find them. There is not a new thought in them.
Four years ago a poet was not to be heard of within a century
of Helpstone, and now there is a swarm. . . .

"*Wed*. Worked in the garden at making a shed for my
auriculas. The Michaelmas daisy is in full flower, both the
lilac-blue and the white, thick-set with its little clustering
stars of flowers."

Here we may pause a moment to scan Clare's garden and
its contents. Elizabeth Kent was doubtless right when she
declared, in her *Flora Domestica* of 1825, that the finest
auriculas were often to be found reared under the tender
solicitude of those who looked after their own small gardens.
Hired servants, she said, in her long and careful account of
the flowers, did not lavish enough parental care on these
delicate "mountain cowslips."

What else Clare had in his garden may be learnt, in great
measure, from his poems, and from what he tells us of his
discoveries in the fields. The pasque flower, or, as he calls it,
"the blue anemone, the anemone pulsatilla of botanists,"
would certainly be there. He liked to fancy it sprang from the
blood or dust of the Romans because it haunted the Roman
banks of the neighbourhood and could be found wild nowhere
else. It used to grow "in great plenty" at Swordy Well, "but
the plough, that destroyer of wild flowers, has rooted it out
of its long-inherited dwelling." He had transplanted some of
the remaining plants to his garden by carefully taking a good
deal of their own soil with them. Perhaps, too, he even managed to coax viper's bugloss out of its stony stronghold there.
There would be white horehound, then growing plentifully
on Cowper Green, still to be found there in 1912, but now not
to be found there because of our modern threateners of the
rarer wayside flowers. Mullein, too, he brought from Cowper
Green, and betony, ploughman's spikenard, and other
flowers of middle summer. Ashton stone-pits, blanketed
with "old man's beard," wild basil, and marjoram, would
supply him with what he needed of these; Glinton's still-
pellitoried church wall would provide him with creepers for

his stones. He brought yellow-wort from the Heath, and oxlips (or, as he preferred to call them, Bedlam cowslips) from under the shady hedges, with harebells, and, in early autumn, clumps of ragwort. Then, "the year growing ancient," there was an "everlasting rose" whose green leaves nodded in at the door all winter; this was the "bastard black hellebore" which, in Culpepper's day, was "commonly found in the woods in Northamptonshire," and, since Clare wrote some verses on it, we may conclude it had done him some good, as the old herbalists held it could, when he was "molested with melancholy."

As well as these wild ones that he had always loved to transplant by the side of his chrysanthemums and auriculas, be sure there were "Lady's laces, everlasting peas"; and, as in Hudson's true cottage garden, "the flowers we know and remember for ever. The old, homely, cottage-garden blooms, so old that they have entered the soul." Clare himself recounts them over and over:

> The pale pink pea, and monkshood darkly blue;
> The white and purple gilliflowers, that stay
> Ling'ring in blossom, summer half away;
> The single blood-walls, of a luscious smell,
> Old-fashioned flowers which housewives love so well;
> The columbines, stone-blue, or deep night-brown,
> Their honeycomb-like blossoms hanging down. . . .
> With marjoram knots, sweet-brier, and ribbon-grass,
> And lavender. . . .

Yet, while he was proud of his own slip of land, "never was there a garden like the meadow." His poems are, after all, far more concerned with the flowers there than with the cultivated ones. Yarrow, for instance, he would not transplant, because

> . . . . on the leas
> Of rough neglected pasture I delight
> More than in gardens thus to stray
> Amid such scenes and mark thy hardy blooms. . . .
> Bidding the loneliest russet paths be gay.

In this period of such poor health his wanderings after flowers were not forgone; so that by 1830 he could annotate a list of orchises made by Henderson of Milton with the names of every place in the neighbourhood where the plants were to be found. But it was as a botanist that he was interested in the orchises. The late Dr. George Claridge Druce, in his *Northamptonshire Botanologia* and in his *Flora of Northamptonshire*, is decisive in his measure of Clare as botanist. Speaking only of Clare's published works, he says:

"In his poems about a hundred and twenty different plants are referred to, and of these about forty-two are mentioned for the first time as Northamptonshire species . . . one has been frequently impressed with Clare's close and accurate information; if the Muse had not claimed him for her own, Natural Science would have gained a devotee."

Clare's contribution as naturalist will be discussed at the end of the Journal.

"*Thur.* . . . Took a walk in the fields. Gathered a bunch of wild flowers that lingered in sheltered places as loath to die. The ragwort lingers still in its yellow clusters, and the little heath-bell or harvest-bell quakes to the wind under the quick banks of warm furze. Clumps of wild marjoram are yet in flower about the mole-hilly banks, and clumps of meadow-sweet linger with a few bushes yet unfaded.

"*Fri.* Read Hazlitt's *Lectures on the Poets*. I admire his mention of the daisy as reminding him of his boyish days, when he used to try to jump over his own shadow. He is one of the very best prose-writers of the present day, and his works are always entertaining, and may be taken up whenever one chooses or feels the want of amusement. His political writings are heated and empty—'full of sound and fury.' I hate politics and therefore I may be but a poor judge.

"*Sat.* Continued to read Hazlitt; I like his *Lectures on the Poets* better than those on the Comic Writers and on Shakespeare; his *View of the English Stage* is not so good as either: they might have remained in their first places—viz. the newspapers for which they were written—without any loss to the world. His other works I have not seen. Read in

Shakespeare, 'A Midsummer Night's Dream,' for the first time. I have still got three parts out of four of the plays to read and I hope I shall not leave the world without reading them.

"*Sun.* . . . Finished another chapter of my Life. Read some passages in Blair's *Sermons*. Looked into Maddox on the culture of flowers, and the *Flora Domestica*, which, with a few improvements and additions, would be one of the most entertaining books ever written. If I live I will write one on the same plan and call it 'A Garden of Wild Flowers,' as it shall contain nothing else, with quotations from poets and others. An English Botany on this plan would be very interesting and serve to make botany popular, while the hard nicknaming system of unutterable words now in vogue only overloads it in mystery till it makes darkness visible.

"*Mon. 25 Oct.* Old Shepherd Newman died this morning, an old tenant of the fields and the last of the old shepherds. The fields are now left desolate and his old haunts look like houses disinhabited; the fading woods seem mourning in the autumn wind. How often hath he seen the blue sky, the green fields and woods, and the season's changes! Now he sleeps unconscious of all. What a desolate mystery doth it leave round the living mind. The end of Gray's 'Elegy' might well be applied to this tenant of the fields—'Oft have we seen him.'

"*Tues.* . . . Looked into Pope. I know not how it is but I cannot take him up often or read him long together; the uninterrupted flow of the verses wearies the ear. There are some fine passages in the 'Essay on Man.' The Pastorals are nicknamed so, for daffodils breathing flutes, beachen bowls, silver crooks, purling brooks, and such like everlasting singsong does not make pastorals. His prologue to the Satires is good; but that celebrated Epitaph on Gay ends burlesquely. . . .

"*Wed.* I have been much struck with some passages in the Poems of Aaron Hill. He seems to struggle to free his ideas from the turnpike hackneyisms of sounding rhymes and tinkling periods then in fashion, for most of the rhymers of that day seem to catch their little inspiration from Pope.

"*Thur.* . . . Read some passages in Shakespeare. Turned over a few leaves of Knox's *Essays*. Read Bacon's essay on the idea of a compleat garden, divided into every month of the year, in which the flowers bloom; what beautiful essays these are! I take them up like Shakespeare and read them over and still find plenty to entertain me.

"*Fri.* Read some poems of Wordsworth. . . , When I first began to read poetry I disliked Wordsworth because I heard he was disliked; and I was astonished when I looked into him to find my mistaken pleasure in being delighted and finding him so natural and beautiful: in his 'White Doe of Rylstone' there is some of the sweetest poetry I ever met with, though full of his mysteries.

"*Sat.* Received a present of two volumes of sermons on 'The Doctrines and Practice of Christianity' from Lord Radstock. He is one of my best friends and not of much kin with the world. The chrysanthemums are just opening their beautiful double flowers: I have five [six] sorts this year, the claret-coloured, the buff, the bright yellow, the paper-white, the purple, and the rose-coloured: lost one—the chocolate or coffee-coloured. Promised more from Milton.

"*Sun.* Took a walk. Got some branches of the spindle tree, with its pink-coloured berries that shine beautifully in the pale sun. Found for the first time 'the herb true love' or 'one berry' in Oxey Wood. Brought a root home to set in my garden. . . .

"*Mon. 1 Nov.* Took a walk to Lolham Bridge to hunt for a species of fern that used to grow on some willow tree heads in Lolham lane when I was a boy, but could find none. Got some of the yellow water-lily from the pits, which the floods had washed up, to set in an old water-tub in the garden, and to try some on land in a swaily corner, as the horse-blob thrives well, which is a water flower. Listened in the evening to Glinton bells at the top of the garden. I always feel melancholy at this season to hear them; and yet it is a pleasure.

I'm pleased and yet I'm sad.' [10]

"*Tues.* Set some box edging round a border which I have made for my collection of ferns. Read some passages in Blair's *Grave,* a beautiful poem, and one of the best things after the manner of Shakespeare. Its beginning is very characteristic of the subject. There are crowds of beautiful passages about it. Who has not marked the following aged companions to many such spots of general decay?

> . . . *a row of reverend elms,*
> *Long lashed by the rude winds. Some rift half down*
> . . . *others so thin atop,*
> *That scarce two crows could lodge in the same tree.*

"*Wed.* Took a walk with John Billings to Swordy Well to gather some 'old man's beard' which hangs about the hedges in full bloom. Its downy clusters of artificial-like flowers appear at first as if the hedge was littered with bunches of white cotton. Went into Hilly Wood and found a beautiful species of fern on a sallow stoven in a pit, which I have not seen before. There are five sorts growing about the woods here; the common brake, the fox fern, the hart's tongue, and the polypody, two sorts, the tall and the dwarf.[11]

"*Fri.* Read in Bishop Percy's poems, the *Reliques of Ancient Poetry.* Take them up as often as I may I am always delighted. There is so much of the essence and simplicity of true poetry that makes me regret I did not see them sooner, as they would have formed my taste and laid the foundations of my judgement in writing and thinking poetically. As it is I feel indebted to them for many feelings.

"*Sat.* Took a walk in the fields. The oaks are beginning to turn reddish brown and the winds have stripped some nearly bare. The underwood's last leaves are in their gayest yellows. Thus autumn seems to put on bridal colours for a shroud. The little harvest-bell is still in bloom, trembling to the cold wind, almost the only flower living, save the 'old man's beard' or traveller's joy, on the hedges.

"*Sun.* Received a packet from London with the Magazine and some copies of MSS. that come very slowly, and a letter very friendly worded. But I have found that saying and doing is a wide difference, too far very often to be neighbours, much less friends. . . .

"*Mon. 8 Nov.* Read over the Magazine. The review of Lord Byron's Conversations is rather entertaining. The pretending letter of James Thomson is a bold lie.[12] I dislike these lapt-up counterfeits mantled in truth, like a

SWORDY WELL

brassy shilling in its silver washings, those Birmingham half-pence passed off as matter of fact moneys. Elia can do better. The rest of the articles are motley matters, some poor and some middling. Magazines are always of such wear.

"*Tues.* Read Shakespeare's 'Henry the Fifth' of which I have always been very fond from almost a boy. I first met with it in an odd volume which I got for sixpence. Yet I thought then that the Welsh officer with two other of his companions were tedious talkers, and I feel that I think so still. Yet I feel such an interest about the play that I can never lay it down till I see the end of it.

"*Wed.* Read 'Macbeth.' What a soul-thrilling power hovers over this tragedy. I have read it over about twenty times and it chains my feelings still to its perusal like a new thing. It is Shakespeare's masterpiece. The thrilling feelings created by the description of Lady Macbeth's terror-haunted walkings in her sleep sink deeper than a thousand ghosts— at least in my vision of the terrible. . . .

"*Thur.* Received a letter from Inskip the friend of Bloom-field, full of complaints at my not writing. What use is writing when the amount on both sides amounts to nothing more than waste paper? I have desires to know something of Bloomfield's latter days, but I can hear of nothing further than his dying neglected; so it's of no use enquiring further; for we know that to be the common lot of genius.

"*Sat.* Looked into Thomson's 'Winter.' There is a freshness about it I think superior to the others, though rather of a pompous cast. How natural all his descriptions from nature are! Nature was consulted in all of them. The more I read them the more truth I discover. The following are great favourites of mine and prove what I mean. Describing a hasty flood forcing through a narrow passage he says:

> *It boils, and wheels, and foams, and thunders through.*
> *Snatch'd in short eddies, plays the wither'd leaf;*
> *And on the flood the dancing feather floats.*

"*Sun.* Read in old Tusser[13] with whose quaint rhymes I have often been entertained. He seems to have been acquainted with most of the odd measures now in fashion. He seems to have felt a taste for Enclosures, and Mavor, that busy note-maker and book-compiler of schoolboy memory, has added an impertinent note to Tusser's opinion, as an echo of faint praise. So much for a parson's opinion in such matters! I am an advocate for open fields and I think that others' experiences confirm my opinion day by day. There are two pretty sonnets in Tusser and some natural images scattered about the book. The four following lines are pretty:

> *The year I compare, as I find for a truth,*
> *The Spring unto Childhood, the Summer to Youth.*
> *The Harvest to Manhood, the Winter to Age,*
> *All quickly forgot, as a play on a stage.*

"*Mon. 15 Nov.* Went to gather pooties on the Roman bank for a collection. Found a scarce sort of which I only saw two in my life, one picked up under a hedge at Peakirk town-end, and another in Bainton Meadow. Its colour is a fine sunny yellow, larger than the common sort, and round the rim of the base is a black edging which extends no further than the rim. It is not in the collection at the British Museum.

"*Tues.* My friend Billings told me that he saw four swallows about the second of this month flying over his house. He has not seen them since and forgot to tell me at the time. Now what becomes of these swallows for the winter? That they cannot go into another country now is certain; but how or where is a mystery that has made more opinions than proofs, and remains a mystery.

"*Wed.* The chrysanthemums are in full flower. What a beautiful heart-cheering to the different seasons nature has provided in her continual successions of the bloom of flowers! . . . The little aconite peeps its yellow flowers, then the snowdrop, and further on the crocus dropping in before the summer multitude; and after their departure the tall hollyhock and little aster bloom in their showy colours; then comes the Michaelmas daisy, and lastly the chrysanthemums; while the China roses

> *all the year*
> *Or in the bud or in the bloom appear.*

"*Thur.* Read in Southey's *Wesley*. He has made a very entertaining book of it; but considering the subject I think he might have made more of it. The character of Wesley is one of the finest I have read. They may speak of him as they please, but they cannot diminish his simplicity of genius as an author and his piety as a Christian. I sincerely wish that the present day could find such a man.

"*Friday*. Had a visit from my friend Henderson, and I felt revived as I was very dull before. He had pleasing news to deliver me, having discovered a new species of fern a few days back, growing among the bogs on Whittlesey Mere; and our talk was of ferns for the day. He tells me there are twenty-four different species, or more, natives of England and Scotland. One of the finest of the latter is called the maidenhair, growing in rock-clefts.

"*Sat*. Went out to hunt the hart's tongue species of fern and fell in with the ruins of the old castle in Ashton Lawn; but found none. Its commonest place is in wells, in the crevices of the walls, but I have found it growing about the badger-holes in Open Copy Wood. Got very wet and returned home. Finished the eighth chapter of my Life.

"*Mon. 22 Nov.* Looked into Milton's *Paradise Lost*. I once read it through when I was a boy. At that time I liked *The Death of Abel* better. What odd judgements those of boys are! How they change as they ripen. When I think of the slender merits of *The Death of Abel* against such a giant as Milton I cannot help smiling at my young fancies in those days of happy ignorance.

"*Wed*. I have often been struck with the tales old men and women relate in their remembrances of the growth of trees. The elm groves in the Staves Acre Close at the town-end, where the rooks build, and that are of giant height, my old friend Billings says he remembers no thicker than his stick; [he] saw my father's uncle set them, carrying a score on his back at once. I can scarcely believe it.

"*Thur*. Received a letter from Hessey. I have not answered his last and know not when I shall. The world's friendships are counterfeits and forgeries. On that principle I have proved it and my affections are sickened unto death. My memories are broken, while my confidence is grown to a shadow. In the bringing out of the second edition of the *Minstrel* they were a twelvemonth in printing a title-page.

"*Sun*. A gentleman came to see me to-day whose whole talk was of Bloomfield and booksellers. He told me to put no

faith in them, and when I told him that all my faith and
MSS. likewise were in their hands already he shook his head
and declared with a solemn bend of his body 'Then you are
done, by God! They will never print them, but will dally you
on with well-managed excuses to the grave, and then boast
that they were your friends when you are not able to con-
tradict it, as they have done to Bloomfield." He then desired
me to get my MSS. back by all means and sell them at a
market-price at what they would fetch. He said that Bloomfield had not a £100 a year to maintain five or six in the
family. Why, I have not £50 to maintain eight with! This is a
hungry difference.

"*Tues. 30 Nov.* An excessive wet day. Read the *Literary
Souvenir* for 1825 in all its gilt and finery. What a number
of candidates for fame are smiling on its pages! What a pity
it is that time should be such a destroyer of our hopes and
anxieties; for the best of us are but doubts on fame's promises
and a century will thin the myriad worse than the plague.

"*Fri.* Found a very beautiful fern in Oxey Wood. Suppose
it the white maidenhair of Hill. It is very scarce here.

"*Tues. 7 Dec.* Another gipsy wedding of the Smith
family; fiddling and drinking as usual.

"*Wed.* Found the common polypody on an old willow
tree in Lolham Lane and a small fern in Hilly Wood scarcely
larger than some species of moss and a little resembling
curled parsley. I have named it the dwarf maidenhair
and believe it is very scarce here.

"*Tues. 14 Dec.* A copple-crowned crane shot at Billings's
pond in the Green. 'Twas four foot high from the toes to
the bill. On the breast and rump was a thick, shaggy down
full of powder, which seemed to be a sort of pounce-box to
the bird, to dress its feathers with to keep out the wet. Its
neck and breast were beautifully stained with streaks of
watery brown. Its back was slate-grey. The down on its
head was of the same colour.

"*Wed.* Went to Milton. Saw a fine edition of Linnaeus's
Botany with beautiful plates, and find that my fern which I
found in Harrison's close dyke, by the wood lane, is the
thorn-pointed fern. Saw also a beautiful book on insects
with the plants they feed on, by Curtis. Found Artis busy
over his fossil plants and Roman antiquities; but his complaints of the deceptions of publishers are akin with mine.

"*Thur.* Saw Henderson's collection of ferns, which is far from complete, though some of them are beautiful. Learned from him of a singular instinct in plants of the creeping or climbing kind, some having a propensity to twine to the left in their climbing, and others to the right; the woodbine seems to twine to the left and the traveller's joy to the right; but this is not an invariable fact.

"*Wed. 22 Dec.* A copple-crowned pheasant shot. Very large and coloured about the breast and back like the cock; but the head was plain.

"*Sat.* Christmas Day. Gathered a handful of daisies in full bloom: saw a woodbine and dogrose in the woods putting out in full leaf, and a primrose root full of ripe flowers. What a day this used to be when [I was] a boy! How eager I used to attend the church to see it stuck with evergreens (emblems of eternity), and the cottage windows and the picture ballads on the wall all stuck with ivy, holly, box, and yew! Such feelings are past and 'all this world is proud of.'

"*Sun.* Found at the bottom of a dyke made in the Roman bank some pooties of varied colours, and the large garden ones of a russet colour, with a great many others of the meadow sort which we called 'badgers' when I was a school-boy, found nowhere now but in wet places. There are a great many, too, of a water species now extinct. The dyke is four foot deep and the soil is full of these shells. Have they not lain here ever since the Romans made the bank? And do the water sorts not imply that the fields were all fen and under water, or wet and uncultivated at that time? I think it does. I never walk on this bank but the legions of the Roman army pass by my fancies, with their mysteries of nearly 2,000 years hanging like a mist around them. What changes hath passed since then!

"*Wed. 29 Dec.* Went with neighbour Billings to Southey Wood and Gees Holt to hunt ferns: found none. Met with a new species of moss fern, striped, growing on a common species like the mistletoe on a thorn. It is a sort of moss mistletoe. Preserved a specimen. Saw a branch of black-thorn, dogrose, and eldern, in full leaf all in one hedgerow. Saw a bumbarrel with moss as if building a nest.

"*Sun. 2 Jan. 1825.* Received a parcel from Mrs. Emmerson. Took a walk to Simon's Wood; found three distinct species of the bramble. Henderson will have it there are but two but I am certain he is wrong, and believe there are four, the common one that grows in the hedges, the larger sort that grows on commons bearing larger fruit called by children 'blackberry,' the small creeping dewberry that runs along the ground in the land furrows and on the brinks of brooks, and a much larger one of the same kind growing in woods. Botanists may say what they will; for though these are all of a family they are distinctly different. There are two sorts of the wild rose, the one in hedges bearing blush-coloured flowers, and the other much smaller in woods with white ones.

"*Wed. 5 Jan.* Gillyflowers, polyanthuses, marigolds, and the yellow yarrow are in flower, and the double scarlet anemone nearly out; crocuses peeping out above ground, swelling with flower. The authoress [Elizabeth Kent] of the *Flora Domestica* says the snowdrop is the first spring flower: she is mistaken; the yellow winter aconite is always earlier, and the first on the list of spring.

"*Fri.* Bought some cakes of colour with the intention of trying to make sketches of curious snail horns, butterflies, moths, sphinxes, wild flowers, and whatever my wanderings may meet with that are not too common.

"*Wed. 19 Jan.* A slight storm of snow for the first time this winter. Just completed the ninth chapter of my Life. Corrected the poem on the "Vanities of the World," which I have written in imitation of the old poets, on whom I mean to father it, and send it to Montgomery's paper *The Iris,* or the *Literary Chronicle,* under that character.

"*Sun. 23 Jan.* Took a walk to Hilly Wood: brought home another plant of the white maidenhair fern that grows on a sallow stoven in a sort of spring. . . . Finished my 'two ballads to Mary' which I intend to send to the *Literary Gazette,* as also my three sonnets to Bloomfield. I am weary of writing.

"*Thur.* Heard the buzz of the black beetle or cockchafer that flies about in the autumn evenings and early in spring. It is different to the brown or summer beetle which is described by Collins:

the beetle winds
His small but sullen horn

and is not so common.

"*Mon. 31 Jan.* Went to Simon's Wood for a sucker of the barberry bush to set in my garden. Saw the corn tree putting out into leaf. A yellow crocus and a bunch of single snowdrops in full flower. The mavis thrush has been singing all day long. Spring seems begun. The woodbines all over the wood are in full leaf.

"*Tues.* A beautiful morning: took a walk in the fields. Saw some birch poles in the quick fencing, and fancied the bark of birch might make a good substitute for paper; it is easily parted in thin layers and one shred of bark round the tree would split into ten or a dozen sheets. I have tried it and find it receives the ink very readily.

"*Wed.* Went to walk in the fields and heard Ufford bells chiming for a funeral: when I enquired I found it was for poor old John Cue of Ufford, a friend of mine with whom I worked some seasons at turnip-hoeing for which he was famous. He knew my Grandfather well and told me many recollections of their young days' follies. John Cue was once head gardener for Lord Manners of Ufford Hall. He was fond of flowers and books and possessed a many curious ones of the latter, among which was Parkinson.

"*Thur.* Received a letter from Hessey, with £5 enclosed and a parcel containing two numbers of the new series of London Mag., and *Walladmor*, a German-Scotch novel. If Job was living now he would stand a chance to gain his wish, 'O that mine enemy would write a book!' for this is the age of book making and like the small-pox almost everybody catches the plague.

"*Fri.* The first winter's day: a sharp frost and a night fall of snow drifted in heaps by a keen wind. There has been a deal of talk about the forwardness of this season, but last season was not much behind. On the third of this month I found an hedge-sparrow's nest in Billings's boxtrees before the window, with three eggs in it. I looked again in March and found two young ones, pen-feathered, starved to death. She laid again in the same nest and brought off a fledged brood.

"Sun. 13 Feb. An odd sort of fellow came today with a bag full of old school summing books, wanting me to buy them, and vowing he was the author of them, and that I might make a good bargain by publishing them. What odd characters there are in the world! The fellow fancied that I was excessive ignorant, to palm such ignorant impudence upon me for truth. After he found his scheme would not take he begged two pence and departed. He is the son of an odd fellow at Baston. He is a little foolish by nature and they put him a long while to school to compleat what she began.

"My dear Anna taken very ill.

"Mon. 14 Feb. In my letter to Van Dyk I inserted the tune of 'Peggy Band.' There are a great many beautiful tunes to these provincial ballads, such as the 'White Cockade,' 'War's Alarms,' 'Down the Burn, Davy' (old and new), 'Through the wood, Laddie,' 'Dusty Miller,' 'Highland Laddie,' and a very beautiful one I forget the title: it begins 'A withered old gipsy one day I espied, Who bade me shun the thick woods and said something beside'; but the old woman that sung it . . , the old 'Guardian Angels,' 'Banks of Banna,' and a thousand others, [is gone].

"Tues. Heard the blackbird sing in Hilly Wood: received a Valentine from Mrs. Emmerson.

"My Anna is something better.

"Sun. Found several pieces of Roman pot in Harrison's top close on the hill over which the road crosses to the Tindhills at the north-east corner of Oxey Wood. One piece was the lettered and Artis says they are Roman. I verily believe some Roman pottery was made there.

"Mon. 21 Feb. A robin busy at building its nest in the garden.

"Sun. 27 Feb. Received a letter in rhyme from a John Pooley—a very dull fooley—who ran me tenpence further into debt, as I had not money to pay the postage.

"Tues. 1 Mar. Saw today the largest piece of ivy I ever saw in my life, mailing a tree which it nearly surpassed in size in Oxey Wood. It was thicker than my thigh and its cramping embraces seemed to diminish the tree to a dwarf. It has been asserted by some that ivy is very injurious to trees and by others that it does no injury at all. I cannot

decide against it. The large pieces were covered all over with root-like fibres as thick as hair, and they represented the limbs of animals more than the bark of a tree.

"*Thur.* This is Patty's Birthday.

"*Sun. 6 Mar.* Received a parcel from Hessey with the magazine and a leaf of the new poems; also a present of Miss Kent's *Sylvan Sketches.* She seems to be a regular book-maker. Parish Officers are modern savages, as the following fact will testify: 'Crowland Abbey.—Certain surveyors have lately dug up several foundation stones of the Abbey, and also a great quantity of stone coffins, for the purpose of repairing the parish roads.'—*Stamford Mercury.*

"Anna taken again for the worse yesterday; had a terrible fever all night and remains in a doubtful state.

"*Wed.* I had a very odd dream last night, and I take it as an ill omen, for I don't expect that the book will meet a better fate. I thought I had one of the proofs of the new poems from London, and after looking at it awhile it shrank through my hands like sand, and crumbled into dust. The birds were singing in Oxey Wood at six o'clock this evening as loud and various as in May.

"*Thur.* Heard an anecdote yesterday of Dr. Dodd[14] which is well known and considered authentic among the common people. It is said that Dr. Dodd was haunted on his way to the place of execution by a lady who had envied his popularity, and looking out of a window as he passed she exclaimed 'Now Dr. Dodd, where's your God?'; when he bade her look in the last chapter of Micah and read the eighth, ninth, and tenth verses for an answer: which she did, and died soon afterwards of a broken heart.

"*Fri.* Intend to call my Natural History of Helpstone "Biographies of Birds and Flowers," with an appendix on animals and insects.

"*Sat.* Received the first proof of the *Shepherd's Calendar* from Hessey to correct, and a letter from Lord Radstock in which he seems to be offended at a late opinion of mine of some newspaper poems that he sent me as specimens of the beautiful; and he thanks his stars that his taste is not so refined as to make him above admiring them. The word refinement has lost its original use and is nothing more than a substitute for fashionable coquette which I thank *my* stars for keeping me too ignorant to learn.

RJ

"*Mon. 14 Mar.* My double scarlet anemone in flower. A sharp frosty morning.

"*Tues.* I have been reading over Mrs. Barbauld's *Lessons for Children* to my eldest child who is continually teasing me to read them. I find by this that they are particularly suited to the tastes of children as she is never desirous of hearing anything read a second time but them.

"*Thur.* Received a letter and present of books from Lord Radstock containing Hannah More's *Spirit of Prayer*, Bishop Wilson's *Maxims*, Burnet's *Life of God in the Soul of Man*, *A New Manual of Prayer*, and Watson's *Answer to Paine*, a quiet unaffected defence of the Bible and an example for all controversialists to go by, where railing has no substitute for argument. I have not read Tom Paine, but I have always understood him to be a low blackguard.

"*Mon. 21 Mar.* Had a double polyanthus and single white hepatica sent me from Stamford, round which was wrapped a curious prospectus of an *Every-Day Book*, by W. Hone. If such a thing were well got up it would make one of the most entertaining things ever published; and I think the prospectus bids fair to do something. There is a fine quotation from Herrick for a motto. How delightful is the freshness of these old poets; it is like meeting with green spots in deserts.

"*Sun. 7 April.* Two gentlemen came to see me from Milton; one of them appeared to be a sensible, well-informed man. He talked much of the poets, but did not like Wordsworth; and when I told him I did he constantly asked me whether I did not like Byron better. I don't like these comparisons to knock your opinions on the head with. I told him that I read Wordsworth oftener than I did Byron, and he seemed to express his surprise at it by observing that he could not read Wordsworth at all.

"*Thur. 14 April.* My mother is sixty-seven years old this day. She has been afflicted with a dropsy for this twenty years and has for all that outlived a large family of brothers and sisters and remains 'the last of the flock.' The snakehead or fritillary in flower; also the light-blue, pink, and white hyacinths; bluebell or harebell in flower; the primrose, violet, and bedlam cowslip fading out of flower.

"*Sat. 16 April.* Took a walk in the field, birds-nesting

and botanizing, and had like to have been taken up as a poacher in Hilly Wood, by a meddlesome, conceited keeper belonging to Sir John Trollop. He swore that he had seen me in act, more than once, of shooting game, when I never shot even so much as a sparrow in my life. What terrifying rascals these woodkeepers and gamekeepers are! They make a prison of the forests and are its gaolers.

"*Mon. 18 April.* Resumed my letters on Natural History in good earnest, and intend to get them finished with this year, if I can get out into the fields, for I will insert nothing but what has come under my notice.

"*Sat. 23 April.* Saw the redstart or firetail today and little willow wren. The blackthorn tree in full flower that shines about the hedges like cloaks hung out to dry . . . .

"*Mon. 25 April.* Heard a terrible kick-up with the rats in the ceiling last night and might have made up a tolerable faith to believe them ghosts. . . . .

"*Tues.* This used to be 'Breakday' when the fen commons used to be broke as it was called, by turning in the stock; it used to be a day of busy note with the villages. But Enclosure has spoiled all.

"*Thur.* Hedge-sparrow finished her nest in Billings's box-tree and laid one egg. Walnut showing leaf: sycamore and horse-chestnut nearly covered. I observed a snail on his journey at full speed, and I marked by my watch that he went thirteen inches in three minutes, which was the utmost he could do without stopping to wind or rest. It was the large garden snail.

"*Fri.* The hedge-sparrow in the box tree has been about twelve days building her nest, the robin in the wall about fourteen, and the jenny-wren near three weeks. Heard all through last night the sort of watch-ticking noise called a death-watch. I observed there was one on each side the chamber, and as soon as one finished ticking the other began. I think it is a call that the male and female use in the time of cohabiting. . . . .

"*Sat.* Received another letter from the editor of Bloomfield's Correspondence, requesting me to alter a line in my sonnet on Bloomfield, 'Thy injured muse and memory need no sigh,' and asking permission to publish only two of them, which I shall not agree with either way. Editors are troubled with nice amendings; and if doctors were as fond of amputation as they are of altering and correcting, the world would have nothing but cripples.

"*Fri. 6 May.* Could not sleep at night. Got up at three o'clock in the morning and walked about the fields. The birds were high in their songs in Royce Wood and almost deafening. I heard the cricket-bird again in full cry in Royce Wood; it is just like a child's 'screecher.' Saw a hawk-like bird that made an odd noise like one of the notes of the nightingale as if to decoy his prey into sight.

"*Tues. 10 May.* Saw a male and female of the treesparrow (as I supposed them) in Royce Close hedge next the lane. The cockbird had a very black head, and its shades of brown were more deep and distinct than the house sparrow. The female when flying showed two white feathers in her tail. They seemed to have a nest in the hedgerow but I could not find it. Saw a pettichap in Bushy Close. Its note is more like 'chippichap'; it keeps in continual motion on the tops of trees, uttering its note.

"*Fri. 13 May.* Met with an extraordinary incident today, while walking in Open Wood to hunt a nightingale's nest. I popt unawares on an old fox and her four young cubs that were playing about. She saw me and instantly approached me growling like an angry dog. I had no stick, and tried all I could to fright her by imitating the bark of a fox-hound, which only irritated her the more, and if I had not retreated a few paces back she would have seized me: when I set up an halloo she started.

"*Sat. 14 May.* The Magazine is very dull. A note also from Miss Kent accompanied the parcel to request my assistance to give her information for her intended History of Birds. But if my assistance is not worth more than twelve lines it is worth nothing and I shall not interfere.

"*Thur. 26 May.* Took up my hyacinth bulbs and laid them in ridges of earth to dry. Made a new frame for my auriculas. Found a large white orchis in Oxey Wood of a curious species and very rare. I watched a bluecap or blue titmouse feeding her young, whose nest was in a wall close to an orchard. She got caterpillars out of the blossoms of the apple trees and leaves of the plum: she fetched 120 caterpillars in half an hour. Now suppose she only feeds them four times a day, a quarter of an hour each time, she fetched no less than 480 caterpillars. . . .

"*Sat. 28 May.* Found the old frog in my garden that has been there this four years. I know it by a mark which it received from my spade four years ago. I thought it would die of the wound, so I turned it up on a bed of flowers at the end of the garden, which is thickly covered with ferns and bluebells. I am glad to see it has recovered. . . .

"*Tues. 31 May.* My dear child Eliza was taken ill of a fever on Sunday night and is as yet no better. Sent a letter and parcel to Mrs. Emmerson with 'The Parish' and my new will for Mr. Clutterbuck to draw up. Mrs. Bellars of Wood-croft Castle came to see my garden. Artis told me he fancied that the place in Harrison's close was a Roman pottery. I have since recollected that there used to be a large hole, about two stones' throw from it, called 'Potter's Hole,' when I was a boy, and filled up since the Enclosure. This may go far for his opinion.

"*Thur. 2 June.* This is my darling Anna's birthday who is five years old, a weakling flower fast fading in the bud,— withering untimely. . . .

"*Fri. 3 June.* Finished planting my auriculas: went a-bot-anizing after ferns and orchises and caught a cold in the wet grass, which has made me as bad as ever. Got the tune of 'Highland Mary' from Wisdom Smith, a gipsy, and pricked another sweet tune without name as he fiddled it.

"*Sat.* Saw three fellows at the end of Royce Wood, who, I found, were laying out the plan for an 'Iron railway' from Manchester to London. It is to cross over Round Oak Spring by Royce Wood corner for Woodcroft Castle. I little thought that fresh intrusions would interrupt and spoil my solitudes. After the Enclosure they will despoil a boggy place that is famous for orchises at Royce Wood end.

"*Mon. 6 June.* Went to see Mrs. Bellars's garden at Wood-croft with Anna. Saw a scarlet anemone and white peony, both very handsome. The moat round the garden has a very fine effect, and the long bridges that cross it [are] made of planks and railed with crooked pieces of oak. I thought of the time of Cromwell while walking about it, and felt the difference. Swallows had several nests under the bridge.

"*Tues.* Received another parcel from Hessey, with another

proof of the Poems, viz. the 'Sorrows of Love.' Taylor has cut out a good deal and some things which I think might have stood. The parcel also brought a present of Ayton's *Essays*,[15] a young writer of great promise, which was killed in the bud. These essays are excellent and contain a great deal more of the human heart than an affectedly written book with that title.

"*Wed. 8 June.* Poor old Coz Day the mole-catcher died tonight after a short illness. He has been a tenant of the meadows and fields for half a century.

"*Fri. 10 June.* Saw the blue-grey or lead-coloured flycatcher for the first time this season. They are called 'Egypt birds' by the common people, from their note, which seems to resemble the sound of the word 'Egypt.' They build in old walls, like the redstart and grey wagtail.

"*Mon. 13 June.* My dear Eliza is three years old today. I feel anxious to insert these memorandums of my affections, as memory, though a secondary, is the soul of time, and life, the principal, but its shadow. . . . .

"*Sun.* Received a letter from Taylor in which he says that there is twice as much as he wants for the *Shepherd's Calendar*, and a few months back one of his causes for delay was that there was not enough to begin on. Nothing has made a wide difference here by time, and left a puzzling paradox behind it, which tells that he is a very dilatory chap. Received a parcel containing a present of a waistcoat and some fine polyanthus, Brompton stock, and geranium seed.

"*Tues. 21 June.* Found a bird's nest in the thatch of a hovel gable-end in Billings's yard; think it a flycatcher's. It resembles in colour and shape something of the chat or whitethroat, or more like the sedgebird than either. The female sits hard and the cock feeds her with caterpillars from the leaves of trees.

"*Sun. 3 July.* Today is Helpstone Feast. Wrestling and fighting. The ploughman's fame is still kept up with the usual determined spirit.

"*Thur. 7 July.* Wrote an answer to Hessey's letter of the 30th of June which contained a draft for my dividend and salary, and enquired after the stoppage of the new poems. Also was forced to solicit them anew to send me £10 which I want to pay off my half-yearly accounts.

"*Tues. 12 July.* Went today to see Artis: found him busy over his antiquities and fossils. He told me a curious thing about the manner in which the golden-crested wren builds her nest: he says it is the only English bird that suspends its nest, which it hangs on three twigs of the fir branch, and it glues the eggs at the bottom of the nest, with the gum out of the tree, to keep them from being blown out by the wind, which often turns them upside-down without injury.

"*Wed.* This day I am thirty, (or thirty-three, I am not certain which) [16] and my health was drunk at Milton by two very pretty girls, Mrs. P—r, and Mrs. B—n, who wished I might treble the number; but I did not drink it in return. . . .

"*Fri.* . . . . Began to teach Eliza Holmes the common rules of Arithmetic at the restless request of her parents who are anxious for me to learn her.

"*Fri. 29 July.* Received a proof from Taylor. The plan is again altered, and he now intends to print the months only and leave out the tales; this plan is one that puts the worst first and leaves the best for a future opportunity. This proof contains 'February' and 'April.' The last is good for nothing and is not worth troubling the printers with. The poem on Spring is the best in the bundle and would supply its place well.

"*Sun. 21 Aug.* Received a letter from Mr. Emmerson which tells me that Lord Radstock died yesterday. He was the best friend I have met with. Though he possessed too much of that simple-heartedness to be a fashionable friend or hypocrite, yet it often led him to take hypocrites for honest friends and to take an honest man for a hypocrite.

"*Tues. 23 Aug.* Found a most beautiful Death's head moth caterpillar in Billings's potatoes. It is about four and a half inches long, of most beautiful rainbow colours.

"*Fri.* Received a letter from the Editor of a new *Almanack of the Muses* or *Souvenir*, or *Forget me not*, some such thing, intended to be published by Messrs. Baynes and Son, of Paternoster Row, requesting me to send a contribution.

"*Wed. 7 Sept.* Received a letter from Hessey telling me that Taylor has been very ill, also one from Messrs. Baynes and Son, and one from Alaric A. Watts, of Manchester. Received in October a letter from J. Power of the Strand requesting permission to publish 'Broomsgrove' with music, for which he gave me two sovereigns.

"*Thur. 8 Sept.* Met old Dacon, the Jew of Cliff, at Billings's, who has the odd notion to believe himself the saviour of the world and in spite of all this is a very sensible and remarkable man, about 5 feet 10 inches high, with a pleasing countenance. His hair and beard is never cut or shaved.

"*Sun. 11 Sept.* Went to meet Mr. and Mrs. Emmerson at the New Inn at Deeping and spent three days with them.

The letters on natural history to which Clare refers in his entry for the 18th of April in the Journal were begun in the very early part of the year. Signs of spring, as well as the desire to put forth as much writing as possible, incited him to begin. No sooner was the old year dead than he was impatiently watching for the return of life in the new year. He noted the bee busy in January. In February he heard blackbird and skylark's song, saw wild violets and Bedlam cowslips in flower. By the 7th of February he had written his third letter on natural history, and it was joyfully concerned with the signals from a reviving earth:

"I always think that this month the prophet of spring brings many beauties to the landscape, though a careless observer would laugh at me for saying so, who believes that it brings nothing because he does not give himself the trouble to seek them.

"I always admire the kindling freshness that the bark of the different sorts of trees and underwood assumes in the forest; the ash with its grey bark and black swelling buds; the birch with its paper rind; and the darker, mottled sorts of hazel; black alder with the greener hues of sallow willow; the bramble that still wears its leaves, with the privet of a purple hue; while the straggling wood briar shines in a brighter and more beautiful green even than leaves can boast at this season. Odd forward branches in the new-laid hedges of whitehorn begin to freshen into green before the arum dare peep out of its hood, or the primrose and violet shoot up a new leaf through the warm moss and ivy that shelter their spring dwellings. The furze, too, on the common, wears a fairer green, and here and there an odd branch is covered with golden flowers. The ling or heath nestling among the long grass below (covered with the withered flowers of last year) is sprouting up into fresh hopes of spring. The fairy rings on the pastures are getting deeper dyes, and the water-weeds, with long, silver-green blades of grass, are mantling the stagnant ponds in their summer liveries. In fact, I find more beauties in this month than I can find room to talk about."

More than a year before this, after he had visited London and had found that the genial understandings he had there could not keep him from loneliness of mind when he was back at home, he had invoked again the *genius loci* of his childhood, realising that his most sure if secret joy was in that spirit's keeping.

> *Live on thou spirit of departed years*
> *And take that voice that cares have rendered dumb!*
> *O tell again those loves and hopes and fears*
> *As when my bosom was thy early home,*
> *Wooing the child to ecstasy. O come,*
> *Though desolate with tears, with troubles torn,*
> *This one lorn blossom may be found to bloom*
> *In the old haunts where thou didst once sojourn;*
> *Then wake and smile anew! Sweet cherubim, return!*
>
> *Thy smiles are sweet to him that needs thy smiles,*
> *He feels thy raptures in no less degree*
> *Than bolder votaries whose ambition toils*
> *Up the steep road of immortality;*
> *And while their souls expand and rise with thee,*
> *On humbler wings, with unpresuming powers,*
> *He shares a portion of thy ecstasy*
> *Wandering around thy valleys, brooks, and bowers,*
> *Cheered by thy sunny smiles with other lowly flowers.*

Back from London a third time, unwell and rather lonely, he began to offer to this childhood's muse descriptions of birds and nests, observations on insects and plants. Like other and greater naturalists, he found an immeasurable content in merely watching. Watching and describing now became his refuge. Not all the poetry and prose which comprise these offerings belong to the year 1825. Some of the poems, though the years are not certain, may be of as late a date as 1830, or 1831; but they are all offered in the same spirit, with the earnestness of a boy, one to whom nothing is so often seen that it has lost its wonder; with the untainted joy of a child whose vision has not "faded into the light of common day"; with the perception of one mature, but one whose thirty years' knowledge of the seasons has only made them more intimate and lovely without divesting them in the least of their freshness. Though he himself stood within the threshold, there are no shades of the prison-house upon these nature musings of Clare's.

Neither were they written after the way of the confirmed naturalist or zoologist. John Lawrence might have welcomed Clare, or J. L. Knapp commended him, if either of these two could have known him or seen his manuscript notes. Clare was fond, at the moment, of writers like Hurdis, John Dyer, and Langhorne. While he went to Pennant for occasional reference, his jottings were nothing akin to the concise information pressed into the *Genera of Birds*. When asked about the cuckoo, he makes clear his attitude in his reply to Hessey:

"Artis has one in his collection of stuffed birds, but I have not the sufficient scientific curiosity about me to go and take the exact description of its head, rump, and wings, the length of its tail, and the breadth from the tips of the extended wings. These old bookish descriptions you may find in any Natural History, if they are of any gratification. For my part I love to look on nature with a poetic feeling, which magnifies the pleasure. I love to see the nightingale in its hazel retreat, and the cuckoo hiding in its solitudes of oaken foliage, and not to examine their carcases in glass cases. Yet naturalists and botanists seem to have no taste for this poetic feeling; they merely make collections of dried specimens, classing them after Linnaeus into tribes and families, and there they delight to show them as a sort of ambitious fame. With them "a bird in the hand is worth two in the bush." Well, everyone to his hobby; I have none of this curiosity about me, though I feel as happy as they can in finding a new species of field-flower or butterfly which I have not seen before. Yet I have no desire further to dry the plant or torture the butterfly by sticking it on a cork board with a pin. I have no wish to do this if my feelings would let me. I only crop the blossom of the flower, or take the root from its solitudes if it would grace my garden, and wish the fluttering butterfly to settle till I come up with it to examine the powdered colours on its wings; and then it may dance off again from fancied dangers, and welcome."

This explanation follows a full and faithful description of the nightingale—of the living nightingale, its habits and characteristics, not of the nightingale dead. He goes on to catalogue, for Hessey's benefit, the authors whose images from nature have moved him to appreciation. He begins with Chaucer and concludes with Cowper, Hurdis, and Bloomfield. He saw and regretted the injustice in that oblivion to which Erasmus Darwin had sunk. He had not yet read White's *Selborne*, but had heard it praised. White certainly, among writers on rural subjects, received his due then, as he receives it now. Clare wished to know whether his description coincided with White's. But White was concerned rather with the distribution of the nightingale, and with its notes after its young are off the nest. On this last point Clare and White did not agree; for Clare takes the plaintive note for alarm and the harsh "chur-chur" as a food-call to the young; while White interprets this "snapping or cracking" sound as "menace and defiance" to passers-by.

It would be ridiculous and impertinent to provoke any comparison between White's finished, justly admired work and Clare's fragmentary descriptions; but it is typical of Clare's unobtrusive observation and tolerance of all creatures that, whereas White, in the cause of science, caused the sparrows to be shot which invaded his martins' nests, Clare entered into the warfare among these birds with impartiality:

"The sparrow is an unfeeling enemy to these birds [the house-martins] and when [their] nest is nearly finished they will take it by storm and make use of it themselves. In these emergencies the martins will both occupy the nest and keep in for days together, while the besieging robbers sit as patiently on the thatch above, watching the opportunity to enter. When the martins are pined out and forced to leave their nest for food the cock-sparrow seizes the chance immediately, and the poor martins find on their return a determined occupant who resists their every effort to regain the lawful possession of their houses. Sometimes they return the insult afterwards by an odd revenge; when the old sparrows leave the nest for food, and they will do when they have been in quiet possession of it awhile, they instantly sally to the nest, where others of their companions, as I have often seen, join helping hand and block up the entrance till the hole is too small for the sparrows to enter; who, on their return, fancy[ing] some strategy is laid to entrap them, leave it with little or no hesitation; for I have observed that the sparrow cannot get into the hole of a finished nest, who always watches to seize possession before [they] have finished the entrance, adding the lining of straw and feathers themselves. And one of these can easily be known by straw hanging out of the hole, as they use more straw than the martin."

He had for many years rescued the sparrows from the onslaughts of the village boys, who used to be paid for all the small carcases they could show, by the overseers of the estate. Other birds suffered for the reward's sake, says Clare.

Supplementing the letters to Hessey, he has left a long and full list of the birds of his neighbourhood, with accounts of those he is familiar with—the nuthatch, the kingfisher, the fern owl, the fire-crest, the grasshopper lark, and the "bumbarrel"; with mention of others now rare—the crossbill, the grosbeak, and the bittern. He tells of the superstitious awe in which the then common "butter-bump" was held during his boyhood; of the birds which, besides his boyhood's pets, he had managed lately to tame—a jackdaw, a raven, four pigeons, and two hawks which he thought were hobbies.

His jackdaw, a thief and a mimicker, through vanity "got
drowned in a well." His hawks, whose flight gave him
such pleasure to watch that he could not cage them, yet

"grew very tame and would come at a call or whistle. When
they were hungry they made a strange noise that pierced the
ear with its shrillness. They were very fond of washing
themselves, often doing it twice a day in winter. After being
fed they would play in the garden, running after each other
and seizing bits of clods or fallen apples in their claws, or
catching at flies. One was much larger than the other and
the large one was the tamer. When I went a-walking in the
fields it would attempt to fly after me and as I was fearful of
losing it I used to drive it back; but one day it took advantage
of watching and following me, and when I got into the fields
I was astonished and startled to see a hawk settle on my
shoulder. It was mine, who had watched me out of the
town and taken a short cut to fly after me. I thought it would
fly away for good, so I attempted to catch it; but it would
not be made a prisoner, and flew to the trees by the road-
side. I gave it up for lost, but as soon as I got out of sight it
set up a noise and flew after me again. When I got up on the
Heath where there are no trees it would settle upon the
ground before me, and if I attempted to catch it, it would
run and hide in the rabbit-burrows. When I left it it took
wing and flew after me, and so it kept on till the end of the
journey, when it found home as soon as I did.

"After this I took no more heed of losing them, though
they would be missing for days together. A boy caught one
by surprise and hurt it so that it died; and the tamer died
while I was absent from home four days. It refused food,
hunted for me every morning, and came to sit in my empty
chair as it would do till I got up.

"They thought it fretted itself to death in my absence, but
I think the meat I gave it was too strong for it, and I believed it was not well a good while before I left it. I felt
heartily sorry for my poor, faithful, affectionate hawk." [17]

Besides his published poems on the nests of birds, the
nightingale's, the yellowhammer's, the pettichap's or chiff-
chaff's, there are many others, hardly inferior, still in manuscript. He may have intended these for a volume made

something after the manner of Tusser's *Husbandry*, in which
the birds and their nests were to be described in short poems
of varying stanzas. The whole collection was to be called
Bird Nesting. In it are pictures of the "small bird of saddened
green," the blackcap; of the reed-bird or sedge-warbler, into
whose covert the boys throw stones to make him start his
song again; of the mysterious and seldom-seen landrail, that

> *sort of living doubt;*
> *We know 'tis something, but it ne'er*
> *Will blab the secret out;*

of the wryneck; of the "teasing melody" from the ventrilo-
quist firetail; of the willow-biters; of the painted red-cap; of
the blackbird's nest with "a snake lapt up within"; of the
magpie, whose reputation, against the fury of gamekeeper
and game-rearer, Charles Waterton also defended, "on
account of its having nobody to stand up for it"; and of the
snipe among the solitudes of Whittlesey Mere:

> *Mystic indeed,*
> *For isles that ocean make*
> *Are scarcely more secure for birds to build*
> *Than this flag-hidden lake.*
>
> *Thy solitudes*
> *The unbounded heaven esteems;*
> *And here my heart warms into higher moods*
> *And dignifying dreams.*
>
> *I see the sky*
> *Smile on the meanest spot,*
> *Giving to all that creep or walk or fly*
> *A calm and cordial lot.*

The Mere's lonely, almost impenetrable reaches were
natural strongholds for many birds and bog-plants which are
now far scarcer than they were then. In 1850 it was laid dry
and the sanctuaries lost. Peter De Wint sketched its "Dutch-
like scene," as well as E. W. Cooke, R.A., and other nine-
teenth-century landscape-painters. In 1825, when the land

was rapidly becoming private properties where trespassers would be prosecuted, the Mere remained for Clare a place to wander by freely and botanize. He made expeditions to it with Artis and Henderson, or with his old friend John Billings. Or, if he was too ill to venture upon so long an excursion, as he often was during that excessively hot summer of 1825, there was still the Heath – or that part of the original common that remained heath – belonging to Lord Fitzwilliam, to which he had open access. There the snakes abounded. There were so many, he says, that often at every step he took by a dyke-side they "dropped into the water by scores." In the Fens they were as numerous as flies, and crept up the milk-pails that were set to cool of an evening at the doors. Clare has a long account of both adder and viper; of how some people believed that a snake-skin worn round the hat was a charm against headache; and of how the French prisoners at Norman Cross Camp during the Napoleonic War used to buy the adders strung on poles from the country people, to eat; of how he had seen snakes "creeping half-erect by the sides of the fallen oaks that were pilled, putting their darting horse-hair-like tongues every now and then to the tree." They were catching the flies that were attracted to the newly peeled tree-trunks, he found. His entry concerning these "wild wormes" might have interested Waterton, sedulous to correct the errors of the zoologist and the post-mortem naturalist. It would certainly have pleased W. H. Hudson, with whom Clare unites, across the century which divides them, in love of the living creature rather than the dead specimen.

It is this outlook of Clare's, and not any comprehensive or classified knowledge in his nature musings, that gives them their value. The nineteenth century, with its taste for game in covert or on table, its rage for further Enclosure and intensive cultivation, with its predilection for dissecting and museums, has, perhaps even more than preceding ages, lessened the abundance and variety of life among wild birds and plants. Clare saw this work of devastation, and felt the deadness that might lie at the heart of scientific knowledge.

He spoke in praise and championship of almost every live creature and every plant, no matter how ordinary, in the country-side.

> *This common dandelion – mark how fine*
> *Its hue – the shadow of the Day's proud eye*
> *Glows not more rich of gold; that nettle there,*
> *Trod down by careless rustics every hour –*
> *Search but its slightest blooms, kings cannot wear*
> *Robes prankt with half the splendour of a flower –*

Perdita herself could not plead for nature against art and science with a more vehement, more thrilling voice. But Clare was scarcely heard.

XIII

POESY IS ON THE WANE
1825-1827

Poetry . . . is not a thing for a man to live upon while he is in the flesh, however immortal it may render him in spirit.

LEIGH HUNT.

MEANWHILE, the preparation of the *Shepherd's Calendar* had been proceeding slowly under Van Dyk's super-vision. It had already been announced in the magazines; in the event, this advertisement harmed rather than helped its chances, for the long delay disappointed those whose in-terest had been aroused. As early as October, 1824, Van Dyk was regretting for Clare's sake that he had taken the work on, since he was too busy to make quick progress. In November, Hessey wrote that Taylor and he were reading the manuscripts with difficulty, and they were by no means fit for the public eye yet; he also criticised the poems because they abounded in description and lacked sentiment and human interest; the world would expect something new from Clare this time. Hessey had seen Dr. Skrimshire, who was attending Clare again and who gave a better account of his health. In December the question of a settlement of accounts was again mooted, Mrs. Emmerson and Van Dyk agreeing with Clare that it was high time he had one. On the 28th of January, Hessey promised that in his next letter he would give an account of the sales of the poems and the profit that might be due to Clare. Taylor was too busy to do anything in the matter, and had been unable to continue reading the manuscripts. He was, in fact, engaged in a last attempt to revive the *London Magazine*, which had declined rapidly of late. He had handed over the editorial duties to Henry Southern, the size of the *Magazine* was increased and the

SJ

price raised; the first number of the new series did not justify the change. "It is whip syllabub, 'thin sown with aught of profit or delight,' " commented Lamb. Taylor had other troubles, among them a fierce dispute with W. S. Landor over the publication of *Imaginary Conversations*. It is not surprising that he had no time left for editing the *Shepherd's Calendar*.

In January, Clare's friend Sharpe called upon the publishers and did not know what to think of the situation. He hoped they were Clare's friends, since he was certainly in their power and kept a strange account with them. On the 10th of February came news from Van Dyk that all the poems were copied except the first one, "January," which had been overlooked; as soon as it was done, Clare should have the first proof sheet and all would go "swimmingly"; the book would be out in six weeks. Clare was already tired of waiting, and wrote in his diary that he would edit his next book himself. A month later the first proof arrived and was sent back corrected; but no more followed. Van Dyk's next letter, of the 15th of March, was not forwarded by the publishers until May. On the 29th of March he wrote again with the news that he now found Taylor had omitted to give him some of the poems in his possession, and the printing was held up while they were being copied. Clare had written in his journal for the 30th of March:

"Received a letter from Van Dyk which proves all my suspicions are well-founded. I suspected that he had not seen those MSS. which I considered my best poems and he says in his letter that he has not."

Clare had other cause for complaint; Artis, who was in London in March, had called on Taylor and Hessey three times and sent oftener for some manuscripts which Clare wanted back; he had written for them himself several times, and Hessey had promised to send them. Then on the 15th of April he heard from Radstock that Van Dyk was going out of town. "This is the man," commented Clare, "that was to get my new book through the press in 6 weeks and with the assistance of Taylor and Hessey has been a month about one proof of it."

His Journal entry for the 17th of April ran thus:

"I have waited 3 weeks for a new proof of the *Shepherd's Calendar* and nothing has come, which was to be in 3 days. I have sent for some rough copies of Poems which I sent up to Taylor when the *Village Minstrel* was in the press, and I have not got them yet and never shall, I expect. I want them to finish some for a future publication and correct others. . . . I have never as yet had a settling. . . . Wrote to Hessey in a manner that I am always very loath to write, but I could keep my patience no longer."

A rough draft of this letter has survived. He set forth his grounds for complaint very soberly, mentioning the retention of manuscripts which he needed, the failure of Taylor either to edit the poems himself or give them into Van Dyk's hands, and the continual delay. "If this is to be the plan of proceeding, I would really from my heart that my MSS. were returned altogether and I left to do them myself." He concluded, "I do not wish to hurt the feelings of anyone, nor do I wish they should hurt mine; but when delay is carried into a system its cause must grow a substitute for a worse name. I will go no further, but I will just ask you to give a moment's reflection to my situation and see how you would like it yourself." He added a note to this letter some years later: "These [the poems he wanted] never were returned nor accounted for."

Taylor replied immediately, saying that Clare's letter had had its intended effect of turning his attention to the manuscript once more. He confessed that his heart was not in the business, because he did not think he could make of the poems a volume equal to the previous books. But he would do his best, for he had never intended to delegate all control to Van Dyk. As to the hints and cautions which Clare had received from his friends, it would be better to terminate their connection at once rather than continue it in distrust.

He dwelt on the difficulties of the work; he had pondered for hours over the first poem.

As was his custom, Taylor answered charges by ignoring them and advancing counter-charges. It had taken him eighteen months to discover that the first poem was full of difficulties. Clare wrote in reply:

"I have felt neglect and delay latterly very keenly and whatever harm may come from complaining of matters that appear to deserve no commendation, I am sure no good can come from speaking in their praise. When I feel anything I must speak it. I know that my temper is hasty and with that knowledge of myself I always strive to choke it and soften it. But put yourself in my place for a minute and see how you would have felt and written yourself, and if you feel that you should have acted differently, then I will strive to correct my feelings and be as perfect as I can. I have no desire to seek another publisher, neither do I believe any other would do so well for me as you may do . . . if you want to get out of the job of publishing my poems you may tell me ; I will seek another and trust to providence. But if you have no desire to turn me adrift, the speedy publication of the new poems will gladly convince me that I was mistaken and that you are my friend as usual."

Taylor accepted the olive-branch, admitting that he had been slow. "Perhaps I have no just cause. . . . Had I been in your place I should probably have complained as much as you." At midsummer, Hessey and he were to dissolve partnership, Hessey retaining the retail business and Taylor the publishing. In July came the news that they had resolved upon selling the *London Magazine* also, as they were worn out with the labour it imposed on them and they had found a purchaser. This was the acting editor, Henry Southern, in whose hands the *London* lingered on for a while, a mere shadow of its former mighty self.

Since his return from London, besides reading widely among the modern poets, Clare had turned with renewed interest to the poetry of the sixteenth and seventeenth centuries as represented in Ritson's *English Songs* and Ellis's

Specimens. Perhaps some talk with Lamb or Darley had inspired him, although his interest in the Elizabethans was firmly established years before through his friendship with Gilchrist. However, the winter of 1824–1825 saw a curious and more active development of his veneration for these poets "of glorious memory." On the 5th of January, 1825, as his Journal tells, he had written to James Montgomery, who had edited the Sheffield *Iris* for many years:

"My dear Sir,

"I copied the following verses from a MS. on the fly-leaves of an old book entitled 'The World's Best Wealth, a Collection of choice Counsels in Verse and Prose, printed for A. Bettesworth, at the Red Lion in Paternoster Row, 1720.' They seem to have been written after the perusal of the book, and are in the manner of the company in which I found [them]. I think they are as good as many old poems that have been preserved with more care; and, under that feeling, I was tempted to send them, thinking they might find a corner from oblivion in your entertaining literary paper the *Iris*: but if my judgement has misled me to overrate their merit, you will excuse the freedom I have taken, and the trouble I have given you in the perusal: for after all, it is but an erring opinion, that may have little else than the love of poesy to recommend it."

There followed nineteen stanzas headed "The Vanities of Life."

The poem duly appeared in the *Iris*, Montgomery cautiously repeating the story of its origin as on Clare's authority, and adding some praise of its "condensed and admirable thought" and "felicity of language." Clare noted in his Journal for the 19th of February:

"Received a newspaper from Montgomery in which is *my* poem "The Vanities of Life," with an ingenious and flattering compliment passed upon it. Praise from such a person as Montgomery is heart-stirring, and it's the only one from a poet that I have met with."

Thus encouraged, Clare decided to keep up the fiction. He wrote to Mrs. Emmerson assuring her that he was not the author, and he proceeded to father some more poems on the older writers. Perhaps, as Cherry suggested, he had Chatterton in mind; he had been reading his poetry again in September, 1824, and the Journal entry for the 14th of that month gives some point to the suggestion.

On the 2nd of July, Clare wrote in his diary: "Sent some verses 'On Death' in imitation of the old Poets to Hone's *Every-Day Book*." There is a draft of this letter among his papers. It is signed "James Gilderoy" and says the verses ascribed to Andrew Marvell were printed in a volume of *Miscellanies* published by the Spalding Society of Literature. On the 27th of July, Clare received the twenty-eighth number of the *Every-Day Book* with the poem in it. "I shall venture again under another name after awhile," he commented. He ventured again on the 2nd of August, this time taking the name of Frederick Roberts of Milton and sending to Hone "A Farewell and Defiance to Love," fathered on Sir John Harington, and supposed to be taken from a small book called *The Court of the Muses*. In another draft of the same letter he said he had found it on the fly-leaves of an old copy of *Reliquiæ Wottonianæ*. The letters were copied out in a disguised hand. This poem was not accepted by Hone, but it appeared later in the *European Magazine*, as did "Thoughts in a Churchyard," written in imitation of Sir Henry Wotton, "The Gipsy's Song," of Tom Davies, and "Go with your tauntings, go," of Suckling. "To John Milton, From his honoured Friend, William Davenant," was printed in the Sheffield *Iris*, May 16th, 1826. By this time, however, Clare had made confession to Montgomery, who had written on the 5th of May, 1826, asking for definite proof of the authenticity of "The Vanities of Life," which he had suspected all along as Clare's work. "I thought that the glorious offence carried its own redemption in itself, and I would not only forgive but rejoice to see such faults committed every day for the sake of such merits." But he now wished to include the verses in a collection of *Christian Poetry* if they were indeed the work of an old writer, and he asked to see the volume in which they were written. Clare replied on the 8th, saying how much Montgomery's kind notice had heartened him.

"But your question almost makes me ashamed to own to the extent of the falsehood I committed; and yet I will not double it by adding a repetition of the offence. I must confess to you that the poem is mine, and that the book from whence it was pretended to have been transcribed has no existence (that I know of) but in my invention of the title. And now that I have confessed to the crime, I will give you the reasons for committing it. I have long had a fondness for the poetry of the time of Elizabeth, though I have never had any means of meeting with it, farther than in the confused channels of Ritson's 'English Songs,' Ellis's 'Specimens,' and Walton's 'Angler'; and the winter before last, though amidst a severe illness, I set about writing a series of verses, in their manner, as well as I could, which I intended to pass off under their names, though some whom I professed to imitate I had never seen. . . ."

"The Vanities of Life" was reprinted in the *Rural Muse*, but this did not prevent its appearing in *Ancient Ballads and Songs of the Peasantry of England*, 1857, with a note by the editor, R. Bell, retelling the story of its discovery, with additions, and making some deductions about the character of the unknown author. In *Notes and Queries*, 1873, J. H. Dixon, LL.D., wrote that he had included the poem in his *Ancient Poems, Ballads, and Songs of the Peasantry of England*, 1846, that it had found its way into various selections, that he did not believe Montgomery ever had any doubts about it as a genuine old poem, and that because of its elegance and lack of any "little slip that detects the forger," he was convinced that Clare's claim to it merely betrayed his mental aberration. "Could it be proved that Clare was really the author," he added, "it would place him beside Burns." After this we can readily sympathise with Clare's desire to escape from the narrow rôle assigned to him as the peasant-poet of nature; if it led someone to place him beside Burns, his attempt to "write for antiquity" seems fully justified. In that same year, 1873, J. L. Cherry closed the discussion by giving proofs of Clare's authorship of the poem.

Another expression of Clare's delight in these old writers, and his recapturing of their spirit, took the form of a fanciful essay which seems to have been the outcome of that day described in his Journal, September 8th, 1824, when he read *The Compleat Angler*. He imagined a day spent "with some delightful company, the latchets of whose shoes I am not worthy to unloose; and yet they were very civil to me and seemed quite at home with my rudeness." They were Izaak Walton, Sir Henry Wotton, Sir Walter Raleigh, Dr. Donne, Charles Cotton, George Herbert, and Richard Hooker. Some of the company repeated fragments of their own sweet verses; a nest of gipsies sang Frank Davison's "Song of the Beggars," "till a sudden sprinkling shower made us leave our angles and seek shelter under a sycamore tree"; there the haymaking damsel sang again "that sweetest of Melodies made by Kit Marlowe," after which the company betook them to a tavern and spent the night in mirth and memories.

Clare continued to write imitations of the older poets for some years; there are a score of them among his manuscripts. "I am still going on with my verses after the manner of the old poets but not with the success I began with," he wrote to Montgomery in 1827. Nor did he put aside the idea of publishing them as originals; in 1829 he had a project for making up a volume of them, but he was dissuaded by Taylor and Cary.

With the publication of the *Shepherd's Calendar* still hanging fire, Clare was glad enough to find any market for the poems which he continued to produce with amazing fertility. In 1825 the outlook for poetry was none too bright; there was every sign that the boom of the first quarter of the century was drawing to an end. "The literary world is dulness itself – scarcely a book of any value published," wrote Hessey in May, and Beddoes had exclaimed in 1824, "If I were the literary weather-guesser for 1825 I would safely prognosticate fog, rain, blight in due succession for its dullard months. . . ." The more prudent editors, like Taylor, restricted their activities in time; the more reckless or unwary went on to suffer in the crash of 1826. In September, Taylor was seriously ill with brain-fever; his recovery marked a new period in his life. His literary interests took second place, and the scientific and theological became predominant. He was no longer proud of his reputation as a free-thinker, and he began to look about for some means of linking his new interests with his business. Overwork and disappointment, culminating in a breakdown, had entirely changed his outlook; but he also discerned a change in the taste of the reading public which fitted in with his own inclinations. For as the general interest in good poetry declined for a decade or more, the demand for works of useful knowledge, for textbooks and novels, continued to increase steadily. And while the best work of poets like Darley, Beddoes, Wade, R. H. Horne, H. Coleridge, and Clare, went almost unregarded, in the magazines and annuals the glow-worm lights of poetry still caught the public eye until the rising star of Tennyson outshone them.

It was through Van Dyk that Clare had his poems inserted in the *European Magazine*, for which Van Dyk himself was writing at this time. Here was published the only one of Clare's essays to see the light of print – the essay on "Popularity in Authorship." In his essays Clare was grappling with an unfamiliar medium; as he himself remarked, he found some difficulty in attempting the orderly exposition of a theme. His mind was like a corner of his woodlands for profusion; thought crowded upon thought. Yet something he did achieve in this essay-form by dint of constant practice – enough to astonish his London friends at his rapid improvement in prose expression. The essay on "Popularity" is simply but brightly written, redeemed from the commonplace by Clare's eye for apt metaphor and his feeling for prose rhythms. In speaking of the fame of nursery rhymes and ballads among the common people, he has something personal and original to say, his comments on the poets reveal sound judgment, and he ends with an eloquent comparison between the fierce blaze of "fashionable popularity" and the "quiet progress of a name gaining ground by gentle degrees in the world's esteem."

Clare had 12s. 6d. a page for his writing in the *European Magazine*; Van Dyk scolded him for giving away poems to Montgomery, Hone, and others. "Do nothing without being paid for it. . . . If I had £10,000 a year I would be paid rather than encourage so dangerous a precedent." He spoke as the professional journalist who saw his market being flooded by the productions of amateurs who desired only to see their writings in print. The spectacular genius of Byron and Scott had raised the taste of the public beyond its usual level. In 1820 there was still a fair demand for good poetry; the tide of enthusiasm ebbed rapidly in the following years. Yet it left behind it a host of readers and writers who dabbled in the shallow pools on the margin of good literature. The curious may study the tastes of this public in the Annuals which came into being in 1823 and 1824, flourished and multiplied in the late twenties, and declined in the thirties.

Although the names of most of the talented writers of the day may be found among the contributors, even Lamb, Scott, and Wordsworth yielding occasionally to the urgings of friendship, the Annuals will attract or repel the modern reader chiefly as literary museums, with a few gems shining here and there among the lumber. As their primary aim was decorative rather than literary, literature became in them the handmaiden of the steel engraving, and the editors, saddled with the heavy expenses of their "sumptuous embellishments," and dependent for success upon their large sales, could afford neither to transcend the tastes of the general reading public nor to pay for much literary work of a high quality. Scott might obtain his £5 a page for the sake of advertisement; but if a Clare could be persuaded to accept a copy of the book in lieu of payment, many of the editors had no scruples about offering it.

Clare began contributing to the Annuals in the summer of 1825. *The Literary Souvenir* for 1826, edited by Alaric Watts, published two poems, one, "First Love's Recollections," a tribute to Mary Joyce, whom he had last seen nine years before. Clare was also represented in the 1827 and 1828 volumes. With Thomas Pringle, editor of *Friendship's Offering*, a sturdy Scotsman, friend of Hogg and Cunningham, Clare's relationship was entirely pleasant. He found Clare, he said, a man after his own heart; they corresponded on very friendly terms between 1828 and 1834, in which year Pringle set the seal on his labours as secretary to the Anti-Slavery Society by signing the document which proclaimed the abolition of slavery. In all, ten of Clare's poems, some of considerable length, appeared in *Friendship's Offering*, and Pringle saw that Clare was paid for them. Clare also had ten poems in *The Amulet*, but had the greatest difficulty in extracting payment for them, despite many promises and professions of friendship on the part of S. C. Hall, the editor. Others appeared in Ackerman's *Forget Me Not* and *Juvenile Forget Me Not*. Marshall, publisher of *A Pledge of Friendship*, was another of those against whom Clare's London friends had to undertake dunning expeditions.

In 1829, two of the *Londoners*, both regular contributors to the Annuals, turned editors, and applied to all their friends for support. Allen Cunningham prepared *The Anniversary* for John Sharpe, in an effort to outshine the popular *Keepsake*. Clare's contribution was that mature and vital poem, "Autumn," of which a later and better version was printed in *The Rural Muse*.[1] The other new venture of 1829 was Thomas Hood's *Gem*, an annual which did not entirely belie its name; for there were several gems among the usual tales and verses of domestic affections and Oriental disaffections. Clare's contribution, "Thou art gone the dark journey," is certainly among the gems. He sent it after Hood had refused "To the Rural Muse," which became the first poem in his last book.

Beside these contributions to the Annuals, we find poems by Clare in several newspapers and magazines of the same period: the *New Monthly* in 1824; the *Literary Magnet*, 1827 and 1828; *The Spirit and Manners of the Age*; the *Morning Post*; and Moxon's *Englishman's Magazine*. He found a place in *The*

Living Poets of Great Britain, Paris, 1827, and his considerable share in *The Naturalist's Poetical Companion*, 1832, shows that he had new admirers here and there to replace the many who had forgotten him. He also supplied a number of songs to the composers Power, Barnett, and Hodgson. All these activities added a little to his income at a time when he badly needed money, though the difficulty of obtaining payment from some of the publishers added not a little to his worries.

Mrs. Emmerson's letters to Clare toward the end of 1825 contain references to incidents in his domestic life which he evidently discussed fully in his letters to her. He was still receiving advice from Dr. Darling, who wrote in December telling him to make his conscience easy about his children, who had been ill, "for however much they may suffer, it is through no voluntary fault of your own." He was not to give way to low spirits or abstain from exercise. When Mrs. Emmerson wrote before Christmas she was waiting for Clare's "unreserved and free explanation of what may have taken place since I was at Deeping . . . your poor heart is alas! too yielding for your general good." The explanation arrived and she replied on the 10th of January, 1826. He had been wandering from home, himself, and happiness; she deeply regretted the cause of his late "outbreaking from propriety"; "but why my dear Clare, will you allow the temper or injudicious conduct of others, to harry you away from your own reason." She averred she was neither prude nor moralist, but would prevail on him "by every gentle kind and reasonable entreaty" to give up his acquaintance with—— "It is an *unworthy* connection and can only bring you a train of miseries." She besought him to return to home and family and hoped —— would do all in her power to make his mind more contented and enable him to pursue his literary labours. In March she again pleaded with him to rid himself of domestic discontents and rouse himself from his infatuated, tortured, besotted, and inactive state.

The letters throw no further light on the subject of Clare's infatuation, and the domestic disharmony which preceded and followed it, until the end of 1827, the occasion of his

next illness. Meanwhile, his relationship with John Taylor
survived yet another crisis. It was now six months since
Taylor had taken over the editing again, yet little progress
had been made. Mrs. Emmerson had a long talk with him
about Clare's affairs in December, 1825, and had mentioned the possibility of another publisher being found. This
appeared to alarm Taylor, who hoped Clare would not risk
his reputation by letting his manuscripts pass into other hands.
He again promised that a statement of accounts would be
sent at once, and said that if Clare needed money he had
only to ask for it. He thought there was about £40 profit
on the *Village Minstrel*. In January, Clare evidently wrote
to remind Taylor of his promise to bring out the *Shepherd's
Calendar* without delay. The publisher replied on the 28th
expressing no little indignation at Clare's "frank censure,"
which had, however, relieved him from the irksome
situation of submission and apology and self-blame to
which he had lately submitted. Now he could speak
out. Clare, and Clare alone, was responsible for the
delay and present total stoppage in the work. The manuscript of "July," on which he was engaged, was almost unreadable, and his copyists could do nothing with it. It was
"slovenly written and slovenly composed." He sent it back
for Clare to judge for himself.

Taylor had not exaggerated. The first draft of "July" is
undoubtedly one of the most difficult of Clare's manuscripts. Clare was not slow to admit it. In his reply he did
not point out, as he might have done with justice, that the
delay since Taylor began on this poem was brief compared
with the delay before he set about it; nor did he mention
that Taylor had definitely asked him to send up his manuscripts as he wrote them and leave copying and correction to
him. He simply agreed that the matter now rested with him
and said that he would do his utmost. He enclosed a new
draft of the poem, and was willing to try again if it was
still unsatisfactory. Taylor was highly delighted with it,
and sent back the remaining manuscripts for transcription.
It seems clear that Clare could have done his own copying

and correcting years before if he had been allowed to do so.

The publication of the essay on "Popularity" had encouraged him to continue his prose-writing. He had finished a character-sketch, "The Farmer and Vicar," which he proposed to remodel as "The Harvest Supper, or a Sketch of Old Customs." He had some idea of making a book of his essays, and Taylor encouraged him, suggesting a criticism of the poets of the last and present ages as a suitable subject, a suggestion which Clare took up. He also began to write a tragedy in the Elizabethan manner, and planned to publish locally his long satiric poem, "The Parish," for which no place could be found in the *Shepherd's Calendar*.

During 1825–1826 Clare corresponded with that ardent botanist, Elizabeth Kent, Leigh Hunt's sister-in-law, to whom Hessey had shown the letters on the natural history of Helpston. Her *Flora Domestica*, published in 1823 by Taylor and Hessey, had contained pleasant mention of Clare. On the 8th of April, Taylor remarked that Darley was much gratified by Clare's opinion of his little book; this, presumably, was *Labours of Idleness: or Seven Nights' Entertainments, by Guy Penseval*, which Taylor published in 1826. Taylor wrote in pessimistic vein; business was flat; he was weary of it, and contemplated retiring to live on his means and amuse himself with his own vagaries as Clare did. He saw none of the *Londoners* now except Lamb, Darley, and Cunningham, and had found that what was called friendship was merely self-interest. In May there came a rumour that Taylor had gone bankrupt, and Clare was worried by it until he heard that it was unfounded. He had been visiting at Stamford and Milton, and had found the change of company beneficial.

But June brought a bombshell in the form of a brusque letter from Edward Drury, demanding settlement of a bill for over £40. Taylor, evidently still engaged in winding up the affairs of the firm of Taylor and Hessey, had sent Drury a claim for £100 which had been advanced by the firm years before in the form of books sent to booksellers to whom

Drury owed money. Drury countered this with a claim for
money and goods supplied to Clare during the writing of the
Village Minstrel, for procuring medical advice for his mother,
and for binding books. Taylor refused to admit this to the
firm's accounts, and advised Drury to settle it with Clare.
Drury's demand for immediate settlement perturbed Clare
greatly. Taylor assured him that Drury had no right to
charge anything, because his account had been received and
allowed by the firm long before. But Drury wrote again,
threatening legal proceedings, so Clare asked Taylor to get
the matter settled for him. This was eventually done by
Hessey, who discovered that some of the money claimed had
in fact been paid already; the balance of some £30 was
placed on the debit side of Clare's account with the firm.
With that his relationship with Drury again lapsed, until the
arrival of the long-delayed statement of accounts in 1829
convinced Clare that he had been not only unkindly but
unfairly treated by his old friend.

During the summer and autumn of 1826, Clare worked
again in the fields and felt happier, although Hessey's envy
of his happy lot as a peasant was scarcely justified. He had
renewed his confidence in Taylor, who was now pressing
forward with the *Shepherd's Calendar* and showed interest in
Clare's prose writings. The scheme for the publication
locally of "The Parish" also showed signs of reaching
fruition; details of printing and costs were being discussed.
In his spare time, Clare was busy making in his garden a
shrubbery of hedge-plants and wild flowers, a plan which he
followed later at Northborough. In June a second son had
been born, and was baptised on the 18th – "John, son of
John Clare, Poet."

> *Two little girls and two little boys*
> *Are quite enough for wedded joys,*

wrote Mrs. Emmerson upon this occasion.

In September the title-page and dedication of the new
book were under discussion; there was some talk of a

frontispiece by Hilton or De Wint, and Hessey suggested that Clare should write a preface himself, as there was little to say except to account for the long delay on the score of ill-health. Thus Clare was to bear the onus of his publishers' shortcomings and provide an excuse which was only partially true. The only illness which had delayed the book was Taylor's own; and that for no more than six months of the four years. At last, toward the end of November, Clare received six copies of the book; but it was not yet ready for the public, for De Wint's first drawing had proved unsuitable, and a second was made and engraved. Thus five more months were added to the long struggle of the *Shepherd's Calendar* toward the light.

During those five months Clare spent some time with his friend Artis, and helped him in his excavation of a Roman villa on the side of the North Road, near Water Newton. Artis had left Milton in August, 1826, through trouble arising out of a love-affair; but he continued his work on the Roman remains in the district, and was preparing for publication his book on the fine mosaic pavements and remains of Roman baths, villas, and potteries which he had unearthed around Castor since 1822. A brief account of these remains, "by far the most curious and extensive that have been explored in Britain," appeared in the *New Monthly Magazine*, October, 1826. The *Durobrivæ of Antoninus*, published in 1828, consists of a series of plates illustrating these finds, but without any letterpress.

Early in the new year, Clare wrote to George Darley, who had just published his text-book of geometry and was busy with others on algebra and trigonometry. Taylor sent a copy to Clare, remarking that it was a subject for which the two poets had a common taste. Darley replied on the 2nd of March in an interesting and characteristic letter. Discussing his mathematical work, he agreed with Clare that the writers of scientific text-books treated the public as babies, designing to titillate their fancy rather than improve their reason. Clare had been unwell again in January, and Darley referred to this :

"I was sorry to hear from Taylor yesterday that you were not in good health. What *can* be the matter with you, so healthfully situated and employed? Methinks you should live the life of an oak-tree, or a sturdy elm, that groans in a storm, but only for pleasure. Do you meditate too much? – or sit too immovably? . . . Poetry, I mean the composition of it, does not always sweeten the mind as much as the reading of it – There is an anxiety, a fervour, an impatience, a vaingloriousness attending it which untranquillizes even in the sweetest-seeming moods of the poet. Like the bee, he is restive and uneasy, even in collecting his sweets."

Writing on the 30th of March to inform Clare that De Wint had finished the frontispiece drawing, which he did gratis, but that the engraver was delaying with it, Taylor remarked that Darley and he had been reading Clare's poems together, and Darley liked "The Dream" best. "Darley is the only good that ever came from the London Magazine – He is a staunch Friend, & one of the gentlest & kindest of Human Beings – It is very odd that I have never seen Reynolds for nearly 2 years. He has lately lost an Infant Child."

By the end of April, the last of the many delays had come to an end and the *Shepherd's Calendar* was ready for the public. Clare's brief preface expressed his long-felt desire to appear before the public simply as a poet.

But the *Shepherd's Calendar* had waited too long. The public, whose memory had lasted just long enough to redeem the *Village Minstrel* from failure in 1821, could not be expected to remember for six years more. By 1829 only 400 copies had been sold. Clare's dream in which he saw the proofs of the book crumble into dust had foreshadowed reality. The reviews were few, and most of them poor. The *Eclectic Review* again gave him a kindly reception and just praise. The *Literary Gazette* thought there was fine poetry in the book, but held out few hopes of its success with the public, since its poetry was not romantic enough; the reviewer added with unconscious irony that there was too much regular routine of comfort in the life of the English peasantry for it to be very

T J

picturesque. It was certainly not a surfeit of comfort that produced the riots of 1831. The *Literary Chronicle* published a favourable review by a friend of Van Dyk's, but it was too hastily written to be impressive; *Blackwood's* mentioned the *Shepherd's Calendar* as the work of the Ettrick Shepherd. Another writer thought it would be manifest injustice to take Clare at his word and view his work apart from a consideration of his rustic character; it would be unfair to judge the poems by too high a standard. Similar notices appeared in the *Monthly Magazine* and the *Magnet*.

Yet, even if the public's memory had been jogged more forcibly by the reviews, there would have been a miracle had it responded in 1827 as it did in 1820. The change in the public's taste was now fully apparent, and from all sides came complaints that there was no demand for poetry. The age was changed, said Taylor. "All the old Poetry Buyers seem to be dead and the New Race have no taste for it." He thought men's circumstances were not so prosperous as formerly and they had no money for luxuries. He intended in future to publish only works of utility; he was busy with Darley's new book, *Sylvia*, which appeared in November, but he had no great hope that it would sell. In August he asked Clare to keep his expenses within bounds, as he had had to pay the late firm of Taylor and Hessey £80 for advances made to Clare and he saw no prospect of getting it back from the new book.

Writing to Montgomery in September, Clare suggested that the rage for novels was perhaps the cause of the decline of interest in poetry. Montgomery replied, "Poetry has had its day in the present age and two more generations must go by before there is such another revival in its favour, as was excited by the agitation of human minds of every degree and order, by the events of the French Revolution."

Van Dyk, too, now struggling hard to avert direst poverty, voiced his complaints; his publisher had failed, and he had lost all his profit on *The Gondola;* he was writing for periodicals and music-setters, but had difficulty in getting payment, and cursed the editors for dolts who preferred the common-place to the original.

It was a double misfortune for Clare that the work of his maturity was written for a generation which had no ear for poetry. It meant that his attempt to earn a livelihood by his pen was foredoomed to failure; and because his finest work was disregarded – much of it, indeed, never published – succeeding generations remembered him only as the peasant-poet of 1820 who had failed to stay the course. The poets who are anathematized in their day, as were Keats and Shelley, may with confidence expect redress from the on-coming generations; but those who are simply neglected or forgotten, as were Clare, Darley, and others, may languish in that obscurity for a century, until some rare admirer with a poet's discernment and a scholar's industry shall undertake a priest-like task of reclamation.

Turning over the leaves of the *Shepherd's Calendar*, we may understand why the reviewer in the *Literary Gazette* omitted to use his common sense about the poverty of the peasantry. His ear had heard, rightly enough, the joy which is audible all through the book. Therefore Clare and his like spent the year in comfortable if unpicturesque routine. Others have made the same mistake since then, and Clare's verse aids and abets such error. In 1827, with troubles and poverty behind it and with little else visible ahead, comes his third volume; and not a month of the twelve which the title-poem celebrates but has its chronicle of delights: January, with winter stories told by the dame round the fire; February, with a lovely day of false spring and a sullen throw-back into winter; March, when the ploughmen were as busy as the birds, and, like them, members of the natural universe, not vain masters of it; May, with its flowers made glorious; June, with the furmety-feast after sheep-shearing; July, with its heavy noon-pause while the white feathers lie still on the still water and the heat shimmers up over the fields; and so on round to December.

The other poems in the book, such as "The Approach of Spring" and "The Last of Autumn," continue the story;

autumn was a season whose triumphant wildness roused Clare's adoration no less than June's dappled sky. "Each year with brighter blooms returned"; he saw every new season more clearly than the last. The eternal spring was "one that weeps Life's faded majesty." These two poems were among the collection of "Village Scenes" which Clare had prepared for the press in 1820.

The book as a whole offered a surer vision of joy to its readers than could be found in the earlier books. It was not only the happiness of his childhood which he was reliving – he *did* relive that at times all through his life – but present things, "grey veined ivy," or the colt knapping his furry hide in winter, gave him present joy, a joy which did not depend on circumstances for its being. It was something that Clare had found in spite of all the difficulties of his manhood.

It seems time, then, to enquire into Clare's philosophy as it is to be gathered from his third book; but "philosophy" is rather a high-sounding term with which to burden the memory of a man like him. Perhaps it would be better to call it the realisation which he had of his own life and his own time and the relation of both these with all life. The core of this realisation lies in that very joy of which the *Shepherd's Calendar* is so full. We shall not expect to find the careful, self-conscious expression of it in intellectual terms, a metaphysic chained beneath the Ætna of his mind. We shall not expect to find him discussing his attitude to the whole of nature or the whole of life. But his attitude is there none the less. It is implicit in every poem. It is almost instinctive, not self-conscious and separate, but perfectly united with his art, and almost perfectly united, as we shall see hereafter, with his life. Yet because we are used to deliberate, extraneous expression of the personal philosophy of poets, Clare's has been overlooked, thought non-existent.

Every sound and shape in nature moved him to ecstasy; so he submitted himself to them and sang of them endlessly. To examine or explain would only have been to desiccate and in the end come no nearer to discovering their reality

or evoking its love and joy again in the hearts of his
readers. His was the

> heart devoted
> *That, wisely doting, ask'd not why it doted.*

So Clare became a voice crying, almost prophetically,
from yon side of the wilderness of the age of the machines,
for tender kinship with every living thing in the natural
universe. As the philosophy of a happy man, comfortably
circumstanced, this might carry weight with the intellectual;
but as the faith of a man with a life like Clare's, it becomes
doubly impressive, a gospel of reality.

Since Clare was living his life according to his faith, and
plying his art according to that faith, his life was bound up
in his art. His faith and art were almost as spontaneous as
his life. Yet his art could not and did not quite escape the
struggle of the intellect. In the *Shepherd's Calendar* his melodies become more truly his own, his phrases more memorable; shapes, colours, and details become clearer. The sense
of life in all things, in dogs, squirrels, even in stones and
flints, is more surely translated. All this implies selection of
words. Clare had always had an instinct for the essence of a
word; he was never led away by its sonority. The ostenta-
tion of its mere sound he definitely avoided; its accuracy
was all, its power as a verbal substitute for the thing it was
to represent. Living near the native ground of Dryden and
Shakespeare, he had inherited a dialect singularly pure, and
rich in Anglo-Saxon. As he discarded dialect words on the
advice of his friends, he applied his instinct more and more
to the search for the words that would inevitably convey the
potency of his many loves, his sources of joy, to a sensitive
reader. There are very few dialect words in the *Shepherd's
Calendar*, and we find this deliberate part of his art almost
perfected. So we read of the "bright glib ice" of January,
and, remembering, too, Hunt's predilection for the word in
"The Nymphs," we know that 'glib' is as inevitable a word
as any that can be used to describe ice. Or to feel the very
re-creation of a July midday, we need no more than this:

The tottergrass upon the hill,
And spiders' threads, are standing still;

.   .   .   .

Hawkweed and groundsel's fanning downs
Unruffled keep their seedy crowns;
And in the oven-heated air,
Not one light thing is floating there,
Save that to the earnest eye,
The restless heat seems twittering by.

As an expression of his faith and as an example of his mature artistic power the *Shepherd's Calendar* is a valuable milestone in Clare's story.

AUTUMN

XIV

SKIES O'ERCAST
1827–1830

Alas! What boots it with uncessant care
To tend the homely slighted Shepherd's trade,
And strictly meditate the thankles Muse, . . .?

"Lycidas."

Damn the Muses.—I abominate them and their works: they are
the Nurses of Poverty and Insanity.

THOMAS CHATTERTON.

In June, 1827, another child was born, but died before it was baptized. Clare was still indisposed, but able to go out with Henderson in search of bee and spider orchis. Early in July, Henry Behnes the sculptor, a friend of the Emmersons, paid him a visit, to which Mrs. Emmerson referred in a letter of the 8th of July: "Harry B. told me of your welcome, of the pleasant hour he spent with you, of your harvest, or rather Botanical pursuits, of your delightfully rustic attire, your 'unshaven' chin and all the etcetera that are so peculiarly the attributes and habits of the genius of solitude." She also mentioned a dinner at the Bishop's, and hoped Clare had been at his ease there. Behnes had evidently been greatly disturbed at the situation in which he found Clare and his family; writing after his return to London, he urged upon Clare, for the sake of Patty and the children, the necessity of making his want known to the people who were too ready to think that poets could live on their own imagination; when he had gained independence he could become a recluse again. Frank Simpson had also seen Clare and was equally impressed; he wrote from London offering to do anything in his power to help. Clare evidently fled to an old friend for comfort; Mrs. Emmerson joked about his recent attachment to John Barleycorn, "yet inasmuch as it made you happy I must be glad."

In October the Bishop of Peterborough visited Clare, and we learn from a letter of Mrs. Emmerson's that he could not invite the Bishop into his cottage because the door was locked against him – whether by accident or design is not clear. The same letter mentions his reading at this time – Dryden, Bell's *Life in London*, Sturm's *Reflections*, and *Boxiana*, a very mixed bag. Despite the poor reception of the *Shepherd's Calendar*, Clare's ambition was undiminished, for he was already planning a new volume for 1828, which was "to beat all his other performances hollow." Taylor proposed that Darley and he should come to Helpston at Christmas, but the visit had to be postponed because Darley was too busy. He was anxious about the reception of his *Sylvia*, and he had just proposed himself as candidate for the Professorship of English Literature at the New University of London. Lamb and Cary had given him handsome letters of recommendation, but Taylor thought that he was too little known as an author, although he had written so much. Whatever the reason, Darley did not get the post. Clare received a charming and characteristic letter from him in December, together with a copy of *Sylvia*, "as a mark of my regard and *brotherly* feeling." Darley spoke with pleasurable anticipation of "the threatened invasion of the Cottage at Helpstone, next Spring." He thought it would please him more than Clare; "For I have no faculty at conversation – dull as a sign post." In this same month, Taylor succeeded where his friend had failed; he was appointed publisher and bookseller to the University of London. Despairing of further success with poetry, he had for some time specialised in the publication of text-books of useful knowledge; he was well fitted for his new post, which assured him freedom from business worries and some leisure to pursue his own curious researches. Although the affairs of the defunct firm of Taylor and Hessey were not finally disentangled until 1829, Clare realised that this new appointment meant that Taylor could publish no more poems for him. From this time he began to look for another publisher, and also to press repeatedly for the long-promised statement of accounts, so that he might know his true position.

On the 4th of November, Clare renewed his correspondence with Cary after a long silence, due, he said, first to his illness, then to shame at having neglected for so long to reply to Cary's last letter. Unless some correspondence has been lost, this was the letter of February, 1825, in which Cary promised to read Clare's memoirs. If so, it would appear that Clare had been unable to finish the memoirs, and that Cary never saw them. There is no reference to them in the renewed correspondence. Clare asked Cary's opinion of the *Shepherd's Calendar*, and spoke of his present "attempts after the manner of the olden Bards in the reign of Elizabeth," mentioning the high compliment paid him by Montgomery. He looked forward to the appearance of Cary's *Lives of the Poets*, for he had always turned first to them in the *London Magazine*.

Clare also renewed correspondence with Taylor in November, after a silence on both sides. He spoke of his indifferent health, and asked for some engravings of De Wint's frontispiece and a copy of the *Eclectic* with the review of the *Shepherd's Calendar*. This review was by Josiah Conder, whose poems Clare admired; he wished to write to him, for praise from a fellow-poet always heartened him. Taylor sent the plates and the magazine, and in his reply Clare spoke of the pleasure with which he looked forward to the proposed visit by Taylor and Darley. He had enjoyed reading *Sylvia;* the characters of the peasantry in it reminded him of those in *As You Like It.*

Toward the end of the year, Clare's indisposition took a more serious turn. Frank Simpson had talked with Patty about her husband's health, and was much concerned. Mrs. Emmerson's letters referred frequently to his distress of mind and pains in the head; Dr. Darling's letters mention eruptions on the body which he thought were due to Clare's eating more and working less and generating bad humours

in his corporeal frame. He thought there was no cause for
alarm, but in January he wrote that in the doubtful character of the complaint it was unsafe to trust to prescription
at a distance, and advised Clare to consult his local doctor.
Clare scribbled these lines on the back of this letter:

> For him the whole wide world contained no friend
> His griefs to sooth or weakness to defend;
> Look where he might, all he possessed had fled,
> And he himself, though living, seemed as dead.

February found him still in this mood of dire depression; he
was unable to accept a second invitation to the Bishop's
Palace, and told Mrs. Marsh, who was most sympathetic and
helpful, that he feared he would not recover. Then Mrs.
Emmerson urged him to go to London to see Dr. Darling
and discuss his affairs with Taylor, and he decided to accept
the invitation. It is noteworthy that one of his finest poems,
"Autumn," was written during this period of acute distress.
He sent it to Mrs. Emmerson, who recognised it as "by far
the best and choicest thing" he had written. Clare had told
her to shut out Collins's "Evening" when she read it, but
she thought no such effort necessary, since the poem itself
obliterated the memory of Collins's ode, "with all due
respect to the harmony of his flowing lines."

Clare's fourth visit to London began in the latter part of
February and lasted about five weeks; he resided with the
Emmersons in Stratford Place, where his "sky-chamber"
at the top of the house had been prepared for him. What
we know of this visit is gleaned from letters. On the 25th
of February he wrote to Patty:

"Mr. Emmerson's Doctor, a Mr. Ward, told me last night
that there was little or nothing the matter with me and yet
I got no sleep the whole of last night; but I hope for better
success to-night. I have as yet taken no medicine and perhaps I shall not, but I shall most likely see Dr. Darling
before long for satisfaction."

It is unlikely that Clare did much visiting during his stay; there were no *London* dinners now, and of that goodly company only Darley, with whom Clare talked of poetry again, had kept in close touch with Taylor. Yet, even if the company had been there, Clare's ill-health would have made a round of visits a painful pleasure. For this reason, perhaps, Clare hesitated to call even upon his old friend Cary, now installed at the British Museum Library. However, Taylor prevailed upon him to go, and Cary was very glad to see him, showing him over the library, where he was at once delighted and overawed at the sight of so many books. With Taylor Clare found occasion to discuss his affairs and the immediate result was a plan, of which more will be heard later, for Clare to take copies of his poems at a reduced rate and try to sell them locally.

Another old *Londoner* whom Clare met again was Allan Cunningham; he paid a visit to Cunningham's home and gave him the poem "Autumn" for the *Anniversary*. Cunningham praised it highly, and advised Clare to try his hand at prose tales. Clare replied by letter just before he left for home, sending a "shake of the hand on paper" by way of good-bye.

Clare did try his hand at prose tales, fragments of which may be found among his manuscripts. In one, called "The Stage Coach," the hero, a courteous gentleman, rescues three ladies, who are travelling by coach, from the insulting attentions of two young fops, and then holds a long discussion with them upon the follies of the day, the arrogance of riches, and the prevalence of bad novels. In another story, "The Two Soldiers, or The Protection of Providence," two soldiers returned from service abroad get lost at night in the country, and, seeking lodging at a large house, are turned away as suspicious characters. These stories are written in a lively, metaphorical style, and it is interesting to find in them, as in many of the essays, a recurrent theme of Clare's thoughts – the exposure of arrogance and discourtesy, especially of the rich toward the poor.

Rippingille was not in London this time, though he wrote while Clare was there, hoping to see him if he stayed for

a month or two. Rippingille had met nothing but disappointments of late, and intended going to Italy "to be among
people guided by passions instead of self-interest." He was
able to achieve this ambition in later years, and became
"one of the best delineators of Italian groups" of his day.
Hilton also wrote soon after Clare's return home, reproach-
ing him for failing to visit him while in London. Of Van
Dyk, Clare saw little, for he was confined to his bed with the
illness to which he was soon to succumb. His last letters in
1827 reveal the story of a brave struggle against misfortune
and poverty. He had ceased to call upon the Emmersons,
being sensitive about his poverty. "Had circumstances permitted, you would have seen me long before this, but I have
found, Clare, that poverty, which divides us from the rich,
makes us even aliens to the poor. Having to cater from day
to day, we are like shipwrecked men who speedily lose all
thoughts of humanity except those that immediately concern themselves." But, despite this preoccupation with his
own troubles, he was still ready to do anything he could on
Clare's behalf. He managed to get some money which was
owed by the editor of the *European Magazine*, and he offered
to try to get a publisher for some "National and Provincial
Melodies" of Clare's. Later in the year he overcame his
scruples and visited the Emmersons again. They had him
moved to better lodgings, where he could receive proper attention, but he declined rapidly and died in June, 1828.

Clare spent some time in the company of Harry Behnes,
who, in 1828, was setting out with great determination to
make his name as a sculptor; to avoid confusion with his
more gifted but degenerate brother, William, he took a new
surname and became Behnes Burlowe. For some years to
come he worked zealously on Clare's behalf, taking his poems
round and extracting money from editors for them. Another
result of the friendship was the fine bust of Clare for which
he sat during this visit. It is of bronze, and rests now in the
Northampton Public Library.

Clare also met some of the editors of the Annuals to
which he was contributing, and visited Marshall and other

publishers to arrange for future contributions and try to obtain payment for past. He had little success, however; he was a poor debt-collector. He met Alaric and Mrs. Watts at the house of Mrs. Emmerson, who suspected lion-hunters and was not impressed by them. Watts, says Clare, was kind to him, and offered to help in procuring a publisher for a new volume of poems. He also made the acquaintance of S. C. Hall, whose letters had been full of friendly professions, but who was unwilling, or unable, to pay for the many poems he accepted. His *Book of Gems*, 1838, contained an appeal for Clare, then at High Beech, with this sketch of the poet as Hall saw him in 1828:

"His appearance, when some years ago it was our lot to know him, was that of a simple rustic; and his manners were remarkably gentle and unassuming. He was short and thick, yet not ungraceful, in person. His countenance was plain but agreeable; he had a look and manner so dreamy, as to have appeared sullen – but for a peculiarly winning smile; and his forehead was so broad and high, as to have bordered on deformity."

Another and less vivid picture was given in *A Book of Memories*, 1871, where Hall, having in mind Clare's sad later years, explained that unhappily he was ignorant, when he had dealings with Clare, of the untoward circumstances in which he was placed. Unhappily – for Hall – we know that Clare's friend Sharpe visited him again and again in 1828 and 1829 to represent Clare's need of the considerable sum then owing to him. April, 1829, found Sharpe still unsuccessful, and his quarry had become evasive. "Hall is as hard to catch as a little eel. I hunted him from place to place." There is no record that the little eel was ever trapped.

Clare seems to have spent most of the five weeks quietly at Stratford Place; as he explained to Allan Cunningham, he was too ignorant of the "great Babel" to venture far without a guide, and a guide was not always procurable. If he went out by himself, he would turn his steps toward Fleet Street and St. Paul's, for that was the only part of London with which he was familiar.

By the end of a month, Clare had grown homesick, as usual, and on the 21st of March he wrote to Patty to announce his return the following week :

". . . I am anxious to see you and the children and I sincerely hope you are all well. I have bought the dear little children four books, and Henry Behnes has promised to send Frederick a wagon and horses, as a box of music is not to be had. The books I have bought them are *Puss in Boots*, *Cinderella*, *Little Rhymes*, and *The Old Woman and Pig*. Tell them that the pictures are all coloured and they must make up their minds to choose which they like best ere I come home. Mrs. Emmerson desires to be kindly remembered to you and intends sending the children some toys. I hope next Wednesday night will see me in my old corner once again amongst you. . . . I have been poorly, having caught cold, and have been to Dr. Darling. I would have sent you some money, which I know you want, but as I am coming home so soon I thought it much safer to bring it home myself than send it. . . . Kiss the dear children for me all round. Give my remembrances to all and believe me, my dear Patty, yours most affectionately,

"J. C."

He evidently departed from London hurriedly, for he left behind his greatcoat and a number of books, which Mrs. Emmerson, who had been ill for the greater part of his visit, had to forward. Soon after his return, a third son was born, and was baptized William Parker, on the 4th of May. Here was another mouth to feed, but Clare's affection for his children outweighed his fears for the future. Apart from that, his visit to London had heartened him considerably. At this time it did appear, as Mr. Emmerson remarked in a letter, that the Annuals would be the means of ameliorating the struggle with poverty. Moreover, the scheme by which Clare was to become his own bookseller at first held promise of some success. He wrote to Taylor on the 12th of April, asking a second time for the books to be sent; he had advertised them, had three orders already, and hoped to sell many sets to visitors. Then the Emmersons sent news of a plan which they thought would bring comfort and security to Clare and realize an ambition which he had nourished for some years. A Mr. and Mrs. Henry Ryde of Burghley had dined with them, and had offered to get Clare a cottage and a few acres of land at Barnack. The plan was mentioned frequently in the letters of the summer of 1828, but nothing came of it.

Meanwhile Clare was tormenting his mind in a personal matter, the aftermath of that infatuation which he had confessed to Mrs. Emmerson in 1826. This time his confidant was Hessey, who replied on the 18th of June. He was glad to find that Clare's alarm in his last letter but one had not so serious a foundation as he then supposed. "But as there is reason for the suspicion you entertain, from the character of the person concerned with you, I think you should not be content without taking the opinion of a Medical man on the case, unless you actually find that all the symptoms have entirely disappeared. On your wife's Account, (whose name I am ashamed to couple with yours in speaking on such a subject,) this is proper and your duty, and I trust you will think with me & act accordingly." Answering Clare's question as to how he should make his peace with God, he advised him to humble himself before the God of Purity, as King David did when he had been led to commit the double crime of adultery and murder. "You have sinned like him in the first instance, and in intention have been guilty of the second, but it pleased God to frustrate your rash design upon your own life, and to afford you time for Repentance."

Clare's repentance was sincere enough; whatever the extent of his sin, he paid for it in mental distress. But his fears for his body's health on this account seem to have been quite groundless, for by the end of the year he was able to report a complete recovery.

In July the question of the long-promised accounts cropped up again. Writing to Taylor on the 2nd, Clare had no good news to communicate: the bookselling business had met with little success, for he had sold only two sets and been paid for

U J

one. He had to request an extra £5 to cover his expenses.
With many apologies, he pressed for a settlement of the
accounts, so that he might know his exact position. Hessey
sent the money, but Taylor himself did not reply; nor could
Mr. Emmerson obtain anything more substantial than promises. Even a letter from Lord Milton, whose influence
Henderson enlisted on Clare's behalf, brought no answer
from the publisher.

In September, Clare paid a visit to Boston, after repeated
invitations from Henry Brooke of the Boston *Gazette*, to meet
the bookworms of the old Lincolnshire town, once the commercial capital of England; its chief pride in Clare's day, as
now, was its tall church tower, Boston "stump," which can
be seen for forty miles across the wide levels of the fen and
the shallow basin of the Wash. Clare's reception by his admirers at Boston warmed his heart; he was introduced to the
literary circle of the town, met all the local versifiers, and
was received by the Mayor, who gave a supper in his honour,
at which Clare resolutely refused to make a speech, so that,
as Mrs. Emmerson remarked, the Bostonians hardly knew
whether to treat him as a Lion or a Lamb. The Mayor's
hospitality was something of a trial at the time: "A lady at
the table talked so ladily of the Poets that I drank off my
glass very often without knowing it and he as quickly filled
it with no other intention than that of hospitality and I felt
rather queer and got off almost directly after finding myself so, but I was nothing like disordered; yet it was wine
and I was not used to the drink and tho' it made me ill for
two days or at least helped to do so for I had a sort of cold
at the same time it was nothing of that kind that caused my
illness after my return." His stay lasted several days, and
he sent home to Patty for sets of his poems which the Mayor
and others had ordered.

He returned home cheered in mind, but for the next few
months he and his family suffered from an illness which was
supposed to be a fen fever, brought back from Boston by
Clare. Taylor thought it might be due to an overdose of
hospitality, but Clare assured him again that John Barleycorn

and he were scarcely nodding acquaintances now. "I don't think I have drunk a pint of ale together this two years; in fact, I can drink nothing strong now in any quantity, and as to spirits I never touch and yet without them I feel hearty and hale and have quite recovered from my last ailments and hope to prolong the lease of life for a good season tho' I don't think I am much qualified for an old man."

Clare wrote this in January, 1829, but his return to health had already been reflected in his plans for a new volume of poems. He sought Taylor's advice, but the publisher, immersed in his work for the University, saw little prospect of making a book of poems pay, and advised Clare to stick to the Annuals. Hessey also had begun a new venture in December, as a publisher of books of religious knowledge. These fresh interests naturally loosened the ties between Clare and his publishers; neither of them was now in a position to entertain plans for a book of verse. "Time," wrote Clare to De Wint thanking him for the frontispiece to the *Shepherd's Calendar*, "has made sad havoc with my little catalogue of friends."

He had mentioned some of his literary projects to Taylor in December. He was contemplating a long poem on the "Pleasures of Spring." "I had some desire to try one on 'The Last Judgement' but expecting I shall be on the wrong side in this world as well as the next by so doing I dare not." He did write this poem later, however. He was also still turning over the idea of a volume of poems in the manner of the old poets, and on the 3rd of January he wrote to Cary for advice on this matter.

"I write to beg your opinion of the inclosed Poem [Death] as one of those I intended to pass off as the writing of others – this I sent to the *Every-Day Book* as the production of Andrew Marvell, and the Editor took it for granted that it was so and paid me a compliment in praising it which he would not have done perhaps had it passed under my own name, and as I still have thoughts of going on with the deception I have sent it to request your opinion of it. ... the old manner is all that I attempt, with sprinkling a few old words here and there – but Taylor wished me not to disguise them under the names of others, but publish them under the title of *Visits of the Earlier Muses*. But I thought if I could succeed well I should like to have published them as old things found in imaginary Books and MSS. There would be no harm in it I think, would there?"

In his reply, dated for the 18th of January, Cary tactfully advised Clare not to attempt any such deception, not that he saw any wrong in it, but because it might injure Clare's reputation with others.

"And in truth I must own I like you better in your own natural guise of John Clare than in the borrow'd trim of Sir Walter Raleigh, Sir Henry Wotton or any other Sir of Elizabeth's or James's days. What you most excel in is the description of such natural objects as you have yourself had the opportunity of observing, and which none before you have noticed, though every one instantly recognises their truth. Now nothing of this sort can be introduced into such imitations as you meditate. They must consist of mere moralizing. Forcible you may indeed make them, but still they will want the livelier touches of your pencil."

It was good advice, and Clare took it; no more is heard of the projected volume. But the problem which it was an attempt to solve remained. Clare was ready enough to write poems in his own style; his manuscripts already contained enough to make several new volumes. But where was the publisher who would undertake to print them or the public who would read them? He had been busy for some months with the long descriptive poem, "The Pleasures of Spring." Taylor judged from the title that it would be too much like poems which had already been published; so Clare asked Darley's advice. Replying in a letter dated the 14th of March, 1829, Darley also criticised the idea of the new poem because the public would be chilled at the prospect of a series of literary scene-paintings such as the title suggested.

"I cannot see why you might not infuse a dramatic spirit into your poem on Spring, which is itself only the development of the living principle in Nature. See how full of life those descriptive scenes in the Midsummer Night's Dream and the Winter's Tale are! . . . Thomson has a little of this, but not enough. Imagine his 'Lavinia' spread out into a longer story, incidents and descriptions perpetually relieving each other: imagine this, and you have a model for your Poem. Allan Ramsay's 'Gentle Shepherd' would be still better; only that his poem *is* cut into actual dramatic characters. Besides, though with plenty of feeling, and a good deal of homestead poetry, he wants imagination, elegance, and a certain scorn of mere earth, which is essential to the constitution of a true poet. You want none of these; but you want his vivacity, character, and action: I mean to say you have not *as yet* exhibited these qualities. The hooks with which you have hitherto fished for praise in the ocean of literature, have not been garnished with *live-bait;* and none of us can get a bite without it."

Clare was not convinced, and defended his own method in a letter to Taylor.

"I think many of the productions of the day that introduce action do it at the expense of nature, for they are often like puppets pulled into motion by strings and there are so many plots, semiplots and demiplots to make up a bookable matter for modern taste that it's often a wonder how they can find readers to please at all." In this letter he spoke of the difficulties of writing for the Annuals: "as what one often thinks good the Editors return back as good for nothing while another gives them the preference, and what one thinks nothing of they often condescend to praise."

In February, 1829, Clare paid a visit to Northampton on the invitation of George Baker, author of a monumental but unfinished history of Northamptonshire, and brother of Anne Elizabeth Baker, whose *Glossary of Northamptonshire Words and Phrases* was to be published in 1854. Clare had much in common with these two retiring and indefatigable students.

When summer came round, he was busy in the harvest-field again, and had little time for writing; then in August he at last received the long-delayed statement of accounts. The firm of Taylor and Hessey, dissolved in 1825, had just succeeded in winding up its business affairs. If all its accounts were kept in the same way as those pertaining to Clare, the length of the proceedings need cause no surprise. These accounts have been more than once held up as models of accuracy and Clare's criticisms of them dismissed as the flounderings of the unbusinesslike mind supposed to be the natural heritage of a poet. In fact the evidence is all the other way; the accounts were very inaccurate, and Clare, consulting the records which he had himself carefully kept in a memorandum book, was able to point out many of these inaccuracies and omissions. In every instance the letters prove that he was in the right.

It may be recalled that Clare's regular income was £40 a year, to which occasional gifts, with the money earned by harvesting and writing for periodicals, may have added £10. Account A, the general account, showed that the money paid out to Clare from 1820 to 1829, together with Drury's bill of 1826 and a book account of £24, exceeded the money received from the dividends, annuities, and profits by £140. Thus Clare and Patty had actually made ends meet on about £60 a year; they can hardly be accused of extravagance or bad management. By way of comparison it may be mentioned that Taylor had been paying Darley £120 a year, a sum which the publisher considered just "enough for his bare subsistence." The £140 adverse balance, however, favoured the firm somewhat; an examination of Account A exposes numerous omissions, which, since they occur on both sides, must be due to careless book-keeping rather than to any intention to defraud. On the debit side, several sums of money sent to Clare and noted in his memorandum book do not appear; others are placed under wrong dates. But there are graver omissions on the credit side, totalling some £50 and including the money due for the poems inserted in the *London Magazine*.

Clare also criticised the book account of £24, chiefly for copies of his own books sent him to sell. He had been charged at a higher rate than that promised by Taylor; he was also charged for the paper on which his poems were copied, and as the originals had never been returned to him, he considered this unfair.

Account B, containing the list of subscribers and details of the Fund-money, needs no further notice, but Account C, which deals with the four editions of *Poems Descriptive*, is an interesting document.[1] On the first three editions, Drury and the publishers shared profits of £88, and Drury was repaid the £20 for the copyright. No profits were shown to Clare; instead, the £100, which still stood in the subscription list as the gift of Taylor and Hessey, was repaid to the firm. Of the fourth edition, 600 copies had been sold at a loss of £5, the advertising costs having risen to £30. Taylor also received commission for his work as editor – £30 in all. The credit side of the account looks straightforward enough; but the appearance is deceptive. One thousand copies at 3s. 7d. are made to yield some £7 less than the true figure. This was evidently due to a system by which the firm counted 25 sold copies as 24 to cover bad debts; for a proportionate discrepancy occurs in all the accounts. It may have been a customary device among publishers, but why should it be thus disguised?

The *Village Minstrel* account, D, showed a profit of £56 on the 1,250 copies sold. The firm and Drury took half, and half was entered on the credit side of the general account for Clare, the only profit actually shown to him on all three books. Commission and advertising ran away with £80, and 15 guineas was put down for a portrait of Clare by Hilton. As Clare pointed out, this portrait was painted for Taylor at his own request; he could not see why it should be charged to the *Village Minstrel* account in addition to the £26 for the engraving of it by Scriven.

Of the *Shepherd's Calendar*, only 425 copies had been sold, and Account E had an adverse balance of £60. In these last two accounts the discrepancy of 4 per cent. on the credit side amounted to £22 on the copies sold.

Having examined the accounts, Clare felt that something must be done to rectify the many errors he found in them. So he decided to write to Taylor as soon as the harvest was

over and he had leisure. It is clear, from the many drafts of
this letter, that he had no taste for the business; he disliked
intensely the idea of haggling about money, and began with
many apologies on this score. Having pointed out the errors
and omissions in the accounts, he went on to speak of his
plans for the future; he was faced with the failure of his hopes
to earn a living by his pen, yet he was glad to know the worst:
"for in losing hope I have cleared the prospect to see a little
further as to how I must proceed for the future. My intention is to get a small farm or cottage as soon as possible and
if I can I should like to purchase Billings's house and land
which will come to the hammer very shortly." He hoped to
use his Fund-money for the purpose, but of course that was
as impossible now as it had been years before. It had already
been suggested by Clare in August, and approved by Henderson, that he should again approach Lord Milton for a
cottage and land, which would enable him, as Henderson
wrote, "to lift a more independent head than the muses,
I fear, will enable you to do; at least you would free your
mind of much of the present harassing uncertainty. . . .
Labouring work is now out of the question and indeed any
kind of employment requiring confinement would not suit
while you continue to write. A cottage with land could be
managed partly by yourself, and partly by your wife." But
Clare had to wait three more years for his cottage and land,
and three more years of anxiety, struggle, and deferred hope
did not leave him unscathed.

Clare's letter to Taylor was written at the end of harvest-
time; Taylor replied on the 6th of January, 1830, sending the
dividend, with the cheerless news that if the Government carried out their intention of lowering the interest rate, Clare's
little income would be still further reduced. He had consulted Hessey, who had failed in his publishing business and
set up as a book and print auctioneer, about the points raised
by Clare, and there were some that ought to be and should
be corrected: "I am much pleased with the manner in
which you have stated them."

When these corrections had been made, Clare still owed

his late publishers a considerable sum, with little prospect of being able to pay it back. Yet he can hardly be held responsible for a debt about which he was kept in the dark for so long. He had done his best years before to get a statement of his position; but, as he wrote to Taylor, "when I expressed a desire to have a settlement, Hessey urged me to patience and told me to wait and that I should be both rich and happy, and I did not like to urge a settlement, though I continually wished it, not caring to give offence." One decision he now made which he might well have made to his advantage earlier if he had been given the information he desired; he would have nothing more to do with the system of half-profits. As he wrote to Sharpe when S. C. Hall had promised to find a publisher for a new book, he would "rather take a small sum for the volume altogether than a large promise in half-profits." He kept to that resolve, and was able in 1835 to get £40 for the *Rural Muse* – a small enough sum, but better than the £28 which his previous two volumes had yielded.

Meanwhile an angry correspondence had broken out between Clare and Drury, which wiped out the last traces of their friendship. Clare's chief cause of complaint was the £20 for copyright repaid to Drury in addition to the £30 allowed in 1826. Clare said he had not received a farthing beyond that £30, and hoped Drury would admit the mistake and have it corrected. He also mentioned that he had not had anything in the way of remuneration for writing songs; he knew that Drury had received payment for some of them. Finally, Drury still had a number of manuscripts which he would like back. Drury replied in November, insisting that the claim was correct and begging to be excused from any further interest in bygone causes, since Clare had long ago transferred all his confidence to Taylor. There is a draft of a reply to this letter in which Clare discussed the strange business of that first agreement in detail. As he now saw it, he had been cheated out of £40 on *Poems Descriptive*, for, instead of receiving £20 for it, as asserted, he had been charged £20 for his own property – "a damnable luxury."

"You never gave me an item of accounts in your life. What had I of you in 'money and goods' to amount to £51, let me ask you."

Whatever the truth of this transaction, it was not likely to be disclosed after ten years. This much is clear; if Clare, in his early innocence, too readily accepted as a bond the word of those who controlled his affairs, Drury undoubtedly took advantage of that trust. He certainly intended at first to serve Clare's interests as well as his own; but he took good care to be well prepared against the day when those interests should clash, and he knew his cousin Taylor well enough to realise that they must clash. So he was able to make good terms for himself, and when there were signs that the business was declining, he hastened to seize what he could from the sinking ship.

The part played by John Taylor cannot be so easily defined. A man of "close designs," who often shrouded his intentions and motives, however innocent, in a veil of secrecy, he remains something of an enigma. The honesty of his motives in his dealings with Clare is not in question. Their friendship had survived many storms and difficulties; nor did it end in 1829. Taylor helped to edit the *Rural Muse;* he contributed toward the cost of Clare's upkeep at High Beech. We do not know how the balance ultimately stood between them in 1864; but up to 1829 the firm had certainly not lost money through their connection with Clare, if we take into account their profits and commissions as publishers, book-sellers, and editors. Taylor also took the copyright of the poems and all the unsold copies of the books, which he eventually remaindered.

Taylor deserves every credit for his introduction of Clare to the public, his conscientious and capable editing, his appreciation of the poet's genius; but there is an imposing list on the other side of the account. When careful allowance has been made for illness and overwork, many of those unfulfilled promises, those chronic delays in the preparation of poems, in the payment of money, in the answering of letters, remain inexplicable except on some such assumption as Clare himself made, that by a defect of character Taylor "erected delays into a system." There is sufficient evidence that he had such a system; he expressed in writing at least twice that he felt justified in holding over an author's profit on one volume to meet possible losses on the next. This inability to distinguish clearly between the firm's property and rights and the author's seems to have been the cause of the amazing lack of tact which Taylor sometimes evinced in his dealings with other men, a complete failure to apprehend their point of view. It was a policy of penury and delayed payment which ruined the *London Magazine* and alienated nearly all its contributors. It was Taylor's tactless exposition of his system of delayed payment which provoked Landor's extravagant outburst. Hood also fell foul of the firm. "Is Taylor or Hessey dead?" he asked, in 1825, telling how he had met a viper in his path and had cut him in two with a stone, a token that he was to overcome an enemy. "I thought of Hessey's long backbone when I did it." Lamb also, faithful *Londoner* as he was, had little admiration for his editor, and criticised his methods in characteristic style. It was Taylor's illegal claim to the copyright of *Elia*, leading to a lawsuit with Moxon in 1833, which brought from Lamb the inspired comment: "The more I think of him, the less I think of him. His meanness is invisible with aid of solar microscope; my moral eye smarts at him. The less flea that bites little fleas! The great *beast*! the beggarly nit!" And this was the publisher whose generosity to Keats was beyond an author's wildest dreams, who had earned a reputation for fair and honest dealing. That was in the firm's prosperous days, but even in the lean late twenties George Darley was given no cause for complaint.

"Firm in counsel but weak in purpose and doing," was Edward Drury's shrewd comment on his cousin's character. In this Hamlet quality, this gap between his intentions and his actions into which the many difficulties of his life as publisher and editor slipped like a wedge, may lie the solution of those puzzling inconsistencies. The editing of the *London Magazine* tried him sorely at his weakest point. That highly individualistic team of writers needed generous and tactful treatment. Taylor was sometimes capable of both; but, when difficulties arose, he was betrayed into procrastination and evasion, became secretive, refused to share his work and responsibility with others, and resented criticism as a personal affront. He did much for Clare; yet his way of doing it often increased the poet's difficulties not a little. In the name of independence he sought to rescue Clare from the attentions of patronage; but the relationship he substituted for it aggravated the very dependence from which the poet was struggling to escape. For ten years he kept him in ignorance of his financial position, assuming full responsibility for the conduct of his affairs and resenting any interference by others. Then at the end of the ten years he withdrew his support and left Clare without a publisher, without a public, without experience in editing his own texts, and without the means of using his own money to better his prospects. He allowed the considerable popularity which Clare had gained by his first two books to be lost in the six years' silence between 1821 and 1827. And in the anxieties, the disappointments, the unceasing struggle for independence during those years, we see the origin of that dark cloud which overshadowed the poet's later days.

XV

A THINKER FROM A BOY
1830–1831

"... *Those who recall the discussions of the time, and the assumption of the upper classes that the only question that concerned the poor was the question whether Enclosure increased employment, will be struck by the genuine emotion with which Clare dwells on the natural beauties of the village of his childhood, and his attachment to his home and its memories. But Clare's day was brief and he has few readers.*"

J. L. HAMMOND AND BARBARA HAMMOND,
The Village Labourer, 1760–1832.

As 1830 dawned in grey uncertainty, Clare may well have looked back wistfully to that January ten years before, when first his "hopes 'gan travel for a glorious day." This mood of retrospect pervades his letter to Cary on the 25th of January, in which he recalls some of the old familiar faces of his earlier London visits:

"Do you ever see or hear anything of Wainewright, that facetious good-hearted fellow? I long to hear something of him again; and where is Charles Lamb? I have never seen him since the year 1824 – what a season! Do you ever see or hear anything of him now, or do you know where he is to be found?"

Cary replied to these enquiries in April:

"I have not seen either Lamb or Wainewright since last summer, when the former spent one day with me here & another day we all three met at the house of the latter, who now resides in a place he has inherited from a relation at Turnham Green. Lamb is settled at Endfield, about seven miles from London, with his sister, who I fear is in a very indifferent state of health, so that his friends see very little of him. When I meet either one or other of your old companions, whom I regard as much as you do, I will not fail to acquaint him with your anxious enquiries."

Cary went on to express his disappointment at the settlement of Clare's affairs with Taylor, whom he had not seen lately, and he had much to say of "this grand Age of Utility," which had little respect for poets and painters. He remarked on the rate of increase of both their families, which was greater than Mr. Malthus would approve; but at least Clare and he had obeyed the command to multiply and replenish the earth.

It was natural enough that Clare should feel that the world had passed on and left him stranded in the quiet backwater of Helpston. The lighter side of this mood is seen in a draft of a very long letter to "Friend Allan" – Cunningham. It is headed, "On the Wonders of inventions and curiosities, strange sights and other remarkables of the last forty days in the Metropolis, in a Letter to a Friend." In this letter, Clare, as the amazed country bumpkin, a rôle he had often assumed to amuse his London friends in the old days, jested about these new wonders, with many a fanciful excursion and digression among the old wonders, now outfaced by them. After reading of Gurney's steam-engine, balloon ascents, schemes for a tunnel under the sea and the building of a "pyramidal sepulchre," Siamese twins and learned pigs, Clare was inspired to prophecy:

"You will have communications with all nations by and by, and steam will be boiling from one end of the world to the other. Yours will be the world's market and sellers will muster like locusts from all quarters on the wings of all the winds . . . methinks with a long pole you'll be shaking hands with Africa and with some patent ear-trumpet be bidding good-night and good-morning to all the world."

One wonder he could not swallow, however, in spite of his great faith. "It is said that the next meeting of the assembly of St. Stephen's is to be for the good of the country."

Clare also enquired after his old friends, Lamb, Reynolds, and Hood.

"Where is friend Lamb, the keenest and wittiest Lampoon in the world and the heartiest fellow upon earth? Where is Charles Lamb? Is he grown into a gentleman and got above us in parading with country esquires? Be as it may, he is not a publisher, and though he had no further interest in our friendship than good wishes, he has no interest to forget us."

Forgotten as he thought himself by those who had "mistaken Collins's Ready Reckoner for a treatise on friendship," little prospect as there now seemed for that new volume of poems, Clare went on planning and hoping. His London friends were looking out for a publisher there; he himself was discussing the publication of a volume locally; he was making a selection from all his unpublished poems, and copying those he considered worthy of preservation into a large manuscript book. He had grown too dependent on Taylor for the correction of his texts; he now set about that task himself, and grimly wooed the minor muses of grammar and punctuation, as may be judged from Mrs. Emmerson's patient answers to his queries. He must have been comforted by her remark that punctuation, at least, was arbitrary, and it was now the fashion not to point at all. Clare had no desire to be unfashionable in that respect. His imprecations upon the pedantic Lindley Murray had amused the *Londoners;* like Linnæus, Clare would undoubtedly rather "have his ears boxed thrice by Priscian than once by Nature." Yet his later manuscripts show clearly enough that he made considerable progress in the uncongenial task.

The spring of 1830 found him botanizing again, alone or with Henderson, renewing acquaintance with all his old friends of field and wood, and searching for rare plants, among whose ancient habitations the changes of Enclosure had lately made such great inroads. The good health which he had enjoyed for some time gave way in July to an illness which lasted in its acute form for two months, and prevented him from harvesting. It was preceded by an incident which increased the mental distress that invariably accompanied his bodily ailments. In June, Mrs. Marsh had invited Clare to dine at the Palace at Peterborough and accompany a party to the theatre, where a touring company performed for three months every summer. The Bishop and his wife were keen playgoers, and Clare made one of their party on several occasions; he was on friendly terms with the manager of the company, Robertson. On the 14th of July, Clare was again invited to dinner and the play. On the 18th, Frank Simpson wrote mentioning that "unfortunate affair at the Theatre." He advised Clare to write at once to his "offended patroness" and apologise. He felt sure it was Clare's frailty and the warm yet unwise conduct of his companions and not his viciousness which had led him into error. According to the traditional story, Clare had risen and cursed Shylock vigorously in the middle of *The Merchant of Venice*.[1]

Letters in August from Behnes Burlowe, Mrs. Emmerson, Hessey, and the Simpsons are full of references to Clare's serious illness. The symptoms were similar to those of his last attack – inflammation and discharges, indigestion, violent pains in the head, and acute misery. Treated by Dr. Darling and local physicians, he found some of the remedies as painful as the disease. A prescription from Darling included leeches applied to the temples, a seton to the neck, cold cloths constantly to the head, and poultices to the body. He was to eat little and drink only water. Clare felt that these remedies were increasing his weakness, but he was assured that they were necessary to carry off "the inflamed humours." There is some record of his mental sufferings in a letter from Taylor, in which he compared Clare's illness with his own in 1825. Taylor had the same "suspicion of those around," but not the "imagination of unreal sights and sounds," being able to form a "tolerably correct judgement of what was going on around," wherein Clare's illness surpassed his in the violence of its effects. But he had the same "convictions of the indestructible nature of my own soul," which had turned his mind toward religion on his recovery.

Clare's own attitude toward religion was in accord with his general mental outlook. Upon those matters of which he had direct personal knowledge, he held decided views; on all others he kept an open mind. Where he saw hypocrisy and insincerity in religion, as elsewhere, he condemned it in good set terms; he was as ready in his praise of sincerity and simple integrity. His scathing criticism of the corrupt churchgoers and officials in his satire, "The Parish," is balanced by his warm appreciation of the old vicar in his prose sketch, whose religion lay rather in his simple week-day honesty and common sense than in his sermons. Clare's feeling for the Bible, which "contains the best Poetry and the best morality in the world," had been the subject of more than one entry in his journal; "Shakespeare," he wrote in a letter, "is the only poet worthy of being placed by the side of the Bible"; for in them alone simplicity and truth to nature were combined with sublimity. His Journal also shows that he did not allow his admiration to obscure his critical eye. He had decided views about the function of sermons and biblical expositions, of which he had a great many sent him by Lord Radstock. "Such things are entertaining but I do not like to see opinions insisted upon as facts, for where exposition is the foundation we must not take it for granted that truth is the fabric. We know that the world was made and we know its architect from no other book than the Bible. But, being a part of the architect ourselves, we cannot go to comprehend the whole. We know but little about the matter of which we ourselves are but a portion, and although new theories may entertain us by their novelty they seldom lead us to truth." The same sturdy common sense marked his attitude toward the different religions and creeds. He admired Montesquieu because "he did not stop at the bounds of creeds as the bounds of right and wrong," but "boldly declared that the basis of all religions ought to be humanity." Of his own faith he wrote, "My creed may be different from other creeds, but the difference is nothing

WJ

where the end is the same. If I did not expect and hope for
eternal happiness I should be ever miserable; and as every
religion is a rule leading to good by its professor, the religions
of all nations and creeds where that end is the aim ought
rather to be respected than scoffed at." His impatience with
what he considered humbug, however, sometimes disclosed
a chink in his armour of tolerance. Although, like his friend
Henderson, he sympathized with the movement for Catholic
Emancipation on grounds of fairness, he noted on one occasion that the Catholics deserved to lose because of the
"sacred humbugs which their religion hoards up and sanc-
tifies"; there follows a list of relics preserved in a Catholic
church. The Established Church, with its soothing ritual and
fine prayers, satisfied Clare's feeling for tradition and poetry,
but, convinced as he was that truth could not be found
within the narrow bounds of any one creed, he committed
himself wholly to none. At one time he had thought of joining the Ranters, whose chapels he had frequented in earlier
days; at another time he talked of becoming a Unitarian.
Because they were content to go their own way in meekness
and humility, interfering with no man, he considered the
Quakers "the prince of sects, the 'Israel,' that seems
pitched nearer the Jordan of Christianity and higher up the
hill of Calvary than any. They have suffered persecutions
and have hardly murmured about them, and certainly
made no boast, but let it pass as a matter of course and were
thankful."

His questionings and doubtings sometimes distressed him
when he was ill; he felt the need then for the comforts of a
steadfast belief, and, as some of the poems written at these
times reveal, he did not always search in vain. But the advice of Mrs. Emmerson and Hessey, that he should simply
believe and question nothing, was not such as he could
accept or wished to accept, save when his mind was distraught with broodings upon his loneliness and he was
assailed with visions of eternal punishment for past errors.

His advice to his children was to avoid controversy, and,
until they could arrive at a creed of their own, to attend

church and hear those prayers, "the best ever written or uttered," in which he had found much comfort. But for Clare's own creed we must search rather among his thoughts about poetry and nature. He was more at home and nearer his God in the fields than in a church; "solitude and God are one to me." There his emotions and intellect were in harmony, and he could accept without question the Creator implicit in all the works of creation. In a poem which combines true religious insight with the exact observation of a naturalist, he developed the idea that our ignorance, the result of being ourselves a portion of the Creator, is a secret of the scheme of things.

> *This blessed ignorance is half the sum*
> *Of providence. Thus all are blessed indeed, –*
> *The weak, the strong, the timid and the bold.*
> *Thus will the hare feel safe in its retreat*
> *Where lay the murdering fox an hour before;*
> *And upon boughs warm with the falcon's feet,*
> *The wren will perch and dream of harm no more.*
> *Kind providence amid contending strife*
> *Bids weakness feel the liberty of life.*

In September, 1830, another daughter, Sophia, the sixth surviving child, was born. As Clare was still too ill to write letters, Mr. Mossop sent the news, with an account of Clare's health, to London. Hessey's reply, dated September the 15th, contained news of old friends. He had seen Elton and Rippingille at Clifton. Darley had gone to France. Lamb was the same kind-hearted creature as ever, and Mary was again suffering from her distressing complaint. "Poor Hazlitt is very ill indeed – I fear on his death-bed. I saw him twice on Monday, but yesterday he was too ill to see me. I fear his Mind is quite as ill at ease as his body." Hazlitt died three days later, and both Hessey and Lamb were at his bedside. Woodhouse was still abroad, in Madeira, seriously ill with consumption. Hessey had not seen Reynolds or Hood lately, and Cunningham only by chance. Taylor was preparing a new edition of Cary's Dante and was interested in Cabinet Cyclopedias, which, with Albums and

Family Libraries, made up the sum of the public's demands at the moment. Hessey ended with a tribute to John Taylor, "that most kind and generous and friendly and disinterested of men," who had been a true friend to him now for thirty years.

In his reply, Clare thanked Hessey for the news. "I am glad to hear the names of my old friends repeated, for I still believe them as such, though I have a heavy catalogue of sins against most of them." He was sorry that Darley had not written before he left; "of that exquisite oddity of friendship, Charles Lamb, I have heard by the excellent sample of patient sincerity and goodness, Mr. Cary, who still writes to me in the kindest manner possible."

Thus by October Clare had renewed his correspondence; he was better in body and spirits, though the recovery was but partial and temporary. It could hardly be otherwise, when he recovered but to face the old anxieties again. The long-continued struggle was beginning to exact a higher toll than Clare could afford to pay, and no year now passed without some record of illness. As soon as he was able, he wrote to Mrs. Marsh, evidently apologizing for the scene at the theatre; her kindly reply of the 9th of October bade him not distress himself; they had been so soon informed of his illness that whatever alarm they felt had long vanished and he was to obliterate the incident from his memory. She sent books, grapes, and gingerbread. Clare's letters to Mrs. Emmerson marked the improvement of his spirits toward the end of 1830. He had sent in December a charming picture of real comfort, "of chimney-corner enjoyment, of winter delight, of social and sweet cottage love," with "an excellent account of the feud and turmoil of party feeling at Stamford." One result of this political agitation was the publication in November of a new local paper, *The Bee or Stamford Herald and County Chronicle*, a Constitutional newspaper, issued as a counter-blast to the Radicals. Both Frank Simpson and Henry Ryde were interested in the venture, and thought that Clare should contribute; he was glad enough to find a new market for his poems now that the

Annuals were failing, so the editor, Clark, paid him a visit, and during the next two years he contributed a considerable number of songs, sonnets, and longer poems to the *Bee*. But the old story was repeated; fair promises were made by Ryde and the proprietors, but in 1831 we find Frank Simpson writing that Clare had done right to discontinue feeding the *Bee*, since he had received none of its sweets. Clare was not altogether sorry to dissociate himself from the "violent and high" politics of the paper, though Mrs. Emmerson pointed out that he had friends on both sides and should not concern himself with such matters. This was true enough; he was contributing as freely to Drakard's *Champion* in 1830 as to the *Bee*. Clare made his position clear in a letter to Simpson: "I hate party feuds and can never become a party man, but where I have friends on both sides there I am on both sides as far as my opinions can find it right; but no further, not an inch."

The many comments on social and political affairs which we find among Clare's manuscripts were all inspired by this same attitude. In politics, as in religion, he desired to stand apart from the strife of parties, and work out his own conclusions from personal experience and direct observation. "I never meddle with politics," he wrote to a friend; "in fact, you would laugh at my idea of that branch of art. For I consider it nothing more or less than a game at hide and seek for self interest, and the terms Whig and Tory are nothing more in my mind than the left and right hand of that monster, the only difference being that the latter lies nearer the windfalls of success than the other; but that there are some, and many, who have the good of the people at heart is not to be doubted." He expressed the same conclusion elsewhere in this form: "Politics may be said to be an art of money-catching. The terms Whig and Tory are only distinctions between the actors in the play. Their discourse is of their country, but when their parts are done we see they only meant themselves." His native shrewdness made him distrustful of all "mouthing spouters," whether politicians or parsons, who sought to impose their beliefs on others, with threats of ruin in this world or damnation in the next. "I think it is very perceivable to common sense that such men only want power to be equal to the greatest tyrants that ever existed and that the basest deeds would not be blushed over to attain their ends, though burnings and bloodshed were the price of its attainment."

Beneath the flaunting banner of the politicians, emblazoned with the devices of patriotism or liberty, justice or progress, he saw arrayed the grim forces of self-interest, hypocrisy, and tyranny. He hated all violence and excess, the blind violence of the mob no less than the disguised and legalised violence of the rich oppressor. "With the mob, freedom and plunder are synonymous . . . thus mobs of every kind should be put down before any remedy is proposed; for anything short of downright pleasure to plunder the peaceable will be despised and rejected." He regarded Cobbett as one of the most powerful prose-writers of the day, and appreciated his arguments; but he regretted that men could not regard these vital questions except through the distorting glasses of party politics. "I am no politician, but I think a reform is wanted; not the reform of mobs where the bettering of the many is only an apology for the injuring of the few, nor the reform of parties where the benefit of one is the destruction of the other; but a reform that would do good and hurt none. I am sorry to see that the wild notions of public spouters always keep this reform out of sight; and as extremes must be met by extremes, the good is always lost, like a plentiful harvest in bad weather."

This was written in a letter to Mrs. Marsh towards the end of 1830, when the southern counties were ablaze with the fires of the last revolt of the English peasantry and there were fears that the Midlands also would be involved in the conflagration. There had been rick-burnings in Northamptonshire and risings of the labourers around Peterborough and Oundle. The Archbishop of Canterbury, by command of the Privy Council, had prepared a special form of prayer to the Almighty to "defeat and frustrate the malice of wicked and turbulent men." But earthly justice did not wait for divine intervention; the prisons of Winchester, Salisbury, and Dorchester already overflowed with men whom *The Times* on the 6th December had described as "industrious, kind-hearted, but broken-hearted beings, exasperated into madness by insufficient food and clothing, by utter want of necessaries for themselves and their unfortunate families." But, for their madness, the only asylum provided by the state was death, or the living-death of the penal settlements.

None understood better than Clare the hardships and degradations which had at last driven the peasantry to this desperate means of calling attention to their lot. He was one of them; he had shared their misfortunes during his youth and early manhood and he still spent several months of the year in their company as a day labourer. If his genius set him a little apart from them, it made him articulate, which they were not, and placed him in the best position for accurate observation and faithful recording. Clare was aware of this distance which his talents and education had placed between him and his fellows, sometimes painfully aware of it, when he smarted under the lash of village gossip; but he did not regret it, and he was grateful to his parents for encouraging his early ambitions. He wrote of his dislike of lawlessness and violence: "I do not know from what cause I inherit this feeling, unless the little wisdom I have gotten imbued me with it. But this I do think; if I had not been taught to read and write, I should not have indulged in such scruples. Though I might not have joined the violence of mobs, I should not have seen the unlawful expression of their notions of right and freedom as I do now; and therefore I feel happy with the little learning that my parents gave me as the best legacy fortune could ever bestow." We find the same thought elsewhere in a wider context: "I should like to see the effect of schools established by government in every village. I should think they would put human life and common sense into the dull and obstinate class from whence I struggled into light like one struggling from the nightmare in his sleep."

The story of Clare's life can only be read aright with that struggle for its background. When Clare was born, the English peasantry had just entered the darkest period of their history since their emergence from feudal serfdom. A wave of Enclosure was sweeping across the country, backed by the powerful interests of the ruling classes, justified in the name of enlightenment and progress, and supported by the moral and æsthetic standards of the eighteenth century. To the landlords and tithe-owners it brought increased rents, to the farmer larger profits, but to the smallholder and the labourer ruin. Their ancient rights of commonage were swept away, and they had to buy commodities which they had previously produced themselves; and the rise in the cost of living far outstripped the increase in wages. The family budgets compiled by Eden and Davies show that even on starvation diet the peasant could not make ends meet. His only choice was between starvation and pauperdom; and, when the Speenhamland system of making up the labourer's wage to bare subsistence level by a parish allowance was generally adopted, he found himself enclosed by a rigid organization of pauperism; the parish which had been his home became his prison.

Undermined by these changes, the very foundations of the village social structure crumbled. The old system, however wasteful and clumsy, had provided a place for each individual in the community, a means of livelihood, and a chance of bettering his condition. The new order removed all incentives, independence, and hope; by 1830 it had smothered even the most primitive of instincts, fear, so that men were ready to risk their necks to assist in the breaking of a machine or the burning of a rick.

Clare had witnessed one of these Enclosures at close quarters, and had suffered with his fellows from the consequences of it. He had spent the impressionable years of his boyhood under the old system; the difficult years of early manhood, when ambition is most ardent, under the new. We have seen how the fortunes of the Clare family reached their lowest ebb in the post-war years of meagre harvests, rising prices,

and unemployment; how John went from place to place in
search of work, even joining the "catch-work" gangs, that
"foul and revolting species of agricultural slave-driving";
how at length unemployment reduced the slender resources
of the family, and the parish brand was set upon their goods.
These events made a deep impression upon Clare's character, and affected the whole course of his life. They quickened his ambition to publish his verses in an effort to escape
from the state of hopeless dependence and sullen apathy
into which his fellows were slipping. Against this background, too, must be set his later struggles for independence
as a writer and as a smallholder, his desire to manage his
own affairs, his occasional touchiness about patronage and
begging-lists, his tirades against pride, pretension, hypocrisy,
and self-interest. He had seen the spirit of the class into
which he had been born crushed within a generation, the
ancient and closely-woven fabric of their society torn asunder, the face of the earth changed and mutilated. He turned
back to his childhood as to a golden age, now vanished, and
he found a never-failing inspiration for his poetry in the
recollections of what had been. Here, as elsewhere, Clare
was a realist, not a romantic; for the world of his youth had
indeed vanished, and Clio owes a little debt to the man who
sighed over its "pleasant names of places" and left his record of the characters and customs, the holiday games and
everyday occupations, of its inhabitants.

These glimpses of the days before

> *Enclosure came and trampled on the grave*
> *Of labour's rights, and left the poor a slave,*

abound in the poems and in the autobiographical prose. The
fullest picture of the new order which had succeeded the old
is to be found in Clare's long satirical poem, "The Parish."
"The Parish" opens thus:

> *The Parish hind, oppression's humble slave,*
> *Whose only hope of freedom is the grave,*
> *The cant miscalled religion in the saint,*
> *And Justice mocked while listening want's complaint,*

The Parish laws and Parish queens and kings,
Pride's lowest classes of pretending things,
The meanest dregs of tyranny and crime,
I fearless sing; let truth attend my rhyme.

Clare then invokes the past, and describes the old-time farm-house, where "master, son, and serving-man and clown" lived as equals in one large family. Now all is changed and the old hospitality vanished, and the farmer apes the squire. His daughter, no longer the rosy-cheeked girl who sang old songs as she milked her cows or shared in the household tasks, now scorns all toil, and, "pale and bedrid," spends her days before a glass, paints "unnatural daubs," "screams a tune," affects learning, dresses fashionably and angles for the favours of young Squire Dandy. The farmer's son is

of this same flimsy class,
Wise among fools, and with the wise an ass.

He struts about like a squire, "braced up in stays as slim as sickly miss," turns the heads of the village girls, and is an easy prey for all flatterers. His relative, young Headlong Racket, "deals more openly in sin"; he brags of his conquests, all his talk is of horses, dogs, and women, and he

Prepares by turns to hunt a whore and shoot,
Less than a man and little more than brute.

Next we meet Dandy Flint, Esquire, whose name has grown into a proverb for bad deeds:

A sot who spouts short morals o'er his gin,
And when most drunk rails most against the sin;
A dirty hog, that on the puddle's brink
Stirs up the mud and quarrels with the stink.

The picture of old Saveall follows; he has grown rich by meanness and professes piety, praises neighbourly goodwill, and locks up his very wells in dry weather.

Religion also has fallen on evil days in the village; for

many, it was but a cloak of outward piety which they slipped on when the bells rang for service and cast off even before they left the church; for the fixing of fresh rates upon the needy poor was regularly discussed in the church porch. Others joined the new church and became "pious maniacs, regularly mad," accounting themselves a chosen race and raving to their hearts' desire. The drunken cobbler left his wickedness and his shoes to save men's souls and unravel mysteries which had puzzled the wise. Old Ralph, "the veriest rake the town possessed," was converted, turned preacher, and was well on the way to sainthood; but a simpering Eve crept into his garden, he fell, and, after leading a double life for some time, was found out by his flock, and the new-born saint became the old sinner again.

Behind the clamour for reform raised by squire-aping farmers lurked the wolf of self-interest; power might change hands, but the poor would not benefit; and, as in France, the cause of freedom would become a tyrant's tool. The village politician, as Clare saw him, was often such a tyrant on a small scale:

> Who votes equality that all men share
> And stints the pauper of his parish fare,
> Who damns all taxes both of church and state
> And on the parish lays a double rate.

Churchwardens, constables, and overseers made up the hierarchy of village government, with the parish clerk to carry out their decisions and do "whatever dirty jobs they choose"; he clapped the parish brand on the goods of the pauper labourer, "On parish bounty rather pined than fed"; he claimed fresh taxes from the needy.

Justice Terror next appears, "a blunt, opinionated, odd, rude man," whose capricious judgments made him feared by all. He leaned somewhat to the stronger side, yet the poor had worse governors than he was; his Christmas gifts were regularly given, he reprimanded farmers as well as paupers, and spoke against luxury and pride on all occasions. His

young kinsman, the curate, was more the tradesman than
the priest; his chief study was the extortion of higher fees
from the parishioners; he would have his half-crown before
he signed the register.

Clare then recalls the old Vicar of the days before hunting
parsons and trading curates arose, a good, plain man with
little wealth, but what he had was at the service of his flock;
now he was almost forgotten, and the parish clerk lived in
his pleasant house, scarcely more pretentious than the surrounding cottages; docks and nettles had usurped the place
of his pinks and roses; the hive bees, his only stock, perished
with their owner; the very churchyard which he tended so
carefully wore a different face. "Who'll feed and clothe us if
the Vicar don't?" asked the children when he died.

In a cold corner with a northerly aspect stood the parish
workhouse, "a makeshift shed for misery."

> *Here dwell the wretched, lost to hopeless strife,*
> *Reduced by want to skeletons in life.*

Over them reigned the overseer, Farmer Thrifty, who
cloaked his roguery in an outward show of honesty and
piety, "an outside Christian but at heart a Jew." He
tyrannized over the poor, gave them curses when they asked
for bread, and pleaded bad times when justice criticized his
methods.

Then we meet the workhouse-keeper, a subject too low
even for satire; the bailiff, Bumtagg, a fawning puppy to his
master and a wolf to the unfortunate; the gamekeeper, king
of the woodland, whose task it was to prevent the poor from
gathering the refuse of the woods, which had been one of
their ancient rights.

Feeling that he had reached the very dregs of tyranny
and oppression, Clare concluded his poem.

Had the process of Enclosure been carried out with some
regard for the rights of the peasantry, there would have
been little ground for criticism; even so, it would not have
found an enthusiastic supporter in John Clare. It was his

conviction that the very earth had its rights, and that beauty was as important as utility. He viewed the ploughing up of heaths and pastures and their enclosure within the fences of private ownership with deep dismay; they were parish slaves now with the rest. Yet Clare arrays his indignation in the garments of pity – pity not only for the spoiled but for the spoiler, for the "poor greedy souls" who, though already blessed with plenty, still hanker after more, and miss peace and beauty in their mad lust for worldly possessions. And despite his losses, material and otherwise, there is nothing of bitterness in Clare's letters to his friends, but the same desire to pierce the clouds of self-deception or hypocrisy and see the plain truth about men and events. He gave Taylor his view of the situation in 1831:

"The Farmer is on the look out for 'high prices and better markets,' as he styles them, though these markets are always curses to the cottager and the poor man. The Parson is now rather stirring into radicalism for a partial reduction of individual taxes, merely because he sees something must be done, and as he wishes to keep his tithes and his livings untouched, he throws the burden on the Government. The Speculator is looking up to a paper currency, which places a false value on his bargains and thereby enables the cunning to cheat the honest. . . . I think a paper currency upon just principles a very commodious way of traffic, much better than gold . . . and I think that a universal reduction of tithes, clerical livings, placemen's pensions, and taxes, and all renovated and placed upon a reasonable income, suitable to the present decreased value of money and property, is the only way to bring salvation to the country. . . . I am no leveller, for I want not a farthing of any one's property. All I want is to keep the little that fortune allowed me to call mine; but if Government goes on taking a little from those who have little and leaving the wealthy untouched, I shall quickly be what I have been. But no matter; times must change, and if for the better I am willing to suffer my little with the rest."

But however times changed, whether prices rose or fell, no relief came to the peasant. The tide of prosperity had flowed over his head, while the ship of justice rode the waters above him; then the tide had ebbed and left him stranded in the quicksands of pauperdom. His wretched position was now apparent enough, but justice had sailed with the tide and was unable to rescue him.

"Every restraint nowadays," wrote Clare, "is laid on poverty, and every liberty is given to luxury. Burthens are constantly laid upon the weak and the strong are left without them. With the weak, they are called useful and necessary laws, and with the rich they are considered as mean and incommodious matters never intended for them.

"Thus every necessary article with the poor is taxed, and every luxury with the rich goes scot free as far as is possible."

And again:

"Our present laws defend the properties of the great, but they often leave the properties of the poor man to the care of providence alone."

Another note deals with the misconceptions of the peasant's lot prevalent among other classes, and recalls how Clare's own friends often envied his supposedly idyllic pastoral life.

"Every discontented tradesman declares the poor peasant's lot to be the happiest in the world and the hardest labour the best exercise, yet he would sooner choose any lot than that of a poor man and any labour but that of hard work."

On one occasion at least Clare's indignation at injustice provoked him to depart from his policy of not meddling with political matters. There is a rough draft of a letter written about this time to the editor of a newspaper. It is headed "An Apology for the Poor." Clare wanted to know whether, amidst all the present stir about taxation, tithes, agricultural distress, and reform, the poor were to benefit with the rest; they had had fine promises made to them before, but fulfilment had not followed. They were to benefit when the tax was taken off leather, yet shoes were dearer now than before. Had the removal of the duty on spirituous liquors reduced the price of gin? Would the reduction of the tax on malt and beer benefit anyone except the farmer and brewer? The poor man was forced nowadays to go to the petty village retailer for all necessities, and was sold the worst articles at the highest price. Clare feared that even the repeal of the corn laws would be of little service to those who were so low in the thermometer of distress that benefits to others never reached them; they remained just a little above freezing-point.

"Some years back when grain sold at five and six guineas a quarter, I can point out a many villages where the farmers, under a combination for each other's interests, would give no more in winter than 10 shillings per week. I will not say that all did so, for in many places and at that very time farmers whose good intentions were 'to live and let live' gave from 12 to 15 shillings per week, and these men would again do the same thing, but they could not compel others; and there it is where the poor man loses the benefit that ought to fall to him from the farmer's better markets and high prices for corn."

This letter was evidently published; for there is another following it which replies to an attack made by a corres- pondent, a clergyman, upon the first letter. He wrote, said Clare, as if he had "all the blood of all the Howards" in his veins. "Who is he? Clear the stage, and let me listen this mountebank." Clare's hatred of tyranny and pretension had been thoroughly roused:

"There was a time when the prosperity of others was universally popular; yet at that very time the poor man was as an alien in a strange land. He was not suffered even to open his mouth about his distresses; for if he had he would have been instantly thrust into jail as a raiser of mobs and seditions. And who were the lords and tyrants of every vil- lage that treated the rights of the poor with such contempt as not even to let the murmurs of sorrow to go unpunished? Why, these very farmers who are now raising up mobs

themselves. They were metamorphosed into special constables and paraded the dirty streets with shouldered muskets
in all the swaggering awkwardness of the raw lobsters that
now infest the metropolis; and if a poor man only smiled
upon the ridiculous groups of armed animals when it was
almost impossible to resist laughter, he was instantly guarded
to prison by these files of ridiculous assumptions, these
treasons upon honour and libels on courage, who would
have retreated from the bray of a jackass as the cannon of
the enemy and turned their backs on a scarecrow if it had
been invested with a red jacket."

That the peasantry had been ruined in the first place by
conditions which brought prosperity to those above them
seemed to Clare, as to other sympathetic observers, the most
distressing aspect of their decline. The poor, wrote Crabbe,

> *Are as the slaves that dig the golden ore,*
> *The wealth around them makes them doubly poor.*

"When farmers become *gentlemen* their labourers become
slaves," was a text frequently expounded by Cobbett.

Clare has left an interesting account of the effect of this
glaring injustice upon the minds of the villagers, or of such
as had not sunk into an apathy of mental servitude. In the
speeches made at the Bone and Cleaver Club, a village
society which met at the Butcher's Arms, rustic philosophers
formulate the principles of conduct for the guidance of those
who lived under a system which, according to the Report
of the Poor Law Commission of 1834, demoralized adminis-
trators and subjects alike, proscribed independence and thrift,
and encouraged immorality. We quote from a speech on
morality which, like Falstaff's honour, is found to be but
a word, and that word, "Air. A trim reckoning!"

"Now to please everybody, Mr. President, we must act
justly to nobody; that's truth. We must praise the church to
the parson, Mr. President, and abuse it to the parishioners.
We must speak well of justice, and belie it in our actions,
Mr. P.; that's fact. We must miscall magistrates wise men

to their faces, Mr. P., and knaves to our neighbours, Mr. P.;
that's truth. We must go to church with farmer Folly to be
good, and get an hour's sleep in the pew, only contriving to
waken to sing Amen with the clerk in the prayer for the royal
family. Only go to church, Mr. P., that's all; go to church,
wait in the porch to make a bow to the priest and praise his
dull sermon, Mr. P.; that's truth. Then go home and drink
to the abolition of English slavery, (applause) tithes, parsons,
and taxes, in the company of radicals, and then we stand in
the praise of all, Mr. P., as good men, good subjects and
good everythings; that's truth, Mr. P. Cant, humbug and
hypocrisy are the three-in-one, grand principles of this age,
Mr. P.; that's truth. If you would be upright, you must suffer
buffets from one party or the other, Mr. P.; that's truth, and
what's the use? If we decline opinions we are insinuators; if
we give opinions we are enemies to our country or infidels
to religion. If we decline to praise ministers we are traitors,
Mr. P.; that's truth, and what's the use? If we fancy patriots
bribe-fishers, the mob worries us for government men, Mr.
P.; that's fact, and what's the use of it? If we say parsons
have great salaries, Mr. P., we are deists and devils and
worse; and what's the use, Mr. P.? But if we say these things
as opportunity offers, we are saints, Mr. P., aye everything,
Mr. P., very Caesars, Mr. P., fit for one of the oracles of
family devotion and public worship, Mr. P., a very saint,
a downright saint, and only inferior to a red-letter saint in
the almanack and a stone and mortar saint in the church;
that's fact, Mr. P. Cant and hypocrisy are the grand necessities of the world, and there's no help for it, Mr. P.; that's
fact. – And now for a song."

XJ

XVI

PILGRIM OF LOVE
1831–1832

PENELOPE: *Whoever writ 'em, he's not the first poet I have made. They may talk and say nature makes a poet but I say love makes a poet.*

RICHARD STEELE, "The Lying Lover."

The muses they get all the praise
But woman makes the poet.
CLARE.

JANUARY, 1831, saw Clare's position unchanged. As we know from Mrs. Emmerson's letters, he had written many new poems since his illness of the previous summer, and he was growing tired of giving them away to the *Bee* and the *Champion*. He sent some to John Taylor, who was reported to be thriving in his business and greatly increasing his connections. Taylor replied that Clare's poems were always interesting to him, but he could not publish any more of them. The situation was growing desperate, for the little money which Clare needed above his regular income was not now forthcoming. Moreover, his half-yearly dividend from the Funds fell to £6 17s. 9d. in January. Even this Clare did not receive till late in the month; Taylor, with one of his strange lapses, tried to pay it in the form of a bill which Drakard and Wilson of Stamford owed him and which Clare was to present. To Taylor's surprise, he refused to accept his dividend in this form; nor was the refusal unnatural, since, apart from Clare's diffidence in such matters, he himself had a small account with Drakard and Wilson which he was unable to pay. It was of this debt that Wilson wrote to Clare in 1832: "You need not be under any apprehension that I could, as one of the agents for the spreading of literature, attempt to lay the iron hand of oppression on a son of the Genius of poetry. I am, in common with most other booksellers, devilish poor, and that was my only reason for making application for payment. You will, I am persuaded, not let me be forgotten in the throng."

But debts had now begun to accumulate on all sides, and few of the creditors were prepared to treat Clare as chivalrously as Wilson treated him. By the end of 1831 two years' rent was owing, and Clare was upset because the landlord had been talking of it in the village; there were unpaid doctors' bills too. So it is not surprising to find him unwell again, suffering from "disordered nerves" and "pains in the head." "I am at the world's end, Harry," he wrote to Behnes Burlowe, "and if you could get Mr. Hall to pay me ever so little of what he promised me, I shall be set up and satisfied." This same letter tells of another commission which Burlowe had undertaken. He had seen George Cruikshank and discussed the possibility of his illustrating some of Clare's poems. Cruikshank, whom Clare may have met in London, wished to see some poems, to decide whether they would be suitable for his pencil. Clare sent "The Summons," which had been printed in the *Champion*, and "The Hue and Cry" – satirical ballads on his favourite theme of callousness and hypocrisy in high places. The scheme seems to have fallen through because Cruikshank wished to have nothing to do with political poems at this time.

Clare had long since learned to temper disappointment with hope, and the spring of 1831 found him engaged with other projects. He was preparing poems for a new volume and arranging his essays and prose. He had begun an essay on "The Sublime and Beautiful in Poetry," with selections to accompany it. Taylor approved of the plan when he wrote in July; he was staying with Hessey, who had now turned schoolmaster and had an establishment in the country three miles from London. Clare was dissatisfied with most of the anthologies he had seen; the selection was too haphazard, as if the selectors were guided by chance rather than judgment.

That he felt able to undertake this work is evidence of the extent of his reading; his library now contained some three hundred books, with the poets well represented. He commented to Taylor on two notable omissions among the modern poets; he had never read a poem by Leigh Hunt, and he knew little of Shelley except that he was "a fine writer." Fragments of the essay on "The Sublime and Beautiful" have survived, but the work of selection appears to have been interrupted by his preoccupation with a venture of a different kind, which promised to ensure that independence which he had sought so long.

Ryde of Burghley, prolific in promises, was still assuring the Emmersons that he would get a cottage and some land for Clare; but more definite news came from Milton. In July, Henderson wrote about a house which was being built at Northborough on the Fitzwilliam estate; there would be land for two cows, and Clare was to apply for it. The application was successful, and the cottage was to be made ready for Clare by January, 1832. From July to October he was ill again, too ill to read or write, so that Parson Mossop had to inform the Emmersons of the promised domain, magnified considerably into five acres of garden, orchard, and meadow, with rights of common. By October, Clare was sufficiently recovered to take stock of his affairs; the Promised Land was in sight, but it lay beyond a river which he could not cross unaided. He was beset by debts, and had no means of stocking his small farm when he took possession of it.

He wrote to Taylor in October, giving him an account of his illness and recovery.

"All I want to go on is a stimulus, an encouraging aspiration that refreshes the heart like a shower in summer. Instead of that, I have nothing but drawbacks and disappointments. I live in a land overflowing with obscurity and vulgarity, far away from taste and books and friends. Poor Gilchrist was the only man of letters in this neighbourhood and now he has left it a desert."

Yet he would leave some old friends behind at Helpston; he expressed his sorrow at the prospect of departing from "the woods and heaths and favourite spots that have known me so long, for the very molehills on the Heath and the old trees in the hedges seem bidding me farewell. Other associations of friendship I have few or none to regret, for my father and mother will be often with me. And though my flitting is not above three miles off, there is neither wood nor heath, furze bush, molehill nor oak tree about it and a nightingale never reaches so far in her summer excursions."

Yet these regrets were but as clouds in the summer sky of his hopeful mood.

"Do you know, I feel as happy at this moment as ever I did in my life, for I am looking forward to a sunny prospect . . . and I think I shall yet live to see myself independent of all but old friends and good health; and as the best way to end well is to begin well, my desire is to start upon a new leaf, to get out of debt before I leave here and to keep out when I commence a cottage farmer."

He was reluctant to meddle with the Fund-money, but could see no other way out of his difficulties; so he asked for Taylor's advice and help.

Taylor did not reply, and Clare's next letter expressed his anxiety.

"In the paralysing suspense, your silence completely stupifies my intentions. I was in hopes that I was at the end of my pilgrimage and that the shadow of independence, if not the substance, was won, as all I wanted was to use my own means to sink or swim as good luck or bad luck might hereafter allow me, and to free myself from talking and writing kindnesses that hung like a millstone about my feelings. I thought that one word to you would procure this and that I should launch into the broad ocean of liberty in my own boat. But no such thing. The conclusion of your letter to my neighbour came like a broad big wave, overpowering every struggle and throwing me back upon the shore among all the cold apathy of killing kindness that has numbed me for years. I am ready to start and not able, for I wish to stand out of debt, and if twopence would do it I could get no such bond here."

The neighbour, no doubt, was Parson Mossop, who frequently wrote letters on Clare's behalf at this time. When Taylor sent the dividend on the 13th of January, he said he could do nothing until Richard Woodhouse returned from Italy in May; but he thought that the trustees had no power to use the principal in the way suggested. Clare replied that if the money was thus tied up it had been done against his intention, and he hoped for better news soon and better advice than that which had been given him by his neighbours, who all thought that he would prosper in any kind of farming – except that in which they were themselves engaged.

"Some tell me that cows are excellent profits and some tell me that pigs are excellent profits, others that ploughed land would be far better than either, and others who have land under the plough say that I am far better off with greensward. Nothing disheartened, I hear this confliction of opinions and strife of tongues with the determination to try, and if God gives me health I have a strong hope in the end that I shall succeed. My whole ambition is to arrive at that climax when I can say I owe no man a shilling and feel that I can pay my way. To me this is independence, nothing else; of money I know no other value than its paying its way and further than that to me it is a worthless matter."

Clare's hope that he might be able to use some of his capital was further dashed when Taylor forwarded him a letter from George Woodhouse, Richard's brother. George had found a draft of the Declaration of Trust made by Taylor and Richard, from which it was clear that the principal could only be used to provide income during Clare's lifetime.

A faint hope remained that something might yet be done when Richard Woodhouse returned, but Clare's inability to pay his debts troubled him not a little in the meantime. He needed £20 to clear himself, and some of the creditors, hearing of his projected removal, were pressing for settlement. He told Taylor that he was feeling the truth of Solomon's remark, "My son, it is better to die than to be poor." "I have some hopes, and they are strong ones, that I shall see the expected haven, but I am so cast down by turns that I don't know that I shall weather the storm." The winter had brought minor ills in the form of rheumatism and colds; Mrs. Marsh supplied him with medicine and provisions as well as books – Cobbett's tracts, and *Robinson Crusoe* for the children. She saw Clare and the family frequently and understood their needy situation; she gave her alms with tact and delicacy: "To show you how much I wish to cheer you, I am trying to make you laugh at sending you Cakes as one does to children."

Another glimpse of Clare's mind during the harassing months of 1832 is provided by his correspondence with Thomas Pringle. Pringle had been making enquiries with a view to finding a new publisher for Clare. He wrote on the 8th of February to report no success; poetry was unsellable. Clare's reply is eloquent testimony that his sense of values had been as unimpaired by poverty and neglect as by his brief prosperity; we discern in it that balance of just pride and simple modesty which inspired respect and affection in his friends.

"I became a scribbler for downright pleasure in giving vent to my feelings, and long and pleasing-painful was my struggle to acquire a sufficient knowledge of the written language of England before I could put down my ideas on paper, even so far as to understand them myself. But I mastered it in time sufficiently to be understood by others. Then I became an author by accident and felt astonished that the critics should notice me at all and that one should imagine I had read the old Poets and that others should imagine I had coined words which were as common around me as the grass under my feet. I shrank from myself with ecstasy and have never been myself since. As to profit, the greatest profits, most congenial to my feelings, were the friends it brought me and the names that it rendered familiar to my fireside, scraps of whose melodies I had heard and read in my corner. But had I only imagined for a moment that I should hold communion with such hereafter, that would have then been to me 'as music in mourning.' But I wrote because it pleased me in sorrow, and when happy it makes me happier; and so I go on, and when they please others whose taste is better than mine the pinnacle of my ambition is attained. I am so astonished that I can hardly believe I am myself, for nobody believed I could do anything here and I never believed that I could myself. I pursued pleasure in many paths and never found her so happily as when I sang imaginary songs to the woodland solitudes and winds of autumn."

Meanwhile Thomas Emmerson had been consulting with Taylor about the Fund-money, but there appeared to be no way out of the difficulty; so he advised Clare to proceed with his plans and make the best of it. Clare was glad enough to take this advice; Henderson and he went to view the cottage in March, and Clare wrote gaily to the Emmersons of his new abode. In April, Henderson sent careful instructions about the laying out of the garden, and told Clare to take no notice of certain Northborough wiseacres who had been indulging in gloomy prophecies. In May, Clare left his native village, the old cottage, the heaths and woods endeared to him by the associations of forty years, and settled in his new house in the fen village of Northborough. "May it be the paradise of health and peace to my friend; may he gather into his garner the fruits of extended years," wrote Mrs. Emmerson to "Farmer John." John's own feelings in these early days were mixed. He found to his delight that the nightingale did sing at Northborough, and in his very orchard; but he found to his sorrow that he must let his pasture for less money than he paid for it, since he had no means of stocking it himself.

However, through the kindly zeal of the Emmersons the situation was relieved. Mr. Emmerson, having again visited Taylor, had realised that the Fund-money was indeed beyond reach, and asked Clare on the 27th of June for an exact account of his circumstances, his debts, and the stock he would require. Then in July came news that the Emmersons had decided to raise a private subscription to provide the necessary stock. They themselves would give £10, which was to be laid out in a cow to be named Rose or Blossom or May;

Taylor had promised £5 for two pigs, and they hoped to raise another £5 for tools. Cary may have helped, for he mentioned the subscription in his next letter.

Grateful as Clare was for this relief, he could not hide his regret that his difficulties could only be solved by means of another "begging-list" and more "killing kindnesses." He had unbosomed himself freely to the Emmersons about the other "begging money," about the way it had been put "into prison for life" without Lord Radstock, the Emmersons, or himself being consulted, about his poor recompense for the poems published by Taylor and Hessey and the depreciation of the interest until "what would make a great coat and full suit and to spare in one ministry will not make out for a spencer in another."

These letters were seen by Taylor, who felt that some personal slight was intended. In his July letter he reminded Clare that he also was out of pocket over the poems, and did not carry on business to have the opportunity of giving away what he did not get. As to the Fund, when Woodhouse returned, he would divest himself of a trust which exposed him to calumny and had become "an odious duty," and Mossop could take his place and lend the money on mortgage, as he had proposed. He thought a new subscription would not easily be raised in these hard times, but he hoped it would answer Clare's needs. This little storm might have ended as usual in mutual explanations, but events were to occur in the summer of 1832 which kept Taylor's resentment alight for some time and placed Clare in an unpleasant position.

Northborough is a small but straggling village between Glinton and Market Deeping. It contains two notable buildings – the little ancient church of St. Andrew's and the Manor House, where once had lived Elizabeth, Cromwell's favourite daughter, wife of Sir John Claypole. The village, which had a population of 227 in 1831, has a pleasant aspect; compared with the bare levels of the surrounding fen, it owns a wealth of trees, and most of the cottages stand apart from their neighbours in gardens and orchards. Clare's thatched cottage, built upon what is known among the villagers as a two-acre piece, is no exception. It contains six rooms, a sitting-room used by Clare as a study, a spacious kitchen, a large back-kitchen, dim and cool on the hottest summer day, and three bedrooms. It stands well back from the street, and, at Clare's request – for the builder was a friend of Henderson's – it was made to face away from the road; thus from his front and only door Clare stepped straight into his secluded garden. Later, when fits of deep melancholy came upon him and he could not bear to meet visitors, he would spy them approaching from his study window and would slip out and escape unobserved through the garden and orchard into the fields beyond. Local tradition still recalls these frequent visitors, driving up to see the poet Clare; and Patty, a moment after her husband had made his escape, would reply that he had just gone out; while sometimes, even as she was denying any knowledge of the way he had taken, Clare would be hiding not two yards away behind one of the three thick yew-trees which he taught his sons to cut into circles and cones. In a district where the cottage gardens are remarkably fine, and, even in those days of poverty, were proudly kept, Clare's garden, with its show of wild and cultivated plants, is remembered still; he was, it is recollected, "a wonderful man with flowers." Beyond the flower-garden and the two patches of kitchen garden lay the orchard; all remains much as it was when he lived there; the apple and pear trees are those he planted, and beneath them were gooseberry and currant bushes; so that he could

> *walk round the orchard on sweet summer eves,*
> *And rub the perfume from the black currant leaves.*

Beyond the orchard, and bounded by pollard-willows, was the pasture for his cow.

A visitor who accompanied Clark of the Stamford *Bee* to Northborough soon after Clare's removal gave a pleasant account of that visit in a sympathetic review of the *Rural*

THE COTTAGE AT NORTHBOROUGH

Muse in the *Druids' Magazine.* After commenting on the commodious cottage and fine flower-garden, the writer continued:

"The first glance at Clare would convince you that he was no common man; he has a forehead of a highly intellectual character; the reflective faculties being exceedingly well developed; but the most striking feature is his eye, light-blue, and flashing with the fire of genius: the peculiar character of his eyes are always remarked by persons when first they see him: his height is rather below the common. His conversation is animated, striking, and full of imagination, yet his dialect is purely provincial; his ideas being expressed in the most simple manner, you can compare his conversation to nothing but the line of Goldsmith –

Like a fair female, unadorned and plain."

Clare took his visitors round the garden and orchard, pointing out in the hedge a nightingale's nest which had been despoiled, and expressing his indignation.

"There is in Clare a simplicity of heart and manner which endears him to you with the first knowledge of him: he is subject to melancholy moments; but when he has a friend with him, he can share the 'flow of soul,' – his manner and conversation are most enchanting and delightful."

Clare went to Northborough with the hope that he would begin there a brighter page of his life. It is true that the Promised Land, on closer acquaintance, proved to be more straitened than it had appeared in the first reports, and its flow of milk and honey somewhat inadequate. The lot of the cottage farmer in the 'thirties was little better than that of the peasant, and, small as was his holding, Clare had not been able to stock it properly; the rent was higher than that of the Helpston cottage. Yet the small farm provided something to eke out his income, Patty was an excellent manager, the house was palatial compared with that he had left, and Clare shook off his melancholy to plunge energetically into a scheme for publishing a new volume by subscription. On the surface there were few signs that within five years he would be snatched from his new home as unfit to carry on the round of everyday life.

Yet when we dip below the surface, and read between the lines of the letters and poems written at this time, we find evidence that the disappointments and cares of recent years had been sapping the foundations of Clare's sturdy mental virility. His later friend and physician, Dr. Allen, recorded that in cases of nervous derangement where the victim is a person of marked individuality and mentality, the first symptoms often make their appearance, not as discrepancies in the character, but as slight exaggerations of already existing traits. So the condition may lurk for years in disguise, and evade discovery until it reaches a stage when cure becomes most difficult. The crisis of the removal to Northborough seems to mark the danger-point in Clare's mental history. His spontaneous power of recovery from severe disappointment has been recorded again and again in this story. That power was still with him, nor did he ever lose it; but something of its elasticity was gone; Clare had to summon all his will to its aid. The letters reveal how the mood of hope, of determination to make a success of his new life, was imposed upon a mood of melancholy and despair. He had to scold himself continually, assure himself that it was absurd and unmanly to feel such misery and regret, to "dwell in trifles like a child," because he was moving a few miles to a new home where he could not be worse off and might well be much better. He succeeded in calming the surface of his mind, but the struggle still went on beneath. The feeling that his life was being uprooted, and would not survive the transplantation, found expression in poetry. It is surely remarkable that "The Flitting," one of the most poignant poems of exile in our literature, should have, as its occasion, not an enforced banishment to some "remote Bermudas," but a voluntary removal to a village three miles away. In the poem he speaks of it as of a foreign land, where "the summer like a stranger comes" and "the sun

e'en seems to lose his way." So he turns from these strange,
shadowy scenes to recall his old haunts,

> *Where envy's sneer was never seen*
> *Where staring malice never comes.*

In "Remembrances," companion poem to "The Flitting,"
Clare compiled a poetical gazetteer of the country of his
boyhood, with many a sigh for the havoc which Enclosure
had wrought among his old friends, Langley Bush, Eastwell
Spring, Lea Close Oak, Crossberry Way, Swordy Well,
Hilly Snow – all those places whose pleasant names rang in
his memory like a peal of bells. Among the remembrances of
past delights which these names evoke threads the recurrent
theme, "Look thy last on all things lovely":

> *But love never heeded to treasure up the may,*
> *So it went the common road to decay.*

Clare was not content to remain for long in this mood of
despair. Even in "The Flitting" we find him reaching
toward a larger hope; the beauty which man heedlessly
destroyed with his innovations would rise again from its
ashes; time would redress the balance. So Clare wrote again
in praise of insignificant flowers and persecuted weeds;

> *All tenants of an ancient place*
> *And heirs of noble heritage,*
> *Coeval they with Adam's race*
> *And blest with more substantial age.*

As the servant of that muse who prefers field flowers and
molehills to towering cities, Clare rose from his despair; he
renewed his feeling of love and joy in nature which "still
can make amends" for the ravages of change:

> *And still the grass eternal springs*
> *Where castles stood and grandeur died.*

There is still further evidence that the removal to Northborough marked a crisis in Clare's inner life, and that his

surmounting of it deeply influenced his later years. The
flitting was but the last stage in the process of the separation of the lover from the objects of his love. Now he was
bidding a long farewell to the dear remnants of that loved
company:

> *Their memory lingers round the heart*
> *Like life whose essence is its friends.*

"A great part of his verse," writes Mr. Blunden, "is a history
of the transference of love in him from woman to Nature."
The records of the crisis of 1832 give a clear glimpse of this
process; it was by the transference of his love for a girl he
had lost long ago to his love for nature, whom he seemed to
be deserting in the midst of her misfortunes, that Clare surmounted his despair and renewed his faith. It was ten
years since he first expressed the belief that in losing Mary
Joyce in the flesh he had won her in the spirit. Since then
she had often been in his thoughts, waking and sleeping.
Poem after poem he addressed to her, and in all the idea of
her nearness to him was dwelt upon, sometimes as a blessing,
sometimes as an intolerable pain:

> *When lovers part the longest mile*
> *Leaves hope of some returning;*
> *Though mine's close by, no hope the while*
> *Within my heart is burning.*
> *One hour would bring me to her door;*
> *Yet, sad and lonely hearted,*
> *If seas between us both should roar,*
> *We were not further parted.*

But despair was foreign to Clare's nature; hope, buried
underground, had germinated in the darkness and thrust
up new leaves into the light.

"Last night, Oct. 13, 1832," he wrote in one of his note-
books, "I had a remarkable dream. That Guardian spirit
in the shape of a soul-stirring beauty again appeared to me,
with the very same countenance in which she appeared

many years ago and in which she has since appeared at intervals and moved my ideas into ecstasy. I cannot doubt her
existence." Clare dreamed that he was in a strange room
among a fine company, and received much kindness and
attention. Yet he was in low spirits until the lovely creature
came to him in a familiar way and with witching voice and
cherishing smiles spoke words which he could not recollect
on waking. He then tells of the first dream in which she
appeared to him. It was many years before, when he had
not published a line. She had led him from his home to an
open field called Maple Hill, near Hilly Wood and Swordy
Well. An immense crowd surrounded them – mounted
soldiers performing evolutions, ladies in splendid dresses,
crowds as at a fair. "I felt shamed into insignificance at the
sight, and seemed to ask her from my own thoughts why I
had been so suddenly brought into such immense company
when my only life and care was being alone and to myself.
'You are only one of the crowd, now,' she said, and
hurried me back." The scene changed to a bookseller's shop
in a city, and there, on a shelf, among a vast crowd of books,
Clare saw three volumes lettered with his name. "I see them
now. I was very astonished, and turning to look in her face
I was awake in a moment; but the impression never left me.
I see her still. She is my good genius and I believe in her
ideally almost as fresh as reality." He then describes yet
another dream of a later date, which he embodied also in a
poem called "The Night Mare." He dreamed he was in
Long Close, and all the villagers were hurrying past him
northward; it was morning, but the sky had a dull, unnatural hue and the sun shone with a pale, moonstruck
light. He felt the sudden conviction that all were called to
judgment, and he followed the crowd into the church, feeling depressed and uneasy. Then his guardian appeared, "in
white garments beautifully disordered, but sorrowful in her
countenance." A light streamed in a corner of the chancel,
and thence appeared to come "the final decision of man's
actions in life." He heard his own name called. "My
conductress smiled in ecstasy and uttered something as

prophetic of happiness. I knew all was right, and she led me again into the open air." Then as he awoke:

> *'Twas Mary's voice that hung in her farewell;*
> *The sound that moment on my memory fell,*
> *A sound that held the music of the past. . . .*

"These dreams of a beautiful presence, a woman deity, gave the sublimest conceptions of beauty to my imagination; and being last night with the same presence, the lady divinity left such a vivid picture of her visits in my sleep, dreaming of dreams, that I could no longer doubt her existence. So I wrote them down to prolong the happiness of my faith in believing her my guardian genius."

Here, then, is the secret of Clare's recovery from that mood of despair which seems, at first glance, so out of proportion to the circumstances of his removal to North-borough. Yet that breaking of so many links with the past led Clare, naturally enough, to take stock of the years since 1820, to weigh his achievements against his hopes; and he saw himself threatened with failure on every side, with the shipwreck of all his "life's esteems" – independence, love, and poetry. Twelve years after his rise to fame, he was still dependent and in debt; he had lost Mary Joyce in the flesh, and could neither regain her nor forget her; he had seen an earlier love, the country of his boyhood, ravaged by change, and he was now losing it too. As poet also he faced failure; he had lost his public; fame had smiled upon him once, then turned away. The waning of mere popularity troubled Clare little, as his essay on that subject shows clearly enough; but the thought that his poems might be forgotten by posterity too, that he might miss the only immortality he valued, troubled him much as he pondered over those

> *future things that burn the mind*
> *To leave some fragment of itself behind.*

It was not "the burning blaze of fame around a restless world" that he desired:

> *I would not be the common song*
> *For all the world to shout and praise,*
> *But just a theme remembered long*
> *By beauty in its sweetest days.*

In recent years he had returned to this theme again and again; sometimes the mood was one of quiet resignation:

> *Alas! to me no home belongs*
> *But what my dreams create;*
> *Vain, cuckoo-like, I sing my songs*
> *And leave the rest to fate.*

Sometimes, when "Fame's hopes with me are faint to look upon," he wished he could give up the struggle:

> *Yet do I follow with unwearied eyes*
> *The shadowy recompense for real toils;*
> *Ah, would the heart cease aching and be wise*
> *And think life vainly spent, staked for a doubtful prize.*

So that vision which came to him again in these dark hours of his doubt and despair was a trinity. She was Mary Joyce, the spirit of love; she was the spirit of nature, the muse who had inspired him to write of his native country; and she was also the guardian of his fame, the pledge of his immortality as a man and as a poet. With her as his guide, he could go forward again; it was enough if she alone praised him:

> *I've heard of Parnass Hill, Castalia's stream,*
> *And in my mind have worshipped beauty long;*
> *I've heard, alas! but never could I dream*
> *That aught of birthright did to me belong*
> *In that rich paradise of sacred song.*
> *Yet have I loved and worshipped; and the spring*
> *Of hope — though not an eagle in the sun —*
> *Did like a young bird to thy kindness cling;*
> *Friend of my vision, though my race be run,*
> *I'll feel the triumph still to know thy praises won.*

Looking before and after, we can see the profound significance of that triumph, snatched from the jaws of despair

YJ

in 1832. For, within five years, the misfortunes which occasioned that despair beset him in a form more dreadful than his blackest fears could have presaged. The Clare who felt so hardly a removal of three miles from his home was to endure an exile which might appal any man. But the triumph of 1832 foreshadowed that greater victory whose story may be read in the asylum poems. In support of this interpretation, we may offer a final piece of evidence, a poem which, if form and spirit alone were considered, would be placed without hesitation among the asylum lyrics. Yet "Song's Eternity" was written in 1832, soon after "The Flitting." It was, indeed, born of the mood which Clare had attained at the end of "The Flitting," when he felt again

> *a love and joy*
> *For every weed and every thing.*

In "Song's Eternity," the mood, purged of all sorrow, soars in a lyrical ecstasy to catch the very tone and accent of the bird-song whose eternity it celebrates, the "mighty songs that miss decay." Someone has remarked that Clare was more interested in the bird than in the eternity. Unaware of Clare's intense preoccupation with thoughts of the ravages of time and change, that writer missed the deeper significance of the poem. The bird is introduced only because Clare hears in its song, untroubled by thoughts of yesterday or to-morrow, an echo of that eternity which man, by inventing time, has forsworn.

> *Bird and bee*
> *Sing creation's symphony;*
> *Other songs will be unknown,*
> *Proud nature's glee*
> *Is in her simplest mood and tone*
> *Eternity.*

The poem is Clare's justification of his conviction that his guardian spirit was no mere phantom; she was the eternal spirit of nature herself, informing all her creatures with love and joy. He had seen that beauty and shared that joy when she walked with him unaware in the careless, time-less hours of boyhood. In manhood, he had wooed her as a mistress, a siren "not incapable of joy" even in her "sullen moods and fading hues." Then came that hour when she had seemed lost to him for ever, when he saw time, the destroyer, defacing her beauty, threatening the poet's own life's work in her service with oblivion, trampling love and joy under-foot. Now, by that process which Stendhal called "*la cristallisation de l'amour*," he had found her again, and "Song's Eternity" was his paean of victory.

Like all victories, it was won at a cost; Clare had exalted the world of dreams over the world of realities, which had threatened the things he held most dear. And, as the years to come brought him no relief in his struggle with adversity, the dreams became more and more real to him. Yet the asylum poems will be found to be a glorious and lasting witness that this sacrifice of the man to the poet was not made in vain.

XVII

UNWEARIED MINSTRELSY
1832-1835

So will I build my altar in the fields,
And the blue sky my fretted dome shall be,
And the sweet fragrance that the wild flower yields
Shall be the incense I will yield to thee.

S. T. COLERIDGE, "To Nature."

ON the 1st of September, 1832, Clare received from a Peterborough printer a hundred copies of his proposals for the publication of a volume of cottage poems, to be entitled "The Midsummer Cushion." He explained this quaint and pleasing title thus: "It is a very old custom among villagers in summer time to take a piece of green sward full of field flowers and place it as an ornament in their cottages; which ornaments are called Midsummer Cushions." This was his letter to the subscribers:

"The proposals for publishing these fugitives being addressed to friends, no further apology is necessary than the statement of facts. The truth is that difficulty has grown up like a tree of the forest, and being no longer able to conceal it I meet it in the best way possible by attempting to publish these for my own benefit and that of a large family.

"It were false delicacy to make an idle parade of independence in my situation; and it would be unmanly to make a troublesome appeal to persons public or private like a public petitioner.

"Friends neither expect this from me nor wish me to do it to others, though it is partly owing to such advice that I have been induced to come forward with these proposals, and if they are successful they will render me a benefit, and if not they will not cancel any obligations I may have received from friends, public or private, to whom my best wishes are due; and having said thus much in furtherance of my intentions I will conclude by explaining them."

The book was to be printed on fine paper and the price would not exceed 7s. 6d. These prospectuses were distributed among Clare's friends and acquaintances, and by the end of October a list of two hundred subscribers had been collected. In this good work the Emmersons, the Simpsons, the Mossops, Mrs. Marsh, and Henderson were prominent. Then, early in November, Clare changed his plans, on the advice of the Emmersons. They had been negotiating with J. How, who was connected with the publishing firm of Whittaker, and suggested that on the security of his two hundred subscribers Clare should sell the volume outright to How and thus relieve himself of the risk and anxiety of its publication.

The manuscript of "The Midsummer Cushion" contains the fruits of Clare's labours during the ten years prior to 1832. For some time now, ever since he had realised that he could no longer rely on Taylor as editor and publisher, he had been constantly revising and re-copying his poems. He had taken the best of them and transcribed them carefully into an expensive, finely-bound manuscript book. By the autumn of 1832 he had collected more than three hundred poems from thirty-five earlier manuscripts. This lovely book, with its neat and vigorous script, offers convincing proof of Clare's ability to edit his own poems. It was used in compiling the *Rural Muse*, and contains nearly all the poems published there. Yet, could it have been printed as it stood, it would have made a finer book than the *Rural Muse*, representing more adequately the work of Clare's maturity; many of the best poems had to be omitted because of their length. Some of these were culled by Mr. Symons from an earlier manuscript for his selection of 1908, while many others have been rescued more recently by Mr. Blunden; but there are still some flowers that blush unseen in the green sward of "The Midsummer Cushion."

Meanwhile, the zeal of some of Clare's friends in giving

publicity to his new scheme had outrun their discretion. A
paragraph in the *Athenæum* for the 25th of August, 1832, stated
that Clare's cottage had been bestowed on him by Lord
Milton rent free for life; the Stamford *Bee* repeated the story.
Clare was naturally annoyed at what might be interpreted
as an attempt to force Lord Milton's hand; commenting on
the folly of such gossip, he wrote to Mossop: "It troubles
me and injures my feelings of a propriety of independence."
He added that he had already told Clark, the editor of the
Bee, that he expected to pay rent as his neighbours did. He
also wrote to his London friends to have the matter corrected there; but the correction gave birth to such a crop of
further errors that Clare felt he had more to fear from his
friends than from his enemies. A notice appeared in the
Alfred giving the correct facts about the cottage, but adding
a most exaggerated account of Clare's situation, suggesting
that he had been cheated out of all profits by his publishers
and that he had only £15 a year on which to maintain his
wife and six children. The *Bee* repeated this story on the
5th of October, and on the 13th the *Athenæum*, correcting
its previous statement about the cottage, also quoted the
Alfred story, and reprinted Clare's proposals as evidence of
its truth. The fountain-head of both these mis-statements
appears to have been Charles Jacob, the Peterborough printer.
He sent them to his relative, How, who supplied them to the
Athenæum and the *Alfred*. The second *Athenæum* notice was
from the pen of Allan Cunningham.

Clare's indignation was tempered by the realization that
his friends had erred in trying to serve him, but he was angry
that Taylor's honesty had been questioned. He wrote at
once to How, stating that he did not want publicity of this
kind, that he "felt a stubborn belief that Taylor was a sincere
friend," and that the trouble had been caused by the double-
dealing of Drury, for Taylor was "utterly above such things
and like myself a man of business only by necessity." He felt
that Clark was less blameless in repeating statements which
he must have known were false. "Had I been aware of his
intentions to meddle in my affairs, I should most assuredly

have treated him as a foe in disguise," he wrote to Simpson;
" I am no beggar; for my income is £36"; and to the editor
himself, "I wish not to have my difficulties trumpeted by
everyone who chooses to pen his spleen in my favour. . . .
Officious interferences as to my adversity add nothing to
my prosperity. . . . I never solicited praise or profit from any
individual in my life. . . .I am not seeking charity but independence." Again and again in his letters to his friends
Clare repeated this last definition of his material ambitions.
To find his latest attempt to achieve independence turned
into an appeal for charity made him indignant, and where
he suspected, as he did with regard to the *Bee*, that he was
being used as a political catspaw, it made him angry too.

Yet, in the height of these annoyances, his larger hopes
and fears remained untouched by what he called the stings
of summer insects. He wrote to Allan Cunningham on the
10th of November, thanking him for his help in advertising
the prospectuses and setting forth his humble ambitions.

"I have those around me that make me turn to the practical matters of pounds, shillings and pence. . . . I have a
strong opinion of Taylor and shall always respect him, and
I think if the matter had been entirely left to business and I
had sold them out and out, even for a trifle, I should have
been better off and much better satisfied. . . . I cannot but
say God protect all hopes in difficulties from the patronage
of trade."

Then there is a draft of what appears to be a letter to Cary,
which well illustrates Clare's ability to regard such troubles
as but minor details in the landscape of his life's work. Cary
had written to him on the 20th of October, "Had you been
as expert an agriculturist or mechanic, as you are a Poet, you
also might by this time have acquired competence or even
wealth. But would you be satisfied to exchange conditions on
those terms?"

"Your philosophy of quietness was better than medicine
to my mind," wrote Clare, and went on to tell of his latest
schemes and difficulties; ". . . your commendation, given

early and continued long, gave me a pride that the ephemeral opinions of unknown interferences cannot take away . . . I wished to be judged of by the book itself, without any appeals to want of education, lowness of origin or any other foil that officiousness chooses to encumber my path with; but it seems I must be encumbered. Never mind; I must write on; for ambition to be happy in sadness, as verses make me, urges me onward." He enclosed a prospectus of his "little cockleshell."

"If you laugh at my ambitions I am ready to laugh with you at my own vanity; for I sit sometimes and wonder over the little noise I have made in the world, until I think I have written nothing as yet to deserve any praise at all. So the spirit of fame, of living a little after life like a name on a conspicuous place, urges my blood upward into unconscious melodies, and striding down my orchard and homestead, I hum and sing inwardly those little madrigals and then go in and pen them down, thinking them much better things than they are ; until I look over them again, and then the charm vanishes into the vanity that I shall do something ere I die. So in spite of myself I rhyme on and write nothing but little things at last."

He thought all his old friends had "gone away with the world," but was glad to find there was still one, "almost the last of the flock," who still remembered him; yet he hoped to see them all again, "as earnest in their affections as ever. . . . And then I shall shake hands with old time and be more happy than when old time was new to me. God bless you, my dear Sir."

The year 1833 opened inauspiciously with reverberations of the newspaper storm of the previous autumn. Taylor's grievances against Clare over the business of the Fund-money had been aggravated by those public aspersions of his character for which he held Clare partly responsible. He had not written since July, 1832; now, on the 9th of January, he announced that he was instituting an action for libel against the proprietors of the papers. The news found Clare in no fit condition to cope with it. He was ill again;

he was much troubled by a hallucination that he was bewitched by evil spirits. Both Mrs. Emmerson and Taylor wrote assuring him that there was no such thing as witchcraft. Meanwhile, the plans for the new volume were at a standstill, and debts began to accumulate again as the months passed. Clare was driven to ask whether How would advance money on the manuscripts already completed; Mrs. Emmerson wrote in June urging him to exert himself, since no publisher would countenance such a proposal. "Good heavens Johnny, how can you sink down to such apathy?" Evidently she did not know that he had been ordered by his doctor to abstain from reading and writing, and he was a little hurt by her failure to understand; for she so rarely failed him.

Not the least of his anxieties at this time was for his family, which had been increased by the birth of a son, Charles, in the previous December. The education of the elder children was a constant theme of his letters to Mrs. Emmerson. He had sent such a formidable list of books for her to procure that she asked if he was about to turn schoolmaster. Another list he sent to Taylor, requesting him to deduct the cost from the next dividend. "For do you know, I wish to make all my children scholars and the expenses for school books make the charges so high that I am troubled often in which way to pay them." He wanted blank summing books, arithmetic text-books, and selections in prose and verse. He had decided ideas about the kind of book he wanted, having talked of such matters years before with Cary and Darley. He did not like Murray's text-books, because they taught set tasks which were not entertaining to children. He wanted books that would please them to read and profit them to remember. We find elsewhere a list of "Christmas Boxes promised to my children"; they were all books, from *Valentine and Orson* for Anna down to *The House that Jack Built* for Sophy. In 1830 the Emmersons had tried to get Fred into Christ's Hospital, but they were unsuccessful.

Clare's interest in his children's education went further

than the provision of schooling and books. In one of his manuscripts is a letter of advice to his sons, written under the impression that he could not live to advise them in person. He warned them against bad company and false friends; they were to consider their master's interests as their own, and value common honesty above all things. He warned them against meddling with political contentions, "for there are many whose superior abilities force them into that storm and strife of opinion, who would give all the wealth they possess for that quiet which you may enjoy for nothing." This need not prevent them from taking an intelligent interest in political questions. "If you can be impartial, read the speeches and they will improve you, and if style or composition or purity of diction delight you, there you will find it in perfection in the orations of both parties; for to me they have been of great benefit."

Clare's affection for his children was deep and sensitive. There is a family tradition that he could not bear to see them punished. Patty, in her flashes of anger, sometimes gave them hearty thrashings, whereupon Clare would plead for them and offer to bear the stripes himself.

In July, 1833, Clare was able at last to write to Taylor, who was "gratified with your expression of friendly Regard and kind recollection of our early and long-continued acquaintance." He had now overcome his feeling of annoyance at the newspaper gossip and had decided to drop the libel action. As soon as his health allowed, Clare completed the copying up of his poems, and by August the manuscript book was in Mrs. Emmerson's hands. She was delighted with it, but suggested changing the title to the *Rural Muse*. Nothing more was effected in 1833, owing to changes in the firm of Whittaker. Among the scanty records of these months is a letter from Cary, sending his translation of Pindar. "It is all about chariot & horse-racing, boxing, running, heathen gods and goddesses, &c., &c.; so I don't expect it will be much to your taste; & therefore don't insist on your reading it. Only it serves to show that you are not forgotten."

In January, 1834, Thomas Emmerson obtained How's

solemn promise to bring out the *Rural Muse* in the spring.
Clare received the good news with gratitude. His situation
was growing desperate; his debts had crept up to £35,
including the £20 which was owing when he left Helpston.
The rent of the Northborough cottage – so Ryde of Burghley
told Mrs. Emmerson – was £15 a year. Some of the children
were ill; even the milch cow, May, whose arrival Mrs.
Emmerson had celebrated with a sonnet, had failed sadly
to perform the duties of its kind, assuming perhaps that a
poet's cow was expected to be ornamental rather than useful. The pressure of these anxieties brought a return of
Clare's illness early in 1834; fears of witchcraft and other
morbid fancies troubled him again. Dr. Darling could do
little more than urge him not to aggravate his ills by these
figments of the imagination, and prescribed verses from the
Psalms. Taylor had at first declined to help with the editing,
but, as Clare felt too ill to assist in the publication, he offered
to look over the proofs.

In March a letter from Thomas Emmerson brought the
much-needed financial relief, and effected a temporary
improvement in Clare's spirits. The copyright had yielded
£40, with which Clare was able to settle nearly all his
accumulated debts. But the clouds of depression dispersed by
this timely wind soon collected again; for, although Clare's
ambition burned no less brightly, though his determination
to struggle through to better days was no less dogged, they
could not now demand the same ready obedience from the
mind and body that served them. Each illness left his mind
less elastic, his body more weary; recovery was slow and
strewn with relapses. There is clear evidence of this in a
series of letter drafts in one of his manuscripts, all dated
1834 and all unfinished. Several of them are mere fragments,
the superscription and one or two lines; then the writing
trails off as Clare found the completion of a brief note too
great a burden. All the fragments tell the same story; he is
very ill, scarcely able to write, cannot even express his
gratitude, wants to see Dr. Darling. In July he made an
attempt to realize this wish, feeling that a visit to London

might benefit his health as it had done in the past. Unfortunately, Mrs. Emmerson was going out of town on a visit to Smallcombe Grove, near Bath, "a spot of exquisite beauty" where they had just purchased a country retreat, and Taylor had no room for him just then.

Clare had managed to write the preface for the *Rural Muse* by August, and the poems were in the printer's hands. A month later Taylor was busy editing the proofs with his usual meticulous care; most of his alterations were made in the interest of grammar or clarity, but occasionally he spoiled a line which did not jump with his personal opinions, as when he changed "Death's long, happy sleep is won" to "Heaven's eternal Peace is won," preferring, he explained, bad divinity to good atheism.

How had now left Whittaker's, but was still active on Clare's behalf. On the 6th of December, he wrote suggesting that Clare should apply to the Literary Fund for help; he was acquainted with some of the committee, and thought Clare might ask for £50, which would keep him in comfort over the winter. The application was successful, and the money arrived in January. Thanks to this gift from the Literary Fund, which had accomplished much good relief-work since its establishment by David Williams in 1780, Clare was able to pay off his remaining debts and face the new year with less anxiety. There was an immediate improvement in his spirits.

Taylor's letter of the 9th of January, 1835, contained news of the death of Charles Lamb in the previous December; Woodhouse also was dead, and had left Taylor all his papers, with many poems by Keats. Taylor said he would like to publish a complete edition of Keats, but he feared that the world did not care enough to buy it. He also pointed out a reference to Clare in Ebenezer Elliott's poem "Love," and another to Keats in "The Letter," where Elliott says that he

> *Lived in melody as if his veins*
> *Poured Music.*

Cary also had commented on Elliott's "words that scald;" Clare was undoubtedly acquainted with the work of the Sheffield poet, though we find none of his books in Clare's library.

Toward the end of 1834, Clare's patron, Lord Spencer, had died, and Clare feared that the annuity of £10 would now be discontinued. Taylor advised him to ask the earl's successor to continue the kindness, and drafted a letter for him; Clare was grateful, "for though I could scarcely do without the money, I had not the resolution to write for it and I think I should never have done so." The new earl responded kindly, and the annuity went on as before.

The publication of the *Rural Muse*, which generously fulfilled the promise of 1820 and should have raised the star of his fame to the second magnitude, produced a very mild and brief Indian summer of interest. For a few months the book sold fairly well, and Whittaker had hopes of disposing of the first edition. A number of old acquaintances looked up from their affairs to applaud. Derwent Coleridge, now a schoolmaster in Cornwall, had visited the Emmersons in July and expressed his appreciation. Mrs. Emmerson hoped – but vainly, it appears – that Henry Nelson Coleridge, Sara's husband, would write a review of it for the *Quarterly*. Alaric Watts had praised it, and James Montgomery too. Rippingille, just returned from a lecturing tour in the north, sent congratulations; there came news of Charles Elton, who was about to publish his *Boyhood*, which included "The Idler's Epistle." Mrs. Emmerson had given a copy of the *Rural Muse* to Harry Phillips, the popular singer and disciple of Izaak Walton. Captain Sherwill, visiting London after years of European travel, revived the memory of old days, and promised books, Dr. Bowring wrote, and from an American bookseller came a letter proposing an arrangement for selling the book there. A new correspondent was George Reid of Glasgow, who showed his appreciation in practical form by sending many books for Clare's library.

In *Blackwood's Magazine* for August, Professor Wilson welcomed the poems with a long and, in the main, sympathetic review; yet, after exhorting the public to buy a book so full of beauties, and commenting, ironically enough, on Clare's comfort beside Bloomfield's and Burns's deaths in poverty, North incurred Taylor's contempt by inviting Clare to imitate Bloomfield. There was a warmly appreciative article in the *Literary Gazette;* the *Athenæum* recommended the book briefly but sincerely, as did the *New Monthly.* The reviewer in the *Druids' Magazine* described his visit to Northborough, and was enthusiastic in praise of the book. He agreed with North that Clare's popularity might be increased if he confined himself to describing the manners and feelings of the lower orders. Critic and public alike were at the moment snubbing Nature for her recent forwardness in English poetry.

Could these critics have seen the manuscript of "The Midsummer Cushion" and the many poems which Mrs. Emmerson had omitted in her selection, they might have revised their statements. Mrs. Emmerson was an enthusiast who knew a good poem when she saw it, but she did not always recognize a poor one. Occasionally her omissions were justified. Sometimes nothing but a personal bias or a strict eye on the dimensions desired for the book could have helped to decide between one poem and another equally good. The sonnets in the manuscript were all far better than those in the *Village Minstrel,* and those included were among the best; yet we miss such excellent ones as "The Firetail's Nest" and "Providence," which, with poems like "Pastoral Poesy," enshrined important articles of Clare's poetic creed. A place for these poems could easily have been found, without lengthening the book, by the omission of a number of album verses, "The Grasshopper," "The Quiet Mind," "Nature's Hymn to the Deity," "Woman's Love," which had been written by Clare to meet the requirements of the editors of the Annuals.

The *Rural Muse* was dedicated to Earl Fitzwilliam, and Clare's preface was short. The poems, he said again, were written to please his own mind; he did not want indulgence for them, but he would be heartily satisfied with the good opinion of his reader. The accuracy and detail of such descriptive

nature-pieces as "The Pettichap's Nest" and "The Sedge-
bird's Nest" could not have been surpassed, as Miss Mitford
later observed, by ornithologists like Audubon, Gould, and
Waterton.[1] He could now imprison the living moment in
nature with a few words; convey the living image, too, of
the "pranking bat," express the very wood-silences with the
"easy thoughtlessness of thought" he claimed for the highest
poetry.

> *I love at early morn, from new mown swath,*
>   *To see the startled frog his route pursue;*
> *To mark, while leaping o'er the dripping path,*
>   *His bright sides scatter dew,*
> *The early lark that from its bustle flies*
>   *To hail his matin new;*
>   *And watch him to the skies.*
>
> *To note on hedgerow baulks, in moisture sprent,*
>   *The jetty snail creep from the mossy thorn,*
> *With earnest heed and tremulous intent,*
>   *Frail brother of the morn,*
> *That from the tiny bent's dew-misted leaves*
>   *Withdraws his timid horn,*
>   *And fearful vision weaves.*

What he had set himself to do he had done. His technique
was finished, his artistic form, as far as he could apprehend
it, perfect.

We have watched Clare, through *Poems Descriptive*, the
Village Minstrel, and the *Shepherd's Calendar*, climbing to this
zenith of his art. In the *Rural Muse* we may see indications
of how he might soar above himself, as if, his art being perfected, something more was to be added unto it. Except for
"Vanities of Life" and "The Quiet Mind," there were no
imitations of other and older writers in the book. Yet his
reading since the compiling of the poems for the *Shepherd's
Calendar* had been continuous and varied. He was still steeped
in the Elizabethans. His unceasing struggle to transcend the
ever-increasing difficulties of his life resulted in the more
intensely emotional writing to be found in the *Rural Muse*; it
let loose a lyricism not present in his work hitherto. A Lear-like
note of tragedy has crept in, of which Clare is unconscious,

and when his subject is still joy. It is as if he had taken
upon himself the "mystery of things," and the Elizabethans
and the king of them had helped him to find his own personal
lyric note. A new dignity and authority, especially when he
returns to the theme of the eternity of nature, is there.

> *Man, Earth's poor shadow! talks of Earth's decay:*
> *But hath it nothing of eternal kin?*
> *No majesty that shall not pass away?*
> *No soul of greatness springing up within?*
> *Thought-marks without? hoar shadows of sublime?*
> *Pictures of power, which, if not doomed to win*
> *Eternity, stand laughing at old Time*
> *For ages, in the grand ancestral line*
> *Of things eternal, mounting to divine?*

In those poems, too, where he considers present and future
fame, like "Pastoral Fancies," "Impulses of Spring," the
sonnets "Memory" and "The Shepherd's Tree," there is
a reflection and sorrow, a lonely and eloquent resignation,
which might foreshow the lyric intensity of "I Am."

And then that something more that is to be added. There
are lines and phrases in these poems which are harbingers
of that almost non-human music of his verse in the asylum
poems to come. He had longed for the wizard voice of the
November storm that he might "breathe a living song" in
praise. It almost seems as if later he acquired the sibylline
melody of that "eternal ditty." Trying to capture some of
the very notes of the robin, and so prolong "the happy
prime" of its "eternal song," he appears to have been granted
this identification of himself with other living things:

> *Giving to stocks and stones, in rapture's strife,*
> *A soul of utterance and a tongue of life.*

His verse music begins to take on some quality beyond words.
If, then, we remember "Song's Eternity" as well as these
poems in the *Rural Muse*, may we not say that Clare has become, even at this time of his life, the truest representative
among poets from the world of nature to the world of
literature?

XVIII

SHIPWRECK
1835-1837

He walks with Nature; and her paths are peace.
 EDWARD YOUNG, *Night Thoughts.*

Are geniuses to be the kings of the earth? Not quite. Geniuses have to be kept in order – like criminals. If there's one thing to be said in favour of the English character, it is that we've known the proper way to treat geniuses.
ARNOLD BENNETT, *Milestones.*

THE tributes which Clare received from old and new acquaintances on their reception of the *Rural Muse* relieved somewhat, but could not entirely remove, the gloom that had clung about his mind since his last illness. He sent an account of his distress to Dr. Darling:

"I write to tell you I am very unwell, and though I cannot describe my feelings well I will tell you as well as I can. Sounds affect me very much, and things evil as well [as] good thoughts are continually rising in my mind. I cannot sleep, for I am asleep, as it were, with my eyes open, and I feel chills come over me and a sort of nightmare awake, and I got no rest last night. I feel a great desire to come up but perhaps I shall not be able and I hope you will write down directly, for I feel you can do me good and if I was in town I should soon be better, so I fancy; for I do assure you I am very unwell and I cannot keep my mind right, as it were, for I wish to read and cannot." He said he had never properly recovered from his last illness, and he added this postscript: "I fear I shall be worse and worse ere you write to me, for I have been out for a walk and can scarcely bear up against my fancies or feelings."

For such a condition of nervous collapse there could be
ZJ   369

but one cure – a complete change of environment, with relief from the anxieties which had caused, and daily aggravated, the disease. The removal to Northborough had not brought the hoped-for relief; it had come too late, and the venture was crippled from the first by his inadequate means. The outlook for 1836 was dismal indeed; he could expect no more windfalls from the Literary Fund; the Annuals had now failed him entirely; with the first edition of the *Rural Muse* unsold, there was no hope of money from his poems.

Yet Clare would not yield himself to his fate. Had he done so, had he accepted his failure to achieve independence both as a peasant and as a poet, he might have been spared the fiercer torments to come; like so many of the peasants of England in those days, condemned to pauperdom, he might have acquired a slave's mentality to make the lot of serfdom endurable. Yet his hopes still glowed, not brightly upon his countenance as once they did, but with an inward flame,

> *Burning the soul to leave behind*
> *The memory of a name.*

So he still made plans for a new volume, though he saw no chance of its appearance in print; and he still wrote on, when he was able, writing to please himself or 'for antiquity.'

The poems written between 1832 and 1836 are notable for the absence of that direct personal reference which inspired many of the poems of the preceding period. The crisis of 1832 had ended with a renewal of faith, a replighting of his troth with his first love, nature. Thereafter, whenever he walked in the fields or took up his pen, Clare turned his back on the world of men and on his own troubles and found serenity and joy in the service of his mistress. The transition from that discord to this harmony was not always easy, and occasionally we find traces of it in his verses:

> *To be and not to be and still to know it,*
> *Like toad, life-buried in the solid rock,*
> *Were a blest lot and happiness to mine,*
> *Possessed of feelings that burn out the mind*

Like to a candle snuff, yet leaving fire
Within that would consume with mad revenge
And with a pagan kiss destroy men's souls.

More often, the discord –

I hate the very noise of troublous man,
Who did and does me all the harm he can –

is but the prelude to a triumphant assertion of his belief that
love and solitude could prevail over all the "scorn and noise."

Yet sometimes the world of men intruded into the haunts
of nature and disturbed the harmony which Clare found
there. He had often raised his voice against the thoughtless
and unnecessary cruelty of man toward his fellow-animals.
It is significant that he became more painfully sensitive to
these acts of cruelty during this period. In a series of poems,
he described without comment, seemingly without emotion,
the baiting of badgers, the harrying of marten, polecat, and
fox, the hunting of hedgehogs and spoiling of birds' nests
by boys. Yet the emotion is there, perfectly subdued to its
medium, expressed dramatically in the contrast between the
laughing, shouting, excited mob of men and boys and the
self-possession and dignity of the badger, "demure and
small," beating off the yelping dogs, driving the crowd before it again and again, unyielding,

Till kicked and torn and beaten out he lies
And leaves his hold and cackles, groans, and dies.

But leaving these poems and turning to the rest, we cannot
over-emphasize the calm serenity and joy which Clare found
in his communion with nature. He leaves us in no doubt as
to his prevailing mood: "Field thoughts to me are happiness
and joy," and "every summer's footpath leads to joy."

Apart from many such assurances, this mood is implicit in
most of the poems written during these years. One remarkable manuscript contains a sequence of some hundred and
fifty poems describing fen scenes and occupations. In the
interests of economy, they were inscribed in ink of Clare's
own brewing, the recipe for which was noted down in the
manuscript. Perhaps he put it there as a warning, for his

home-made ink did its work only too well. It ate into the paper, as the desire to be remembered burned the poet's mind, and some of the pages are blurred and almost illegible.

These poems are all very short, most of them of sonnet length; Clare had always used the sonnet form with little respect for tradition; he now adapted it so freely to the requirements of a purely descriptive poem that we must hesitate to call them sonnets. His choice of the sonnet length for these poems was certainly deliberate; in the first place, the strain of composing a long poem was too much for him during these years; but he made a virtue of the necessity. It was always his aim to present nature, which included man in harmony with nature, exactly as he found them, "unadorned and plain." It was an item of his creed that every moment and every object in the fields was significant; as a field naturalist he realized that it is fatal to go out expecting something rare and strange, that nature reserves her richest rewards for those who have patience to "stand and wait," delighting the while in whatever she offers. These short poems, when Clare found so many joys in such a small circuit of experience, remind us of the short lyrics of Emily Dickinson. If Clare had ever been "inebriate," it was surely chiefly of the air, as he was now; if ever "debauchee," as some have hinted, it was surely chiefly of the dew. Furthermore, in these poems of his, that everyday prodigality and variety is conveyed with the simplicity and economy of technique which is the mark of maturity in a poet.

The subjects of these vigorous sketches suggest that Clare's muse, in answer to his entreaties, had left her former haunts to live with him at Northborough. Heaths, woods, and pastures no longer fill the background of his scenes; now he writes of river meadows, of swollen dykes, and the naked levels of the fen. As befits the more cultivated, reclaimed fenland, few of his scenes are unpeopled: a farm-yard at daybreak; a group of bramble-pickers; breakfast-time in the fields; a wasps' nest near a path; a game of blind man's buff; stick-gatherers in the snow; a boy playing truant; the

Morris dancers; a fowler shooting birds; a pedlar with his ass
and panniers; a ploughman lobbing along; a harassed boy
scaring birds; a soldier returning to his native village; a
gipsies' camp; a shepherd-boy building mud castles; a mole-
catcher at work. In these intimate sketches of the everyday
lives of ordinary people Clare accomplished that task which
Wordsworth had set himself in the *Lyrical Ballads*.

On the 18th of December, 1835, Clare's mother died, at
the age of seventy-eight. His parents had not accompanied
him to Northborough; they had left the Helpston cottage to
live elsewhere a few years before Clare's removal, presumably to make room for the growing family. A visitor to
Helpston some time after 1832 had found Clare's mother
gleaning in the fields. Parker Clare, who came to Northborough after Ann's death, lived on until 1846, and reached
his eighty-second year. There is little sign here of the feeble
stock from which the poet was supposed to have sprung.
Rather does he seem to have inherited from his parents a
physical tenacity and, if not a robust, a wiry frame, which,
like one of his sturdy trees, resisted the storms that stripped
from it its blossom and foliage.

The year 1836 renews the story of Clare's illness, which,
in the absence of adequate treatment, gradually tightened
its grip on his mind. There are, however, few traces of it in
the correspondence except reports that he is still no better;
in dealing with most of the business of everyday life, Clare
was, as he remained, quite normal and rational. His letters
to Mrs. Emmerson became shorter, often mere notes; in
March she sent him a waistcoat – chequered, as flowers
were out of fashion – and a volume of Allan Cunningham's
early *Songs*, given her by Henry Phillips. Clare was still
greedy for books, and wrote to Sherwill to remind him of
his promise to send some. In June, Rippingille wrote from
London – a much more serious man than the Rippingille of
Clare's memory, sobered by family troubles and some years of
waiting on fortune to little purpose. Any hope that the *Rural
Muse* might bring about a revival of Clare's fame vanished
completely during the autumn; Whittaker wrote that no

new edition would be required, as the first was still unsold.

On the 29th of November, John Taylor sent word from Retford that he hoped to visit Northborough on his way back to town. Fortunately, he left an account of this visit, which occurred about the 6th of December:

"The following morning at seven I set off to see Clare in a chaise accompanied by a medical gentleman of Stamford, who was to give me his opinion respecting poor Clare's health. We found him sitting in a chimney corner looking much as usual. He talked properly to me in reply to all my questions, knew all the people of whom I spoke, and smiled at my reminding him of the events of past days. But his mind is sadly enfeebled. He is constantly speaking to himself and when I listened I heard such words as these, pronounced a great many times over and with great rapidity – 'God bless them all,' 'Keep them from evil,' 'Doctors.' But who it was of whom he spoke I could not tell – whether his children, or doctors, or everybody. But I think the latter. His children, seven in number, are a very fine family, strongly resembling him; the youngest, a boy of three or four years old; the eldest, a girl, sixteen. There are three boys and four girls. The medical man's opinion was that Clare should go to some asylum. His wife is a very clever, active woman, and keeps them all very respectable and comfortable, but she cannot manage to control her husband at times; he is very violent, I dare say, occasionally. His old father is still living with them. We went thence to see a clergyman who had been always kind to Clare for twenty years, and he has promised to see Earl Fitzwilliam about an asylum."

Family and local tradition, and the records of Clare's condition in the following years, help us to fill in the impression of these last Northborough days. As Taylor remarked in a letter after his return to London, and as several other visitors noted, Clare's outward appearance showed few signs of his illness; from his general mood of melancholy brooding he could usually be coaxed to talk rationally and with animation of the things that interested him. Occasionally the thread of his discourse would be abruptly broken by some irrelevancy born of his delusions, and at times the quiet

melancholy plunged downward into complete apathy or
rose into outbursts of fierce anger. Such outbursts, fed by
his conviction of injustice and frustration, made life at the
Northborough cottage difficult, almost impossible. By the
very nature of his chief delusion, Patty could not soothe him
and might irritate him. It was the theme of Dante, Beatrice
and Gemma, re-written in a minor key and with some varia-
tions. For the projection of Clare's dreams into his waking
life had now been completed; the visionary guardian spirit
and the real Mary Joyce, united in dreams, had now been
transferred to the plane of everyday existence, and the Mary
he had lost nearly twenty years before became his wife. Yet
he had no wish to discard Patty, even in his dream life; he
could not have written, with Dante,

> *Me, my wife*
> *Of savage temper, more than aught beside,*
> *Hath to this evil brought.*

Despite Patty's quick tongue and her imperfect sympathies
regarding his writing, his affection for her and his appreciation of her many admirable qualities remained unchanged.
So, with an inner logic which ignored social law, he made
Mary his first wife and Patty his second. This solution, however satisfactory in the world of dreams, did not make for
domestic peace; Patty could not be expected to understand
it or approve of it; and Clare could not comprehend why
his first wife, whom he said he had seen, was kept from him.
It is not, in fact, impossible for Clare to have seen Mary
Joyce, for she lived until 1838[1]; but the sight of her, real or
imaginary, excited him. One of his grandsons tells how, when
Patty could do nothing with her husband in his fits of irrita-
tion, one of the elder boys would take him aside and soon
calm his anger by talking quietly to him of other things.
There is another story that sometimes when out walking
he would rush into a pond; he "felt better in the water."

One who sought information of Clare at a time when some
personal memory of him still lingered in Helpston and
Northborough gathered the impression that he was moody,

erratic, of a strong temper, not averse to female company, occasionally given to strong drink and strong language. Just such a reputation for strong drink clung too long to the name of Henry Kingsley, seer and neglected genius, who again, for a moment in memory, may stand beside Clare in the tragedy of ill-health and poverty. Such Clare may well have appeared to the village gossips, quick to see failings, niggardly of praise; on the debit side of Clare's character, this impression is not unjust, if it is ungenerous. In fairness, we may place beside it some remarks of Clare's upon his own character, which have special reference to the question of honour in his own country. This first extract was written some years before 1836, and when he was smarting under the lash of gossips' tongues:

"I have been accused of being a drunkard and of being ungrateful toward my friends and patrons by a set of meddling trumpery . . . who never gave me further notice than their scandal, which is too weak or foolish for me either to notice or reply to. . . . Most of them have known me from childhood and could never find that I had any faults till now. I possessed their good word eighteen years and it did me no service, and if I should live to wear their bad one as long it will do me no harm. . . . I have felt all the kindness I have received, though I did not make a parade of it. I did not write eternal praises, and I had a timidity that made me very awkward and silent in the presence of my superiors, which gave me a great deal of trouble and hurt my feelings. I wished to thank them and tell them that I felt their kindness, and remained silent; neither did I trumpet the praises of patrons eternally wherever I went. . . . I was never utterly cast down in adversity; I struggled on. Neither was I at any time lifted up above my prosperity. I never attempted to alter my old ways and manners. I harboured no proud notions nor felt a pride above my station. I was courted to keep company with the 'betters' in the village, but I never noticed the fancied kindness. The old friends and neighbours in my youth are my friends and neighbours now, and I never spent an hour in any of the houses of the farmers since I met with my [success], or mixed in their company as equals."

He was answering definite charges there; in this second passage, he discusses his character more calmly and judicially:

"Every friendship I made grew into a warm attachment. I was in earnest or I was nothing, and I believed everything that was uttered came from the heart, as mine did. When I made a familiar friend I gave him my confidence and un-bosomed my faults and failings to him without hesitation and reserve, putting my all into his hands and thereby making myself bare to his tempest without caring to en-quire into his own as a holdfast or earnest to keep secrets.

"On the other hand I have a fault that often hurts me, though I cannot master it. I am apt to mistake some foibles that all men are subject to as breaches of friendship, and thereby grow dissatisfied and lose my sincerity for them; and when I feel disappointed in my opinions of them, I never can recover my former attachment, though I often try. I always wear the silent enmity of an enemy when I can no longer feel the sincerity of a friend. I know I am full of faults, though I have improved and tempered myself as well as I was able; but these that stick to me were born with me and will die with me."

We turn again to the correspondence for light on the events of the first half of 1837 – Clare's last months at home. Mrs. Emmerson, suffering from a long and painful illness, had not written since the previous August. In March she thanked Clare for his letters, which she thought gave proof of improvement in his health. But her next letter mentioned the "afflicting malady" in his head. She had obtained from How the manuscript book used for the *Rural Muse*; Clare wanted to use some of the unpublished poems in a new volume which he was preparing; he had given Mrs. Emmerson an account of some poems he had recently written. His ambi-tion was as valiant as ever; but it was too late now; the bright period in which he had begun the task passed, and as he turned over that vast collection of manuscripts, from finely-bound books to fragments of letter-paper and edges of newspapers, from poems but lately jotted down to verses of his early youth, he felt that for the present the task was beyond him.

George Reid of Glasgow was a constant correspondent during these months; he sent more books and some donations from friends whom he had interested in Clare.

In March, Clare had been reading and pondering about religious problems; he should not trouble his mind, wrote Mrs. Emmerson, about Unitarianism; Richard Wright, though a clever writer, might be in the wrong; he should believe without questioning.

By June arrangements had been made for Clare's removal to his new home, but of these the records show no trace. Taylor had mentioned that Mr. Mossop might approach Earl Fitzwilliam about an asylum; but, before anything came of this plan, Taylor must have met Dr. Matthew Allen, whose *Essay on the Classification of the Insane* he published in this year, and concluded that here was the very man to help Clare. He could not fail to be impressed by Allen's enthusiasm and experience. The plans were made with Taylor's habitual secrecy; Mrs. Emmerson knew nothing about Clare's removal until months later, and then her information was incorrect.

Thus, one day in June, 1837, a man presented himself at Clare's cottage with a note from Taylor, dated the 13th. "The bearer will bring you up to town and take all care of you on the way." It was hoped that "the medical aid provided near this place will cure you effectually." Clare needed all his faith in this happy termination of his pilgrimage as he journeyed to London with his attendant, leaving all that he loved behind him. It was well for him that he could not presage the nature and extent of his exile. His last letter to Mrs. Emmerson, written before he knew of the plans for his departure, had been gloomy. She replied on the 13th of July, urging him to new endeavour, suggesting that he should write a poem on the Maiden Queen. "Up, up brave Spirit," she implored. But the appeal was unheard; the brave spirit still wrestled with despair; but in another clime, where the voices of his friends and the noises of the world were faint and distant sounds, muted by the barrier of his prison walls.

WINTER

XIX

WITH SHADOWS TOST
1837–1841

So Man's insanity is Heaven's sense; and wandering from all mortal reason, Man comes at last to that celestial thought, which, to reason, is absurd and frantic; and weal or woe, feels then uncompromised, indifferent as his God.

MELVILLE.

MATTHEW ALLEN, M.D., asylum physician, lecturer, writer, a man of wide interests and personal charm, was in the forefront of those reformers of the early nineteenth century who lifted the asylums of England from the confines of hell to the brighter plains of humanity. Under his kindly care Clare was to remain for four years, during which he came within sight of the hoped-for recovery; the student of literature may encounter Allen elsewhere; he tended and cured of derangement the only son of Thomas Campbell, and it was his strange fate, after a life devoted to the rescue of unfortunates stricken with madness, to end by driving the future Poet Laureate to the verge of insanity.

From 1819 to 1824 he was medical resident and superintendent at York Asylum, and earned the thanks of the governors for his "constant and successful efforts in establishing and perfecting the mild system of treatment there." The York Lunatic Asylum, after some thirty years of the mismanagement, dishonesty, and cruelty then all too common in institutions of the kind, had adopted the new system in 1814. On leaving York, Allen decided to embody his theories in an institution of his own, and in 1825 he fixed upon High Beech,[1] Epping, as the most suitable situation near London for his purpose: "for here, together with domestic comfort, diversity of occupations and amusements suited to their various states, the retirement, pure air and sweet scenery around, afford ample scope for walks without annoyance, and apparently without restraint, which, with judicious moral and medical management combine many acknowledged requisites to assist the disturbed and diseased mind to regain its tranquillity."

In his *Cases of Insanity*, 1831, and *Essay on the Classification of the Insane*, 1837, Allen set forth his observations, conclusions, and methods. The patient was to be encouraged in every kind of healthy amusement and occupation for mind and body, and moral restraint was to take the place of physical. In the application of this aim, Allen made his most original contribution to the cause. The first essential for the encouragement of self-control in the patient was a relationship of absolute confidence and friendship between patient and attendant; the truth must never be violated nor deceit resorted to even to get the sufferers from their homes. Many had been cured by this candour and honesty alone. The moral effect of this personal relationship was strengthened by social amenities; but careful organization was necessary here. To plunge a patient among a crowd of fellow-sufferers, each with his own derangement and at a different stage of control, might be as harmful as solitary confinement. Allen emphasized the need for discrimination, for an elastic organization which would enable patients to be divided into suitable small groups according to their needs.

Allen had chosen his situation well; the buildings lay in a wooded valley on the south-west borders of Epping Forest. The asylum consisted of three separate buildings, with cottages and grounds; Fair Mead House was demolished some sixty years ago; Leppitt's Hill Lodge, four hundred yards distant but connected by the grounds, still stands; and just across the road was Springfield, now a farmhouse. One of the buildings was reserved for the women, tended by Mrs. Allen, while the doctor himself took charge of those cases which required the most careful attention – chiefly incipients, convalescents, and the partially deranged. But the organization of all three houses was similar. Each was divided into two parts; the back consisted of small rooms and galleries, inhabited by those not sufficiently recovered to share all the social privileges; the front or family part was planned to look exactly like an ordinary home, where the convalescent patients could share the family life of the doctor and his assistants. The removal from back to front was an important element in recovery; the patient was cut off from his old associations, was solaced and encouraged; he appreciated his privileges, and realized that failure to control himself meant social disgrace. These family parties exchanged visits, played games together, edited newspapers, and shamed in conduct and pursuits many sane families. Many of these convalescents were placed on parole and allowed to frequent the grounds and forest unattended, using a passkey to go in and out as they pleased. Allen recorded that scarcely any took advantage of this freedom to make their escape; fortunately for his plans, few of his patients had the acute nostalgia of John Clare.

But Clare could not have fallen into better hands than Matthew Allen's. The doctor had, indeed, made a special study of those forms of affliction which resembled Clare's. Such cases, where the sufferer had been able to exert control and retain his individuality for long after the trouble arose, required the most delicate attention. He emphasized the need for early diagnosis and expert treatment; when it was delayed, recovery was a long and difficult process. We recall those careful descriptions of his symptoms which year after year Clare sent to his London friends, and we deplore the chance that kept Dr. Allen from the scene until 1837.

Allen also observed that it was a common practice to discourage all mental exertion in the insane; this was wrong; the judicious exercise of the mind, as well as of the body, was conducive to mental improvement. Thus Clare at High Beech was encouraged both to wander in the forest and to write his poems; and these, the stolen delights of his youth, the happy occupations of his maturity, became the chief solace of his years of exile, and enabled him to place the keystone in the arch of his achievement.

Dr. Allen was not long in discovering the chief cause of Clare's derangement. Writing in 1840 of his much improved condition, he contrasted it with his appearance in the early days of his stay:

" He was then exceedingly miserable, every instant be-moaning his poverty, and his mind did not appear so much lost and deranged as suspended in its movements by the oppressive and permanent state of anxiety, and fear, and vexation, produced by the excitement of excessive flattery at one time, and neglect at another, his extreme poverty and over exertion of body and mind, and no wonder that his feeble bodily frame, with his wonderful native powers of mind, was overcome.

" I had then not the slightest hesitation in saying that if a small pension could be obtained for him, he would have re-covered instantly and most probably remained well for life."

Under the doctor's sympathetic guidance, Clare was soon led from the gloomy labyrinths of his despair and was able to avail himself of all the occupations and diversions that High Beech afforded. "The place here is beautiful . . ." he wrote to Patty, in November, "the country is the finest I have ever seen."

Thence until 1840 records of Clare's life and mind are scanty. A letter from Mrs. Emmerson to Patty in April, 1838, mentioned his improved health of which Frederick had written to her. She had just paid £5 to Taylor as her portion of the subscription for Clare's maintenance at High Beech. With this token of her still unfailing kindness and solicitude – she was now almost a permanent invalid – leave may be taken of Mrs. Emmerson, for Clare never saw her again. One of the first to hail Clare's genius, for seventeen years she had advised, befriended, and encouraged him; if there was often more honest enthusiasm than critical judgment in her counsel, Clare needed it all in his later years of neglect and disappointment. She was the only friend to whom he could unbosom himself entirely and be sure of sympathetic praise or admonition in return. It was her ardent hope to occupy a quiet corner of immortality in the shadow of her friend; Clare would be glad to greet her among the asphodel.

A letter from Allen to Taylor in December, 1839, reported Clare's continued improvement; he was stout and rosy in appearance, and in good spirits, all life and fun; he was now working. A similar letter is extant for July, 1840. "He is looking very well and his mind is not worse," wrote Allen, and mentioned the publicity being given to Clare's cause in the newspapers. In 1838, S. C. Hall, in his *Book of Gems*, had appealed for some Good Samaritan to rescue Clare from the "Cave of Despair" into which penury had led him. In 1840, a report was inserted in the *Halifax Express*, presumably by Clare's friend Crossley, of the poet's death in York Asylum. This report strayed into *The Times* for the 17th of June, 1840. On the 23rd, that newspaper published a letter from Allen, contradicting the report, giving an interesting account of Clare, and appealing for subscriptions. The *London Saturday Journal* for the 25th of July printed this letter, too, and added a poem which Clare had given Dr. Badely, one of the visiting physicians at High Beech. The *Athenæum* for the 27th of June also called attention to the scheme to improve the poet's fortunes.

Dr. Allen wrote: "He is at present in excellent health, and looks very well, and is in mind, though full of many strange delusions, in a much more comfortable and happy state than he was when he first came." The attempt to obtain the additional small pension had as yet had no success.

"It is most singular," continued Allen, "that ever since he came, and even now at almost all times, the moment he gets pen or pencil in hand he begins to write most beautiful poetic effusions. Yet he has never been able to maintain in conversation, nor even in writing prose, the appearance of sanity for two minutes or two lines together, and yet there is no indication whatever of insanity in any of his poetry."

With deference to Allen's intimate knowledge of Clare, we suggest that all the statements of the last sentence need qualification. Yet it is certainly true that, despite Clare's

AAJ

remarkable improvement at High Beech in physical well-being, in spirits and mental vigour, that little crop of hallucinations which he had brought with him remained uneradicated, even flourished and blossomed on the alien soil of his captivity. Weeds they were, stubborn and tenacious of life; yet had not Clare celebrated in many a verse the beauty of a despised weed? That he wrote so many poems without hint of insanity is proof that, except for these particular delusions, he was essentially sane when relieved of his eating cares and daily anxieties. There, indeed, lay the tragic dilemma in which Clare was now placed. Worry and penury at home had planted the seeds of those delusions and brought him to the verge of mental and physical breakdown; absence from home, with relief from those anxieties, supplied every condition essential for a cure except one – home. Between Clare's Scylla and Charybdis there was no passage, unless, indeed, that charted for him by Allen should prove navigable.

For, the doctor told Cyrus Redding, if Clare could be at home with his family but without the corroding anxieties of former years, there was every hope of complete recovery; at the least he would be happier there than elsewhere, so slightly was his mind affected. It was proposed, therefore, that an appeal be made for £500, sufficient to raise the income to £60 a year and place the family beyond need. It was a reasonable hope; in earlier years Clare had made ends meet on this sum, though it had meant overdrawing his account with his publishers to supplement what he could earn by field labour and writing for periodicals. The scheme was commended to the public by Cyrus Redding in two eloquent and discerning articles in his *English Journal*, May, 1841, by James Devlin in the same, and by an unknown writer in a collection of verse entitled *Poetry*, 1841. Only a small sacrifice by a few people was needed to keep Clare's name from that sad scroll whereon the names of Smart, Burns, Bloomfield, Chatterton, Boyce, Dermody, and Tannahill gave warning of the tragic alliance of genius with poverty. Matthew Allen himself delivered some shrewd blows for the cause he had at heart, as the refreshing plain-speaking of a letter to P. S. Ackerman may bear witness:

"My dear Sir,

"I enclose at your request some of Clare's writing. Why show respect to the mere hand writing, and no humanity to the man nor his family.

"I pledge myself, that if a small annuity could be secured for him, he will very soon recover and remain so – and yet people desire the autograph of a man who but for me would have been a hopeless case permanently confined and lost in the mass of paupers in some public Establishment or perhaps what is worse exposed to the idle gaze of fools.

"You have never fulfilled your promise."

The appeal was not entirely unheard; according to a notice printed later in the *English Journal*, the Queen Dowager had sent 20 guineas, Lord Fitzwilliam a handsome subscription, and the Marquis of Northampton had promised £5 per annum. No doubt there were some pence as well as pounds, for Clare still had some faithful admirers. Whatever the final amount subscribed, it fell far short of the £500 appealed for. Presumably the small sum was used to help pay for Clare's upkeep at High Beech.

Thus, as the fourth year of exile dragged slowly by, and the hope of a return home to more comfortable circumstances faded, it was but natural that Clare should grow restive. Conscious of restored health, and longing for home, he could see little reason for his continued stay at High Beech; he came to regard it more and more as a captivity, and his thoughts turned to the possibility of escape. A letter to Patty has survived to show clearly enough the trend of his thoughts in the spring of 1841. The only eccentricity in this letter is that every word begins with a capital:

"Leppit's Hill.
" *17 March, 1841.*

"My Dear Wife Patty,

"It makes me more than happy to hear that you and my dear family are all well, and you will all be as well pleased to hear that I have been so long in good health and spirits as to have forgotten that I ever was any otherways. My situation here has been even from the beginning more than irksome but I shake hands with misfortune and wear through the storm. The spring smiles and so shall I, but not while I am here. . . . As soon as I get relieved on duty here, I shall be in Northamptonshire; though Essex is a very pleasant county, yet to me 'there is no place like home.' . . . For what reason they keep me here I cannot tell, for I have been no other ways than well a couple of years at the least, and never was very ill, only harassed by perpetual bother. And it would seem, by keeping me here one year after another, that I was destined for the same fate again; and I would sooner be packed in a slave ship for Africa than belong to the destiny of mock friends and real enemies. Honest men and modest women are my friends.

"I had three separate dreams about three of my boys, or your boys, – Frederick, John and William; not anyways remarkable, only I was in a wreck with the latter. Such things never trouble me now; in fact, nothing troubles me, and thank God it is so. I hope the time is not long ere I shall see you all by your own fireside, though every day in absence seems to me longer than years."

In this same spring, Cyrus Redding paid a visit to High Beech and recorded it in his *English Journal*, the 15th of May, 1841.

"We were informed that Clare was in an adjacent field, working with four or five of the other patients.

"We accordingly proceeded thither, and saw the 'Peasant Poet,' apart from his companions, busily engaged with a hoe, and smoking. On being called, he came down at once, and very readily entered into conversation. Our friend was surprised to see how much the poet was changed in personal appearance, having gained flesh, and being no longer, as he was formerly, attenuated and pale of complexion. We found a little man, of muscular frame and firmly set, his complexion clear and forehead high, a nose somewhat aquiline, and long full chin. The expression of his countenance was more pleasing but somewhat less intellectual than that in the engraved portrait prefixed to his works in the edition of 'The Village Minstrel,' published in 1821. He was communicative, and answered every question put to him in a manner perfectly unembarrassed. He spoke of the quality of the ground which he was amusing himself by hoeing, and the probability of its giving an increased crop the present year, a continued smile playing upon his lips. He made some remarks illustrative of the difference between the aspect of the country at High Beech and that in the fens from whence he had come – alluded to Northborough and Peterborough – and spoke of his loneliness away from his wife, expressing a great desire to go home, and to have the society of women. He said his solace was his pipe – he had no other: he wanted books. On being asked what books, he said Byron; and we promised to send that poet's works to him.

"The principal token of his mental eccentricity was the introduction of prize fighting, in which he seemed to imagine he was to engage; but the allusion to it was made in the way of interpolation in the middle of the subject on which he was discoursing, brought in abruptly, and abandoned with equal suddenness, and an utter want of connection with any association of ideas which it could be thought might lead to the subject at the time; as if the machinery of thought were dislocated, so that one part of it got off its pivot, and protruded into the regular workings; or as if a note had got into a piece of music which had no business there. This was the only symptom of aberration of mind we observed about Clare; though, being strangers to him, there might be something else in his manner which those who knew him well could have pointed out. To our seeming, his affection was slight; and it is not at all improbable that a relief from mental anxiety might completely restore him."

After commending the subscription scheme, Redding printed a number of poems recently composed by Clare. In these poems there are few traces of mental aberration; many record Clare's zestful appreciation of more spacious prospect than that from Langley Bush, heaths more colourful than those near Helpston, grander woods than Oxey's hazel bowers; there is evidence too of a mind enriched and strengthened rather than deranged by experience.

> *I love the Forest and its airy bounds,*
> *Where friendly Campbell takes his daily rounds:*
> *I love the break-neck hills that headlong go,*
> *And leave me high, and half the world below;*

> *I love to see the Beach Hill mounting high,*
> *The brook without a bridge and nearly dry,*
> *There's Bucket's Hill, a place of furze and clouds,*
> *Which evening in a golden blaze enshrouds.* . . .

Redding's necessarily limited selection of poems yet attests the variety of Clare's interests and inspirations. Old scenes are revisited, old themes retouched, and the pencilling is as vigorous, the emotion as fresh, as when he roamed his native fields from Glinton to Walkherd. Distance has renewed the old enchantment of his early love; he calls upon the Maid of Walkherd to meet him in the old haunts:

> *By thy hand of slender make,*
> *By thy love I'll ne'er forsake,*
> *By thy heart I'll ne'er betray,*
> *Let me kiss thy fears away!*
> *I will live and love thee ever,*
> *Leave thee and forsake thee never!*
> *Though far in other lands to be,*
> *Yet never far from love and thee.*

In this simple chronicling of past days, Mary Joyce is but the girl he had loved and lost; there is not an echo from that strange, troubled underworld of which she was queen.

> *In Love's delight my steps were led,*
> *I sang of Beauty's choice;*
> *I saw her in the books I read, –*
> *All then was Mary Joyce.* . . .

> *Till Patty, lighting in my path,*
> *Did fonder love recall;*
> *She stood a flower in Beauty's way,*
> *The Lily of them all!*

He renews acquaintance with his old friends the gipsies, that "quiet, pilfering, unprotected race"; the scene in this poem, "The Gypsy Camp," would have suited the pencil of one of those artists whom he recalls in another poem:

> *There's pleasant Cruikshank, hearty Rippingille,*
> *And quiet Hilton, of diviner skill;*
> *There's simple Etty, never vain or proud . . .*
> *And Cruikshank is what Hogarth would have been.*

An acquaintance of less happy memory is recorded in a song to John Barleycorn. No breath of inward storm troubles the quiet waters of Clare's meditation in these verses, whether he speaks of God, who "lives alone in quiet thoughts," whose love is

> *the kindest love,*
> *To be the friend of all,*

or whether he muses upon earthly change and decay:

> *Time, like a robber, every year*
> *Takes all the fame he gives;*
> *While Beauty only goes away,*
> *And Virtue only lives.*

He welcomes the firstlings of spring in the forest: the chestnut's green-and-white, the wood-spurge, "with caper-flowers of yellow green," dog's mercury, sloe, willow, furze "like myrtle, scarce a finger long," butterflies, those flowers of the insect world, "as if the wind had blown them from their stalks." Then he returns to his Helpston fields to gather cowslips – "they're everybody's flowers " – lady-smocks, water-blobs, Bedlam cowslips, and tells how he played at "mock-bird" in the woods, but had to yield to the nightingale. He sings in praise of men of great mind, who are always kind and "more like common men than others are," though "Fame makes them giants with her idle praise." There is a poem to Wordsworth:

> *Wordsworth I love: his books are like the fields,*
> *Not filled with flowers, but works of human kind.*

He could see London in the distance; it was only half a day's journey away, but he did not wish to go there now:

> *Thus London, like a shrub among the hills,*
> *Lies hid and lower than the bushes here.*

Clare's letter to Patty in March had shown clear signs of an approaching crisis; the thought that he might remain for the rest of his days a captive in a madhouse built a new dam across the current of his mind, behind which the flood rose steadily, strengthening the barrier with the piled debris left stranded by former floods. The return of spring to the forest had quickened his home-sickness. Even chance meetings with strangers left wistful thoughts of home. The small pocket-book, which he carried with him to favourite haunts like "Fern Hill at the back of the chapel, a beautiful retreat from a mad-house," contains two journal entries among the poems:

"Easter Sunday, 1841. Went in the morning to Buckhurst Hill Church and stood in the Churchyard, when a very interesting boy came out while the organ was playing, dressed in a slop-frock like a plough boy and seemingly about nine years of age. He was just like my son Bill when he was about the same age and as stout made. He had a serious, interesting face and looked as weary with the working days as a hard-working man. I was sorry I did not give him the last half-penny I had and ask him a few questions as to his age and name and parents, but perhaps I may see him again.

"Easter Monday. At the Easter Hunt I saw a stout, tall, young woman, dressed in a darkish fox-red, cotton gown as a milkmaid or farm-servant. I stood agen her for some minutes near a small clump of furze. I did not speak to her, but I now wish I had and cannot forget her."

Between these two entries, seemingly in stark irrelevance, stands this inscription, in which the name of Byron is transplanted to *Boxiana* and coupled with that of Tom Spring:

"Boxer Byron
made of Iron, alias
Boxiron
at Springfield."

In similar manner the topic of prize-fighting had appeared in the conversation with Cyrus Redding, thrust up by some stray eddy in the under-current of Clare's consciousness. In that conversation we also meet the name of Byron, whose poems Clare asked Redding to send him. The note-books enable us to define clearly enough the significance of the Boxer Byron theme in the underworld of Clare's mind.

For all his gentleness, Clare had never lacked pugnacity; he had challenged the public again and again with his poems, and to each disappointment and rebuff he had responded with a new plan and a new volume. Now he "came up to the scratch" again; the world would not listen to John Clare, but surely it would pay heed to a challenge from Jack Randall. In the same small note-book he inscribed his challenge in appropriate phrases:

"Jack Randall's Challenge to All the World.

"Jack Randall, the champion of the prize ring, begs leave to inform the sporting world that he is ready to meet any customer in the ring or on the stage to fight for the sum of £500. [This sum, it may be remembered, was what Allen had asked for in his appeal for Clare.]

"He is not particular to weight, colour or country; he wishes to meet with a customer who has pluck enough to come to the scratch.

"So let thine enemies perish, Oh Lord!"

The same subterranean logic which turned the gentle poet of nature into a prize-fighter brought Lord Byron to Springfield as the Poet Laureate of Clare's underworld. Both delusions sprang from seeds sown years before and lying dormant until at High Beech they found an atmosphere in which they could germinate. It was with curiosity and wonder rather than with envy that Clare had regarded Byron's high rank, his wealth, his romantic life, his universal popularity. But now not only were his own simple ambitions all frustrated, but Fortune had taken from him more than she had ever given; and as he pondered over his fate, forgotten and friendless, an exile from home and a captive in a madhouse, Clare turned again to that poet whose star still shone as brightly as ever. So he read in the collected edition of Byron's works which Cyrus Redding sent him, and the reading inspired him to write in imitation of Byron. In the 1823 edition of Byron's works which Clare presented to Mrs. Emmerson we find some verses written on the fly-leaf and headed "Stanzas omitted in the first Canto of Childe Harold." Now, as then, Clare enjoyed using the Byronic tricks and devices, the familiar tone, the outspoken criticism, invective, bathos, and curious rhymes. The general theme of the *Don Juan* verses he had developed before in "The Parish" and in his essays – the triumph of hypocrisy and injustice, while truth and honesty were left to starve or locked up in a madhouse.

> *O glorious constitution! what a picking*
> *Ye've had from your tax-harvest and your tithe. . . .*
> *Truth is shut up in prison while ye're licking*
> *The gold from off the gingerbread. Be lithe*
> *In winding that patched, broken, old, state clock up,*
> *Playhouses open – but madhouses lock up.*
>
> *Give toil more pay where rank starvation lurches*
> *And pay your debts and put your books to rights;*
> *Leave whores and playhouses and fill your churches;*
> *Old cloven-foot your dirty victory fights. . . .*

There are comments on the Court Circular:

> *Here's Albert going to Germany they tell us*
> *And the young queen down in the dumps and jealous –*

with an excursion on the hollow mockery of marriage, "a drivelling hoax," but one which did not prevent Clare from wishing repeatedly that he could see his two wives again. We also find here and elsewhere references to sodomy and other sexual aberrations to which some of the inhabitants of "Allen's Hell" were addicted.

Most of these verses were written in deliberate imitation of *Don Juan;* but occasionally some casual reference to Byron crept in, and for a space Clare wrote as if he were that poet. The transition is indicated here:

> *Though laurel wreaths my brows did ne'er environ,*
> *I think myself as great a bard as Byron.*

And a little farther on we hear that Byron, the disperser of
lies,

> *Who has been dead – so fools their lies are giving –*
> *Is still in Allen's madhouse caged and living.*

The *Childe Harold* verses lead us from the outskirts to the
innermost recesses of Clare's underworld, to the very source
of that secret stream which waters the yet undivided terri-
tories of "the lunatic, the lover and the poet." The indebtedness to Byron here is little more than that legitimate debt
which one poet may owe to another; *Childe Harold* inspired
Clare to this saga of his own mind's wanderings, and provided a verse form suitable for such personal narrative. But
the theme is Clare's own; it is the story of his soul's pilgrimage in the spring of 1841, of how hope sickened and died
under the shadow of his captivity and rose again miracu-
lously from its ashes to soar to regions where only those who
have suffered as Clare suffered can follow to share his
triumph.

The poem opens with a mood of black despair and
misery; spring has returned, not with "the joyous melody
and happy praise" of early years, but with

> *Quicksands and gulfs and storms that howl and sting*
> *All quiet into madness. . . .*

The mood is defined:

> *My mind is dark and fathomless, and wears*
> *   The hues of hopeless agony and hell;*
> *No plummet ever sounds the soul's affairs,*
> *   There, death eternal never sounds the knell,*
> *   There, Love, imprisoned, sighs the long farewell,*
> *And still may sigh in thoughts no heart hath penned,*
> *   Alone, in loneliness, where sorrows dwell*
> *And hopeless hope hopes on and meets no end,*
> *Wastes without springs and homes without a friend.*

He sees nothing but frustration in the past, despair and
madness in the future:

My life hath been one love – No, blot it out –
My life hath been one chain of contradictions,
Madhouses, prisons, whore-shops, – Never doubt
　　But that my life hath had some strong convictions
　　That such was wrong. Religion makes restrictions
I would have followed; but life turned a bubble
And clomb the giant stile of maledictions.
They took me from my wife, and to save trouble
I wed again, and made the error double.

Yet absence claims them both and keeps them too
　　And locks me in a shop in spite of law
Among a low-lived set and dirty crew –
　　Here let the Muse oblivion's curtain draw . . .
Now stagnant grows my too-refined clay;
I envy birds their wings to fly away.

He speaks again of his two wives; nor does he miss the significance of their names, Martha and Mary, names which define the limits of Clare's love, as Walkherd and Glinton limit the Clare country to west and east: Walkherd, with its wooded plain between river valleys, is pleasing and homely; Glinton's spire soars from the bare, flat earth to the vast dome of the fen sky.

In his dark hour, Clare could only remember that he had lost both his wives:

Mary and Martha, both an evil omen;
Though both my own, they still belong to no man.

His children too were lost, "The children of two mothers, born in joy." In this same mood, he wrote down in his notebook among the verses a letter for Mary Joyce:

"MY DEAR WIFE MARY,

"I might have said my first wife, first love and first everything, but I shall never forget my second wife and second love, for I loved her once as dearly as yourself and almost do so now; so I determined to keep you both for ever, and when I write to you I am writing to her at the same time and in the same letter. God bless you both forever and both your families also. I still keep writing though you do not write to me. . . .

"No one knows how sick I am of this confinement, possessing two wives that ought to be my own and cannot see either one or the other. If I was in prison for felony, I could not be served worse than I am. Wives used to be allowed to see their husbands anywhere; religion forbids them being parted; but I have not even religion on my side. . . .

"I wrote a new canto of Don Juan to pass the time away, but nothing seemed to shorten it in the least, and I fear I shall not be able to wear it away. Nature to me seems dead and her very pulse seems frozen to an icicle in the summer sun. . . . I daresay, though I have two wives, if I got away I should soon have a third, and I think I should serve you both right in the bargain by doing so; for I don't care a damn about coming home now. So you need not flatter yourselves with many expectations of seeing me nor do I expect you want to see me or you would have contrived to have done it before now. [A change in the writing and the mood suggests that the letter was finished off later.] My dear Mary, take all the good wishes from me as heart can feel for your husband, and kiss all your dear family for their absent father, and Patty's children also; and tell her that her husband is the same man as he was when she married him 20 years ago, in heart and good intentions. . . ."

In the verses also the mood changes, and hope lifts its head again as Clare muses on the nature of love:

> *Yet love lives on in every kind of weather,*
>   *In heats and colds, in sunshine and in gloom;*
> *Winter may blight and stormy clouds may gather,*
>   *Nature invigorates and love will bloom;*
>   *It fears no sorrow in a life to come*
> *But lives within itself from year to year,*
>   *As doth the wild flower in its own perfume;*
> *As in the Lapland snows spring's blooms appear,*
> *So true love blooms and blossoms everywhere.*

His love for Mary has revived his love for all things; the shades clear above his head:

> *Yet here my prison is a spring to me,*
>   *Past memories bloom like flowers where'er I rove.*

And although

> *Friends' cold neglects have froze my heart to stone*
> *And wrecked the voyage of a quiet mind,*

yet will he turn to those friends who will not betray – his verse,

> *Thou fire and iceberg to an aching soul . . .*
> *Far better opiate than the draining bowl,*

and the glades and woods, "Where nature is herself and loves her own," where solitude "becomes my wedded mate."

So he celebrates again the beauties of the forest, the song of birds that restores "the soul to harmony, the mind to love," the hill of fern where "the chapel peeps between the hornbeams" and "the fern-owl chitters like a startled knell."

> *These solitudes my last delights shall be.*

In the light of this renewal of his love for all things, Clare began to see, as Keats had seen, that he who accepts life fully must accept death also[2]; that when death is accepted, all fear falls away:

> *Cares gather round, – I snap their chains in two,*
> *And smile in agony and laugh in tears,*
> *Like playing with a deadly serpent who*
> *Stings to the death; there is no room for fears*
> *Where death would bring me happiness; his shears*
> *Kill cares that hiss to poison many a vein;*
> *The thought to be extinct my fate endears;*
> *Pale death, the grand physician, cures all pain;*
> *The dead rest well who lived for joys in vain.*

This tone of resolution and defiance rings through the last poem which Clare wrote at High Beech. The title gives both the occasion and the date: "Written in a Thunderstorm, July 15th, 1841." The last four verses read thus:

> *My soul is apathy, a ruin vast,*
> *Time cannot clear the ruined mass away;*
> *My life is hell, the hopeless die is cast,*
> *And manhood's prime is premature decay.*

Roll on, ye wrath of thunders, peal on peal,
  Till worlds are ruins and myself alone;
Melt heart and soul, cased in obdurate steel,
  Till I can feel that nature is my throne.

I live in love, sun of undying light,
  And fathom my own heart for ways of good;
In its pure atmosphere, day without night
  Smiles on the plains, the forest and the flood.

Smile on, ye elements of earth and sky,
  Or frown in thunders as ye frown on me;
Bid earth and its delusions pass away,
  But leave the mind, as its creator, free.

Within three days of writing that last word, Clare had pushed aside, for the time being, his resignation, deciding to be free in body as well as in mind, and within five he was tramping northward toward home and Mary. Here is his story of his eighty-mile journey out of Essex, set down in a note-book soon after his arrival at Northborough:

"July 18, 1841. Sunday. Felt very melancholy; went a walk in the forest in the afternoon; fell in with some gipsies, one of whom offered to assist in my escape from the madhouse by hiding me in his camp; to which I almost agreed, but told him I had no money to start with, but if he would do so I would promise him fifty pound; and he agreed to do so before Saturday.[3] On Friday I went again, but he did not seem so willing, so I said little about it. On Sunday I went and they were all gone. I found an old wide-awake hat, and an old straw bonnet of the plum-pudding sort was left behind. I put the hat in my pocket, thinking it might be useful for another opportunity, and, as good luck would have it, it turned out to be so.

"July 19. Monday. Did nothing.

"July 20. Reconnoitred the route the Gipsy pointed out and found it a legible one to make a movement, and having only honest courage and myself in my array, I led the way and my troops soon followed. But being careless in mapping down the route as the Gipsy told me, I missed the lane to Enfield Town and was going down Enfield Highway, till I passed the Labour in Vain public-house where a person I knew, coming out of the door, told me the way.

"I walked down the lane gently and was soon in Enfield Town and by and by on the great York Road, where it was all plain sailing and steering ahead, meeting no enemy and fearing none. I reached Stevenage, where, [it] being night, I got over a gate [and] crossed over the corner to a green paddock, where, seeing a pond or hollow in the corner, I [was] forced to stay off a respectable distance to keep from falling into it; for my legs were nearly knocked up and began to stagger. I scaled some old rotten palings into the yard, and then had higher palings to clamber over to get into the shed or hovel, which I did with difficulty, being rather weak. To my good luck, I found some trusses of clover piled up about six or more feet square, which I gladly mounted and slept on. There were some rags in the hovel, on which I would have reposed had I not found a better bed. I slept soundly but had a very uneasy dream. I thought my first wife lay on my left arm and somebody took her away from my side, which made me waken rather unhappy. I thought as I woke somebody said, 'Mary'; but nobody was near. I lay down with my head towards the north to show myself the steering point in the morning.

"July 21. Daylight was looking in on every side, and fearing my garrison might be taken by storm and myself be made prisoner I left my lodging by the way I got in and thanked God for his kindness in procuring it; for anything in a famine is better than nothing, and any place that giveth the weary rest is a blessing. I gained the North Road again and steered due north. On the left hand side, the road under the bank was like a cave. I saw a man and boy curled up asleep, which I hailed, and they woke up to tell me the name of the next village.

"Somewhere on the London side the Plough public-house, a man passed me on horseback in a slop-frock and said, 'Here's another of the broken-down haymakers,' and threw me a penny to get a half-pint of beer; which I picked up and thanked him for. When I got to the Plough, I called for a half-pint and drank it and got a rest and escaped a very heavy shower in the bargain by having a shelter till it was over. Afterwards I would have begged a penny of two

drovers, who were very saucy, so I begged no more of anybody, meet who I would.

"Having passed a Lodge on the left hand within a mile
and a half or less of a town (I think it might be St. Ives⁴ but
I forget the name), I sat down on a flint heap where I might
rest half an hour or more, and while sitting here I saw a tall
Gipsy come out of the Lodge Gate and make down the road
towards where I was sitting. When she got up to me, on
seeing she was a young woman with an honest-looking
countenance, rather handsome, I spoke to her and asked
her a few questions which she answered readily and with
evident good humour. So I got up and went on to the next
town with her. She cautioned me on the way to put something in my hat to keep the crown up and said in a lower
tone, 'You'll be noticed;' but not knowing what she hinted,
I took no notice and made no reply. At length she pointed
to a small tower-church, which she called Shefford Church,
and advised me to go on a footway, which she said would
take me direct to it, and I should shorten my journey fifteen
miles by doing so. I would gladly have taken the young
woman's advice, feeling that it was honest and a nigh guess
towards the truth; but fearing I might lose my way and not
be able to find the North Road again, I thanked her and
told her I should keep to the road, when she bade me 'Good-
day,' and went into a house or shop on the left hand side
the road. I passed three or four good built houses on a hill
and a public house on the roadside in the hollow below them.
I seemed to pass the milestones very quick in the morning,
but towards night they seemed to be stretched further
asunder. I got to a village further on – I forget the name. The
road on the left hand was quite overshaded by some trees
and quite dry; so I sat down half an hour and made a good
many wishes for breakfast; but wishes were no hearty meal,
so I got up as hungry as I sat down. I forget here the names
of the villages I passed through, but recollect at late evening
going through Potton in Bedfordshire, where I called in a
house to light my pipe; in which was a civil old woman, and
a young country wench making lace on a curtain as round
as a globe, and a young fellow, all civil people. I asked them
a few questions as to the way and where the clergyman and
overseer lived, but they scarcely heard me, or gave me no
answer.

"I then went through Potton and happened with a kind

BBJ

talking country man, who told me the parson lived a good way from where I was (or overseer, I don't know which). So I went on hopping with a crippled foot, for the gravel had got into my old shoes, one of which had now nearly lost the sole. Had I found the overseer's house at hand, or the parson's, I should have given my name and begged for a shilling to carry me home; but I was forced to brush on penniless and be thankful I had a leg to move on.

"I then asked him whether he could tell me of a farmyard anywhere on the road where I could find a shed and some dry straw, and he said, 'Yes, and if you will go with me, I will show you the place; it's a public house on the left hand side the road at the sign of the Ram.' But seeing a stone or flint heap, I longed to rest, as one of my feet was very painful. So I thanked him for his kindness and bid him go on. But the good-natured fellow lingered awhile as if wishing to conduct me; and then suddenly recollecting that he had a hamper on his shoulder and a lock-up bag in his hand, cramful to meet the coach, which he feared missing, he started hastily and was soon out of sight. I followed, looking in vain for the countryman's straw bed; and not being able to meet it, I lay down by a shed side under some elms between the wall and the trees, being a thick row some five or six feet from the building. I lay there and tried to sleep; but the wind came in between them so cold that I lay till I quaked like the ague. I quitted the lodging for a better at the Ram, which I could hardly hope to find. It now began to grow dark apace and the odd houses on the road began to light up and show the inside tenants' lots very comfortable and my outside lot very uncomfortable and very wretched. Still I hobbled forward as well as I could, but at last came to the Ram. The shutters were not closed and the lighted windows looked very cheering; but I had no money and I did not like to go in. There was a sort of shed or gig-house at the end, but I did not like to lie there, as the people were up. So I still travelled on. The road was very lonely and dark in places, being overshaded with trees. At length I came to a place where the road branched off into two turnpikes, one to the right about and the other straight forward; and on going by, my eye glanced on a milestone standing under the hedge, so I heedlessly turned back to read it to see where the other road led to. On doing so, I found it led to London and then suddenly forgot which was North and which was South; and though

I narrowly examined both ways, I could see no tree or bush or stone heap that I could recollect I had passed. So I went on mile after mile, almost convinced I was going the same way as I came; and these thoughts were so strong upon me that doubt and hopelessness made me turn so feeble that I was scarcely able to walk. Yet I could not sit down or give up but shuffled along till I saw a lamp shining as bright as the moon, which, on nearing, I found was suspended over a toll-gate. Before I got through, the man came out with a candle and eyed me narrowly; but having no fear I stopped to ask him whether I was going northward and he said, 'when you get through the gate you are.' So I thanked him kindly and went through on the other side and gathered my old strength as my doubts vanished. I soon cheered up and hummed the air of 'Highland Mary' as I went on. I at length let in with an odd house, all alone near a wood; but I could not see what the sign was, though the sign seemed to stand, oddly enough, in a sort of trough or spout. There was a large porch over the door, and being weary I crept in and glad enough I was to find I could lie with my legs straight. The inmates were all gone to roost, for I could hear them turn over in bed; so I lay at full length on the stones in the porch. I slept there till daylight and felt very much refreshed as I got up. I blessed my two wives and both their families when I lay down and when I got up; and when I thought of some former difficulties on a like occasion I could not help blessing the Queen. I have but a slight recollection of my journey between here and Stilton, for I was knocked up and noticed little or nothing. One night I lay in a dyke bottom from the wind and went to sleep half an hour; when I suddenly awoke and found my side wet through from the sock⁵ in the dyke bottom, so I got out and went on. I remember going down a very dark road, hung over with trees on both sides, very thick, which seemed to extend a mile or two. I then entered a town and some of the chamber windows had candle lights shining in them. I felt so weary here that I was forced to sit down on the ground to rest myself; and while I sat here, a coach that seemed to be heavy-laden came rattling up and stopped in the hollow below me, and I cannot recollect its ever passing by me. I then got up and pushed onward, seeing little to notice, for the road very often looked as stupid as myself and I was very often half asleep as I went. On the third day I satisfied my hunger by eating the grass by the roadside, which seemed to taste something like bread. I was hungry and eat heartily till I was satisfied; and in fact the meal seemed to do me good. The next and last day I recollected that I had some tobacco, and my box of lucifers being exhausted I could not light my pipe; so I took to chewing tobacco all day, and eat the quids when I had done, and I was never hungry afterwards. I remember passing through Buckden and going a length of road afterwards, but I don't recollect the name of any place until I came to Stilton, where I was completely foot-foundered and broken down. When I had got about half way through the town, a gravel causeway invited me to rest myself; so I lay down and nearly went to sleep. A young woman (so I guessed by the voice) came out of a house and said, 'Poor creature,' and another, more elderly, said, 'O he shams.' But when I got up, the latter said, 'O no he don't,' as I hobbled along very lame. I heard the voices but never looked back to see where they came from. When I got near the Inn at the end of the gravel walk, I met two young women, and I asked one of them whether the road branching to the right by the Inn did not lead to Peterborough, and she said yes, it did so. As soon as ever I was on it, I felt myself in home's way and went on rather more cheerful, though I [was] forced to rest oftener than usual. Before I got to Peterborough a man and woman passed me in a cart, and on hailing me as they passed, I found they were neighbours from Helpstone, where I used to live. I told them I was knocked up, which they could easily see, and that I had neither eat nor drunk anything since I left Essex. When I told my story they clubbed together and threw me fivepence out of the cart. I picked it up and called at a small public house near the bridge, where I had two half pints of ale and two penn'orth of bread and cheese. When I had done I started quite refreshed; only my feet were more crippled than ever and I could scarcely make a walk of it over the stones; and being half ashamed to sit down in the street, I [was] forced to keep on the move and got through Peterborough better than I expected. When I got on the high road, I rested on the stone heaps as I passed till I was able to go on afresh. By and by I passed Walton and soon reached Werrington and was making for the Beehive as fast as I could, when a cart met me with a man and a woman and a boy in it. When nearing me, the woman jumped out and caught fast hold of my hands and wished me to get into the cart;

but I refused and thought her either drunk or mad. But when I was told it was my second wife Patty, I got in and was soon at Northborough. But Mary was not there, neither could I get any information about her further than the old story of her being dead six years ago; which might be taken from a brand-new, old newspaper, printed a dozen years ago. But I took no notice of the blarney, having seen her myself about a twelvemonth ago, alive and well and as young as ever. So here I am, homeless at home, and half gratified to feel that I can be happy anywhere.

> *May none these marks of my sad fate efface*
> *For they appeal from tyranny to God.*
> —Byron.

Clare directed that the following note be placed at the bottom of the page:

"Note: On searching my pockets after the above was written, I found part of a newspaper side, *Morning Chronicle*, on which the following fragments were pencilled soon after I got the information from labourers going to work, or travellers journeying along to better their condition, as I was hoping to do mine. In fact I believed I saw home in everyone's countenance, which seemed so cheerful in my own. 'There is no place like home.' The following was written by the road side. '1st day. Tuesday. Started from Enfield and slept at Stevenage on some clover trusses; cold lodging. Wednesday. Jack's Hill is past already, consisting of a beer shop and some houses on the hill, appearing newly built. The last Milestone 35 miles from London. Got through Baldock and sat under a dry hedge and had a rest in lieu of breakfast.' "

On the 24th of July, the day after his arrival at Northborough, Clare made this entry in the same note-book:

"Returned home out of Essex and found no Mary. She and her family are nothing to me now, though she herself was once the dearest of all; and how can I forget?"

Then for three days he was occupied in writing down the story of his journey; when all was finished, he added this letter, addressed "To Mary Clare – Glinton":

"Northborough,
"*July 27, 1841.*

"MY DEAR WIFE,

"I have written an account of my journey, or rather escape, from Essex for your amusement, and I hope it may divert your leisure hours. I would have told you before now that I got here to Northborough last Friday night; but not being able to see you or to hear where you were I soon began to feel homeless at home and shall by and by feel nearly hopeless, but not so lonely as I did in Essex. For here I can see Glinton Church, and feeling that Mary is safe, if not happy, I am gratified. Though my home is no home to me, my hopes are not entirely hopeless while even the memory of Mary lives so near me. God bless you, my dear Mary; give my love to your dear beautiful family and to your Mother; and believe me as I ever have been and ever shall be,

"My dearest Mary,
"Your affectionate Husband,
"JOHN CLARE."

At the end of August, Clare wrote to Dr. Allen; the draft of this letter, written round the edges of a local newspaper, throws light both on the High Beech period and on the brief interlude at Northborough.

"Having left the Forest in a hurry I had not time to take leave of you and your family, but I intended to write, and that before now. But dullness and disappointment prevented me, for I found your words true on my return here, having neither friends nor home left. But as it is called the 'Poet's Cottage' I claimed a lodging in it, where I now am. One of my fancies I found here with her family and all well. They met me on this side Werrington with a horse and cart, and found me all but knocked up, for I had travelled from Essex to Northamptonshire without ever eating or drinking all the way – save one pennyworth of beer which was given me by a farm servant near an old house called 'The Plough.' One day I eat grass to keep on my [feet], but on the last day I chewed tobacco and never felt hungry afterwards.

"Where my poetical fancy is I cannot say, for the people in the neighbourhood tell me that the one called 'Mary' has been dead these eight years: but I can be miserably happy in any situation and any place and could have staid in yours on the Forest if any of my old friends had noticed me or come to see me. But the greatest annoyance in such places as yours are those servants styled keepers, who often assumed as much authority over me as if I had been their prisoner; and not liking to quarrel I put up with it till I was weary of the place altogether. So I heard the voice of freedom, and started, and could have travelled to York with a penny loaf and a pint of beer; for I should not have been fagged in body, only one of my old shoes had nearly lost the sole before I started, and let in water and silt the first day, and made me crippled and lame to the end of my journey. . . .

"You told me something before haytime about the Queen allowing me a yearly salary of £100, and that the first quarter had then commenced – or else I dreamed so. If I have, the mistake is not of much consequence to any one save myself, and if true I wish you would get the quarter for me (if due), as I want to be independent and pay for board and lodging while I remain here. I look upon myself as a widow[er] or bachelor, I don't know which. I care nothing about the women now, for they are faithless and deceitful; and the first woman, when there was no man but her husband, found out means to cuckold him by the aid and assistance of the devil – but women being more righteous now, and men more plentiful, they have found out a more goodly way to do it without the devil's assistance. And the man who possesses a woman possesses losses without gain. The worst is the road to ruin, and the best is nothing like a good cow. Man I never did like – and woman has long sickened me. I should like to be to myself a few years and lead the life of a hermit: but even there I should wish for her whom I am always thinking of – and almost every song I write has some sighs and wishes in ink about Mary. If I have not made your head weary by reading this I have tired my own by writing it; so I will wish you good-bye. . . ."

Allen replied on the 18th of November with much friendly advice. He said Clare was mistaken about the income from the Queen, it was a single donation of £50 towards the annuity fund, but nothing more had been contributed since Clare left High Beech.

"Whenever you like a little change you are welcome to
come here and get Bed and Board for nothing, and be at
liberty to go and come as you choose, provided you do
nothing to make you unpleasant as a Visitor. You might
lead the life of a Hermit as much as you choose and I would
contrive to give you some place for the purpose."

If Clare had been able to avail himself of this generous
offer and return to High Beech, he would have witnessed the
misfortunes which led within a few years to the ruin and
untimely death of his friend Dr. Allen. The story has been
preserved in the biography of that poet who at last, in 1842,
took literary England by storm and restored to poetry a
popularity which it had not known since the days of Byron.
Soon after Clare's departure from Epping, Allen took up a
scheme for carving wood by machinery. With his usual enthusiasm, he sought to enlist his acquaintances and neighbours in the venture, among them the Tennyson family, then
residing at Beech Hill. The Patent Decorative Carving and
Sculpture Company was formed, and Alfred Tennyson was
persuaded to invest in it all the available family funds. To
judge by his letters, his enthusiasm equalled Allen's. The
enterprise soon collapsed; Allen became a bankrupt in 1843,
and for the Tennysons a period of hardship ensued, during
which Alfred suffered from such severe hypochondria that
his life was despaired of. Dr. Allen did not long survive his
misfortune; he died in 1845, and, as Edward Lushington
had insured his life for part of the debt, his death brought
relief to the Tennysons. The curious may find an echo of
this strange business in the poem "Sea Dreams."

The only other correspondence during these months at
Northborough of which we have any record was with George
Reid of Glasgow. It is probable that Clare made no attempt
to revive old friendships; his removal to Epping had broken
the slender threads of such as then remained as effectually
as if he had entered the tomb; and in the past which Clare
had constructed out of the ruins of his hopes few of his old
friends had place. There was only one whom he now desired

to meet, and her he could not find anywhere, though Glinton spire tantalized him with vain hopes whenever he walked in the fields.

But if other records are scanty, the note-books yield a rich harvest, and it is difficult to select quotations where every verse illuminates the changing moods of that inner life which was more real than the world of men about him.

It was inevitable that the failure to find Mary should plunge Clare once more into despair. The excitement of planning his escape and the privations of the journey had called deeply upon his resources, and as he neared home only the thought that he would see Mary sustained him.

Home, he found, was as distant from Northborough as from Epping.

> *Nor night nor day, nor sun nor shade,*
> *Week, month, nor rolling year*
> *Repairs the breach wronged love hath made;*
> *There, madness – misery here.*
> *Life's lease was lengthened by her smiles*
> *– Are truth and love contrary? –*
> *No ray of hope my fate beguiles,*
> *I've lost love, home, and Mary.*

But he rose from this despair, as he had risen before; while he could walk in fields and woods, and especially in those of his own country, John Clare could always find consolation and wrest happiness from the strongholds of sorrow. True lover as he was, he had always wooed nature as a mistress infinite in her variety; and never was this clearer than now, when his love for nature and his love for Mary met and mingled in every verse he wrote.

We glance at some verses he added to the *Childe Harold* canto. He is walking in the fens with sweet solitude for his partner:

> *These meadow flats and trees, the autumn air*
> *Mellow my heart to harmony; I bear*
> *Life's burden happily; these fenny dells*
> *Seem Eden in this Sabbath-rest from care. . . .*

Then the music of Glinton bells falls on his ear, and he recalls those early days when he wooed nature and Mary together:

> *For she was nature's self, and still my song*
> *Is her, through sun and shade, through right and wrong.*

He revisits after long absence the haunts of his youth:

> *thorn hedges and old walls,*
> *And hollow trees that sheltered from the blast,*
> *And all that map of boyhood, overcast*
> *With glooms and wrongs and sorrows not his own,*
> *That o'er his brow like the scathed lightning passed,*
> *That turned his spring to winter, and alone*
> *Wrecked name and fame and all . . .*

> *So on he lives in glooms and living death,*
> *A shade like night, forgetting and forgot;*
> *Insects that kindle in the spring's young breath*
> *Take hold of life and share a brighter lot*
> *Than he . . .*
> *Parted from one whose heart was once his home.*

> *And yet not parted; – still love's hope illumes,*
> *And like the rainbow, brightest in the storm,*
> *It looks for joy beyond the wreck of tombs,*
> *And in life's winter keeps love's embers warm. . . .*

So the verse ebbs and flows; so the lover's mood, as he paces the fenny meadows sadly, but intensely alive to all things seen and felt, suddenly soars like Glinton spire in an ecstasy that transcends earth and its delusions:

> *e'en these fens where wood nor grove*
> *Are seen – their very nakedness I love,*
> *For one dwells nigh that secret hopes prefer*
> *Above the race of women. . . .*

> *Mary, the muse of every song I write,*
> *Thy cherished memory never leaves my own;*
> *Though care's chill winter doth my manhood blight,*
> *And freeze like Niobe my thoughts to stone,*
> *Our lives are two, our end and aim is one.*
> *. . . Thy name is joy, nor will I life bemoan;*

Midnight, when sleep takes charge of nature's rest,
Finds me awake and friendless — not distressed.

. . . Oceans have rolled between us, not to part;
E'en Iceland's snows true love's delirium warms,
For there I've dreamed — and Mary filled my arms.

Fame blazed upon me like a comet's glare,
Fame waned and left me like a fallen star . . .

My life hath been a wreck, and I've gone far
For peace and truth and hope, for home and rest;
Like Eden's gates, fate throws a constant bar . . .

But still I read and sighed and sued again,
And lost no purpose where I had the will;
I almost worshipped when my toils grew vain;
Finding no antidote my pains to kill,
I sigh, a poet and a lover still.

Another small note-book was used by Clare as a nature journal. Some of the entries are dated:

"Oct. 19, 1841. William found a Cowslip in flower.
"4 Nov. An immense flock of starnels settled on an ash-tree in the orchard, and when they took wing it was like a huge roll of thunder."

We find here the same keen observation and delight as of old; he records again the appearance of flowers, the habits of birds, the occupations of the countrymen, sensitive to the changing rhythm of days and seasons. These observations, jotted down in his walks through the meadows toward Glinton or down the Welland bank to West Deeping and Lolham Bridges, were often used again in his verses. The finer scenery of Epping had certainly not lessened his appreciation of his own country, even though he was now restricted to the fenny levels north and east of Helpston.

"'Tis pleasant as I have done to-day to stand upon a length of Bridges and notice the objects around us. There is the fine old Northborough castle peeping through the scanty foliage of orchards and thorn hedges; and there is the beautiful spire of Glinton Church towering high over the grey willows and dark walnuts, still lingering in the churchyard like the remains of a wreck, telling where their fellows foundered on the ocean of time, – place of green memory and gloomy sorrows. Even these meadow arches seem to me something of the beautiful . . .

"To a man who has had his liberty they would appear nothing more than so many tunnels thrown over a few puddles that are dry three parts of the year, but to me they are more interesting than a flight of arches thrown over a cascade in a park, or even the crowded bridges in a great city."

Among these nature passages, there is a fragment of an essay on self-identity, a subject which troubled Clare's mind at intervals during succeeding years. The utter neglect of him by a world that had once applauded and lionized evidently suggested the idea that there was a conspiracy to make him forget and deny his own identity. "Forget not thyself and the world will not forget thee. Forget thyself and the world will willingly forget thee, till thou art nothing but a living-dead man, dwelling among shadows and falsehood." Clare's awareness of those occasional delusions in which he did forget himself, his stubborn clinging to the stark reality of his own individual existence when everything that he held dear had been taken from him, is characteristic of the man. We seem to see him faced with the final temptation to slip into the happy oblivion of utter insanity; but he put it behind him and fought on, and the song of his triumph will indeed keep his name alive among men in later days.

The little nature note-book has many empty pages; the last descriptive passage – an autumn wood-scene – is followed abruptly by these lines: [6]

> *To live with others is not half so sweet*
> *As to remember thee.*
> *Mary.*

On the next page the last entry in the book records the
season's triumphant vagary:

"Found a Cowslip in flower, Decr. 12, 1841."

But Clare was never again to see his native pastures turn
from green to gold at the touch of spring. With Lord Fitzwilliam's approval, Dr. Skrimshire of Peterborough, who
had often attended him in the past, now examined him
again. He certified him insane,[7] and arrangements were
made for his immediate removal to the Northampton
General Lunatic Asylum. Here he was entered as a farmer,
to be paid for by Lord Fitzwilliam at the rate of eleven
shillings a week, the amount charged for pauper patients.
On the 29th of December, 1841, he was removed from his
cottage at Northborough, never to return.

XX

BEYOND THE TOMB
1841–1864

Perhaps the only comfort which remains
Is the unheeded clanking of my chains,
The which I make, and call it melody!
(Cancelled fragment of) "Julian and Maddalo."

So a second time Clare was exiled from home and cut off from freedom. What he had written of himself years before was now more tragically true than ever. Time had indeed "had a hand" with him and "left an altered thing." However Patty might have wished to keep him, there was sure to be a half-sense of relief once the memory of his pitiful reluctance to be forced away had faded. The situation was too difficult to be supported in a small cottage hovered over by poverty. True, even now "his infirmities were not noxious to society," though not of so devout a character as Smart's. He had lost his identity and could not, as Keats could when the identity of others pressed *him* to annihilation, find it again at will. There was no telling where such a state of affairs might end. He was best in a place where he could be looked after and be under medical care. Had there been, on this occasion, another "Saint Charles" to come forward and, with sufficient money at his back, engage his life upon the recapture, even if occasional, of that lost identity, Clare's story might have been different and subsequent anguish at least diminished. Had there been a Mary Unwin to give herself up "body and soul to his service," twenty-three years' suffering might have been changed to twenty-three years' comparative peace. But there was neither of these. If Clare could have received adequate attention, bodily comforts, and freedom from anxiety over money

matters within his home, his mind would have been contented, and in his rational periods he might have been as
tranquil as Mary Lamb was in similar circumstances. Or,
alternatively, if his mind had not been so constructed that,
after twenty years of enforced absence, the impress of his
home heaths, the trees there, the changing seasons over them,
were as vivid as they had ever been, it might permanently
have recovered its balance once his bodily strength was
restored. But the very means by which he might secure personal ease deprived him of the scenes necessary to his
spiritual contentment. We know that, ultimately, during the
times when the clouds lifted, he grew to accept his second
alienation from home with a serenity which he had never
achieved at High Beech. He even went beyond that. Yet, to
be sane, even for short periods, while confined within a
madhouse, is perhaps one of the most exquisite horrors that
could be imagined for any man; and Clare, in the years to
come, must have endured this often. How, in such extremity,
could there be any hope of a cure after this?

The building of St. Andrew's Hospital for Mental Diseases,
then the Northampton General Lunatic Asylum, was begun
in 1836. The third Earl Spencer, Clare's patron, laid the
foundation-stone. It was opened in August 1838 to accom-
modate fifty-two pauper patients and thirty private patients.
Not the sumptuous building which it is to-day, it yet had
a pleasant situation, about a mile from the town, standing
high, with wooded grounds that sloped to the valley of the
Nen. Its superintendent in 1841 was Dr. Thomas S. Prichard,
a remarkable man, as the editor at that time of the *Northampton Mercury* testifies, "not mad, but just on the other side
of that thin partition by which madness is said to be bounded.
A tall, athletic, handsome man, impulsive, energetic, daring,
he possessed a peculiar faculty of influencing his patients,
even when they were far from his presence."[1] Like Matthew
Allen, he was among the earliest mind-specialists to improve
on the harsh methods of treating the insane. Instead of
cowing the poor irresponsibles into docility by inflicting
suffering on them, he seems to have exerted an almost

mesmeric influence over them, and to have obtained their
obedience that way. As at High Beech, all those of the
patients of St. Andrew's who were classed as "harmless"
were allowed a certain freedom. Here they might go to the
town, or wander about by themselves, while Dr. Prichard
remained assured that they would not abuse this liberty.
Immediately on his arrival Clare was classed as one of these
"harmless" ones, and allowed the same privilege in spite
of his record escapade six months before. But he sank back
into apathy and blank madness. His bodily health steadily
improved, as it had done at Epping, as it was sure to do with
good and sufficient nourishment. Had he not been of wiry
stock, even if of slight frame, he must have died years before
from continued under-feeding. Now he grew sturdy, so that
"The Sherwood Forester," Spencer T. Hall (who, admir-
ingly wishful to be like Clare in some way, often claimed
that his own education "did not cost so much as a guinea"),
saw him in May, 1843, and "instead of the spare, sensitive
person he appears in the portrait of him from Hilton's
painting . . . found him rather burly, florid, with light hair
and somewhat shaggy eyebrows, and dressed as a plain but
respectable farmer, in drab or stone-coloured coat and
smalls, with gaiters, and altogether as clean and neat as if
he had just been fresh brushed up for market or fair."²

But if his person had grown stout and sturdy in these two
years, his mind had not recovered one whit from the blow
of his second estrangement from home. Prichard, whose influence probably took some time to gain its full sway over his
patient, was bound to confess in this same year that the state
of Clare's mind was not improved, but appeared to have
"become more and more impaired." On his first arrival,
before the endless succession of days and years became
apparent in their hopelessness, he wrote, but rarely finished,
many poems. By 1843 he was writing little, and his delusions
were almost always with him. He could not talk to anyone
without revealing them in a few minutes. To "The Sherwood
Forester" on their first meeting he exhibited two of his hallucinations as soon as they had exchanged greetings.

"On my asking him how he was, he said 'Why, I'm very well, and stout, but I'm getting tired of waiting here so long, and want to be off home. They won't let me go, however; for, you see, they're feeding me up for a fight; but they can get nobody able to strip to me; so they might as well have done with it, and let me go.' 'But, Mr. Clare,' said I, 'are you not more proud of your fame as a poet than your prowess as a prize fighter?' When, rather abstractedly, as if considering or trying to recollect something, he answered, 'Oh, poetry, ah, I know, I once had something to do with poetry, a long while ago: but it was no good. I wish, though, they could get a man with courage enough to fight me. . . .'

"Next I asked him if he remembered ever receiving from me at High Beach a copy of the 'Sheffield Iris' and a letter I had sent him. ' "Sheffield Iris" ' he exclaimed: 'Oh, of course, I know all about the "Iris." You know I was editor of it, and lived with the Misses Gales, and was sent to York Castle, where I wrote that "Address to the Robin" ' – thus identifying himself with James Montgomery. On my saying that I was going to London, and would have a pleasure in doing anything I could for him there, he seemed for a moment a little uneasy, and then replied, 'Ah, London; I once was there, but don't like it. There is one good fellow there: if you happen to see him you may remember me to him very kindly – and that's Tom Spring!' Such was the talk of a man who would not have hurt a fly or bruised a flower, much less have been one of the fraternity of Tom Spring, the greatest bruiser, of his day, in England!" ⁹

On this, the first of his three visits, Hall met Clare when the latter had been to visit an acquaintance, one of the tobacconists in the town. Here, often in return for some scrap of verse, he received tobacco, which he used both to smoke and to chew. What impressed Robert Barringer, the brother and assistant of the tobacconist, was the small, keen, blue eyes, the massive, broad forehead, and the country gait. But he remembered, too, the tales his visitor had frequently to tell of great encounters in which he had come off victorious, and how he would double his fists and put himself in an attitude to show how fields were won.

G. J. De Wilde, Editor of the *Northampton Mercury*, who, in

Cc J

1847, tried to help Leigh Hunt, but had to be "content with resuming the money, and leaving the obligation" on Hunt's heart only, often met Clare about the town. Being asked by him some question one day, De Wilde, too, remarked the heavy countryman's tread, the thick eyebrows penthouse-wise over the sad yet eager eyes, the expression as of habitual contemplation. His forehead, too,

"was like that of Napoleon as described by Browning – 'oppressive with its mind.' So towering a forehead had Shakespeare. The question answered was followed by another, rational enough and commonplace, but some re-mark about the scenery led me to think my querist was not an ordinary commonplace man. I did not then know he was Clare. We walked side by side towards Kingsthorpe, and at last he startled me with a quotation from *Childe Harold* and then one from Shakespeare. I do not recall what the pas-sages were, but I was still more startled when he said they were his own. 'Yours,' I exclaimed, 'Who are you? These are Byron's and Shakespeare's verses, not yours!' 'It's all the same' he answered, changing a quid from one cheek to the other. 'I'm John Clare now. I was Byron and Shake-speare formerly. At different times you know I'm different people – that is the same person with different names.' And then he went on to identify himself with a most miscellaneous and unselect lot of celebrities – great warriors, prize fighters, and some eminent blackguards. I saw him very often after that in the Asylum, and on his favourite seat under the portico of All Saints Church. He was very taciturn, and as a rule unsocial in his manner, which seemed to, and very probably did, arise from embarrassment. His answers were the briefest possible. You won his heart, however, with a screw of tobacco, of which he never lacked a store. People out of doors were very kind to him, too kind sometimes, and at the Asylum he had, one may say, boundless liberty so long as Dr. Pritchard⁴ was its Superintendent. . . . Clare believed him to be possessed of some supernatural power which made it as unsafe to disobey him when he was absent as when he was present. There was once a conspiracy among some of his fellow-patients the object of which was to ab-scond. Clare was invited to join in the project, but he steadily refused. They did not know, he said, the length of that man's arm, nor his far-seeing as to their whereabouts, and the only result of their attempt would be that they would be haled back to their confinement with no more liberty to ramble where they listed. So they went without him and got into Hertfordshire. There was some reason for what Clare said. Pritchard spared neither money nor pains to recover an absconded patient, and he usually succeeded in regaining him. Accordingly the two culprits were discovered and brought ignominiously back. Clare was present when they were brought in. 'I told you how it would be, you fools,' said he." ⁵

There is no doubt that Dr. Prichard's influence helped Clare to resignation in his saner periods. W. F. Knight, too, the steward, had his confidence and regard; but Knight soon left to superintend an asylum at Birmingham. J. L. Cherry remembered that "he was always addressed deferentially as 'Mr. Clare,' both by the officers of the Asylum and the townspeople. . . . There was something very nearly akin to tenderness in the kindly sympathy which was shown for him, and his most whimsical utterances were listened to with gravity, lest he should feel hurt or annoyed." The townspeople gave him tobacco in exchange for a song, and eventually he kept his paper and pencil always in his pocket to write, however idly, when required. In time great numbers of these scraps were current in the town.

Hall, in 1843, was the first of a line of visitors for Clare. These visitors were not the friends of his youth nor of his famous days; for Lamb was dead, Cunningham was dead, and Cary and George Darley were soon to die. Clare was alone, a poet who had known all these, but now mad and among strangers. Most of his visitors felt as Frances Burney felt towards another mad poet; they "never knew him in his glory, but ever respected him in his *decline*." Some found him in good humour, and lightened the burden of time by an hour or two's talk, while others, perhaps by too personal questions, angered him. So some found him almost reconciled, cheerful and talkative, others reported him silent and taciturn. In the Northborough days he had been subject to

fits of melancholy and of anger; he was not free from them
now, but he was mainly docile and quiet. In a letter to his
children which probably belongs to this time he explains:

"I am in a Prison on all hands that even numbs common
sense. I can be civil to none but enemies here, as friends are
not allowed to see me at all."

It is likely that in these early years his family were requested not to visit him lest they should arouse in him a
desire to escape a second time.

On the 16th of July, 1844, Mary Howitt, Quaker and miscellaneous writer, devoted a few hours out of a busy life to
a visit to St. Andrew's, and received from Clare a manuscript of "The Sleep of Spring." Shortly before August,
"J. N." from Worcester, hearing that Clare was "on most
subjects, tolerably rational," saw him, learned that the productions of the uncharted mind were often coarse and vulgar,
witnessed as to Clare's unlimited supply of books, commented on his objections to the present Royal succession and
his pugilistic fancies, and pronounced his delusions to be
"protean." Writing some years later, in 1851, Mary Russell
Mitford, in her *Recollections of a Literary Life*, mentions a visit
of a friend of hers, which, according to a reference within,
must have taken place in 1844. The friend, "himself a poet
of the people," may have been William Howitt; what he had
to relate establishes an interesting comparison between
Clare's aberrations and the vagaries of Mary Lamb's "fine
brain." As Talfourd said:

"She would fancy herself in the days of Queen Anne or
George the First, and describe the brocaded dames and
courtly manners, as though she had been bred among them,
in the best style of the old comedy. It was all broken and
disjointed, so that the hearer could remember little of her
discourse; but the fragments were like the jewelled speeches
of Congreve, only shaken from their setting."

Whereas, in Clare, Miss Mitford's friend was struck
"with a narrative of the execution of Charles the First,
recounted . . . as a transaction that occurred yesterday, and

JOHN CLARE IN 1844
From the portrait by Thomas Grimshawe in the Northampton Public Library

of which he (Clare) was an eyewitness – a narrative the most graphic and minute, with an accuracy as to costume and manners far exceeding what would probably have been at his command if sane. It is such a lucidity as the disciples of Mesmer claim for clairvoyance. Or he would relate the battle of the Nile, and the death of Lord Nelson with the same perfect keeping, especially as to seamanship, fancying himself one of the sailors who had been in the action, and dealing out nautical phrases with admirable exactness and accuracy, although it is doubtful if he ever saw the sea in his life." [7]

On the 12th of November, 1844, the Queen and Prince Albert made a Royal Progress through Northampton, on their way to visit the Marquis of Exeter at Burghley House. Shops were closed, the town garlanded for the occasion, and Clare was given an excellent place from which to view the procession; but "The Raree Show," some doggerel verses, was all that the occasion inspired him to produce. Another "nature" poet looked on at this Progress through Northampton. William Wordsworth had been to Cambridge. "I much regret that it did not strike me at the moment to throw off my feelings in verse," he wrote later to Henry Reed. A letter from Prichard in July, 1845, disclosed the fact that, though Clare was in excellent health, his mind was "becoming more and more impaired." "He enjoys perfect liberty here," the superintendent added, "and passes all his time out of doors in the fields or town, returning home only to his meals and bed." But *perfect* liberty the "woe-worn prisoner" could not have, estranged from the woods of his home, and in an incoherent letter to Patty, dated for this year, perhaps half the reason for this deepening cloud upon his mind is explained . . . "this is the English Bastile . . . where harmless people are trapped and tortured till they die – English bondage more severe than the slavery of Egypt and Africa." He had not yet reconciled himself to his fate.

But that he was approaching a supreme acceptance, in which peace, and even joy, though intermittent, would emerge with sanity out of angry melancholy, hopelessness,

and madness, is proved by the poems which belong to this
year 1844, "The Sleep of Spring" and "Graves of Infants."
Such poems are not written when a man is completely sub-
jugated by life; they cannot be composed out of blank
despair, but must be the result of some kind of triumphant
conquest of circumstances. The year 1844 marked the beginning of such an acceptance or conquest in Clare during
his last long torture at Northampton.

The years 1845 and 1846 continued with the same outward monotony. Some days the flowers cannot please; he is
too sad; his life seems a "trouble without end." Sometimes
"the tear drops on the book" he is reading; "prison," with
whatever kindliness accompanied, "injures health," when
"love is clippit o' the wing." The whitethorn bushes, the
field-corners, the brooks he sees, taunt his memory; they
are so like those at home. Nor can he forget the old, stooping,
mossy-walled cottage where he was born.

But at other times the flowers suffice. He can take pleasure
because of them even in the midst of his anguish. They are
nature's

> *very Scriptures upon earth,*
> *And teach us simple mirth where'er we go.*
> *Even in prison they can solace me,*
> *For where they bloom God is, and I am free.*

In June, 1846, the power of his eyes and mind to revel in
"the rising lily's snowy grace" is with him again, and he can
re-create for his own delight the scene of forty years ago by
Round Oak Spring, with the arum and the magpie's nest.
Sometimes he hears music beyond the wood-voices, the bird-
song, and the lore of the flowers. He does not recognise the
full meaning of the music yet, but he knows that by some
alchemy it changes the deepest sorrow a life can hold into
joy:

> *O haud yer tongues, ye sylvan elves!*
> *Yer gladness is but waes,*
> *And keep yer songs within yerselves*
> *For may-be better days.*

> *Another birdie sings to me,*
> *[That makes your] music vain,*
> *And fills my heart with sorrow's glee,*
> *Till pleasure springs from pain.*
> *Sae haud yer tongues, ye sylvan elves,*
> *And keep yer singing to yerselves.*

From this time onward Clare comes into line with his true predecessors, Chatterton and Blake.

Meanwhile Patty and her children lived on in the cottage at Northborough. It was thought among the villagers, since Earl Fitzwilliam paid for Clare's maintenance at St. Andrew's, that they lived rent free, but that supposition was as untrue as it had been when Clare contradicted it in 1832. Patty did not speak of these things even to her nearest neighbour, and nothing conclusive was known. She was still a comely woman, of medium height, plump rather than stout, with a full, rosy face, and well-liked because of her pleasant chatter and her good heart. She did not, to all appearances, make a great trouble of her husband's madness; she rarely spoke of it, and so the tradition grew that she cared little. She was known to the villagers as 'Widow Clare.' Anna, Clare's eldest daughter, died as early as 1844. Eliza Louisa was confined to her own home many years through ill-health. Frederick, too, was so delicate that he died in 1843 before he reached manhood. In March, 1846, old Parker Clare died and was buried at Helpston. It is likely that the news of his children's deaths was kept from Clare, but amid the confusion of a letter to his youngest son Charles, dated for the 15th of June, 1847, there is a philosophic comment on the old man's departure. He also warned Frederick and John against coming to that "Bastile of Hell" to see him. They might "get trapped as prisoners." But by the time of the next letter, February, 1848, he had forgotten that his father was not still alive. Among the eleven letters of Clare for the following years, there are two to Patty and the rest are to Charles, who, almost up to the time of his death in 1852, sent soothing, if short and uncoloured, replies. Among Clare's there is illustration of his madness, with ample proof of some "method in't."

To Patty, in July, 1848, he wrote:

"MY DEAR WIFE,

"I have not written to you a long while, but here I am in
the land of Sodom where all the people's brains are turned
the wrong way. I was glad to see John yesterday and should
like to have gone back with him, for I am very weary of
being here. You might come and fetch me away, for I think
I have been here long enough. I write this in a green
meadow [by] the side of the river agen Stokes Mill⁸ and I
see three of your daughters and a Son now and then. The
confusion and roar of Mill-dams and locks is sounding very
pleasant while I write it, and it's a very beautiful evening;
the meadows are greener than usual after the shower and the
rivers are brimful. I think it is about two years since I was
first sent up in this Hell and not allowed to go out of the
gates. There never was a more disgraceful deception than
this place . . . keep yourselves happy and comfortable and
love one another. By and by I shall be with you, perhaps
before you expect me. There has been a great storm here
with thunder and hail that did much damage to the glass in
the neighbourhood. Hail-stones the size of Hen's eggs fell in
some places. Did your brother John come to Northborough
or go to Barnack? His uncle, John Riddle, came the next
morning, but did not stay. I thought I was coming home
but I got cheated. I see many of your little brothers and
sisters at Northampton, weary and dirty with hard work,
some of them with red hands, but all in ruddy good
health . . ."

There is no knowing whether "your brother John" is
Patty's brother, or Charles's brother, *her* son and Clare's.
Certainly by October the young John had been to see his
father at Northampton, because W. F. Knight, adding a
note to a home letter of Clare's dated for that month, requests that some manuscripts should be sent him from
Northborough, and wishes to be remembered to John.
Knight was trying to get together poems enough for a
publication for the benefit of Clare's family. S. T. Hall, in
this year, paid a second visit to the asylum, gave Clare his
volume of poems *The Upland Hamlet*, after which he carried
to Patty at Northborough news of Clare's evident devotion

to home and her, and brought tears to her eyes over that.
In April, 1849, Clare liberally advised Charles on a subject
which might well have called forth bitterness or reviling
from him.

". . . read books of Knowledge; don't forget you[r] Latin
and Greek and Hebrew, nor your Mathematics and Astronomy, for in them you have Truth. When I was a day-
labourer at Bridge-Casterton and courted your Mother I
knew Nine Languages and could talk of them to Parsons
and Gentlemen and Foreigners, but never opened my mouth
about them to the Vulgar, for I always lived to myself. Don't
forget you have Bibles and Prayer Books; and never act
Hypocrisy, for Deception is the most odious Knavery in the
World. Stick to Truth and 'shame the Devil.' Learning is
your only Wealth. . . ."

Concerned about their reading, and forgetting all his early
book-loves, he keeps on enquiring whether the boys have a
"Harry Phillips." Probably the musical-poetic *True Enjoyment of Angling* was his pocket companion just now, and the
struggle and achievement of the versatile ballad-singer and
English Opera House favourite attracted him by comparison
with his own tragic superannuation. His next home-letter
has a host of names of acquaintances at Helpston and
Northborough after whom he enquires; and "all I have forgotten remember me kindly to, for I have been a long while
in Hell. . . . How is Thomas Porter of Ashton? He used to
be my Companion in my single Days when we loved Books
and Flowers together." By September, 1849, as we learn
from a tribute to his memory in the *Bedford Times*, another
of Clare's old acquaintances was dead. This was Thomas
Inskip, the friend and champion of Bloomfield, a poor
enough poetaster himself, but pious in his fervour for the
memory and genius of Keats, and one, says Clare, who
"loveth the green recess." Some record of his visits, if he
made any, to Clare at Northampton would be acceptable.
His first letter to Helpston had been written nearly a quarter
of a century before. Round about 1846, he was lingering in

illness at Ramsgate, but by December, 1847, having obtained
MS. scraps from Clare either by letter or when on a visit, he
had published the poem "Hesperus, the day is o'er" in the
Bedford Times. Then followed, in the next month, a carelessly made publication of "I Am," ' three weeks after that
the "Invite to Eternity," and in August, 1848, the happy
poem beginning "Come, gentle Spring, and shew thy varied
greens," which goes on to beckon the

> *Meadow-pinks and columbines,*
> *Kecksies white, and eglantines,*
> *And music of the bee that seeks the rose.*

In May, 1849, Inskip published "Mary Byfield" in the same
paper. "I Am" has been written of as Clare's last poem and
his best poem, when really it is only his saddest reflection on
the "shipwreck" of his life. Some have heaped more sadness
and loneliness over him by attempting to deduce from this
poem neglect on his family's part. But this must not be done.
Besides the probability that they were, during the first two
or three years, asked not to visit him, there was the expense
of the journey to hold them back. Before 1845, the best way
to get to Northampton would have been to hire a gig to
Thrapston and there catch the Cambridge coach, which ran
in connection with the coach at Oxford; it might cost, says
a writer on old Peterborough, £4 to get there and back. In
1845, the railway to Northampton was completed, and the
journey might be made for 3s. 6d. one way. The impression
of one living representative of the family is that John and
William went as often as they could, and even the invalid,
Eliza Louisa, who best understood and sympathized with her
father's poetry, went once. As far as they could, after so long
a separation, his children regarded Clare with affection,
and it is plain from his letters that he felt little lack of it
in them.

Apart from its lyric intensity, and its dignity of sorrow, "I
Am" is important because it marks a return of his struggle to
keep a grasp on his elusive identity. Following it, in the same

manuscript, there are fourteen lines in a free sonnet-form in which the same mental contest goes on.

> . . . *I was a being created in the race*
> *Of men, disdaining bounds of place and time,*
> *A spirit that could travel o'er the space*
> *Of earth and heaven, like a thought sublime*
> *Tracing creation, like my Maker, free!*
> *A soul unshackled, like eternity!*
> *Spurning earth's vain and soul-debasing thrall;*
> *But now I only know I AM.   That's all!*

In the "Invite to Eternity" the conquest is his; aware of his own madness, his "sad non-identity," he asks some nameless one, Love herself perhaps, to dare all in life and death and so reach eternity with him. Though the poem is known, it may not be superfluous to quote one of its verses here:

> *The land of shadows wilt thou trace?*
> *And look, nor know each other's face?*
> *The present mixed with reason gone,*
> *And past and present all as one?*
> *Say, maiden, can thy life be led*
> *To join the living and the dead?*
> *— Then trace thy footsteps on with me —*
> *We are wed to one eternity!*

In the mass of poems, unpublished and published, which belong to these desolate years, while to most of them we can assign no date, there is to be observed an order and coherence which make, out of a life so tragically hard for him, an inspiration for us who examine. With a loyalty that must be admired, he holds unshaken to the artistic motive and the principles of his youth. The unpublished poems represent a long and in the main successful effort to find comfort in writing verses. Writing sometimes at the direct request of visitors or townspeople, he dashed off "Halfpenny Ballads" so carelessly that very few have been included in the two volumes of asylum transcripts. Mary Joyce lost for ever now, he still wrote poems to innumerable Marys – Lucy Mary, Mary Ogilvie, Mary Featherstone, Mary o' the Plough; or sometimes he did not call her Mary, though he hid her under names as pretty – Irish Kitty, Helen, and Jean, Caradora, Ann Bodenham, and Alice Grey. These are not good poems, but only in a very few out of the seven or eight hundred is there any instance of irrational thought. This fact may give some indication of the many hours of sanity Clare passed among the mad. Though the people for whom they were written might have thought them proper enough poetry, they are, for us, sad proof of Clare's estrangement from the world. Had he not been where he was they would not have been written. Besides these unpublished poems, there are the published ones. Among them are verses for children and about children, poems like "Little Trotty Wagtail,"[10] "Graves of Infants," "The Dying Child," and "Clock-a-Clay," which no child should miss. There are poems where he returns to his early poetic aim and effaces himself wholly to bring before his readers the thing in nature which he wants them to see and love as he sees and loves – the nightingale, "clod-brown," a bean-field full of blossom, "feathered to one's feet." What Miss Sitwell has said of Christopher Smart might here be said of Clare. There was now "no room in the Heaven of this madman's mind for cruelty or injustice, or for anything but love." There are other poems in which his descriptions are not for themselves alone; he wishes then to bring all the praised together in a macrocosm of praising. He misses nothing even from the confines of his prison – the suthering wind, the rusted chestnut leaves, the earth sobbing under a thunderstorm, gnats in the still time o' day, the purple wood-bell, and the bee asleep upon the thistle. All these are praised, and in turn praise their Maker; Clare's watching eye is never at a loss. Again he reminds us of Smart:

> *We never are deserted quite;*
> *'Tis by succession of delight*
> *That love supports his reign.*

And Smart's constant marshalling of all flowers and beasts in their Creator's praise is akin to Clare's all-embracing gestures "without grudging or regret" from *his* madhouse.

Again there are happy songs which contain scarcely a hint of what he is enduring, like "I saw her crop a rose," and the one which Professor Abercrombie[11] praises for its "irresistible poignancy of expressiveness in metre":

> Come hither, my dear one, my choice one, and rare one
>   And let us be walking the meadows so fair,
> Where on pilewort and daisies the eye fondly gazes,
>   And the wind plays so sweet on thy bonny brown hair.
>
> Come with thy maiden eye, lay silks and satins by;
>   Come in thy russet or grey cotton gown;
> Come to the meads, dear, where flags, sedge, and reeds appear,
>   Rustling to soft winds and bowing low down.
>
> Come with thy parted hair, bright eyes, and forehead bare;
>   Come to the whitethorn that grows in the lane;
> To banks of primroses, where sweetness reposes,
>   Come, love, and let us be happy again . . .

Once more, there are poems among this asylum work, like " Mary Bateman," intolerably sad, on the old theme, first love:

> Are flowers the winter's choice?
> Is love's bed always snow?

We are reminded of Ophelia's songs. The girl Clare had loved as a boy, in spite of all estranging agony, still "blooms the sweetest woman." But he can never have her now. He is, for the last time, driven back upon himself, upon his own strength. His love becomes secret, unseen as the myriad amours of the creatures, yet pervading all nature. "Secret Love" is unforgettable in its tenderness, but it is no more written in madness than was the "mad Maid's song" by a mad Herrick.

Finally, there are poems which contain ideas in the view of which it would be wrong to say that Clare had not progressed in thought even since his mind began to play him tricks. These are the poems which round off, and give beauty to, his life. Through all his long sufferings he remained so united with nature that

My pulse beats calmer while his lightnings play!
My eye, with earth's delusions waxing dim,
Clears with the brightness of eternal day! . . .

In obscurity and inner discord he could find enduring clarity
and harmony. He did it by a process of change which
was intuitively rather than intellectually wrought. His
early love of Mary Joyce had, as we have said, been
identified with his love of nature. Now the sadness of
his loss of her became joy in finding her everywhere. He
"met her in the greenest dells"; she was the spirit, abroad
in spring or winter, in the white-nosed bee, the "fitful
gust," and the rain, that roused his love. From this the truth
followed that love was essentially pure; it cannot "live with
lust"; it is connected with the truest morality, which idea
Richard Jefferies nearly half a century later repeated. Out
of his asylum Clare wrote in correction of the old fallacy
that weighs us down even to-day:

> *In crime and enmity they lie*
> *Who sin and tell us love can die,*
> *Who say to us in slander's breath*
> *That love belongs to sin and death.* [12]

And then his final discovery. Man might decay; earth fade
out of his sight; but love, this all-pervasive, pure, natural
love, is immortal. His love, the joy of it, born of grief and
tragedy, has at last conquered death itself. Clare's voice from
the grave, passionately describing all that he loved, surely
makes stedfast the truth of his idea.

> *Love lives beyond*
> *The tomb, the earth, the flowers and dew.*
> *I love the fond,*
> *The faithful, young and true.*

These poems have been grouped and discussed now, in
order only to observe Clare's final achievement. Some may
have been written after the year at which we have arrived
in this biography. Perhaps between the writing of some of

them there were months of melancholy or madness. There were years still to come during which his ageing body as well as his mind troubled him. But the unity among the poems remains. His life's triumph is apparent. His achievement as man and as poet becomes manifest.

Composition would put a strain on him for which he must have known he would suffer afterwards, but, as his guardians knew, the writing solaced him while the long afternoon dragged on. Just after Christmas, 1849, he wrote to his eldest son, admonishing him, "think, Fred – for yourself." Fred had no use for thought, having been dead six years, and, getting no reply, Clare wrote to John; but the letter trailed off into a list of his children's names. Then, as if he revelled in the very sound of names, he added in his note-book of "Halfpenny Ballads" that bears the date "Dec. 26th, 1849":

"My dear Mary Collingwood, . . . my dear Betsey Avery, Mary Ann Avery, there is no faith here, so I hold my tongue and wait the end out, without attention or intention."

Another note-book, with the printed date 1850 in it, has names of friends too (among them that of long-lost Betsey Newbon), whom perhaps he found pleasure in recollecting. In January, 1850, after an entry here in which he divulged that Lord Byron wrote the fourth canto of *Childe Harold* whilst courting one Martha Turner, he recorded reasonably that he had seen his "Wife Patty in a Dream . . . with little Billy, and an Infant carried by someone else. All looked healthy and happy."

Another letter, this one actually sent, asked Charles to "take care of my Books and MSS. till I come," and in April, 1850, he tells the boy, destined to die from consumption years before his father, "I rather fancy I shall see you shortly." In this letter he is dull, has seen nobody, and heard nothing for a long time, but, though he was long ago shut out from youth, and is now thrust away even from the company of the sane, he can console himself in his own Valley of Humiliation by quoting to Charles the song of Bunyan's Shepherd Boy.

The cottage into which these letters were received had other troubles beside an absent husband and father. There are preserved, with date for March, 1850, two or three false starts at an evidently difficult letter from Charles to Patty's landlord, to say that the interest from the Fund-money must be stopped to pay her backward rent. She is ill; William is out of work; her home is in danger, and bills for Clare's doctors are not yet paid. Another letter begs Lord Milton – "Rev'd Sir" – to wait a little longer. Patty cannot sell her cow till July. John Taylor, who still kept an interest in Clare and his family, was applied to, and in his reply commented on William's unemployment as a "Shame." But Charles defends him, at the same time disclosing some details of the difficulties against which the agricultural poor were still contending:

". . . My Brother . . . would not be Idle if he could get any Employ. He has been to Labouring work the last winter when he could get a day's employ for 1s. 6d., and perhaps has got one in a fortnight."

Perhaps Taylor's compliance with the request for help provoked another plea; but the draft letter we have is un-dated and unaddressed:

"My Eldest Brother is now in journey work. My Second Brother has no work at all, and has been living at the ex-pense of my Mother. . . . My salary is but £4 per annum, which scarcely finds us shoes. If you could advance us a few pounds on the money that is in the Funds. . . ."

In another letter, also without the name of any addressee, Charles, on whom fell the task of answering all the corres-pondence of the family, offered to discharge a debt of his mother's in monthly instalments, presumably to be paid out of his own purse – replete with £4 per annum! This prom-ising boy was at this time articled to a solicitor.

Patty struggled on at her making of a livelihood, getting what profit she could out of her fruit, her cow, and her marketing. Very very occasionally she was asked by a visitor for a copy of *Poems Descriptive* or the *Village Minstrel*. In this year, 1850, as we learn from letters, Knight, the steward of St. Andrew's who had gone to an asylum at Birmingham, was proposing a volume of Clare's poems for publication by subscription, for the benefit of those at North-borough. He himself had, in manuscripts that he had taken away with him from Northampton, "many pieces that are very choice." However, time passed, no more was heard of the project, and one more hope of Clare's, that his name might be heard again outside Northampton, was lost.

In 1852, at the age of nineteen, Charles died. Of all the children of Clare and Patty, only John and William were robust; there was consumption among them, probably through under-nourishment or overcrowding in the early days at Helpston. John eventually went to Wales and obtained a good position on the railway. William stayed longest of any of them at home with his mother; in time he managed to keep a seed-drill, hiring himself and his machine out to the neighbouring farmers.

Sophia wrote to tell her father that Charles was ill, and Clare replied hoping the boy would be "very soon able to write me a letter." After this she wrote only occasionally. So Clare continued to visit his favourite seat under the portico of All Saints' Church in the town square with less frequent news of home. Here he would "sit for hours, musing, watching the children at play, or jotting down passing thoughts in his pocket note-book." Here Claridge Druce, author of *The Flora of Northamptonshire* and other county floras, as a child saw him, "a little, pathetic, distraught figure gazing into the sky."

In 1854, Dr. Prichard, because he could not persuade the governors to support him wholeheartedly, founded an institution of his own at Abington Abbey; Dr. Edwin Wing and Dr. Nesbitt took his place at St. Andrew's; Clare's freedom was further restricted, and he was confined

DDJ

to the asylum grounds. Perhaps the townspeople were too liberal with ale in return for verses; or perhaps the new superintendents had different methods. Dr. Nesbitt, who remained until 1858, while he believed Clare's affliction had its origin in dissipation, has yet left an appreciative account of his patient's good-nature, of his general tranquillity, and of the solace the poets gave him. Dr. Wing, who remained after Dr. Nesbitt, had not the influence with Clare which Dr. Prichard had had.

Another matter which might well have troubled Clare had he known of it was a scheme of John Taylor's – the publication of a complete edition of the poems. The ageing publisher purchased from How the copyright of the *Rural Muse* for £10, after which the scheme, like many another, fell to earth, and no more was heard of it. Routledge, too, wished to produce a complete volume, but there were difficulties which were not surmounted. However, for the moment Clare was occupied. He had been helping Anne Elizabeth Baker, one of the best of the provincial glossarists, to enrich with quotations from his published and unpublished poems her *Northamptonshire Words and Phrases*. The glossary, which had grown out of her devoted help with her brother's splendid but unfinished county history, was issued by subscription in this year 1854. One half of the strictly North-amptonshire words were furnished by Clare, "who," she said in her preface, "beautifully clothes his ideas in his own rustic idiom." Her two volumes, which collect so many instances of the unlettered man's nimble wit at word-making, have plentiful quotations from Chaucer, Tusser, Dryden, and others, as well as from Clare.

In March, 1856, the Rev. Thomas James of Thedding-worth lectured on Dryden and Clare. He had lately visited Clare, and the year preceding that had seen Patty at North-borough. A letter from his friend De Wilde which he read informs us of someone's indiscretion in having plied Clare with drink. James admired Clare's poetry, and left his rather homiletic account of the poet's life to be later drawn on by J. L. Cherry in 1873.

In November, 1857, there appeared in the *London Journal*
verses by some well-meaning visitor concerning Clare, an
"inoffensive lunatic." The next news of him, almost entirely
forgotten now in the throng of mid-century music-makers,
is in 1860. It is to be suspected that Dr. Wing's further confinement of him produced a deeper melancholy than ever,
which had its consequence in thickening the darkness over
his mind. Entries in the case-books for these years have
nothing to report except his good bodily health and the
irrationality of his mind. But he was now approaching
seventy, and his physical powers were declining. For some
years before 1860 he had not written a line of poetry.
Deprived of the power to roam in the fields or talk to the
sane in the town, what was there to write about? On the
7th of March, however, he resuscitated the dead Anna and
Frederick, even old Parker and Ann, added another daughter
to his list, and wrote to Patty:

"This comes with my kind Love to you and the children
and my Father and Mother, hoping it will find you all
well. . . . How is Champion John Junr. and Frederick and
also William Parker Clare, and . . . Anna Maria, Eliza,
Louiza, Sophia, and Julia. Give my love to Mrs. Kettle,
Fanny Temps, and all enquiring friends."

The next day, in answer to an enquiry from the outside
world by Mr. Jas. Hipkins, Wing, noting that his patient
was "very feeble in mind and still the subject of many
mental delusions," persuaded him to write a letter to be
enclosed with his. Clare wrote in a shaky hand:

"March 8, 1860.
"DEAR SIR,
"I am in a Madhouse and quite forget your Name or who
you are. You must excuse me for I have nothing to commu-
nicate or tell of, and why I am shut up I don't know. I have
nothing to say so I conclude.
"Yours respectfully,
"JOHN CLARE."

On the 9th he answered a letter from his "dear daughter" Sophia, saying: "I want nothing from Home to come here. I shall be glad to see you when you come."

A very sympathetic description of him in these later years by a lawyer, Robert Walton, in *Random Recollections of the Midland Circuit*, shows again the burden that his close imprisonment laid on him. Having dined with his friend the former governor, or housekeeper, and four harmless lunatics who were parlour-boarders, Walton "was attracted by the appearance of a man who sat on a stone bench, his hands clasped before him, his eyes looking listlessly towards the ground. Inquiring who he might be, I was told it was no other than John Clare, formerly well-known as the 'Northamptonshire poet.' And this wreck before me was the man who, from the position of a common labourer, had, by his own unaided exertions, raised himself to a position which, but for the mistaken kindness of friends, might have led to great results. Yes, here was the man whose poetry had charmed me in boyhood by its sweetness and simplicity, the talent of which had drawn to this tiller of the soil the notice of Charles Lamb . . . and others of that stamp."

Another visitor reveals that Clare's taste for the true and simple in poetry remained with him to the end.

"Ingenious Della Cruscan rhymes and florid poetry made no impression on Clare. On one occasion he was visited by two gentlemen,[12] one of whom read him some lines of 'fine writing,' written by a friend, and evidently expected his approval. The old man sat listless in his chair and his visitors thought he was unconscious of the reading and not in a poetic mood. But Mr. Godfrey, the secretary, knew more truly how to touch his heart.

" 'John,' he said, 'do you know these lines –

The curfew tolls the knell of parting day?'

" 'Oh, yes,' said Clare, 'I know them, they are Gray's.' And then, . . . with that appropriativeness which we have already remarked, 'I know Gray. I know him well.' "

On the 28th of August, Clare had another visitor. Miss Agnes Strickland, documentary historian and joint author with her sister of the *Lives of the Queens of England*, saw and talked with him when she went over St. Andrew's with Lord Spencer and General Spencer. She found him silent and sad but not violent.

"I told Clare I had been much pleased with his lines on the daisy.

" 'Ugh! it is a tidy little thing,' replied he, without raising his eyes or appearing in the slightest degree gratified by my praise.

" 'I am glad you can amuse yourself by writing.'

" 'I can't do it,' replied he, gloomily; 'they pick my brains out.' I enquired his meaning.

" 'Why,' said he, 'they have cut off my head, and picked out all the letters of the alphabet – all the vowels and consonants – and brought them out through my ears; and then they want me to write poetry! I can't do it.'

" 'Tell me which you liked best, literature or your former avocation?'

" 'I liked hard work best,' he replied, with sudden vehemence, 'I was happy then. Literature has destroyed my head and brought me here.' " [14]

Here is, as there was in Bridget Elia's ramblings, "a vein of crazy logic." Despite his bitter words to his visitor, the old man, in the spring of 1860, had rallied and had risen above his sufferings again. The lover of "the brook's soft sound," the swallow, and "the evening rack," was persuaded to write again. The first production was 'a sheet full of grotesque heads, no two alike. He then, after many protestations that he had forgotten how to write and that he did not know how to begin, produced "The Daisy" and "The Address to John Clare." At intervals, in the spring of the same year, he produced two more sonnets, viz. "Early Spring" and "The Green Lane." ' There are two poems on the daisy, both written between February and July of 1860, and the second one presented to Agnes Strickland. What he wrote was not about his present hopelessness and the wreck of his life – even the "Address to John Clare" was a happy picture of himself at home and of the visit of the "bookman." These poems are the work of a lover, who has lost himself in the daisy, seeing in it spring's whole loveliness again.

In 1860 or the early part of 1861 he had a visitor, John Plummer, a verse-writer from Kettering, who found him reading a book from the asylum library in the sitting-room, "cosy and comfortable, with its mahogany chairs, table, and couch, warm soft carpets, and cheerful fire." Plummer remarked, in a well-meaning and energetic attempt to bring notice to the "forgotten poet," on Clare's "very large forehead, and mild, benevolent-looking features."

"We found him taciturn," he says in a later account of this visit; "in vain we strove to arrest his attention. He merely looked at us, with a vacant gaze for a moment, and then went on reading his book."

But the attendant informed the visitor that Clare was generally good-humoured and obedient. In a letter to the editor of the *Northampton Mercury* on the 24th of June, 1861, Plummer goes further; Clare was said to be "very frequently blithe and talkative." There is no reason to think that his indifference and reticence on that occasion was an attitude of the insane. He was probably engrossed in his book. Besides, from other evidence it is clear that this spring of 1861 found him at intervals sane and tranquil, as he had been during some parts of the preceding year. His last lines – on nature, as they were sure to be – show the calm amid the melancholy and gentle aberration of these closing years. Clare wrote:

> *'Tis Spring, warm glows the south,*
> *Chaffinch carries the moss in his mouth*
> *To filbert hedges all day long,*
> *And charms the poet with his beautiful song;*
> *The wind blows bleak o'er the sedgy fen,*
> *But warm the sun shines by the little wood,*
> *While the old cow at her leisure chews her cud.*

Two more visitors called on him before the end – Paxton Hood, the Nonconformist and writer of *The Peerage of*

Poverty, and John Askham of Wellingborough. Among Askham's *Sonnets on the Months*, published in 1863, there is one to Clare, revealing him after his pen was laid by for the last time and when he could no longer walk even into the garden. As his strength diminished further, Clare was wheeled about the grounds of the asylum in a bath-chair. Sometimes, as two or three have recorded, he would say, "I want to go home," or "I have lived too long." Dr. Wing, who died a few months after Clare and so was unable to make his intended study of Clare's mind, describing his derangement in the case-books of St. Andrew's as "a deep melancholy," added, "Latterly his intellect had become sadly clouded, yet there were periods when the shadow would be temporarily lifted." The case-books from 1862 to 1864 tell of Clare's "tendency to apoplexy, his delusions about his identity . . . his being haunted by phantoms of his own creation, his bad language to these chimeras, his habit of chewing tobacco, [and] his eventual insensibility to the flowers and sunshine into which he was taken." Still, his "insensibility" was neither so deep nor so continuous as to prevent him from reaching his favourite window-seat, to look out on the garden beyond, which he did, says Cherry, to within three days of his death. On Good Friday of that year he was taken out for the last time. On the 10th of May—the month was notable for its excessive heat—he had a paralytic seizure, and Patty was notified of his illness. For Friday, the 20th of May, 1864, the case-books record again – and finally: "This morning on being visited he was found to be completely comatose, and never rallied, but died quietly late in the afternoon."

Forty years before, craving friendship and rightful recognition, Clare had written for the *Rural Muse* a sonnet concerning his end.

> *I would not that my being all should die,*
> *And pass away with every common lot;*
> *I would not that my humble dust should lie*
> *In quite a strange and unfrequented spot,*
> *By all unheeded and by all forgot;*

With nothing save the heedless winds to sigh,
And nothing but the dewy morn to weep
About my grave, far hid from the world's eye: . . .

And ten years before that, thinking of his death, he had
directed:

"I wish to lie . . . where the Morning and Evening sun
can linger the longest on my Grave. I wish to have a rough
unhewn stone, something in the form of a milestone, so that
the playing boys may not break it in their heedless pastimes,
with nothing more on it than this inscription: 'Here rest the
hopes and ashes of John Clare.' I desire that no date be
inserted thereon, as I wish it to live or die with my poems
and other writings, which, if they have merit with posterity
it will, and if they have not it will not be worth preserving."

Mr. Spencer of Woodcroft Castle and the Bellars took steps
to ensure that Clare should be buried in the churchyard at
Helpston, as he had desired. So he took his first and his last
train journey, from St. Andrew's to the Exeter Arms, an
inn in the village. Godfrey, the secretary, took the news to
Northborough. That was on Tuesday, the 24th, the day
before the funeral. Strange tales were current in the village
because the coffin was not opened for the family to look at
the dead. It was not John Clare who lay there, the people
held.

Patty, Eliza Louisa and her daughter, and William and his
wife, mourned him, with Charles Mossop, Mr. and Mrs.
Bellars, and a few more friends of his youth. Up and down
beside the grave Tom Clare, a kinsman, is said to have
walked, growling out: "Vanity of vanities; all is vanity."
Yet perhaps all is not so vain but that Clare's poems, and
the tale of his life's triumph, may find listeners while literature and man continue.

XXI

SONG'S POSTERITY

I see him there, with his streaming hair
And his eyes
Piercing beyond our human firmament,
Lit with a burning deathless discontent.

EDMUND BLUNDEN, "Clare's Ghost."

IF this *Life* does not enable the reader to come to his own conclusions about many of the troubled problems both of Clare's life and of his after-fame, it will have failed in its purpose. If the character of the man does not shine through the lines of his own verse and prose, we shall look for it elsewhere in vain. It is time that the "shades of the prison house" which closed about him in mid-life were lifted. He has suffered too long from the over-insistence upon certain traits and circumstances in his life at the expense of others, equally important. Thus his failures have been allowed to obscure his triumphs, his gifts of exact observation and poetic utterance to outweigh his intellectual qualities, his gentleness and humility to mask the quiet self-confidence and sturdy independence which lay beneath them. Thus he has been depicted as the sport of circumstance, with "no gifts except his dreamy sweetness of character, his child-like simplicity, and his redundant flow of verses."

It is true that Clare had an impressionable and receptive mind, which enabled him to enter so intimately into the life of nature and men about him; we observe the same qualities in his relationships with his fellows as in his poetry. He enjoyed the company of all sorts and conditions of men and women; he was received by most of them as one of themselves, whether they were villagers or nobility, gipsies or men of letters. Wherever pretension and arrogance were absent, there Clare was at home. It was his aim to keep his mind open to impressions and ideas, and form his own judgments at first hand. He was a good listener; but when he spoke, he was listened to; the many quotations and references in his note-books attest his careful and appreciative reading of the books in his considerable library, but in his own prose, as in his poetry, he wrote only of the things which his experience had illuminated. As we read the story of Clare's life we become aware of a remarkable consistency, a tenacity of character beneath the impressionable surface, a reflection of that stubborn wiriness which underlay his rather frail and sensitive body. For the themes shaped in his youth reappear continually in his maturity and age, transposed by experience into new and often strange keys; but they are the same themes still. His youthful joys and loves and ambitions remained with him to the end.

They remained because he would not give them up, however circumstances conspired to wrest them from him. The boy who found freedom, love, and poetry in his native fields became the man who sang in praise of love and freedom when the walls of an asylum hemmed him in; and he sang of them, not as of a past dream only, but as of a present reality too. In them we see the ultimate triumph of a life spent in a vain struggle for independence. The desire for independence was implanted in him by the changing scenes of his youth, when he saw the village society disorganized and broken up by Enclosure, and his fellow-peasants reduced to casual labour and dependence on the parish. He suffered with the rest in that change, and it strengthened his ambitions to escape from a servitude which was destroying the spirit of a race. Then the clouds parted, he stood for a moment in the full blaze of fame, and his modest hope seemed realized; he could enjoy as a poet the freedom denied him as a peasant. For many years he strove diligently to earn his living by his pen; had his publishers been able to bring out a new volume a year, they would not have found poems wanting; he set himself to master what was to him the

much more difficult art of writing prose. When his hope of
literary independence faded, he turned again to the profession he had never entirely left, and sought independence as
a cottage-farmer. Here too it was denied him.

But his failure gives the measure, not of his lack of effort
or determination, but of the odds against him. Each of the
roads which he as poet and as peasant saw before him in
1820 ended in impenetrable forest. Where were the peasants
or cottage-farmers who escaped penury and pauperdom between 1820 and 1830? And where was the nature poet who
could increase by the proceeds of his books a pension of £40
sufficiently to support his family in comfort?

It is no wonder that the flame of Clare's desire for independence, since he would not let it die, consumed his own
mind for lack of other fuel; and, by this supreme sacrifice
of the man to the poet, it was kept alight triumphantly to
the end. If the flame had died, there would have been no
asylum poems, or, perhaps, he would have been content to

> *Murmur a little sadly, how love fled*
> *And paced upon the mountains overhead*
> *And hid his face amid a crown of stars.*

But Clare had long known how to turn molehills into mountains and find a star in the petals of a flower; so now he could
walk with freedom in the confines of his captivity, and in his
inspired moments, like some captive bird with eyes pierced,
sing his songs, wherein, by a secret of melody known to birds
but rarely to men, sorrow was transformed into joy, and
failure soared to triumph.

> *I snatched the sun's eternal ray*
> *And wrote till Earth was but a name.*

> *In every language upon earth*
> *On every shore, o'er every sea*
> *I gave my name immortal birth*
> *And kept my spirit with the free.*

APPENDIX

ACCOUNT C (*Poems Descriptive*)

1st Edition

Dr.	£	s.	d.	Cr.	£	s.	d.
1819—July				By 1000 Copies at 3/7 .	172	0	0
To Paper 22 Reams at 35/–	38	10	0				
1820—Jan. 3							
Printing 1000 Copies .	45	1	6				
Advertising . . .	14	14	0				
Sundry Expenses . .	3	3	0				
27 Copies given away, 33							
do. to Author at 4/– .	12	0	0				
Sundries . . .	1	14	2				
10 Copies to Hall . .	1	15	10				
Cash paid Mr. Clare for							
Copyright p. Drury[1] .	20	0	0				
Commission 5 pr. Cent. .	8	12	0				
Half profit to Drury's							
account . . .	13	4	9				
Half profit to T. & H. .	13	4	9				
	£172	0	0		£172	0	0

2nd and 3rd Edition

	£	s.	d.		£	s.	d.
Feb 21							
To Paper 43¼ Reams at 35/–	75	13	9	March—By 2000 Copies			
. . . .				2nd & 3rd Edn. .	344	0	0
Printing 2000 Copies .	55	5	0				
Advertising 2nd and 3rd							
Editn. . . .	25	0	0				
Cash for Clare's Subscrip-							
tion	100	0	0				
Sundry Expenses . .	5	5	0				
Deductions allowed to							
Agents . . .	4	3	3				
Commission 5 pr. Cent. .	17	4	0				
Half Profit to Drury .	30	14	6				
Half Profit to T. & H. .	30	14	6				
	£344	0	0		£344	0	0

Fourth Edition

	£	s.	d.		£	s.	d.
1821—Jan.				By 616 Copies sold at 3/7	105	17	9
To Paper 22 Reams at 34/–	37	8	0	384 do. on hand . .	66	2	3
Printing 1000 Copies .	37	1	0	Balance carried forward	5	1	0
6 Copies to Authors bds..	1	4	0				
Advertising . . .	30	0	0				
Commission 5 p. Cent. on							
616 sold . . .	5	5	9				
384 Copies on Hand car-							
ried forward . .	66	2	3				
	£177	1	0		£177	1	0

	£	s.	d.		£	s.	d.
To Balance brought for-				By 384 copies carried			
ward	5	1	0	forward . .	66	2	3

BIBLIOGRAPHICAL

(A selection of the more important books and articles consulted)

WORKS

✓ *Poems Descriptive of Rural Life and Scenery.* London: Printed for Taylor and Hessey, and E. Drury. 1820. Second and third editions, 1820. Fourth edition, 1821.

✓ *The Village Minstrel, and Other Poems.* London: Printed for Taylor and Hessey, and E. Drury. Two volumes, 1821. Second issue 1823.

✓ *The Shepherd's Calendar; with Village Stories, and Other Poems.* London: Published for John Taylor, by James Duncan. 1827

✓ *The Rural Muse.* London: Whittaker & Co. 1835.

SELECTIONS, BIOGRAPHIES, AND MISCELLANEA

Four Letters from the Rev. W. Allen to the Right Honourable Lord Radstock, G.C.B., on the Poems of John Clare, the Northamptonshire Peasant. Hatchards'. 1823.

Three Very Interesting Letters (two in curious rhyme), by the celebrated poets Clare, Cowper, and Bird. With an Appendix (Clare's "Familiar Epistle to a Friend"). Charles Clarke's private press, Great Totham, 1837.

✓ *The Life of John Clare.* By Frederick Martin. London and Cambridge: Macmillan & Co. 1865.

✓ *Life and Remains of John Clare.* By J. L. Cherry. London: Frederick Warne & Co. Northampton: J. Taylor & Son. 1873. Issued in *Chandos Classics,* 1873-1877.

The John Clare Centenary Exhibition Catalogue. Introduction by C. Dack. Peterborough Natural History, Scientific, and Archæological Society. 1893.

✓ *Poems by John Clare.* Selected and introduced by Norman Gale. With a Bibliography by C. Ernest Smith. Rugby: George E. Over. 1901.

✓ *Poems by John Clare.* Edited, with an introduction, by Arthur Symons. London: Henry Frowde. 1908.

Northamptonshire Botanologia: John Clare. By G. Claridge Druce. 1912. (Includes a memoir and a classification of the flowers described in Clare's poems.)

447

John Clare: Poems Chiefly from Manuscript. (Edited by Edmund Blunden and Alan Porter. With an Introduction by Edmund Blunden.) London: Richard Cobden-Sanderson. 1920.

Madrigals and Chronicles. Being newly found poems written by John Clare. Edited, with a Preface and Commentary, by Edmund Blunden. London: The Beaumont Press. 1924.

More Footnotes to Literary History. By Edmund Blunden. Tokyo: Kenkyusha. 1926.

John Clare's Library. By Reginald W. Brown. Northampton-shire Natural History Society and Field Club. 1929.

Sketches in the Life of John Clare. By Himself. With an Intro-duction, Notes, and Additions by Edmund Blunden. London: R. Cobden-Sanderson Ltd. 1931.

INCIDENTAL REFERENCE VOLUMES

Abbott, Claude Colleer	*Life and Letters of George Darley*	1928
Abercrombie, Lascelles	*The Theory of Poetry* . .	1924
Baker, A. E.	*Glossary of Northamptonshire Words and Phrases* . .	1854
Blunden, Edmund	*Nature in English Literature* .	1929
Cary, H.	*Memoir of H. F. Cary* . .	1847
Chambers, R.	*Cyclopædia of English Literature* .	1861
Dennis, J.	*Studies in English Literature* .	1876
De Quincey, T.	*Works: London Reminiscences* .	1890
De Wilde, G. J.	*Rambles Round About* . .	1872
Dictionary of National Biography.		
Dobell, B.	*Sidelights on Charles Lamb* .	1903
Elton, Oliver	*Survey of English Literature, 1780–1831*	1912
Forster, —	*Life of Charles Dickens, Vol. III* .	1874
(Galignani's)	*Living Poets of England* . .	1827
Gosse, Edmund	*Silhouettes* . . .	1925
Hall, S. C.	*Book of Gems* . .	1838
	A Book of Memories . .	1871
Hall, S. T.	*Biographical Sketches* . .	1873
Hammond, J. L. and Barbara	*The Village Labourer, 1760–1832.*	1927
Heath, R.	*The English Peasant.* . .	1893
Hewlett, Maurice	*Last Essays ("Peasant Poets")* .	1924
Hone, W.	*Every-Day Book* . .	1832
Hood, E. P.	*The Literature of Labour* . .	1851
	The Peerage of Poverty . .	1870
Hood, T.	*Hood's Own, No. 12* . .	1839
James, T.	*MS. Lecture on Dryden and Clare*	
Kent, Elizabeth	*Flora Domestica* . . .	1823
	Sylvan Sketches . . .	1825

King, R. W.	*The Translator of Dante* .	. 1925
Lamb, Charles	*Letters* (Everyman). .	. 1909
Lucas, E. V.	*Life of Charles Lamb* .	. 1905
Lynd, Robert	*Books and Authors.*	
Marsh, G. L.	*John Hamilton Reynolds* .	. 1928
Mitford, M. R.	*Recollections of a Literary Life*	. 1857
Northampton County Asylum Case-Books.		
Redding, Cyrus	*Fifty Years Recollections* .	. 1858
	Past Celebrities Whom I Have	
	Known. II. .	. 1866
Robinson, Henry Crabb	MS. Journal.	
Sternberg, Thomas	*Dialect and Folk Lore of North-*	
	amptonshire .	. 1851
Strickland, Agnes	*Life of, by her Sister.*	
Symons, Arthur	*The Romantic Movement in Eng-*	
	lish Poetry .	. 1908
Taylor, John	*Bibliotheca Northantonensis.*	. 1869
Walton, Robert	*Random Recollections of the Mid-*	
	land Circuit .	. 1869
Wilson, John	*Recreations of Christopher North*	. 1864

ARTICLES AND REVIEWS

1820	*London Magazine* .	. January, March
	Quarterly Review . .	. . May
1821	*London Magazine* . .	. November
1823	*London Magazine* .	. January, February
1840	*Athenæum* . .	. June
	London Saturday Journal	. . July
1841	*English Journal* . .	. May
1847–1849	*Bedford Times.*	
1861	*Once A Week* .	. May
1864	*Gentleman's Magazine* .	. July
1873	*Manchester Guardian* .	. July
1886	*Northamptonshire Notes and Queries.*	
1920	*Athenæum* . March, April, October, November
	London Mercury .	. July
	Nation .	. February
	Peterborough Citizen .	. March, September
1921	*Athenæum* .	. January
	Times Literary Supplement	. January, June, July
1922	*Nation.*	
	Bookman .	. October
1923	*London Mercury.*	
1924	*Spectator* .	. August
	Times Literary Supplement	. August
1925	*Spectator* .	. September, October
1925	*London Mercury* .	. June, July

EEj

NOTES

CHAPTER I

1. The correct spelling is "Helpston," though Clare almost always, in common with the custom about a century ago, spelt it "Helpstone." We are indebted to Professor F. M. Stenton for a note on the word. The first element, he says, "is the personal name Help, a short form of some such compound as Helpric or Helparic."

2. This rustic wrestling included kicking, and the feet were shod with heavy boots studded with the sharpest nails procurable.

3. Clare's *Journal* for Thursday, the 14th of April, 1825: "My mother is sixty-seven years old this day. . . ." But we know from the baptismal registers of Castor that she was baptized on the 17th of April, 1757. In his *Life of John Clare*, 1865, Frederick Martin says that she was eighteen in the autumn of 1792, when, he says, the marriage with Parker took place; she was, of course, thirty-five.

4. *Quarterly Review*, May, 1820.

5. Statute-time, from the 14th to the 21st of May. There was another Statute in September.

CHAPTER II

1. *Quarterly Review*, May, 1820.

2. "The Resignation," no doubt, the poem which James Montgomery admired, and not "Resignation," on the Duke of Grafton's resigning the premiership.

3. Of Milton; Milton Abbey, about two miles from Helpston, was, at this time, the seat of William Wentworth, Earl Fitzwilliam.

4. In Scott's *Woodstock*, Mr. Holdenough's story of his friend's death is based on the historical story of Dr. Michael Hudson's tragic end at the hands of the Roundheads at Woodcroft Castle.

5. Hazlitt in the *New Monthly Magazine*, Vol. IV., 1822.

CHAPTER III

1. The manuals of John Abercrombie were all very popular, and it is difficult to tell which Clare means. Perhaps the most widely read were *Every Man his Own Gardener* and *The Gardener's Pocket Journal*.

2. 49 Geo. III; from the copy of the Helpston Extract of the Award.

3. The enlistment papers, which Cherry saw in 1873, and which would have given Clare's exact height and other details, have unfortunately been lost sight of.

4. Under Castlereagh's scheme, every man of Militia age was compelled, under penalty of a fine of ten shillings, to be perfect in the use of the firelock.

CHAPTER IV

1. He usually wrote it "Cowper Green." It is now known as "Copy Green."

2. Clare was probably below 5 ft. 2 in. at the age of seventeen, as we may conclude because of his first rejection from the Army of Reserve.

3. May be "in a hip for." – MS.

4. Charles William Wentworth Fitzwilliam; after 1833 the 5th Earl Fitzwilliam.

5. *Maggots: or Poems on several Subjects never before Handled*, 1685, by Samuel Westley (Wesley) contains "To my Gingerbread Mistress," "The Lyar," and "A King turn'd Thresher," all of which had some influence on Clare's early metres.

CHAPTER V

1. Morton says of it: "The spire of this chapell of Glinton, for a Chapell, is certainly the finest in England, 'tis so tall, and yet so very slender and neat."

CHAPTER VI

1. Of Finedon Place, Northamptonshire. The Church there contains the library founded by him in 1788. He was an ancestor of the poet and friend of Robert Bridges, D. M. Dolben.

CHAPTER VII

1. From "The Woodman," dedicated to Holland and published in the *Village Minstrel*. Clare's letters to Holland, among the earliest he wrote, were preserved, and are to be found in *Sketches in the Life of John Clare*.
2. November 13th. A lively account of this ancient ceremony may be found in Hone's *Every-Day Book*, 1832, Vol. I., p. 1483.
3. Brother-in-law of the Marquis of Exeter.
4. *A History of Newfoundland*, D. W. Prouse, 1896.

CHAPTER VIII

1. Kean was playing at Drury Lane in *The Hebrew*, a drama based on Scott's *Ivanhoe*, Macready at Covent Garden in *Ivanhoe, or The Jewess*, a musical drama on the same theme. Emery and the others appeared in the farces which accompanied these plays.
2. The Beggars' Bush, properly the Hare and Hounds, a wild music-hall and inn, demolished about 1844 with the rest of the Rookery in Holborn.
3. Robert Waithman, linendraper and vociferous political reformer, M.P. for the City of London for several years, and Lord Mayor in 1823. An obelisk stands in Ludgate Circus as a tribute to his talent and energy in the cause of reform.
4. The points of contact – and the divergences – between them were noted by Mr. Middleton Murry in "The Poetry of John Clare," *Countries of the Mind* (First Series).
5. This was the original spelling of the name. Chauncy changed it to Townshend later.
6. The Right Honourable George John Spencer, 2nd Earl Spencer and Viscount Althorpe, Privy Councillor, Trustee of the British Museum, and collector of the finest library in Europe.

CHAPTER IX

1. Lines 293–4, *Lamia*, Part 2, H. Buxton Forman's Edition. The earlier lines are given in a footnote.
2. Taylor made several quotations from this piece of autobiography. The full text is given by Mr. Blunden in *Sketches in the Life of John Clare*.

CHAPTER X

1. In the August number, 1824. It is an ingenious exercise in punning.
2. Lamb's earliest recorded reference to Clare is in a letter to B. W. Procter, written in the Spring of 1821: "The *Wits* (as Clare calls us) assemble at my Cell . . . this evening at ¼ before 7."
3. We are indebted to Mr. Charles Johnson for a suggestion. Did Clare mean to write "Packwood's" (Packwood being then famous for the poetical advertisements of his strops), instead of "packman's"?
4. *London Magazine*, September 1821. "C. Van Vinkbooms, his Dogmas for Dilettanti. No. 1: Recollections in a Country Churchyard." The pictures mentioned by Clare were exhibited at the Royal Academy in 1822 and 1824 respectively.
5. *The Flood of Thessaly*, 1823.

CHAPTER XI

1. An Exhibition of Mexican Curiosities at the Egyptian Hall held by W. Bullock, F.L.S.

2. Helen Maria Williams, the poetess whom Wordsworth had admired.

3. Sketches of actors and actresses, with album verses and translations, published in 1822. He collaborated with John Bowring in *A Batavian Anthology*, or *Specimens of the Dutch Poets*, 1824, and a novel, *The Gondola*, appeared in 1827.

4. We have omitted twelve verses here. The Poem was reprinted in Elton's *Boyhood*, and Cherry quotes it in full, though, as often, he takes liberties with the text.

5. Charles Lamb.

6. Julius Hare.

7. J. H. Reynolds. The *Boyhood* version has Janus (Wainewright) here.

8. Allan Cunningham.

9. From here to the end of the next verse is omitted in the *London*, perhaps because Taylor was very partial to De Quincey at this time, at the expense of the "poet true" (Barry Cornwall) and others.

10. The Rev. Charles Strong, translator of Italian sonnets.

11. Rippingille.

12. Philip Astley was the founder of the modern circus. His famous amphitheatre stood near the south end of Westminster Bridge.

13. *Times Literary Supplement*, "Clare and Wordsworth," August 21st, 1924. See also *Times Literary Supplement*, January 1921, reprinted by Mr. Murry in *Countries of the Mind* (First Series).

CHAPTER XII

1. An anonymous collection of tales published by Taylor and Hessey in 1824.

2. "A Plea for Female Genius."

3. H. N. T. S.

4. "Julius" – probably Darley.

5. 3rd edition, 1824, by the author of the *Four Letters* on Clare's poetry.

6. *Remarks on the Internal Evidence for the Truth of Revealed Religion*, 1820.

7. *The Miseries of Human Life, or the Groans of Samuel Sensitive and Timothy Testy, with a few supplementary sighs from Mrs. Testy*, new edition, 1806.

8. By "Billy O'Rourke," perhaps the ubiquitous Darley.

9. Published in *Sketches in the Life of John Clare*, 1931.

10. See Kirke White's "When twilight steals along the ground."

11. In a letter to Cary, written in December of this year, he says he has found eight sorts.

12. But it was in fact a genuine letter of Thomson's.

13. *Five Hundred Points of Good Husbandry*, by Thomas Tusser, ed. W. Mavor, 1812.

14. William Dodd [1729–1777], a forger who yet preached "very eloquently and touchingly," says Horace Walpole. He wrote *Thoughts in Prison* while under sentence of death.

15. *Essays and Sketches of Character*, by the late Richard Ayton, Esq., 1825.

16. Wrong both times. He was of course thirty-two.

17. They could hardly have been hobby-hawks, since these are birds of passage; more probably they were young male and female sparrow-hawks.

CHAPTER XIII

1. A full account of this poem and its significance is to be found in Mr. Blunden's *Nature in Literature*. See also Mr. Murry's *Countries of the Mind* (First Series).

CHAPTER XIV

1. See Appendix.

CHAPTER XV

1. Frederick Martin places this incident in 1836, and takes it for a sign of Clare's mental breakdown. The evidence of the letters seems conclusive, however, and Martin's dating is often very inaccurate.

CHAPTER XVII

1. It is not clear why Clare followed Shakespeare and Barnfield in speaking of the singing nightingale as "she" in "The Nightingale's Nest." He uses the correct pronoun in other poems, and discusses that very error in his prose notes on the bird.

CHAPTER XVIII

1. Frederick Martin killed Mary off years before, thus adding a dramatic touch to the story of Clare's seeing her. But the Glinton register admits of no doubt; she was baptized on the 10th of January, 1797, died unmarried, aged forty-one, and was buried on the 16th of July, 1838.

CHAPTER XIX

1. This is the spelling usually adopted to-day. High Beach and Highbeach were as common in Clare's day.

2. The genesis of this idea, too, may be traced in the crises of 1832 ; in a first draft of " To the Rural Muse " we find ;

> *And if so be that death's the price of fame,*
> *Should but a portion of thy prize befall*
> *To him who dies to live, 'tis recompense for all.*

But by 1841 Clare has outgrown even " that last infirmity of noble mind," and is nearer to the Keats who wrote :

> *Verse, fame, and Beauty are intense indeed,*
> *But Death intenser—Death is Life's high meed.*

3. Clare is evidently referring to the 17th here. His first meeting with the gipsy must have taken place in the previous week.

4. It was St. Neots. (Clare's note.)

5. Dialect word used for water that rises, through winter rains, in well or dyke.

6. A translation of Shenstone's Inscription X, "AH MARIA . . . HEU QUANTO MINUS EST CUM RELIQUIS VERSARI, QUAM TUI MEMINISSE."

7. Unfortunately, the papers of his admission to his second asylum are lost. By an extract from them, however, we know that Fenwick Skrimshire, who has been maligned for counting Clare insane because of "years addicted to poetical prosings," although he did use this unfortunate phrase, used it in answer to the question, "Was it [Clare's mental collapse] preceded by any severe or long-continued mental emotion or exertion?" Skrimshire was the author of books on medicine, chemistry, and natural history.

CHAPTER XX

1. From a letter of G. J. De Wilde's, printed in the *Times Literary Supplement* for the 30th June, 1921.

2. *Biographical Sketches of Remarkable People, chiefly from Personal Recollections* (1873), Spencer T. Hall.

3. *Biographical Sketches*, S. T. Hall.

4. The writer spells the superintendent's name Pritchard throughout his account; but the name was Prichard.

5. From De Wilde's letter to J. W. Dalby, Hunt's friend, *Times Literary Supplement*, 30th June, 1921.

6. From the *Life of Charles Lamb* (4th ed., 1907), E. V. Lucas.

7. From *Recollections of a Literary Life* (1852), Mary Russell Mitford.

8. Probably Spokes's Mill, near Weston Favell, about a mile from St. Andrew's.

9. S. T. Hall also had a copy of this in manuscript.

10. True, the naturalist in him slept when he wrote this; but, cut off from nature's freedom as he was now, may he not be forgiven?

11. *The Theory of Poetry*, Lascelles Abercrombie (1924).

12. It is true that the first line of Southey's then popular verse on *Love's Immortality* finds an echo here. But Clare's poem, voicing his conviction about love's purity, seems modern in idea beside Southey's conventional words.

13. One of these was Grimshawe, who painted Clare in 1844.

14. *Life of Agnes Strickland* (1887), Jane Margaret Strickland.

APPENDIX

1. *Clare's note:* "How can this be? I never sold the Poems for any price. What money I had of Drury was given me on account of profits to be received; but here it seems I have got nothing and am brought in minus twenty pounds of which I never received a sixpence – or it seems that by the sale of these four thousand copies I have lost that much; and Drury told me that 5,000 copies had been printed though 4,000 only were accounted for."

INDEX

The initial C. in this index represents John Clare.

A

ABERCROMBIE, John, 59 and *n*.
Abercrombie, Lascelles, 429 and *n*.
Accounts, C.'s with his publishers, 202, 273, 286–7; examination of, 309–14
Ackerman, P. S., Allen to, 387
"Address to Echo," by E. V. Rippingille, 182 and *n*., 229
"Address to John Clare," 437–8
"Address to Plenty," 139
"After Repentance, An," 105
Alfred, The, false reports about C. in, 358
Alice W——, Lamb's, 189, 192
Allen, Dr. Matthew, 348, 378; views on treatment of insanity, 381–3; description of C. in 1840, 384; reports on C.'s health, 385; letter to *The Times* on C., 385; C.'s letter to, 406–7; letter to C., 408; and Tennyson, 408
Allen, Rev. W., *Four Letters* to Lord Radstock, a critique of C.'s poetry, 204; *Grammar*, 240 and *n*.
Amulet, The, 283
Analectic Magazine, The, 118
Ancient Ballads and Songs of the Peasantry of England, 279
Anniversary, The, C.'s "Autumn" in, 283
Annual Register, The, for 1820, 118
Annuals, C. and the, 282–3
"Antiquity," 205
"Apology for the Poor," C.'s, 334–6
Arnold, Dr., treats C., 36, 209
Artis, E. T., archæologist friend of C., 116, 176, 202, 205, 239, 252, 256, 261, 263, 274; his *Durobrivæ*, 288
Askham, John, visits C. at Northampton, 439
Astley's Theatre, C. visits, 222 and *n*.
Athenæum, The, 222; reports of C. in, 358, 366, 385
Autobiography, C. writes his, 230, 234, 242, 246, 251, 254
"Autumn," 283 and *n*., 300
Ayton, R., *Essays*, 262 and *n*.

B

"BACHELORS' HALL," 77–8, 80, 177–8

Bacon's *Essays*, 200, 246
Badely, Dr., 385
Baker, Anne Elizabeth and George, 309, 434
Baker, "Tant," 60
Baldock, 405
Ballads, 35, 41, 256, 281
Banton, John, *Excursions of Fancy*, 243
Barbould, Mrs., 258
Barnack, 18, 175, 305
Barringer, Robert, on C., 417
Barton, Bernard, 120
Beattie's *Minstrel*, and C.'s *Village Minstrel*, 141–2; 161, 171
Beddoes, T. L., on Darley, 215; on literary outlook in 1824, 280; 281
Bedford Times, The, Asylum poems in, 425–6
Bee, The, C.'s poems in, 83, 324, 358
Beggars' Opera, The, a public house, 131 and *n*.
Behnes, Henry, visit to C., 297; 302, 339
Bell, Dr., of Stamford, 103, 144
Bell's *Life in London*, 298
Bellamy, Counsellor, of Wisbech, 48
Bellars, of Woodcroft, 48, 261, 440
Bennion, Thomas, describes London dinners, 192, 214; letter to C., 202; C.'s guide in London, 200, 213
Billings, James and John, 77–81, 177–8, 250, 253, 255, 259, 262, 312
Birds, C. on, 44, 53, 79, 125, 233, 239, 240, 248, 250, 251, 252, 253, 255, 259, 260, 262, 263, 266, 268–70, 367
Blackwood's Magazine, 150, 166, 175, 194, 241, 290, 365
Blair, Hugh, *Sermons*, 246.
Blair, Robert, *The Grave*, C. on, 247
Blake, William, 195, 220, 423
"Blakesmoor in H—shire," Lamb's, 223, 234
Bloomfield, Hannah, 208
Bloomfield, Robert, 88, 119, 122, 138; letter to C., 155; 189, 197; correspondence with C., 207; C. on, 207–8; 228, 229, 233, 241, 251–2, 254, 259, 425
Blunden, Edmund, *John Clare: Poems Chiefly from Manuscript*, 1920, 12; account of "Village Scenes," 155; on C., 350; 357

457

466 INDEX

DATE DUE